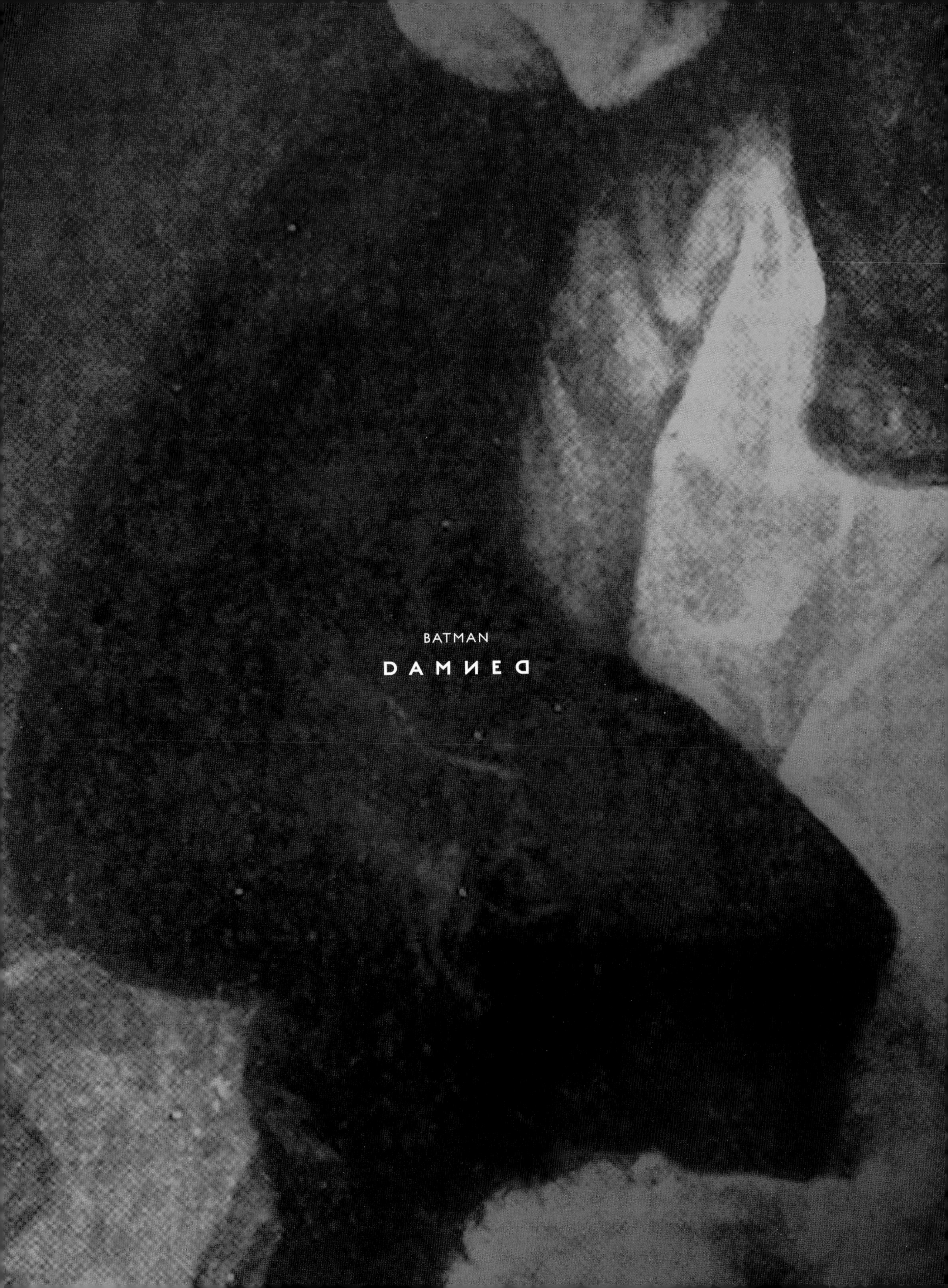
BATMAN
DAMNED

BATMAN

DAMNED

BRIAN AZZARELLO
WRITER

LEE BERMEJO
ART AND COVERS

JARED K. FLETCHER
LETTERER

MARK DOYLE Editor - Original Series
WILL DENNIS Editorial Consultant – Original Series
AMEDEO TURTURRO Associate Editor - Original Series
MAGGIE HOWELL Assistant Editor – Original Series
JEB WOODARD Group Editor – Collected Editions
ERIKA ROTHBERG Editor – Collected Edition
STEVE COOK Design Director – Books
MONIQUE NARBONETA Publication Design
KATE DURRÉ Publication Production

BOB HARRAS Senior VP – Editor-in-Chief, DC Comics

DAN DiDIO Publisher
JIM LEE Publisher & Chief Creative Officer
BOBBIE CHASE VP – New Publishing Initiatives & Talent Development
DON FALLETTI VP – Manufacturing Operations & Workflow Management
LAWRENCE GANEM VP – Talent Services
ALISON GILL Senior VP – Manufacturing & Operations
HANK KANALZ Senior VP – Publishing Strategy & Support Services
DAN MIRON VP – Publishing Operations
NICK J. NAPOLITANO VP – Manufacturing Administration & Design
NANCY SPEARS VP – Sales
MICHELE R. WELLS VP & Executive Editor, Young Reader

BATMAN: DAMNED

DC Comics, 2900 West Alameda Ave., Burbank, CA 91505
Printed by Transcontinental Interglobe, Beauceville, QC, Canada. 8/2/19. First Printing.
ISBN: 978-1-4012-9140-2 | Barnes and Noble Exclusive Edition ISBN: 978-1-77950-145-5

Library of Congress Cataloging-in-Publication Data is available.

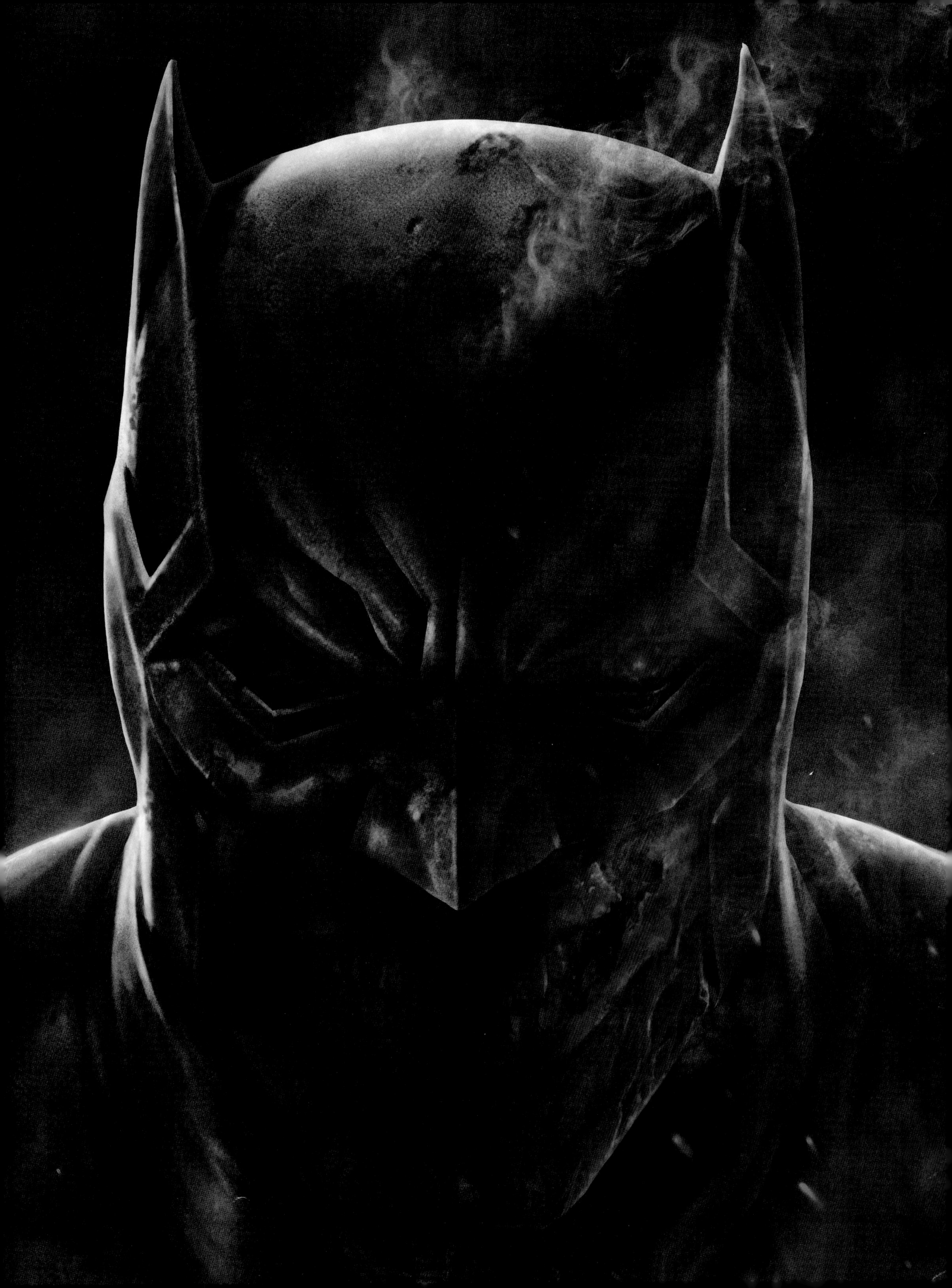

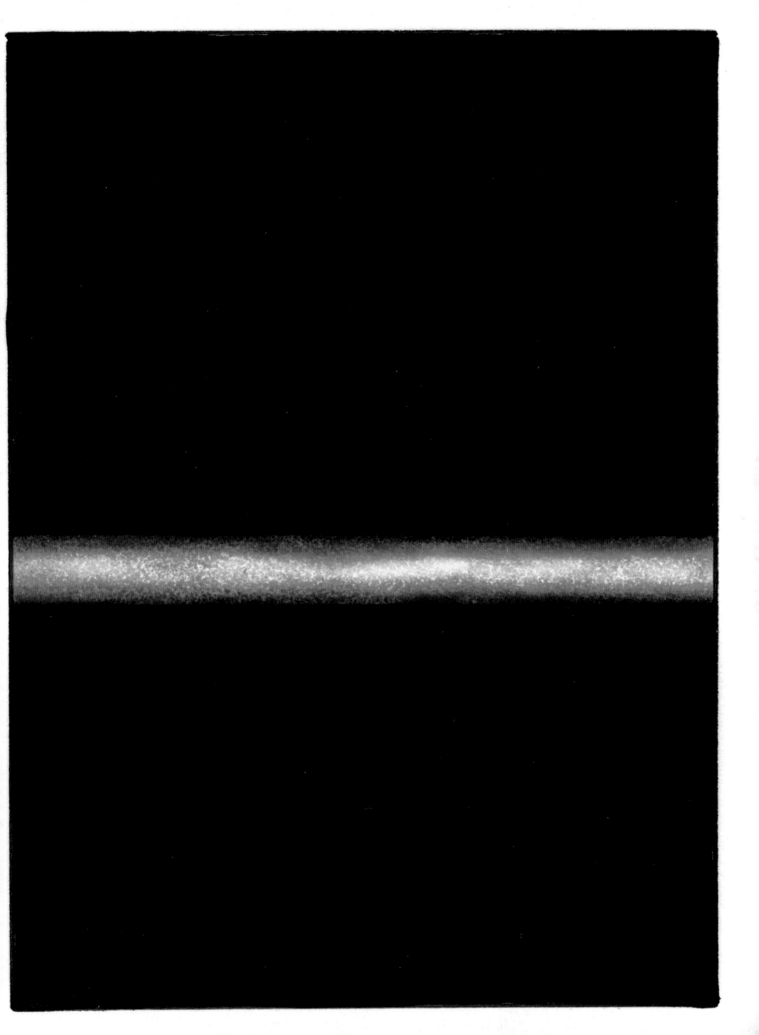

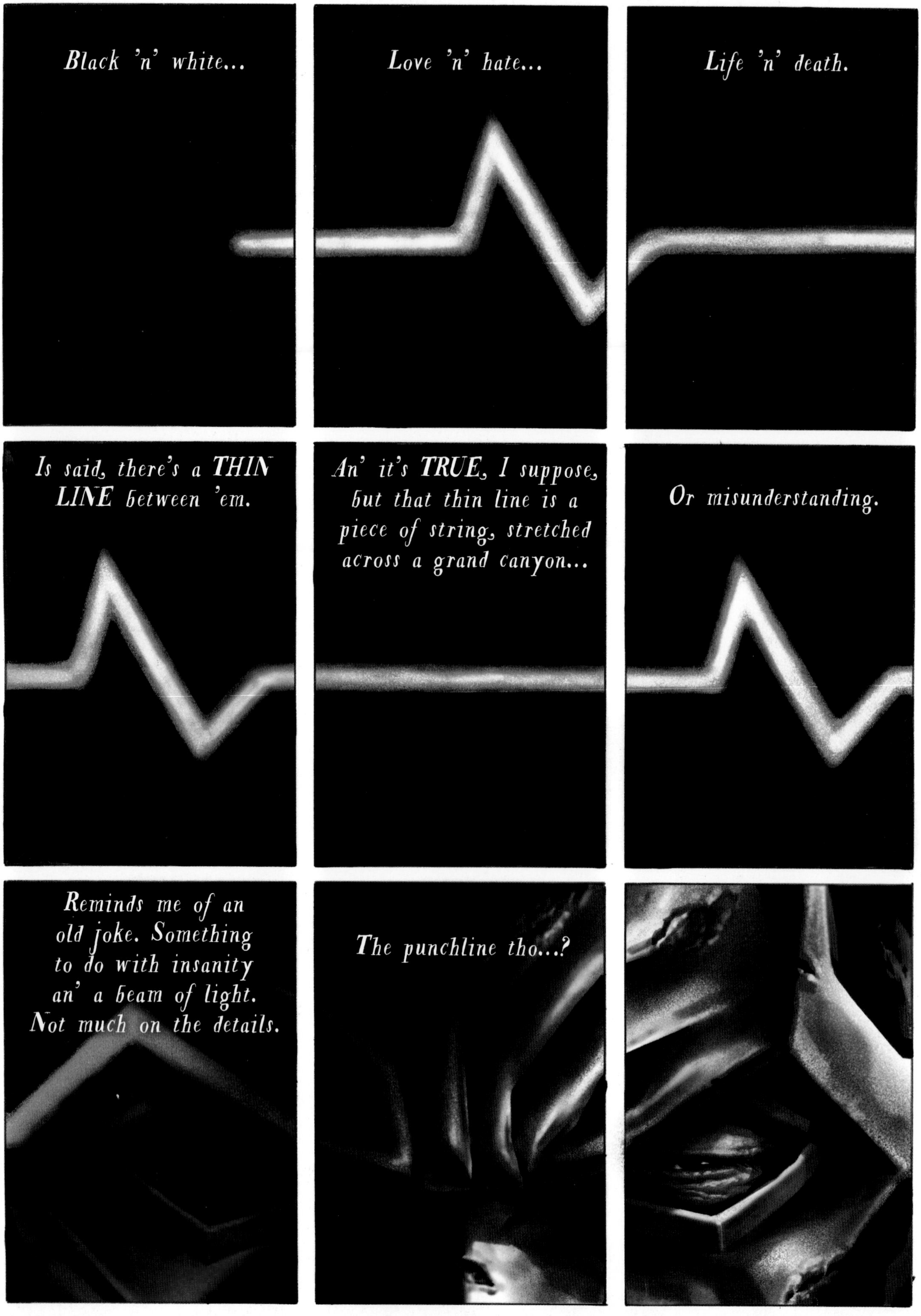
Black 'n' white...
Love 'n' hate...
Life 'n' death.
Is said, there's a THIN LINE between 'em.
An' it's TRUE, I suppose, but that thin line is a piece of string, stretched across a grand canyon...
Or misunderstanding.
Reminds me of an old joke. Something to do with insanity an' a beam of light. Not much on the details.
The punchline tho...?

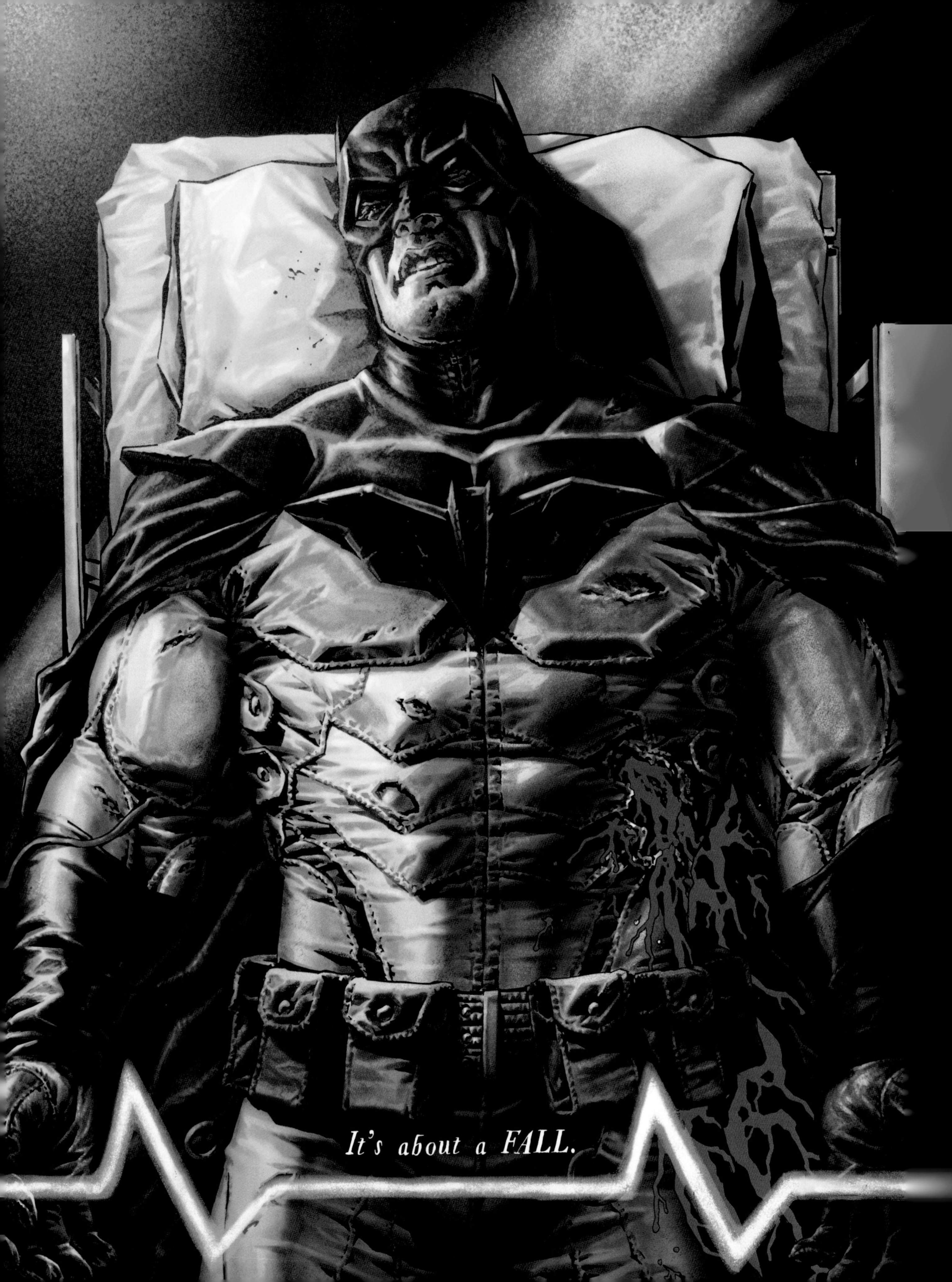
It's about a FALL.

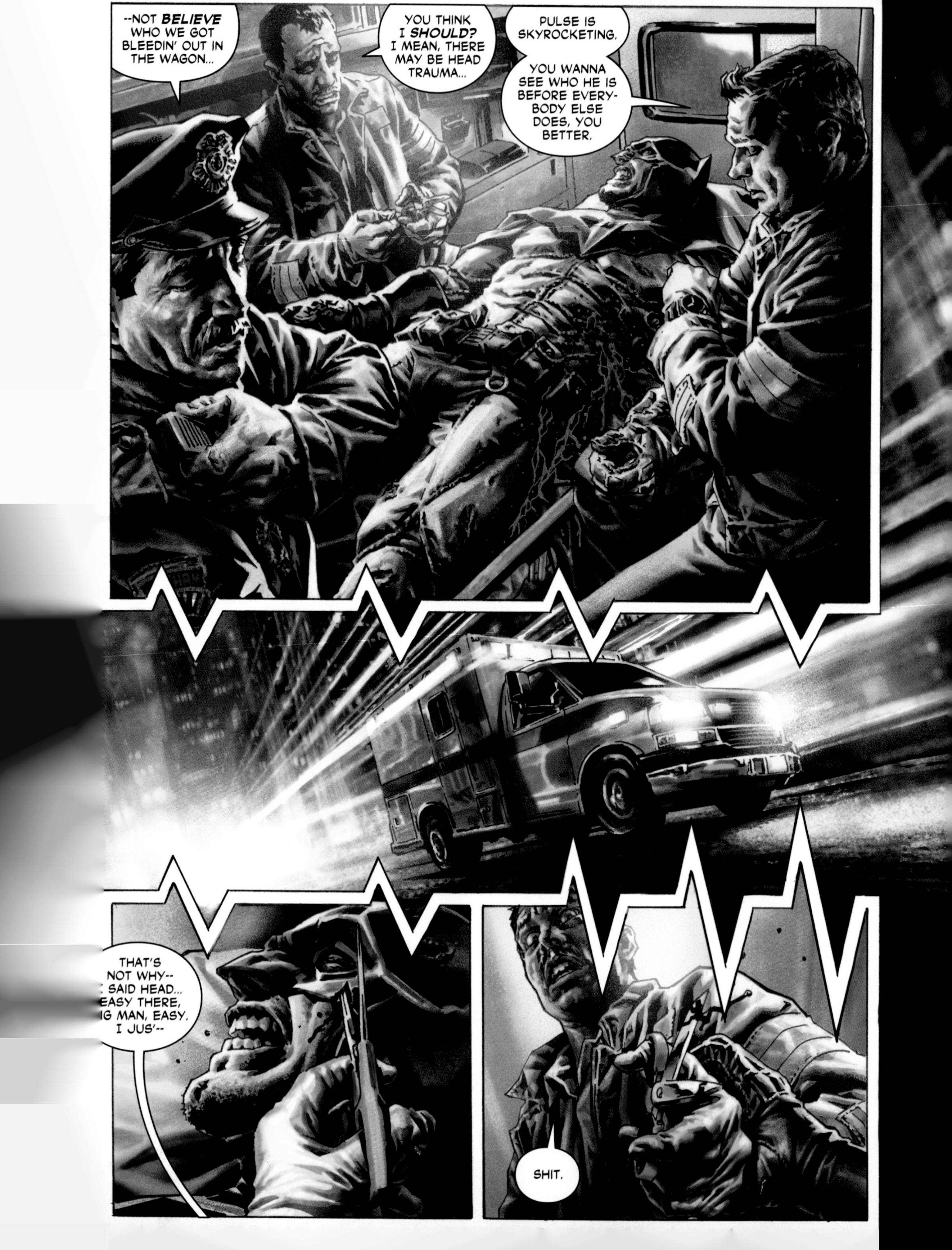
--NOT *BELIEVE* WHO WE GOT BLEEDIN' OUT IN THE WAGON...
YOU THINK I *SHOULD?* I MEAN, THERE MAY BE HEAD TRAUMA...
PULSE IS SKYROCKETING.
YOU WANNA SEE WHO HE IS BEFORE EVERY-BODY ELSE DOES, YOU BETTER.
THAT'S NOT WHY-- SAID HEAD... EASY THERE, IG MAN, EASY. I JUS'--
SHIT.

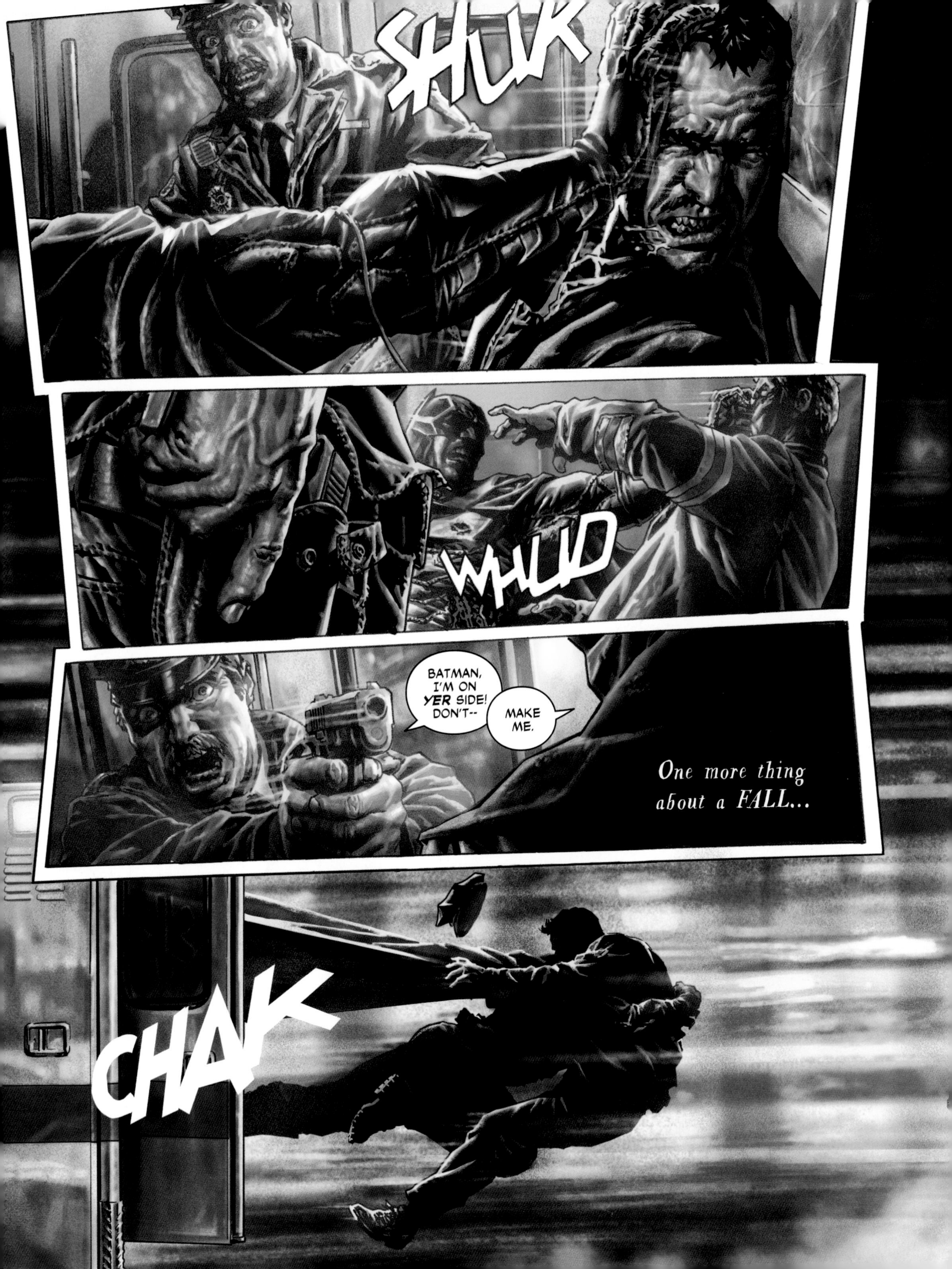
SHUK
WHUD
BATMAN, I'M ON YER SIDE! DON'T--
MAKE ME.
One more thing about a FALL...
CHAK

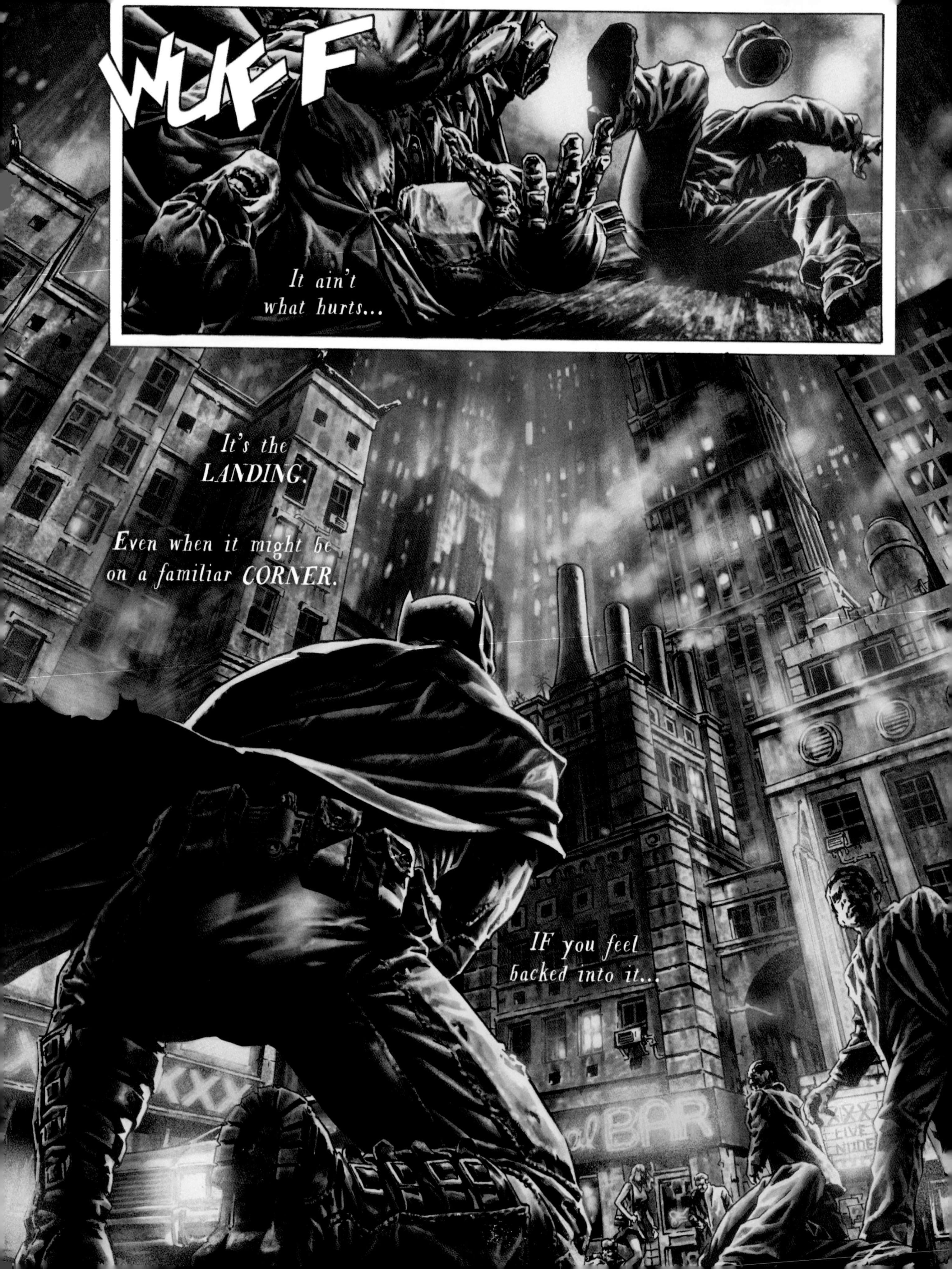
WUFF
It ain't what hurts...
It's the LANDING.
Even when it might be on a familiar CORNER.
IF you feel backed into it...
BAR
XXX LIVE NUDE

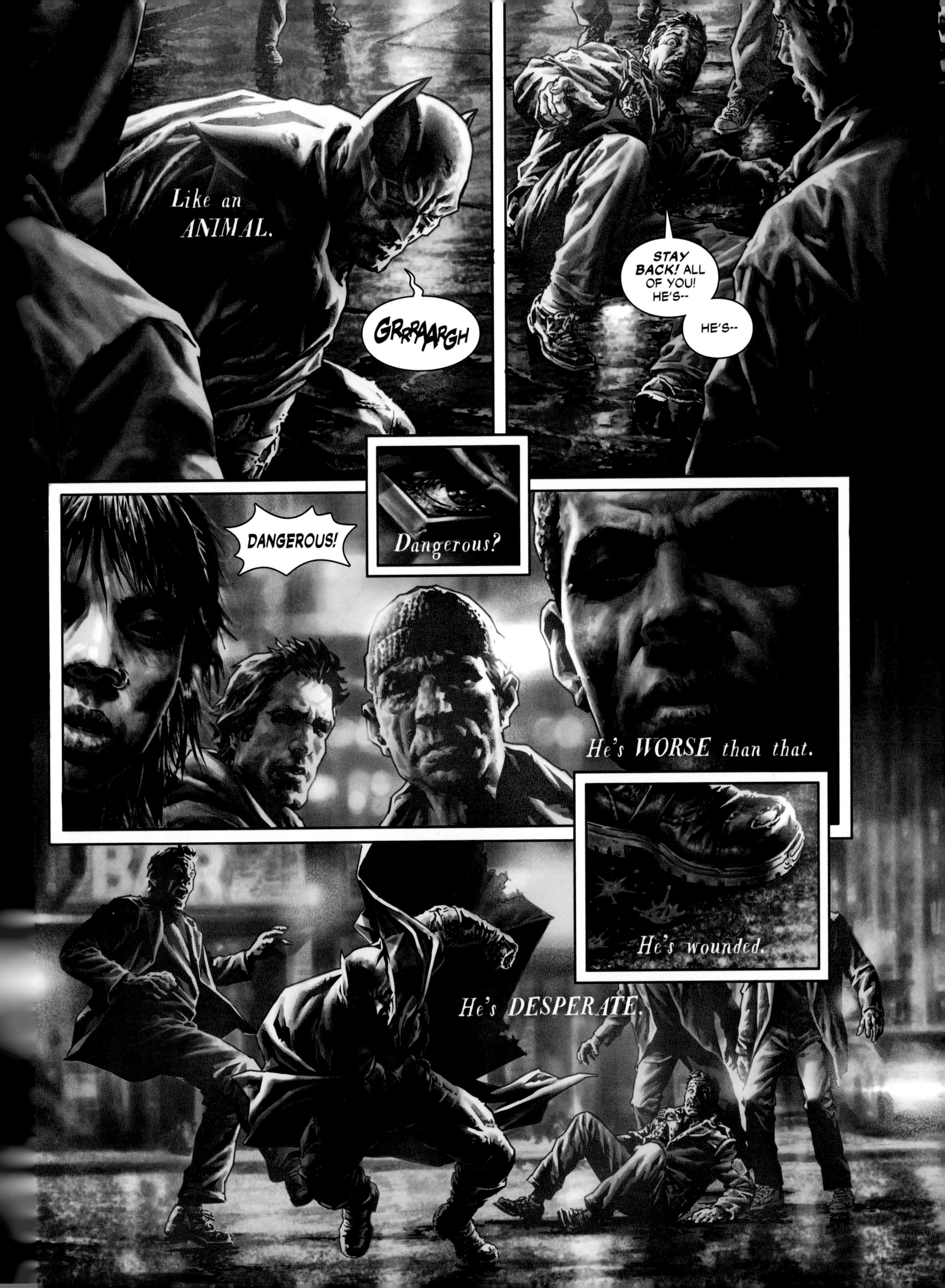
Like an ANIMAL.
GRRRAARGH
STAY BACK! ALL OF YOU! HE'S--
HE'S--
DANGEROUS!
Dangerous?
He's WORSE than that.
He's wounded.
He's DESPERATE.

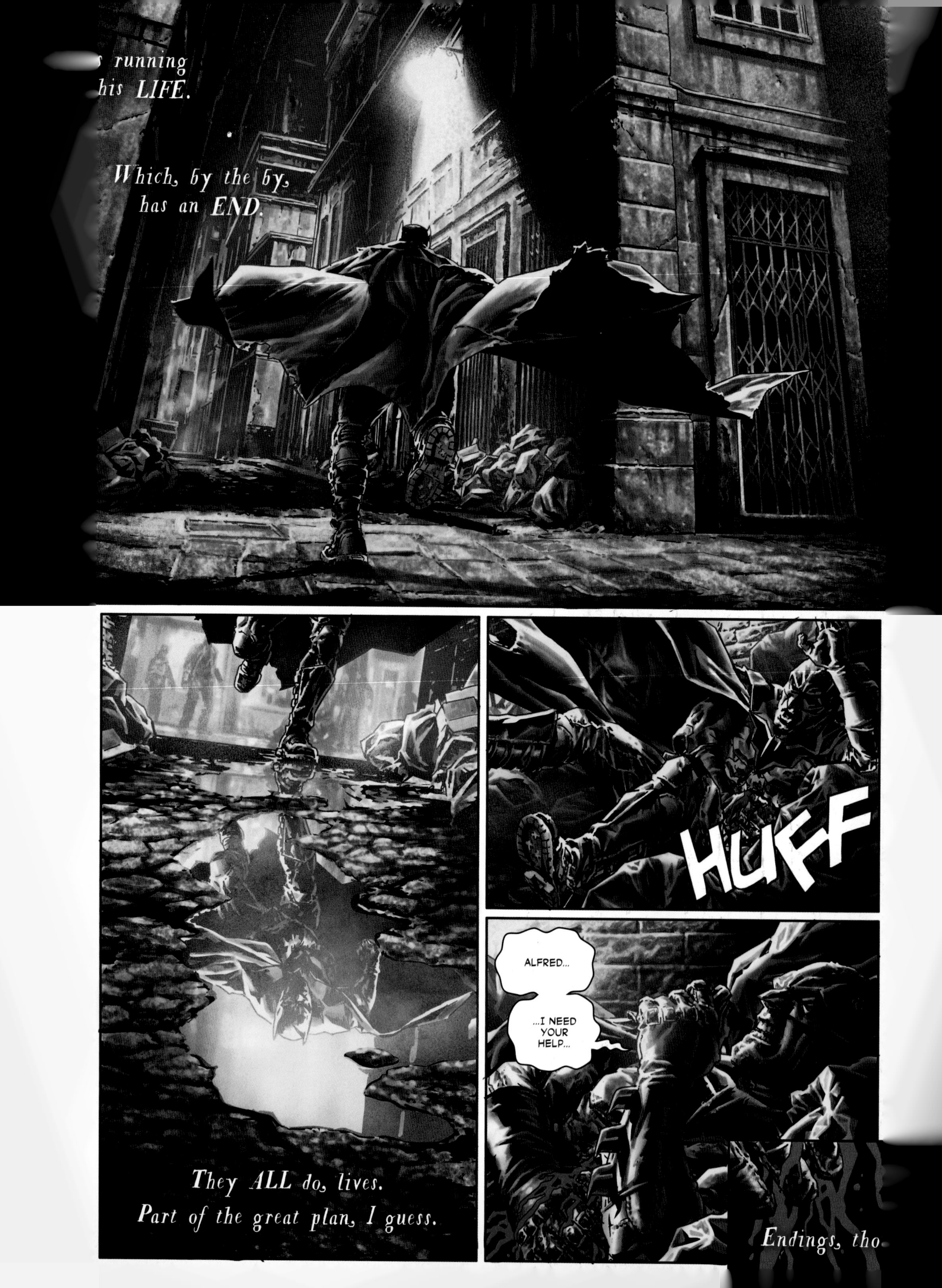
running
his LIFE.
Which, by the by, has an END.
They ALL do, lives. Part of the great plan, I guess.
HUFF
ALFRED...
...I NEED YOUR HELP...
Endings, tho

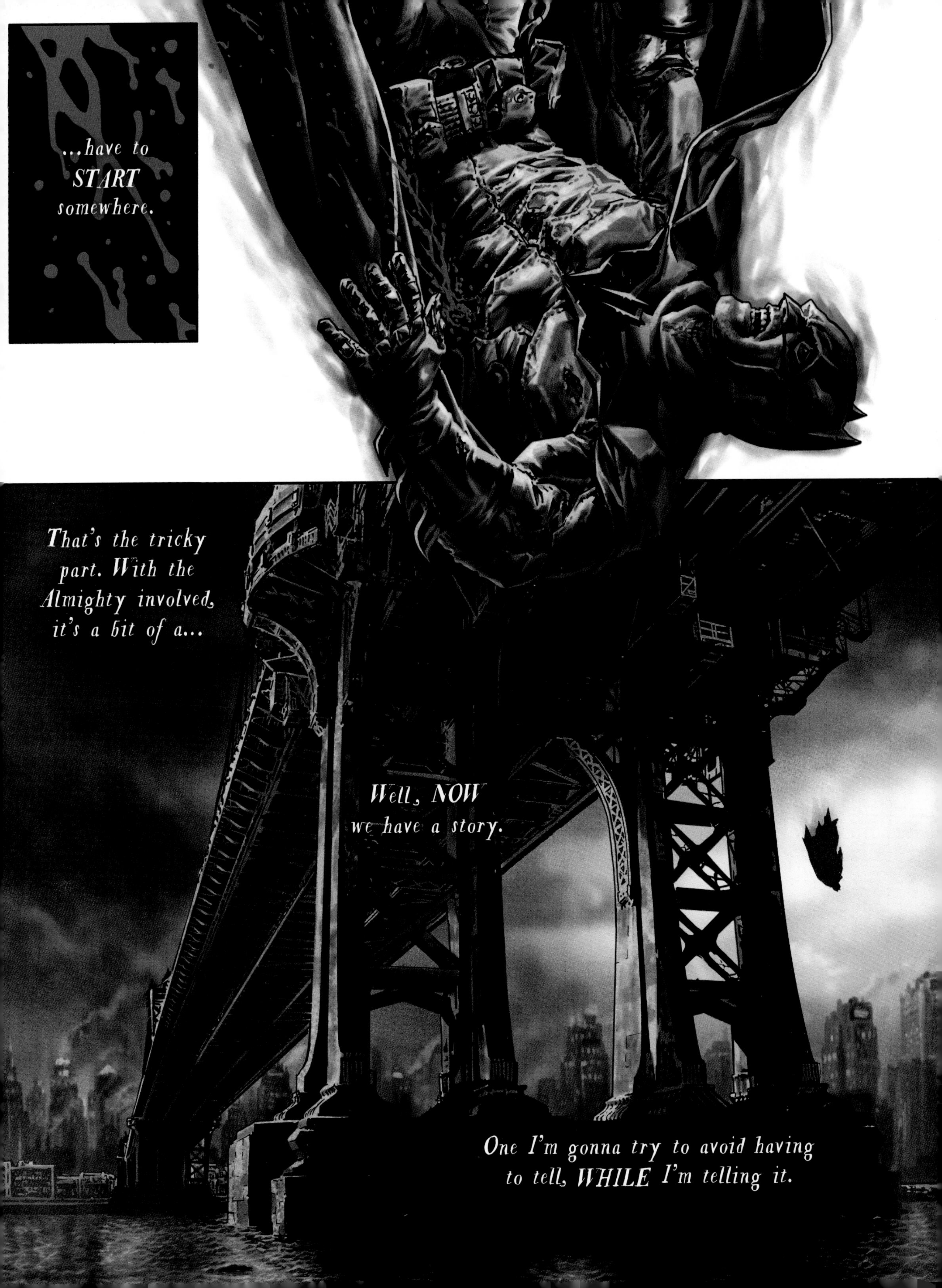
...have to START somewhere.
That's the tricky part. With the Almighty involved, it's a bit of a...
Well, NOW we have a story.
One I'm gonna try to avoid having to tell, WHILE I'm telling it.

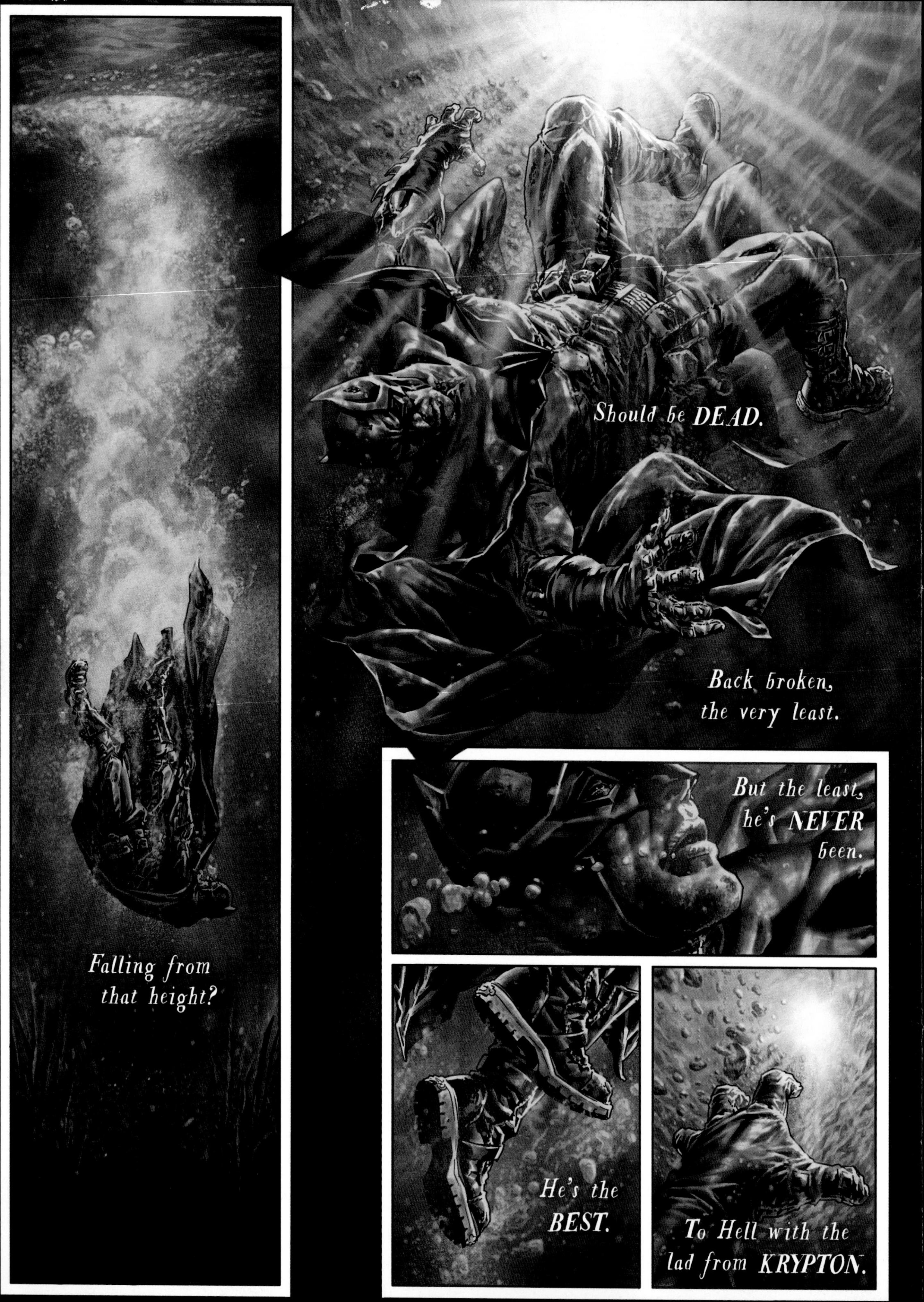

Falling from that height?
Should be DEAD.
Back broken, the very least.
But the least, he's NEVER been.
He's the BEST.
To Hell with the lad from KRYPTON.

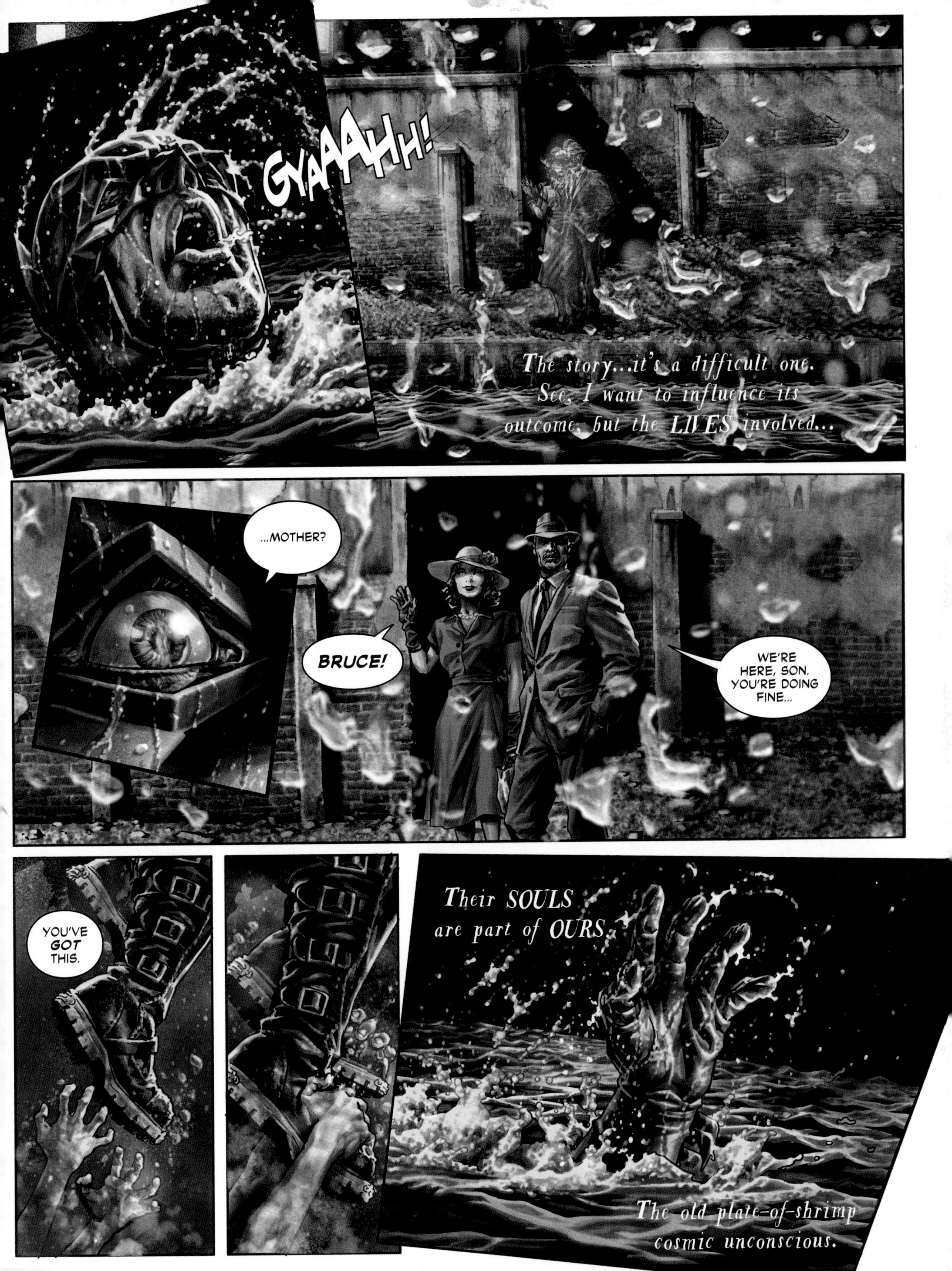
GYAAAHH!
The story...it's a difficult one. See, I want to influence its outcome, but the LIVES involved...
...MOTHER?
BRUCE!
WE'RE HERE, SON. YOU'RE DOING FINE...
YOU'VE GOT THIS.
Their SOULS are part of OURS.
The old plate-of-shrimp cosmic unconscious.

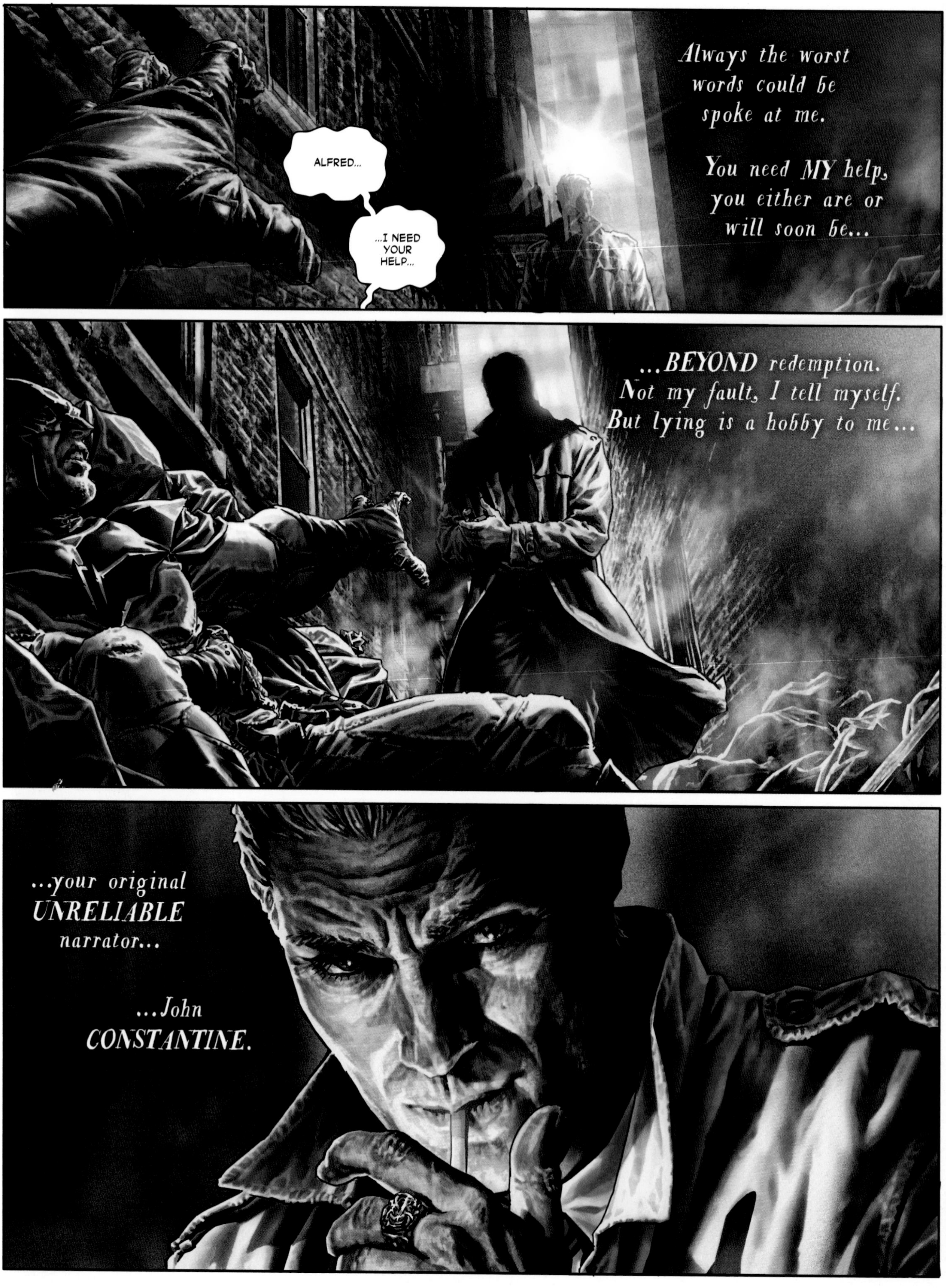
ALFRED...
...I NEED YOUR HELP...
Always the worst words could be spoke at me.
You need MY help, you either are or will soon be...
...BEYOND redemption. Not my fault, I tell myself. But lying is a hobby to me...
...your original UNRELIABLE narrator...
...John CONSTANTINE.

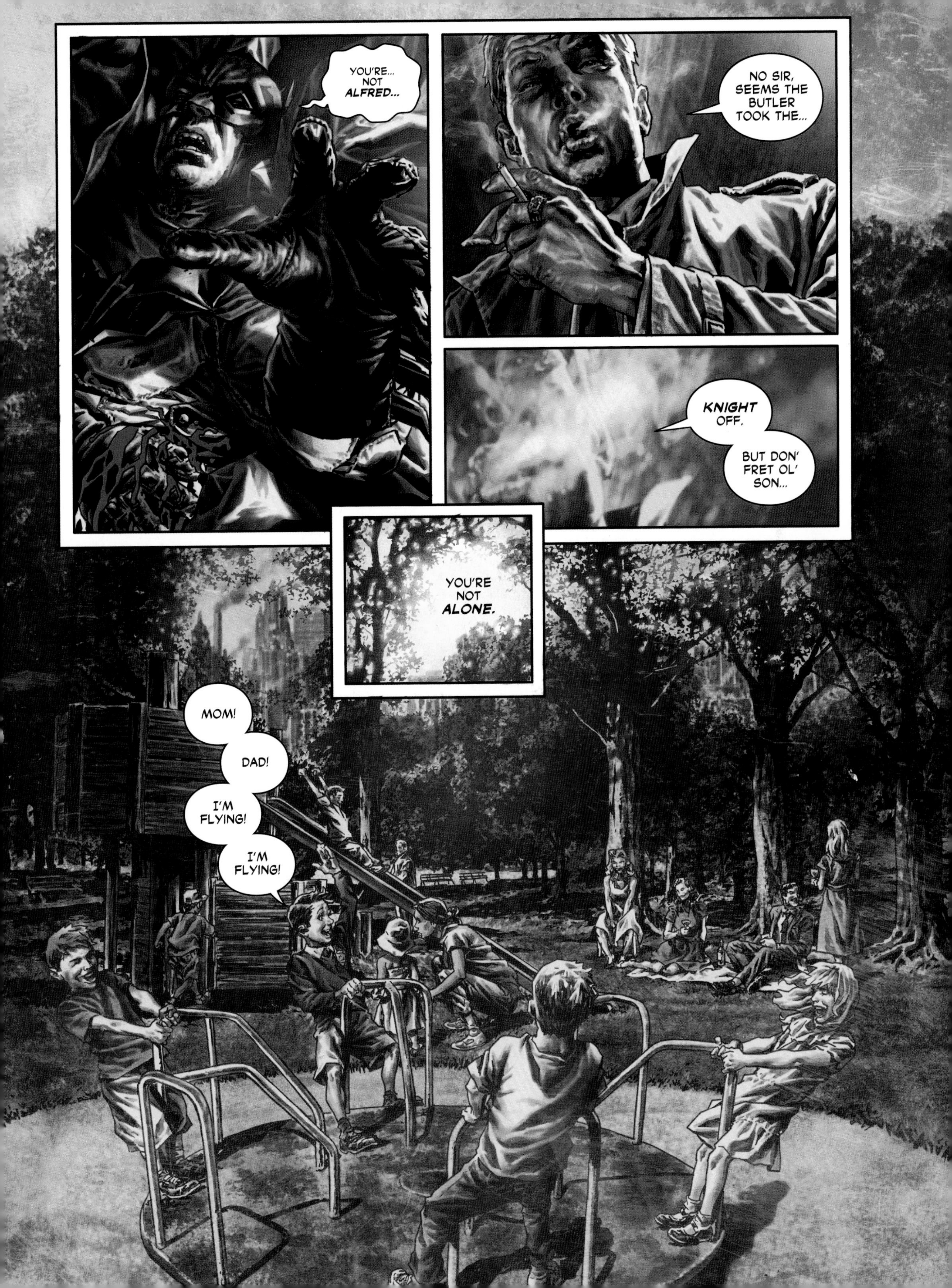

YOU'RE... NOT ALFRED...
NO SIR, SEEMS THE BUTLER TOOK THE...
KNIGHT OFF.
BUT DON' FRET OL' SON...
YOU'RE NOT ALONE.
MOM!
DAD!
I'M FLYING!
I'M FLYING!

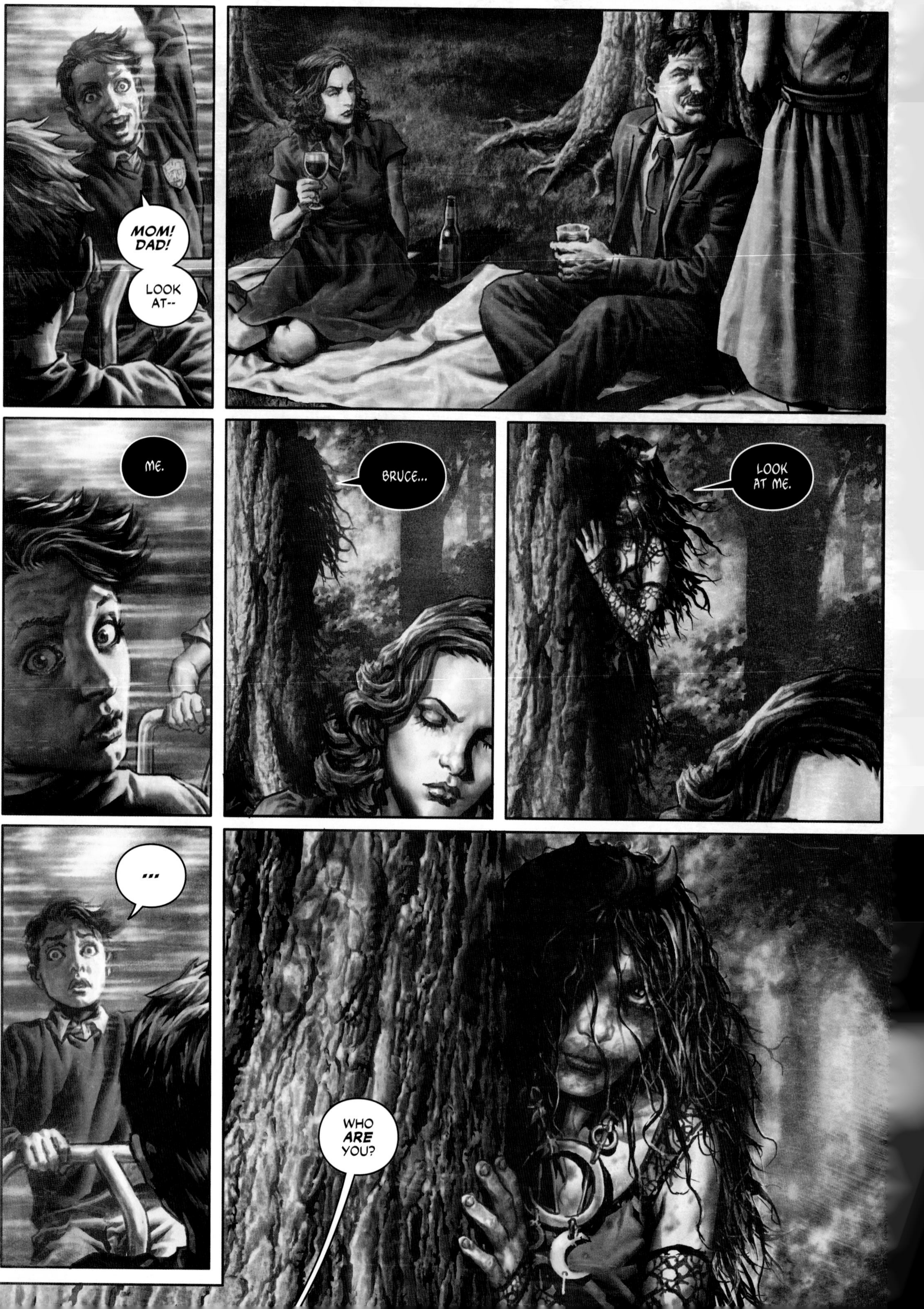

MOM! DAD!
LOOK AT--
ME.
BRUCE...
LOOK AT ME.
...
WHO ARE YOU?

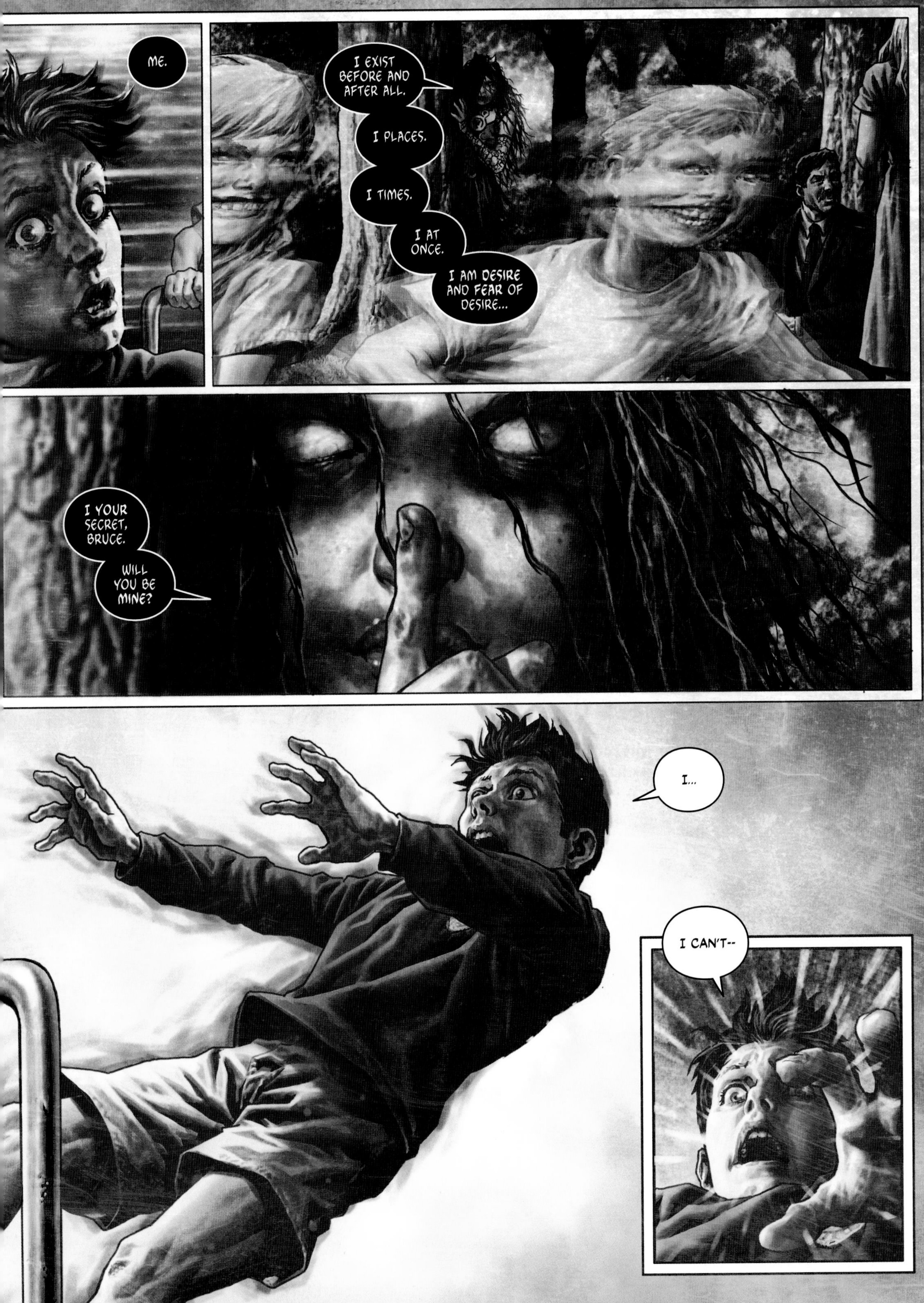
ME.
I EXIST BEFORE AND AFTER ALL.
I PLACES.
I TIMES.
I AT ONCE.
I AM DESIRE AND FEAR OF DESIRE...
I YOUR SECRET, BRUCE.
WILL YOU BE MINE?
I...
I CAN'T--

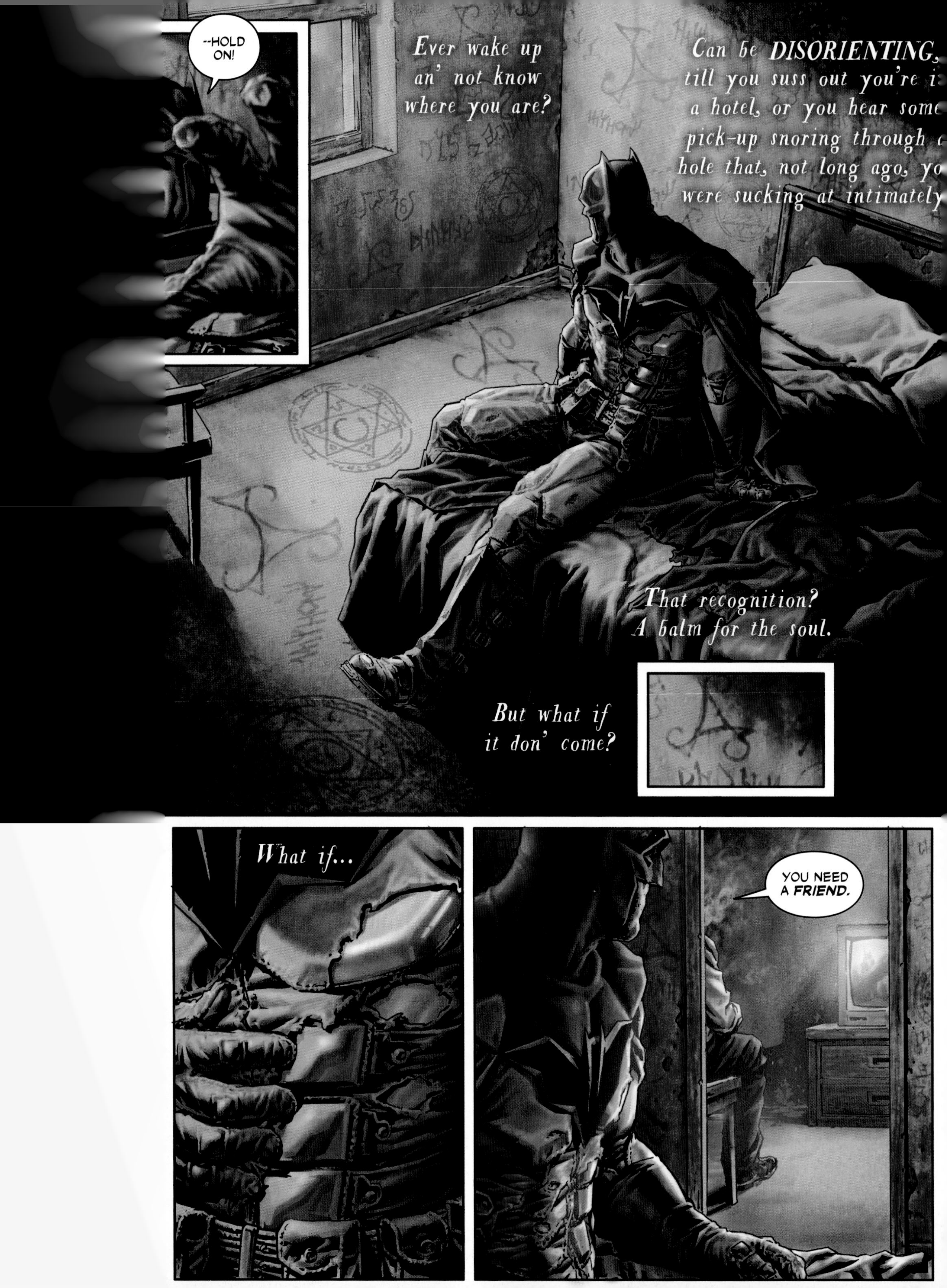
--HOLD ON!
Ever wake up an' not know where you are?
Can be DISORIENTING, till you suss out you're i a hotel, or you hear some pick-up snoring through a hole that, not long ago, yo were sucking at intimately
That recognition? A balm for the soul.
But what if it don' come?
What if...
YOU NEED A FRIEND.

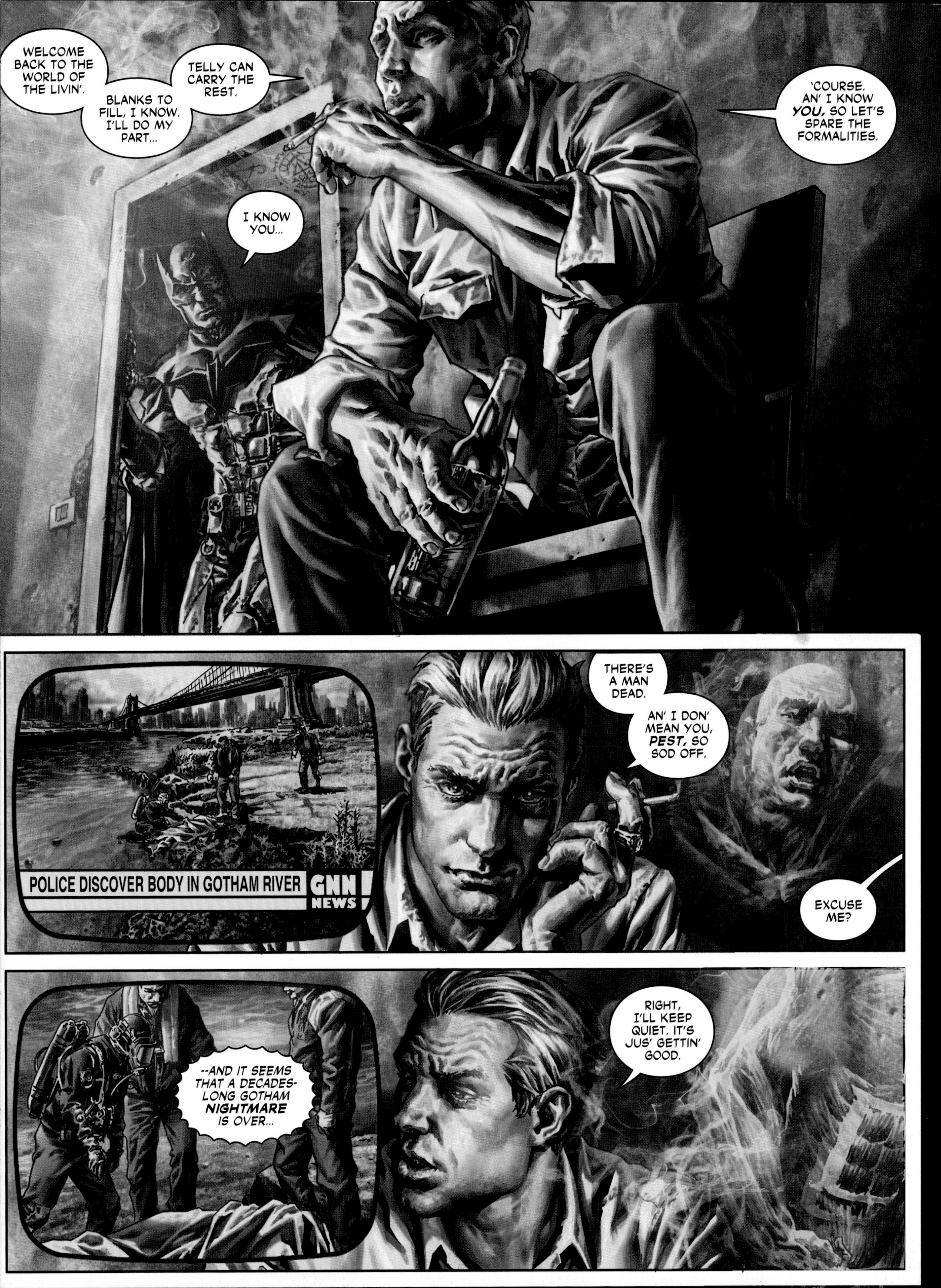
WELCOME BACK TO THE WORLD OF THE LIVIN'.
BLANKS TO FILL, I KNOW. I'LL DO MY PART...
TELLY CAN CARRY THE REST.
I KNOW YOU...
'COURSE. AN' I KNOW YOU, SO LET'S SPARE THE FORMALITIES.
POLICE DISCOVER BODY IN GOTHAM RIVER
GNN NEWS
THERE'S A MAN DEAD.
AN' I DON' MEAN YOU, PEST, SO SOD OFF.
EXCUSE ME?
--AND IT SEEMS THAT A DECADES-LONG GOTHAM NIGHTMARE IS OVER...
RIGHT, I'LL KEEP QUIET. IT'S JUS' GETTIN' GOOD.

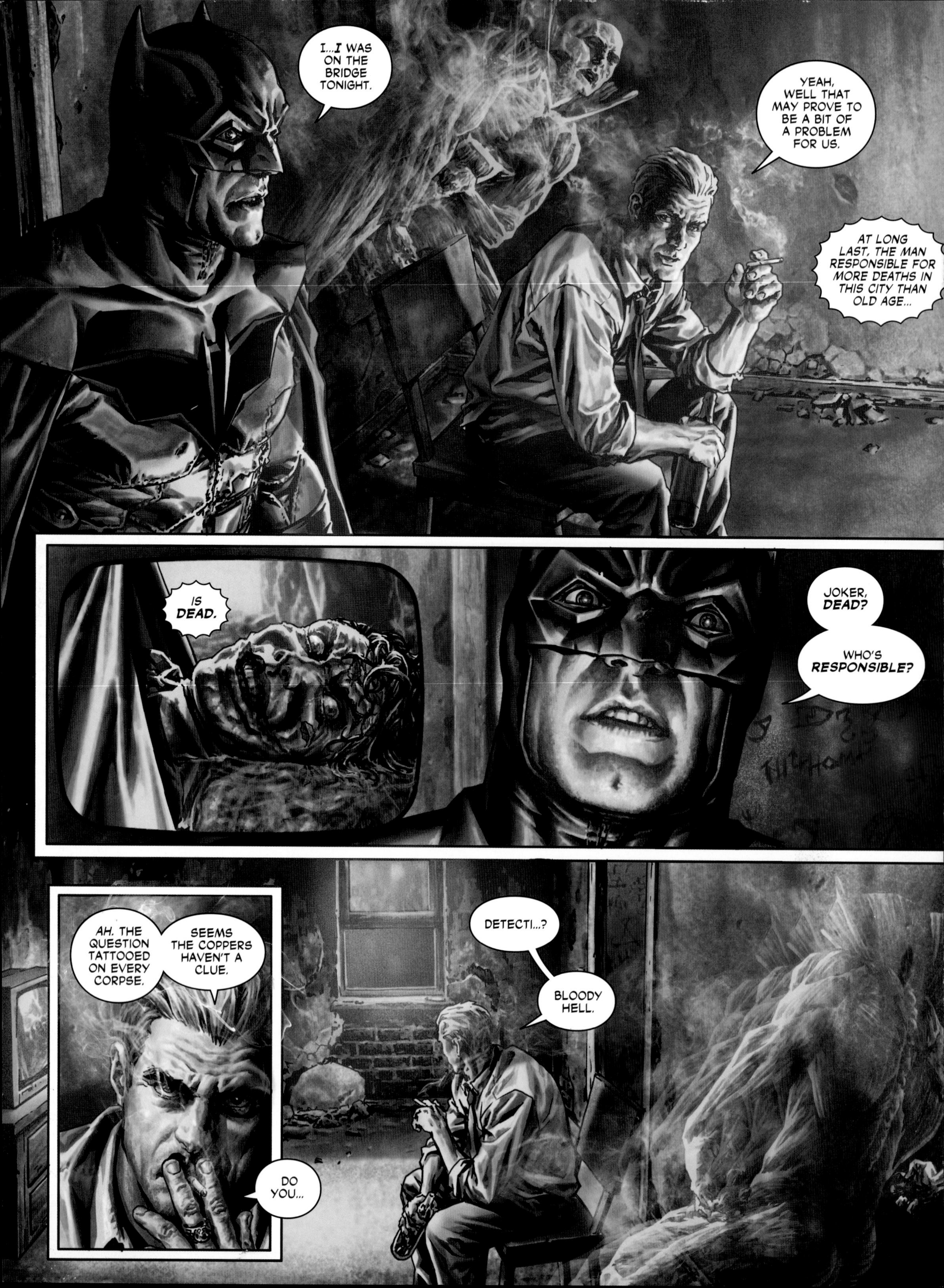
I...I WAS ON THE BRIDGE TONIGHT.
YEAH, WELL THAT MAY PROVE TO BE A BIT OF A PROBLEM FOR US.
AT LONG LAST, THE MAN RESPONSIBLE FOR MORE DEATHS IN THIS CITY THAN OLD AGE...
IS DEAD.
JOKER, DEAD?
WHO'S RESPONSIBLE?
AH. THE QUESTION TATTOOED ON EVERY CORPSE.
SEEMS THE COPPERS HAVEN'T A CLUE.
DO YOU...
DETECTI...?
BLOODY HELL.

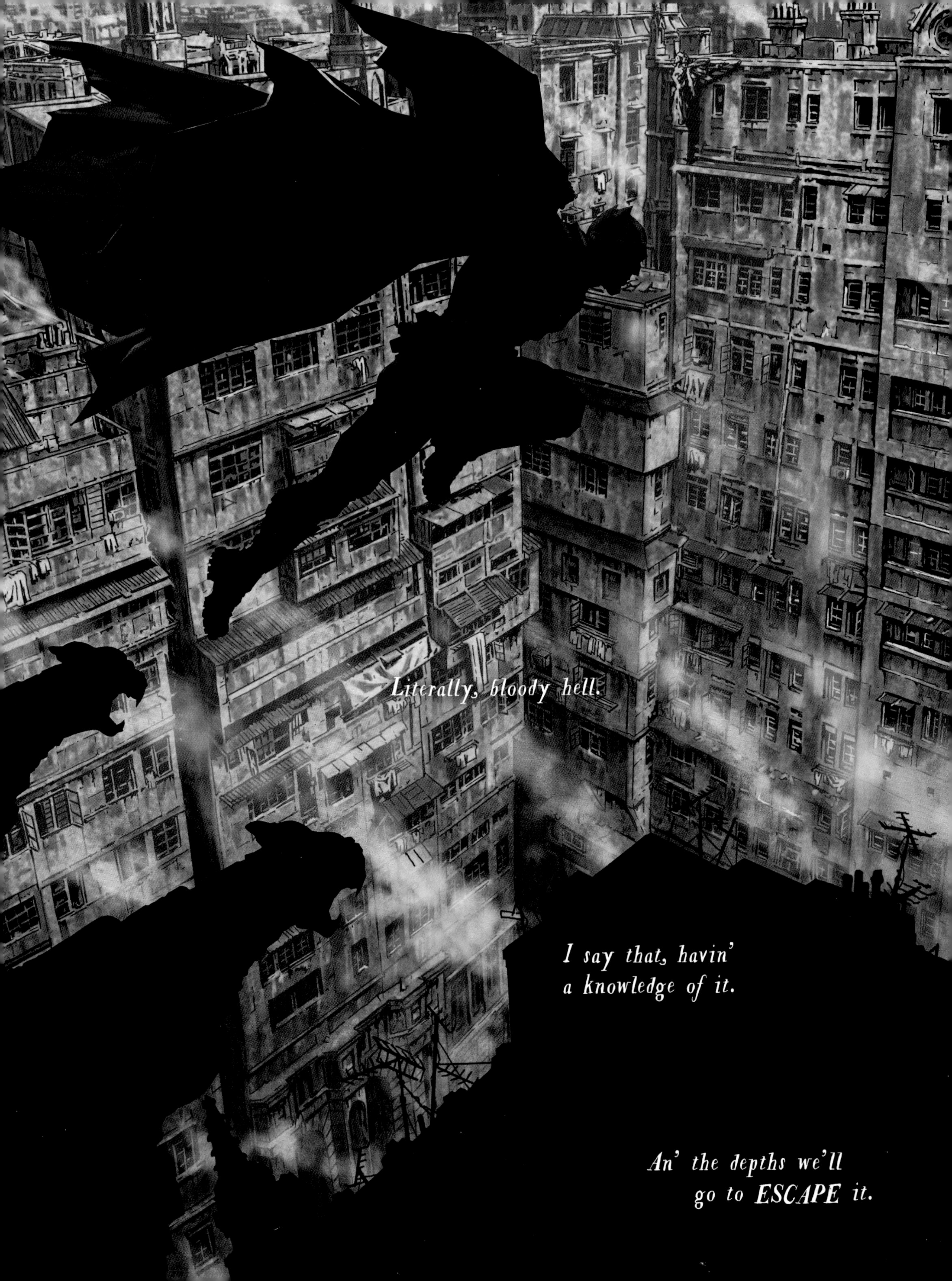
Literally, bloody hell.
I say that, havin' a knowledge of it.
An' the depths we'll go to ESCAPE it.

This night, gonna fall DARKER 'fore we through.
LOOK, IT'S NOT A GOOD IDEA. MY SON IS...
...
...
...

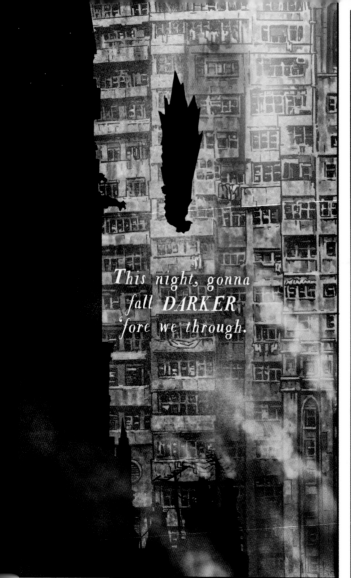

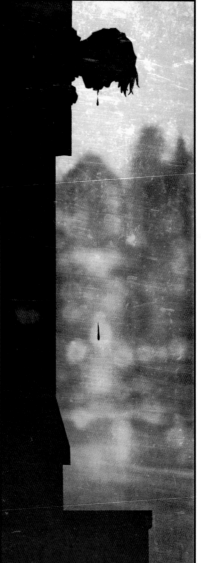

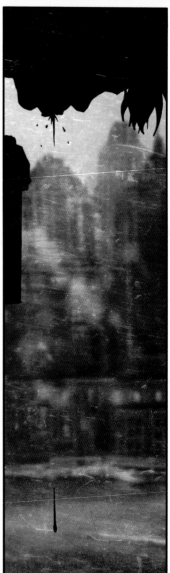

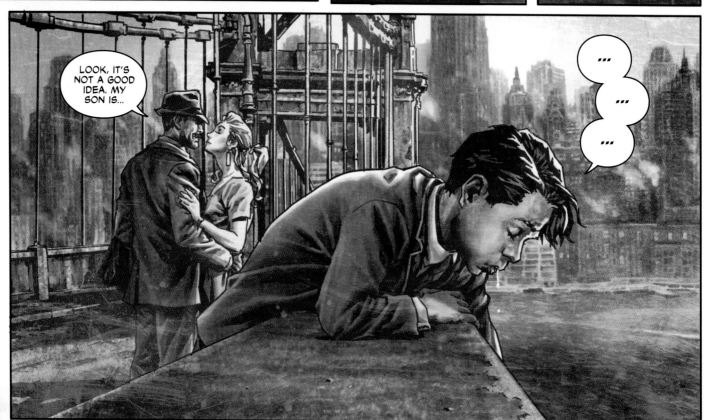

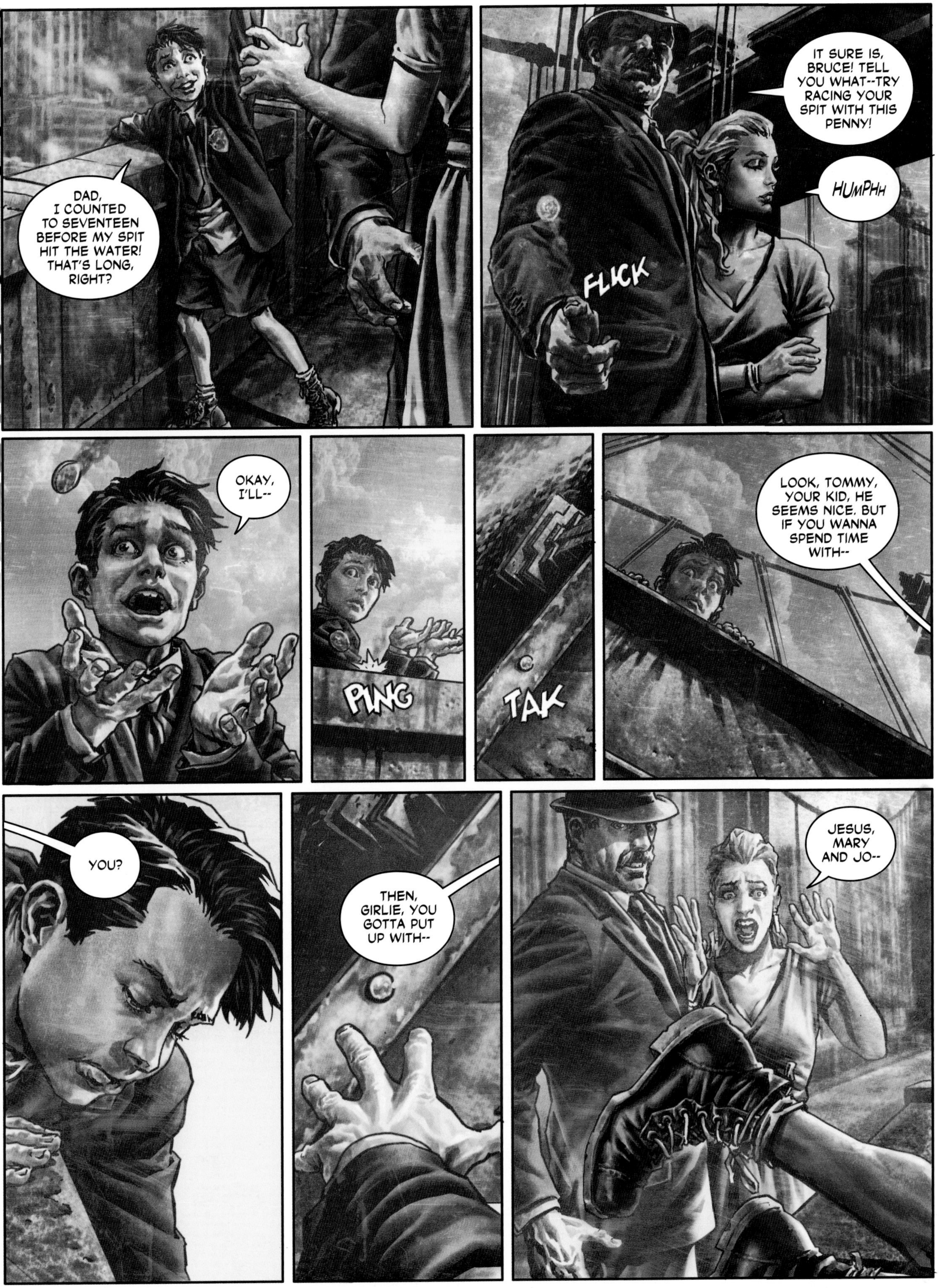
DAD, I COUNTED TO SEVENTEEN BEFORE MY SPIT HIT THE WATER! THAT'S LONG, RIGHT?
IT SURE IS, BRUCE! TELL YOU WHAT--TRY RACING YOUR SPIT WITH THIS PENNY!
HUMPHH
FLICK
OKAY, I'LL--
PING
TAK
LOOK, TOMMY, YOUR KID, HE SEEMS NICE. BUT IF YOU WANNA SPEND TIME WITH--
YOU?
THEN, GIRLIE, YOU GOTTA PUT UP WITH--
JESUS, MARY AND JO--

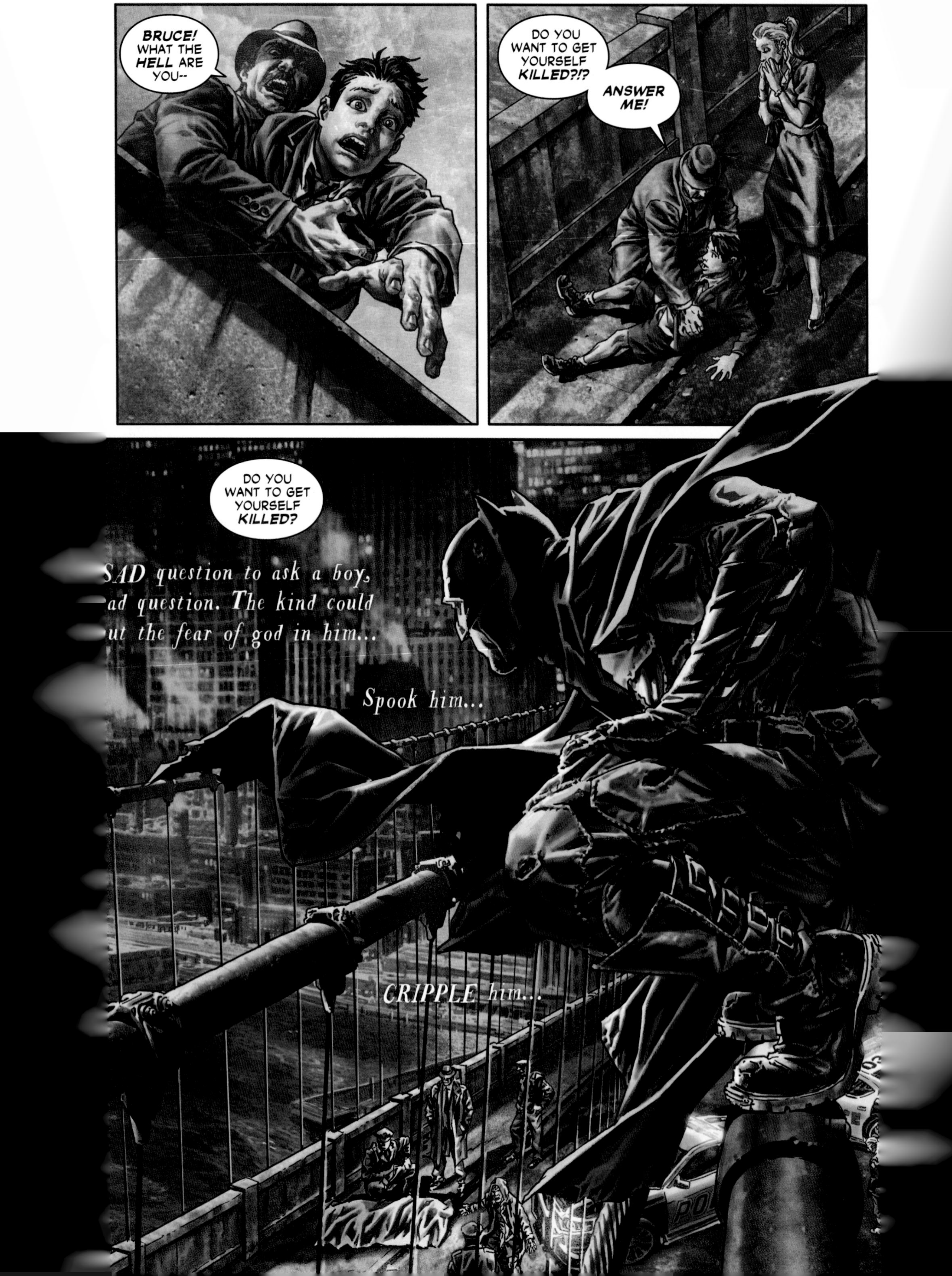

BRUCE! WHAT THE HELL ARE YOU--
DO YOU WANT TO GET YOURSELF KILLED?!?
ANSWER ME!
DO YOU WANT TO GET YOURSELF KILLED?
SAD question to ask a boy,
ad question. The kind could
ut the fear of god in him...
Spook him...
CRIPPLE him...

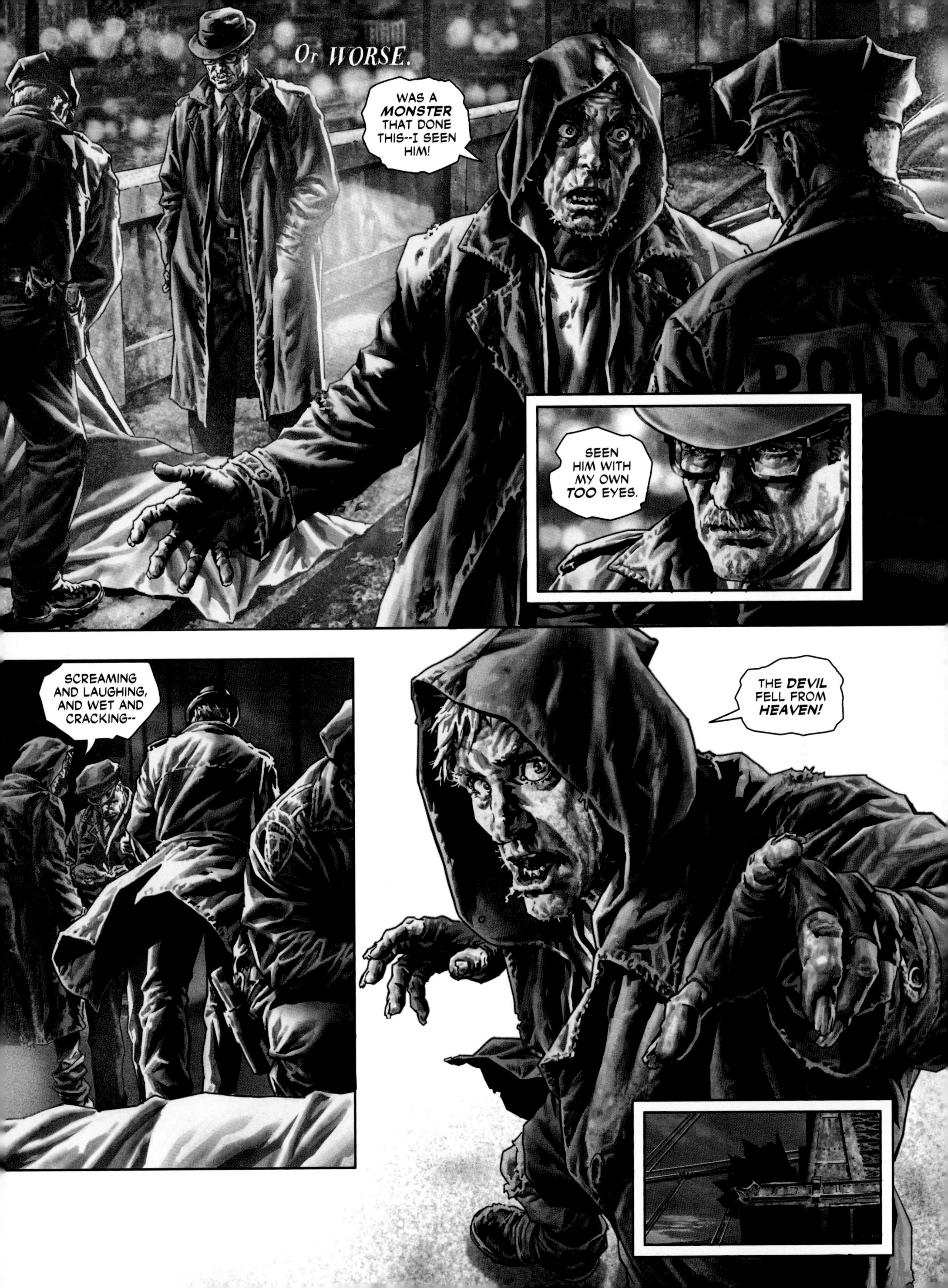
Or WORSE.
WAS A MONSTER THAT DONE THIS--I SEEN HIM!
SEEN HIM WITH MY OWN TOO EYES.
SCREAMING AND LAUGHING, AND WET AND CRACKING--
THE DEVIL FELL FROM HEAVEN!
POLIC

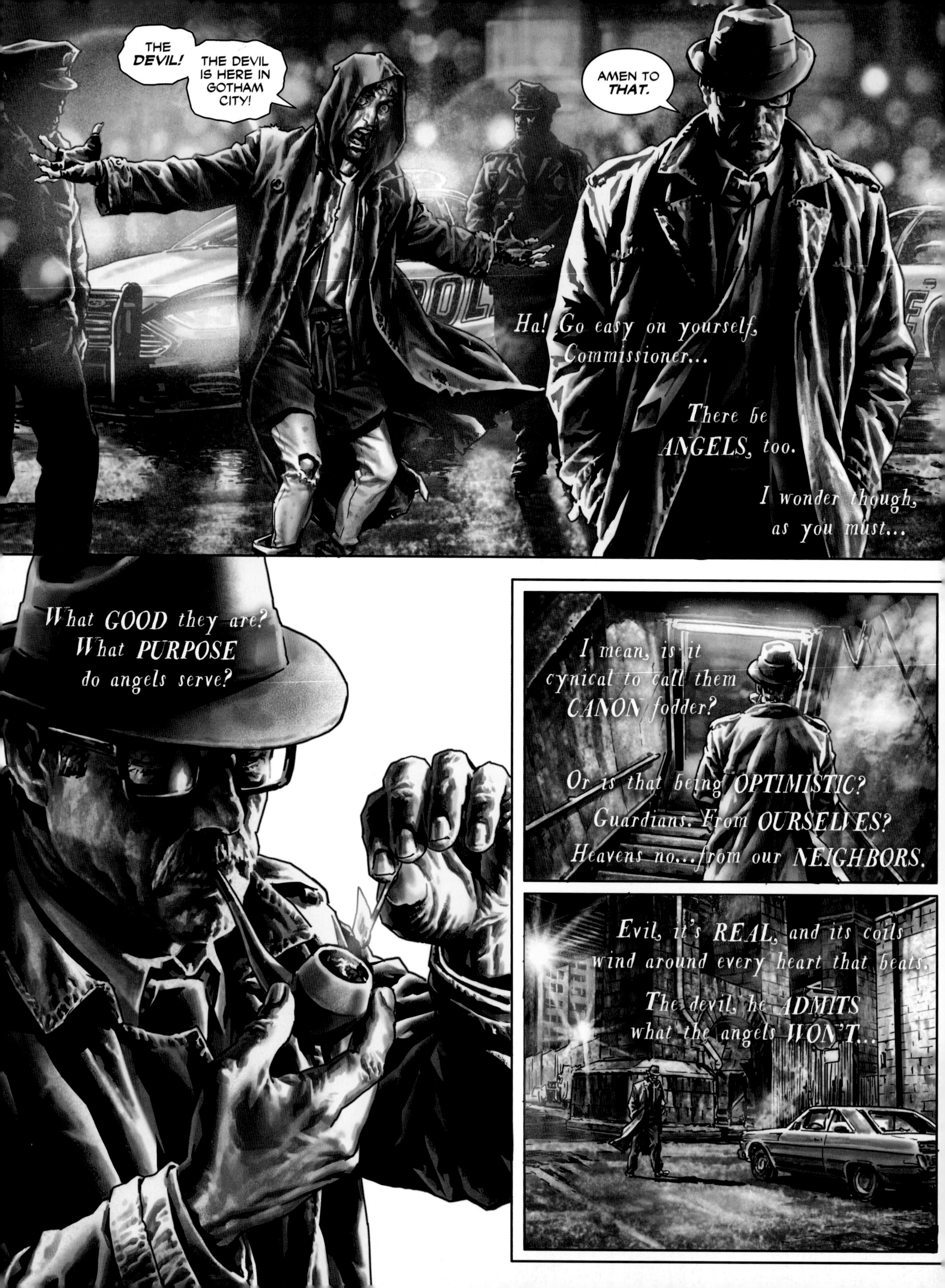
THE DEVIL!
THE DEVIL IS HERE IN GOTHAM CITY!
AMEN TO THAT.
Ha! Go easy on yourself, Commissioner...
There be ANGELS, too.
I wonder though, as you must...
What GOOD they are? What PURPOSE do angels serve?
I mean, is it cynical to call them CANON fodder?
Or is that being OPTIMISTIC? Guardians. From OURSELVES? Heavens no...from our NEIGHBORS.
Evil, it's REAL, and its coils wind around every heart that beats.
The devil, he ADMITS what the angels WON'T...

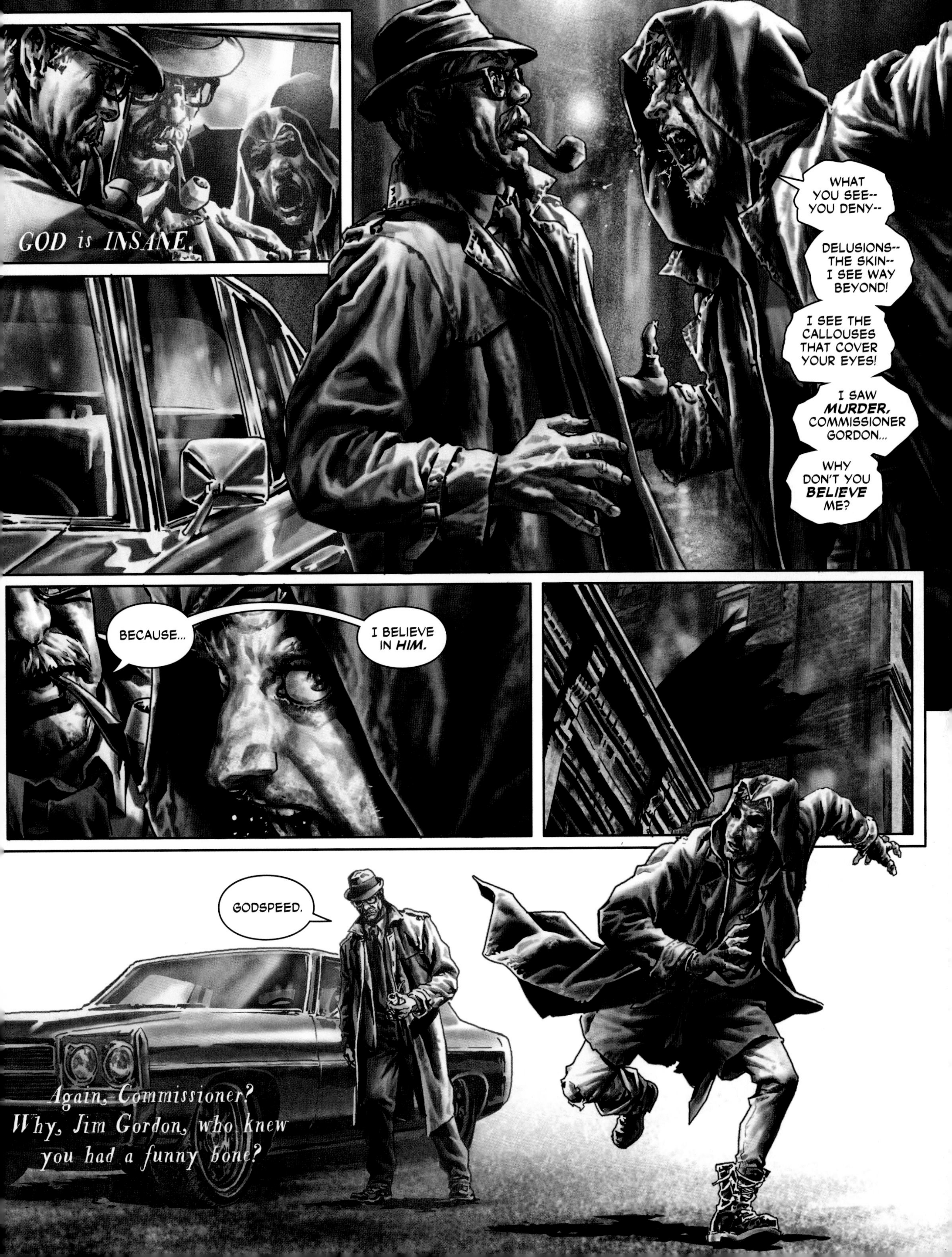
GOD is INSANE.
WHAT YOU SEE-- YOU DENY--
DELUSIONS-- THE SKIN-- I SEE WAY BEYOND!
I SEE THE CALLOUSES THAT COVER YOUR EYES!
I SAW MURDER, COMMISSIONER GORDON...
WHY DON'T YOU BELIEVE ME?
BECAUSE...
I BELIEVE IN HIM.
GODSPEED.
Again, Commissioner? Why, Jim Gordon, who knew you had a funny bone?

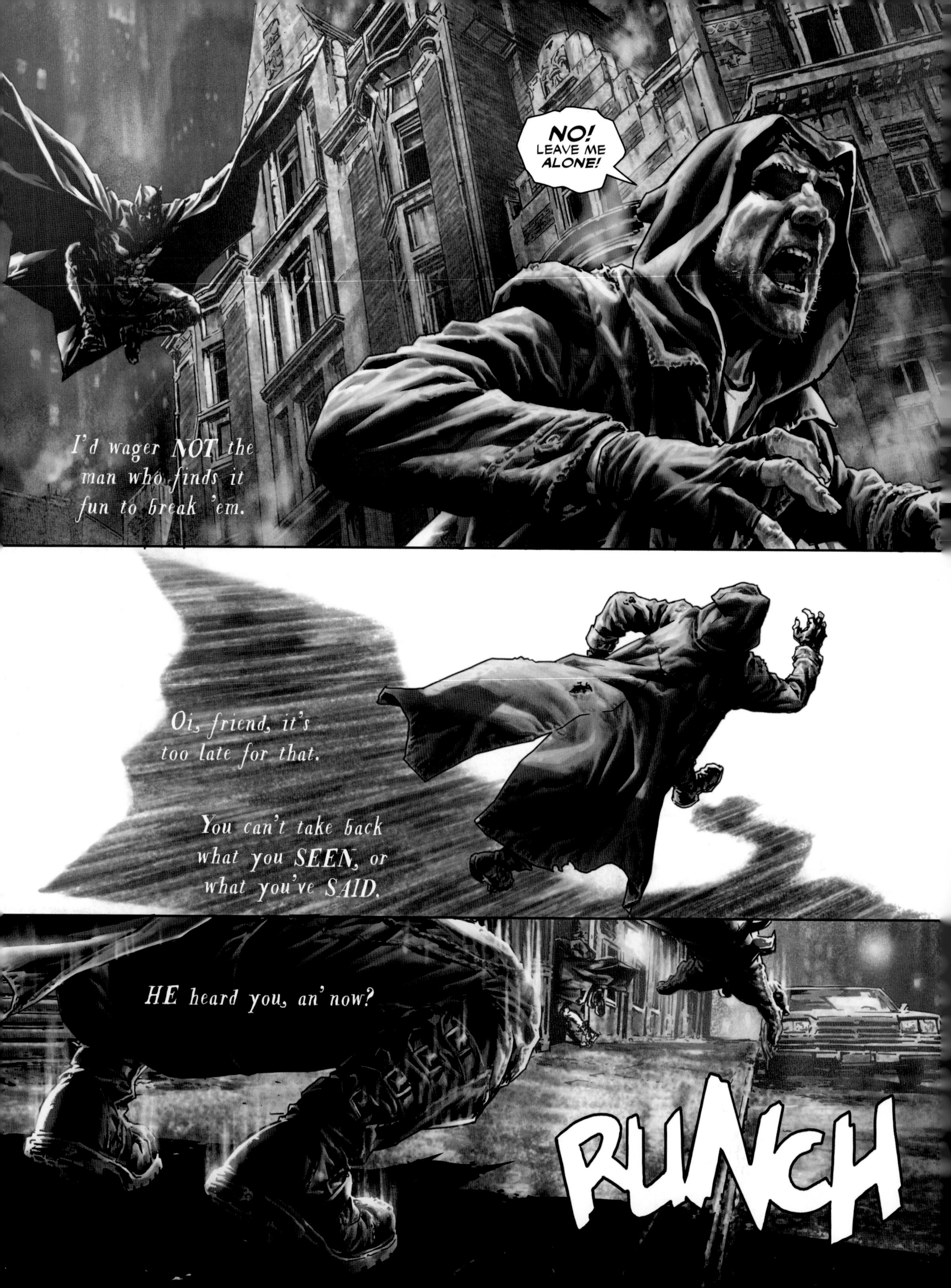
NO! LEAVE ME ALONE!
I'd wager NOT the man who finds it fun to break 'em.
Oi, friend, it's too late for that.
You can't take back what you SEEN, or what you've SAID.
HE heard you, an' now?
RUNCH

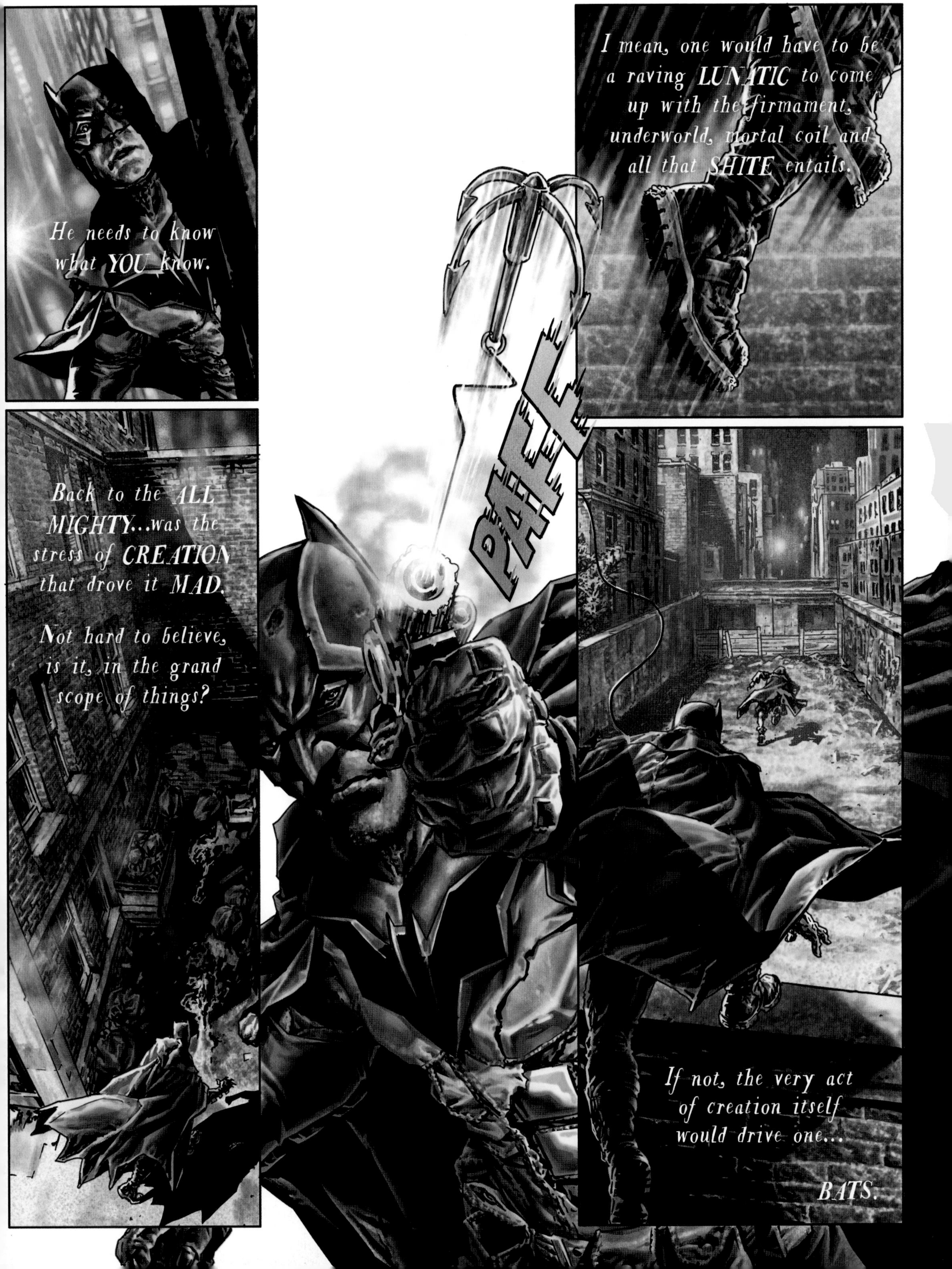
He needs to know what YOU know.
I mean, one would have to be a raving LUNATIC to come up with the firmament, underworld, mortal coil and all that SHITE entails.
PAFF
Back to the ALL MIGHTY...was the stress of CREATION that drove it MAD.
Not hard to believe, is it, in the grand scope of things?
If not, the very act of creation itself would drive one...
BATS.

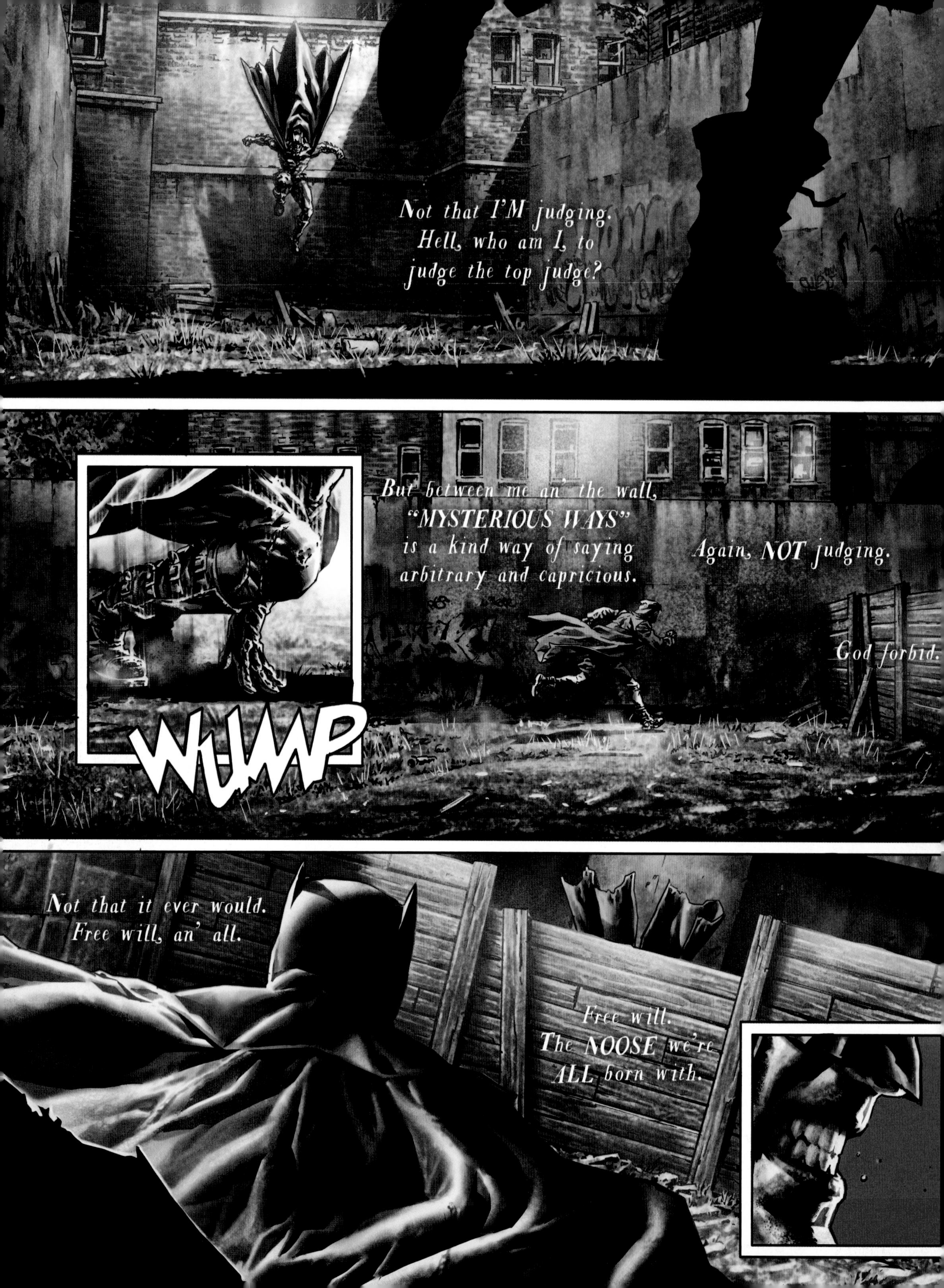

Not that I'M judging.
Hell, who am I, to judge the top judge?
But between me an' the wall, "MYSTERIOUS WAYS" is a kind way of saying arbitrary and capricious.
Again, NOT judging.
God forbid.
WUMP
Not that it ever would. Free will, an' all.
Free will. The NOOSE we're ALL born with.

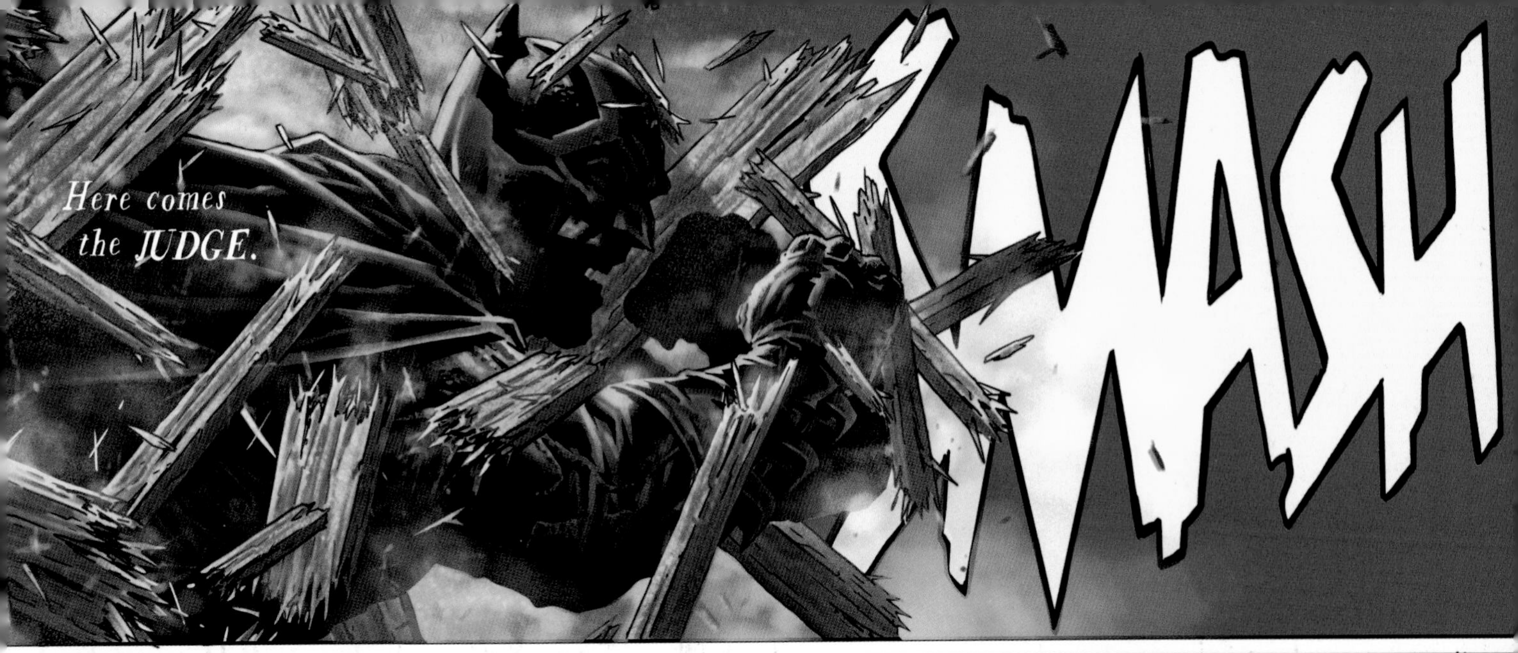
Here comes the JUDGE.
MASH

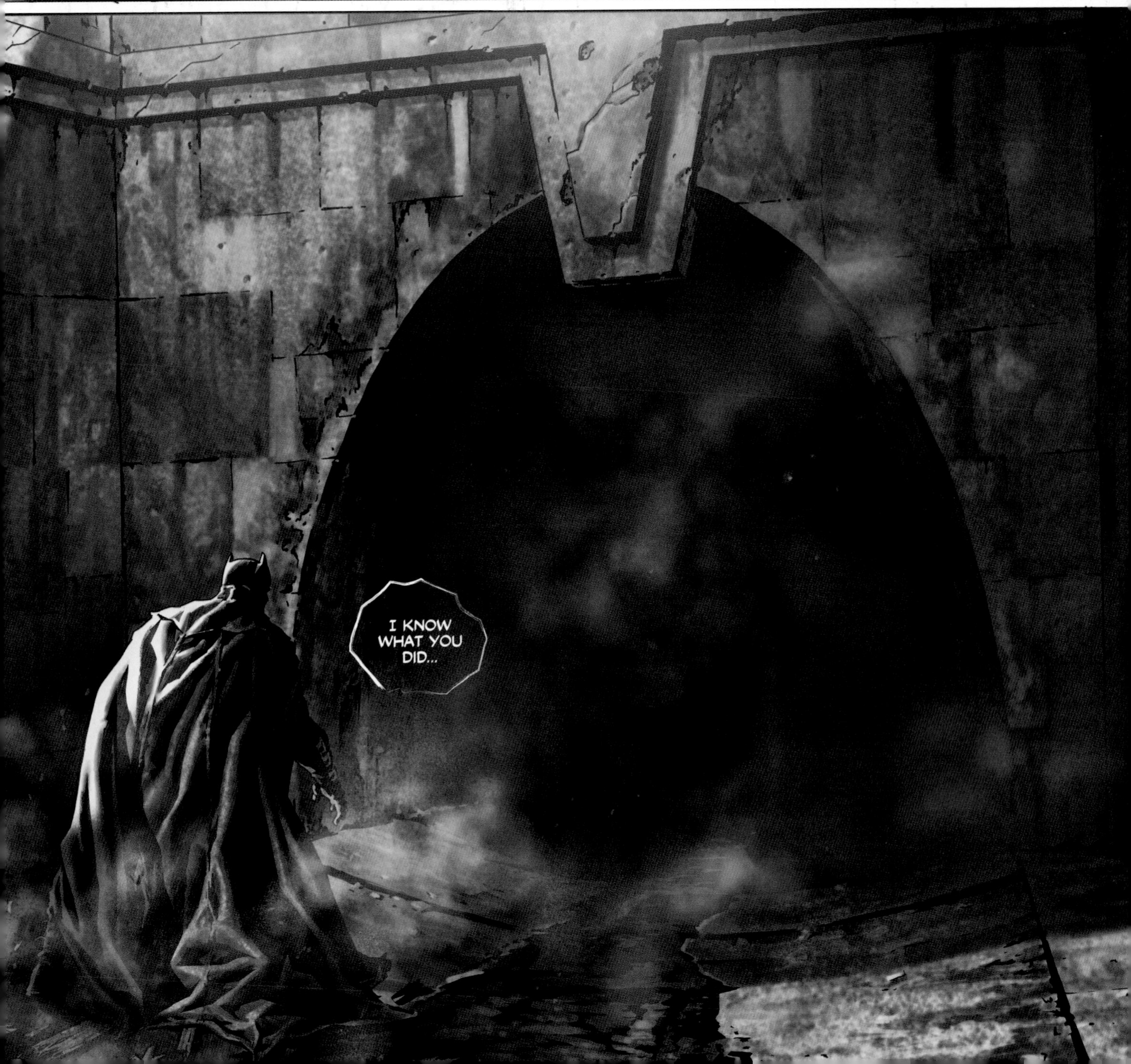
I KNOW WHAT YOU DID...

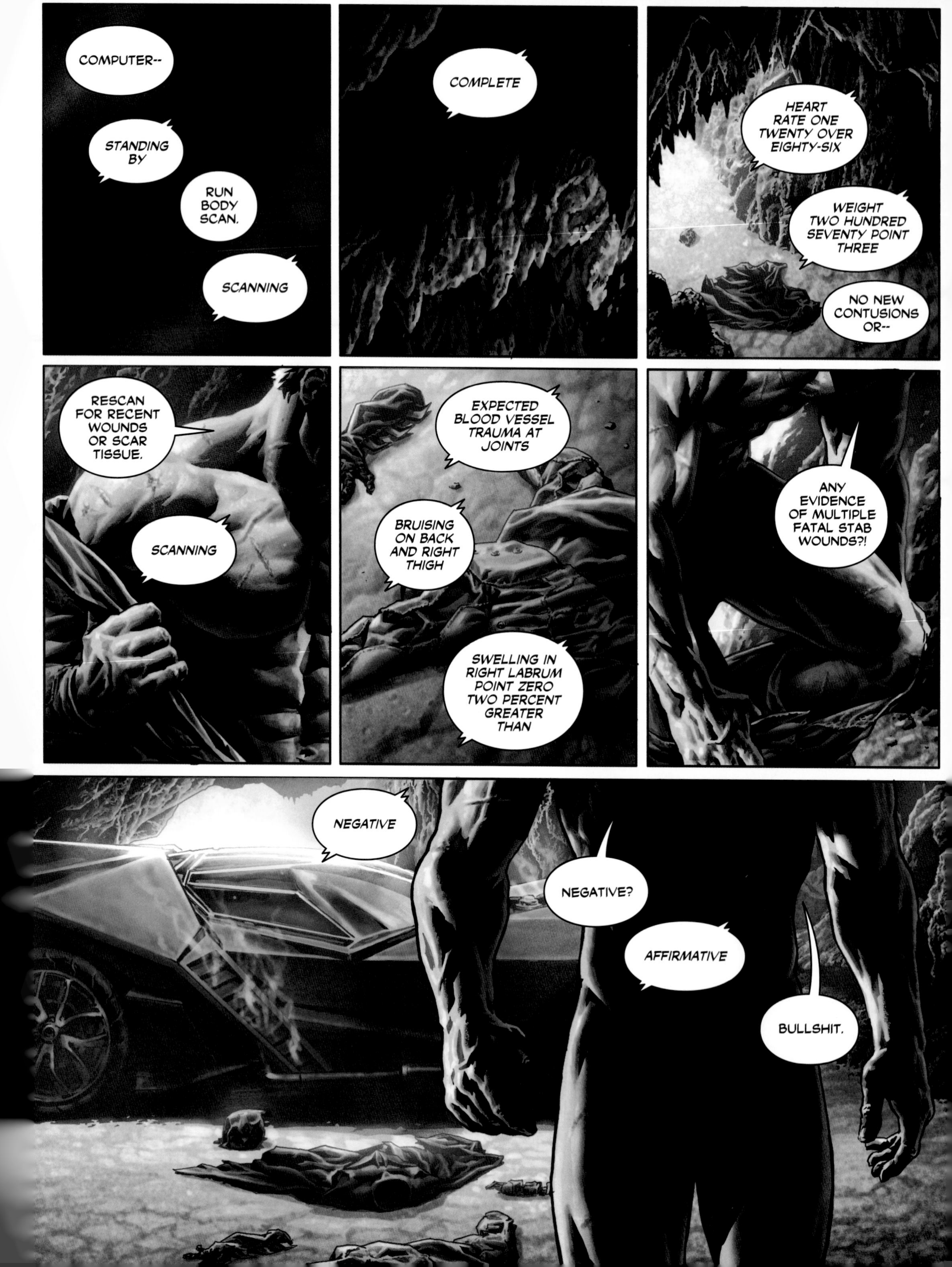
COMPUTER--
STANDING BY
RUN BODY SCAN.
SCANNING
COMPLETE
HEART RATE ONE TWENTY OVER EIGHTY-SIX
WEIGHT TWO HUNDRED SEVENTY POINT THREE
NO NEW CONTUSIONS OR--
RESCAN FOR RECENT WOUNDS OR SCAR TISSUE.
SCANNING
EXPECTED BLOOD VESSEL TRAUMA AT JOINTS
BRUISING ON BACK AND RIGHT THIGH
SWELLING IN RIGHT LABRUM POINT ZERO TWO PERCENT GREATER THAN
ANY EVIDENCE OF MULTIPLE FATAL STAB WOUNDS?!
NEGATIVE
NEGATIVE?
AFFIRMATIVE
BULLSHIT.

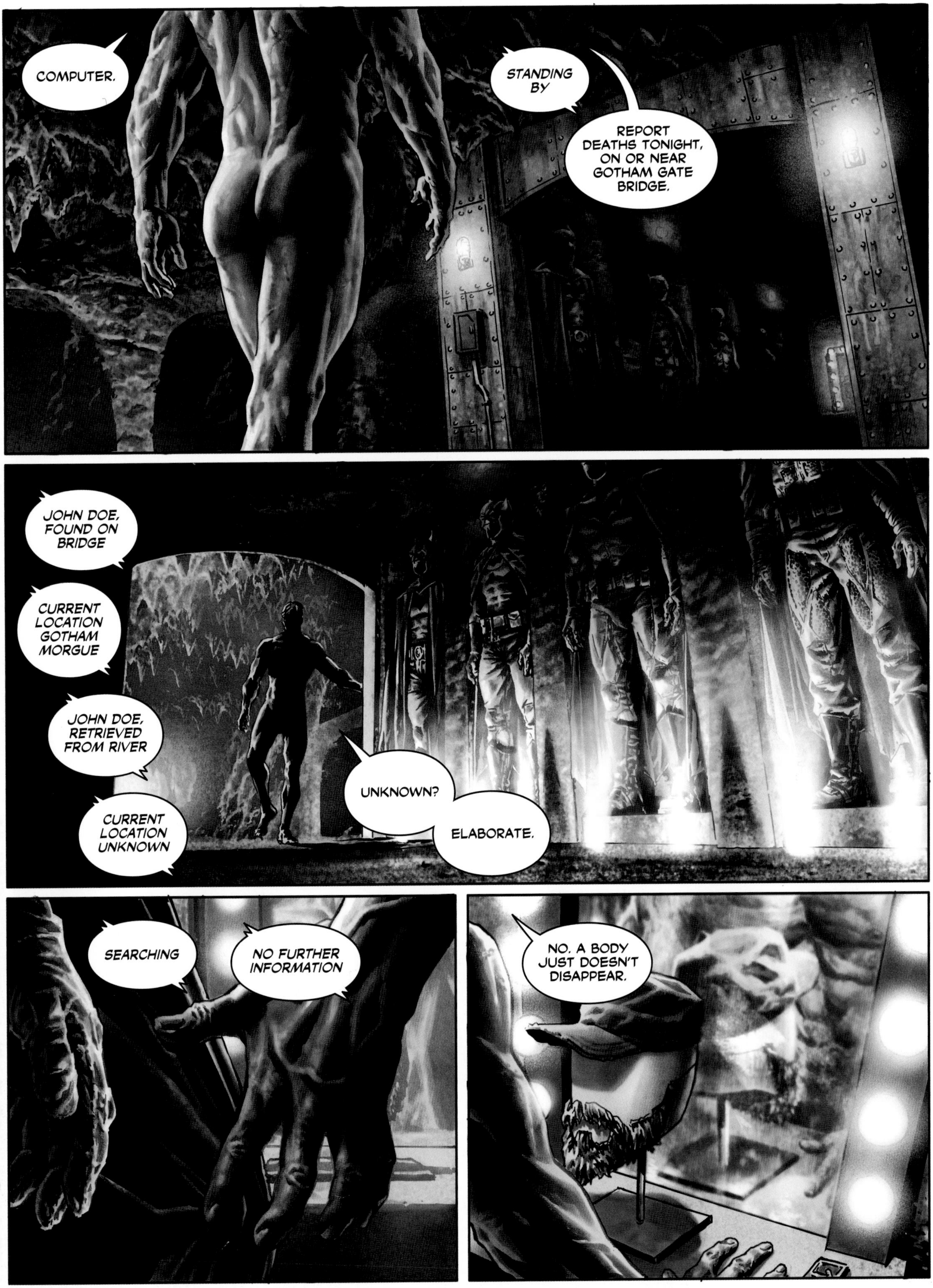
COMPUTER.
STANDING BY
REPORT DEATHS TONIGHT, ON OR NEAR GOTHAM GATE BRIDGE.
JOHN DOE, FOUND ON BRIDGE
CURRENT LOCATION GOTHAM MORGUE
JOHN DOE, RETRIEVED FROM RIVER
CURRENT LOCATION UNKNOWN
UNKNOWN?
ELABORATE.
SEARCHING
NO FURTHER INFORMATION
NO. A BODY JUST DOESN'T DISAPPEAR.

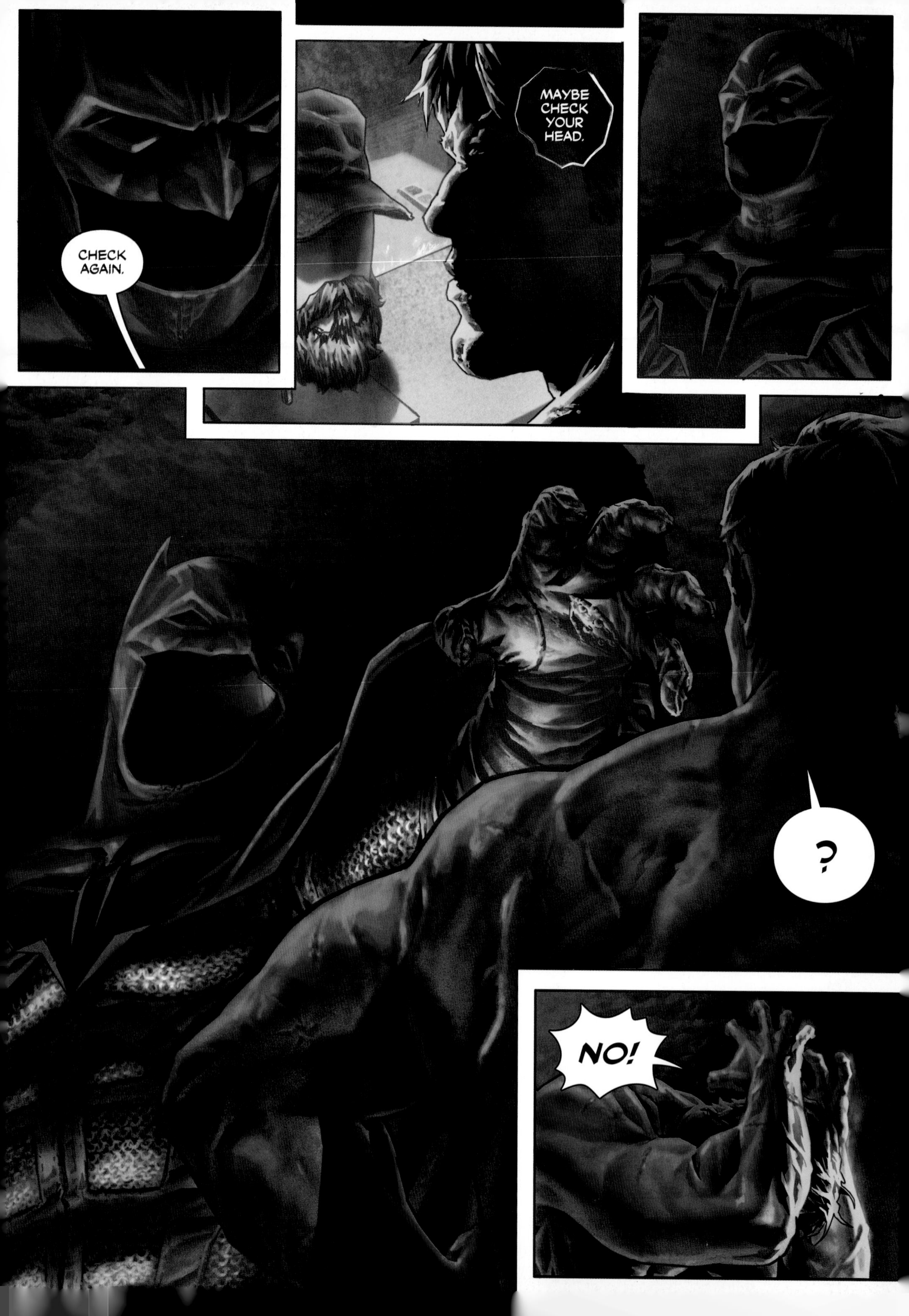
CHECK AGAIN.
MAYBE CHECK YOUR HEAD.
?
NO!

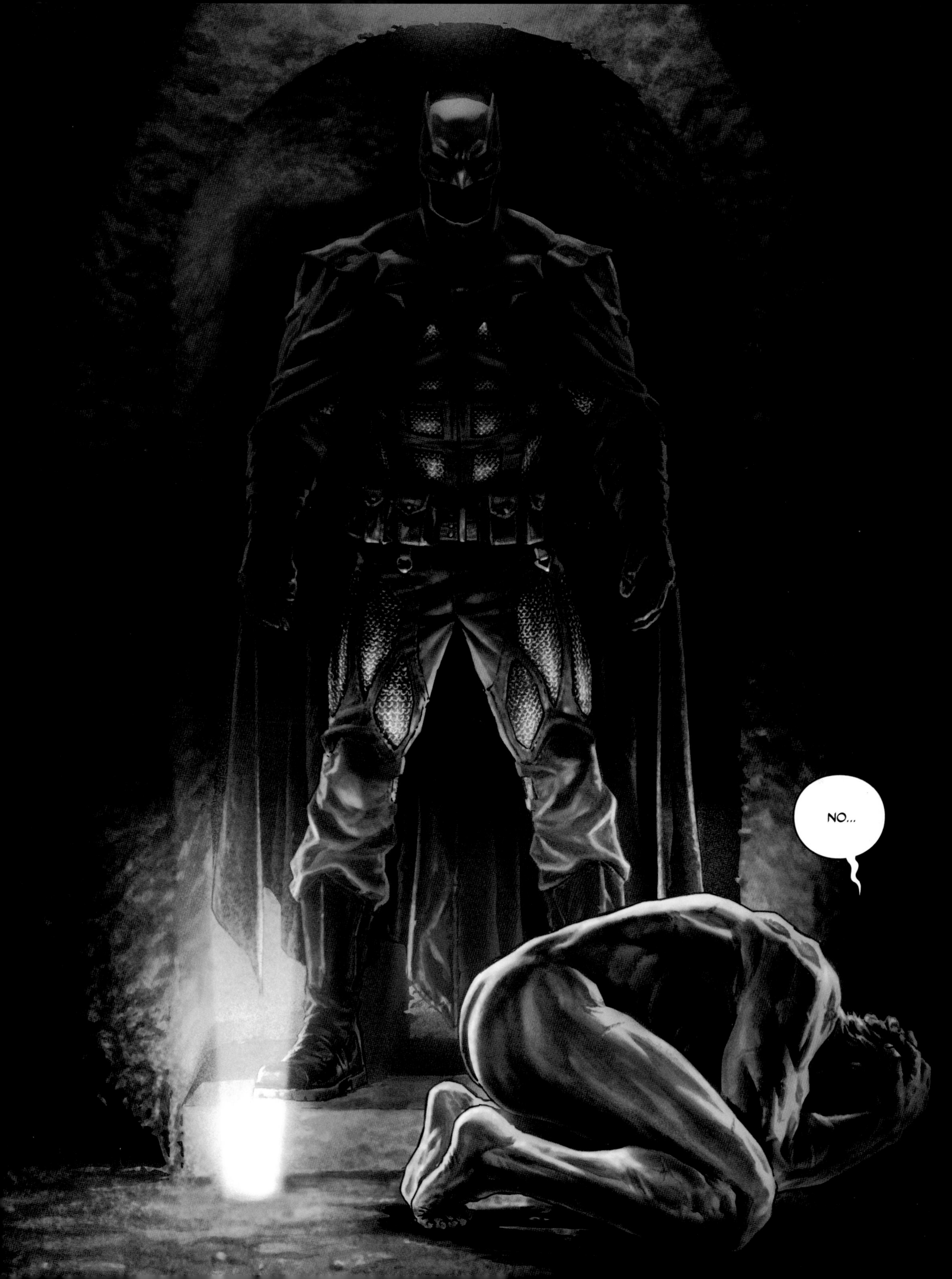
NO...

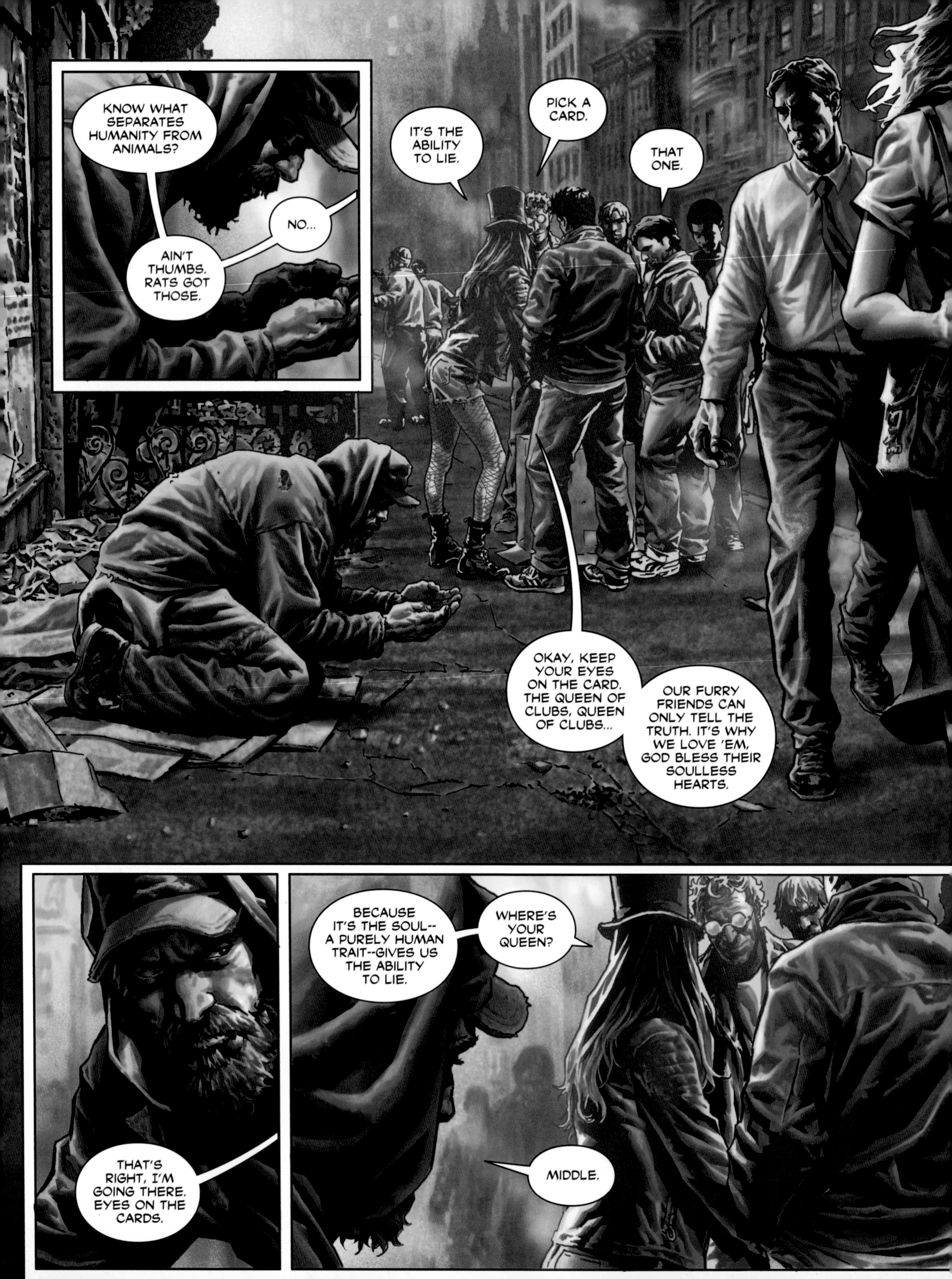
KNOW WHAT SEPARATES HUMANITY FROM ANIMALS?
AIN'T THUMBS. RATS GOT THOSE.
NO...
IT'S THE ABILITY TO LIE.
PICK A CARD.
THAT ONE.
OKAY, KEEP YOUR EYES ON THE CARD. THE QUEEN OF CLUBS, QUEEN OF CLUBS...
OUR FURRY FRIENDS CAN ONLY TELL THE TRUTH. IT'S WHY WE LOVE 'EM, GOD BLESS THEIR SOULLESS HEARTS.
BECAUSE IT'S THE SOUL-- A PURELY HUMAN TRAIT--GIVES US THE ABILITY TO LIE.
WHERE'S YOUR QUEEN?
MIDDLE.
THAT'S RIGHT, I'M GOING THERE. EYES ON THE CARDS.

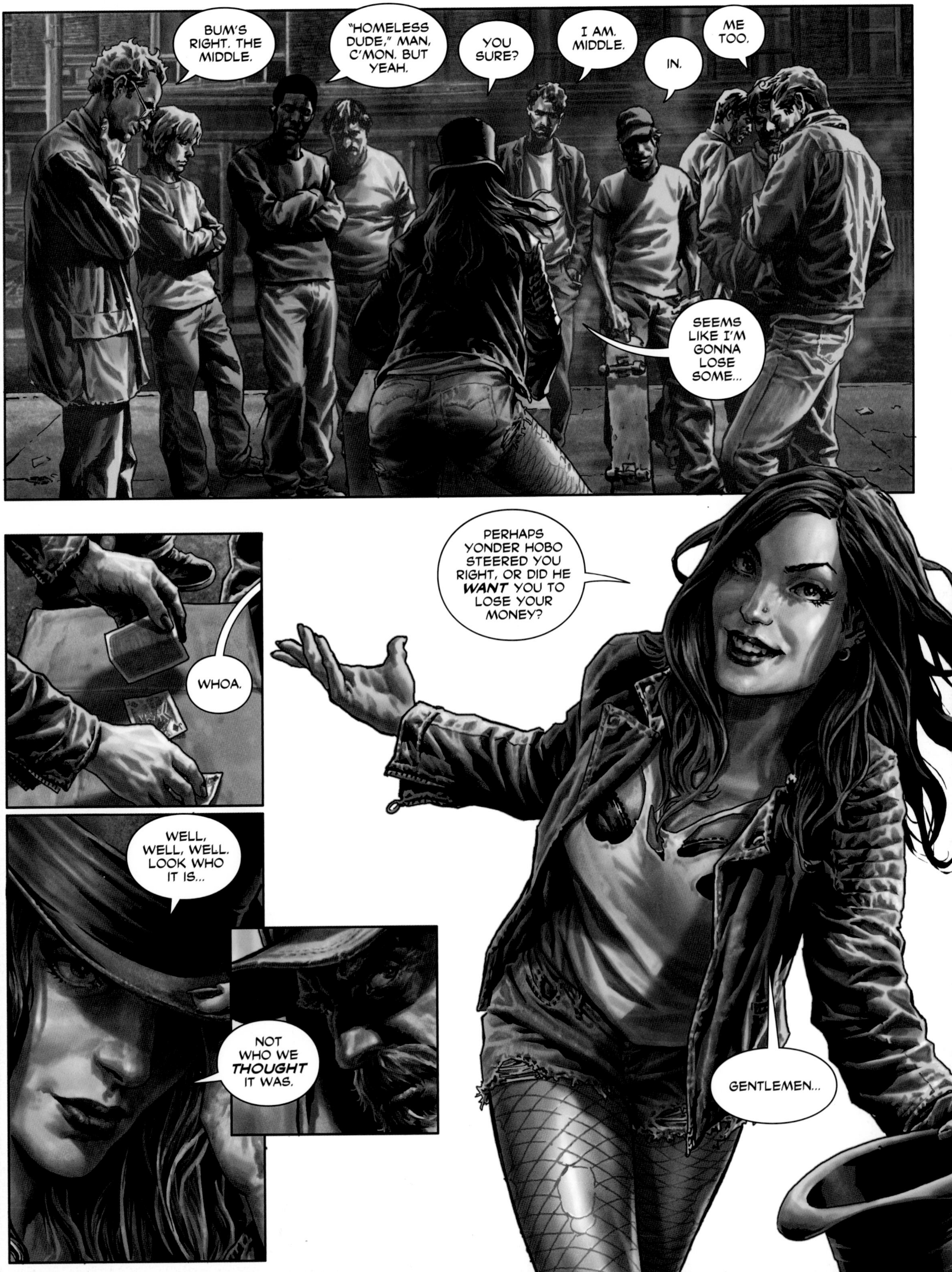
BUM'S RIGHT. THE MIDDLE.
"HOMELESS DUDE," MAN, C'MON. BUT YEAH.
YOU SURE?
I AM. MIDDLE.
IN.
ME TOO.
SEEMS LIKE I'M GONNA LOSE SOME...
WHOA.
PERHAPS YONDER HOBO STEERED YOU RIGHT, OR DID HE *WANT* YOU TO LOSE YOUR MONEY?
WELL, WELL, WELL. LOOK WHO IT IS...
NOT WHO WE *THOUGHT* IT WAS.
GENTLEMEN...

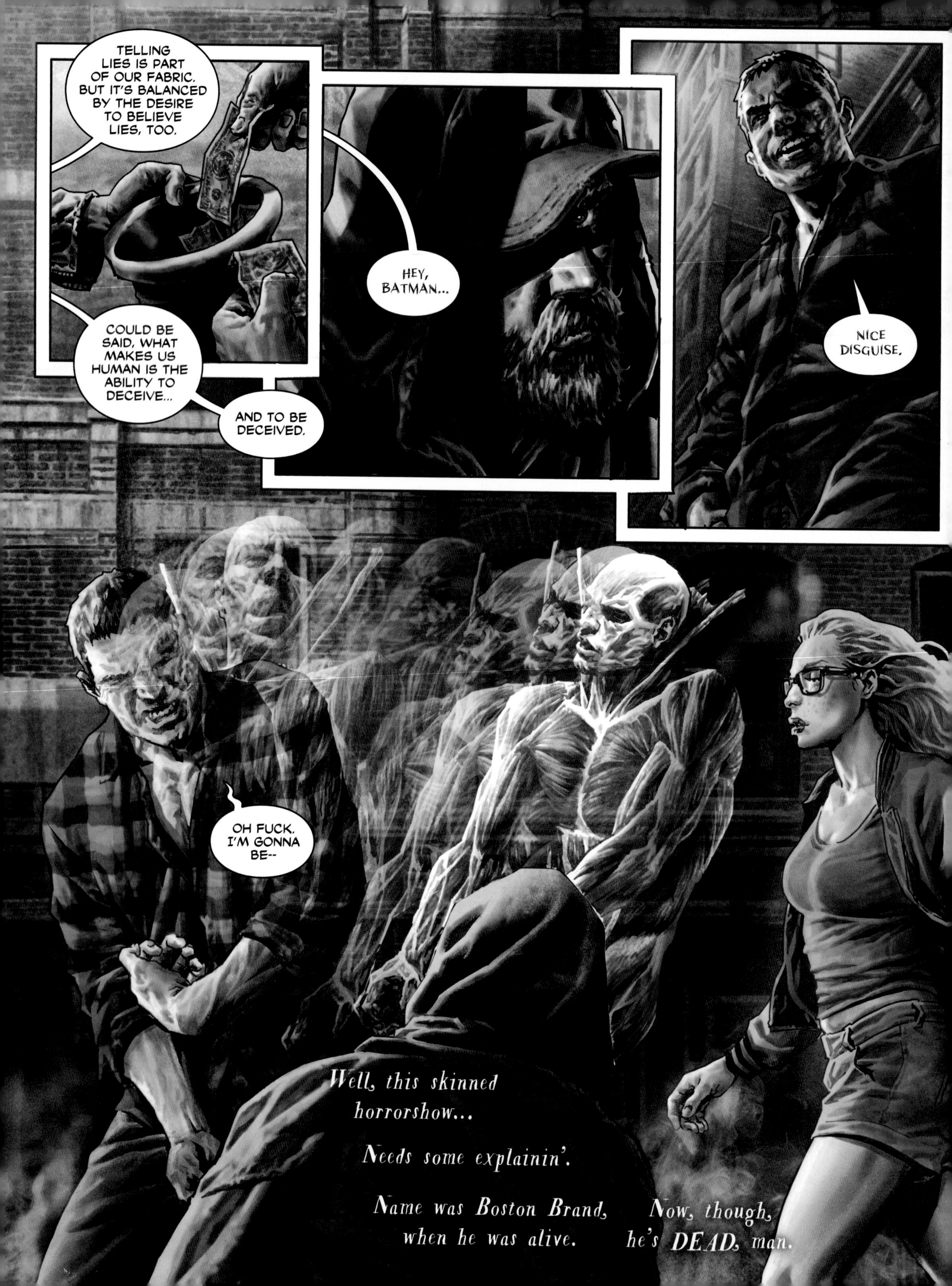
TELLING LIES IS PART OF OUR FABRIC. BUT IT'S BALANCED BY THE DESIRE TO BELIEVE LIES, TOO.
COULD BE SAID, WHAT MAKES US HUMAN IS THE ABILITY TO DECEIVE...
AND TO BE DECEIVED.
HEY, BATMAN...
NICE DISGUISE.
OH FUCK. I'M GONNA BE--
Well, this skinned horrorshow...
Needs some explainin'.
Name was Boston Brand, when he was alive.
Now, though, he's DEAD, man.

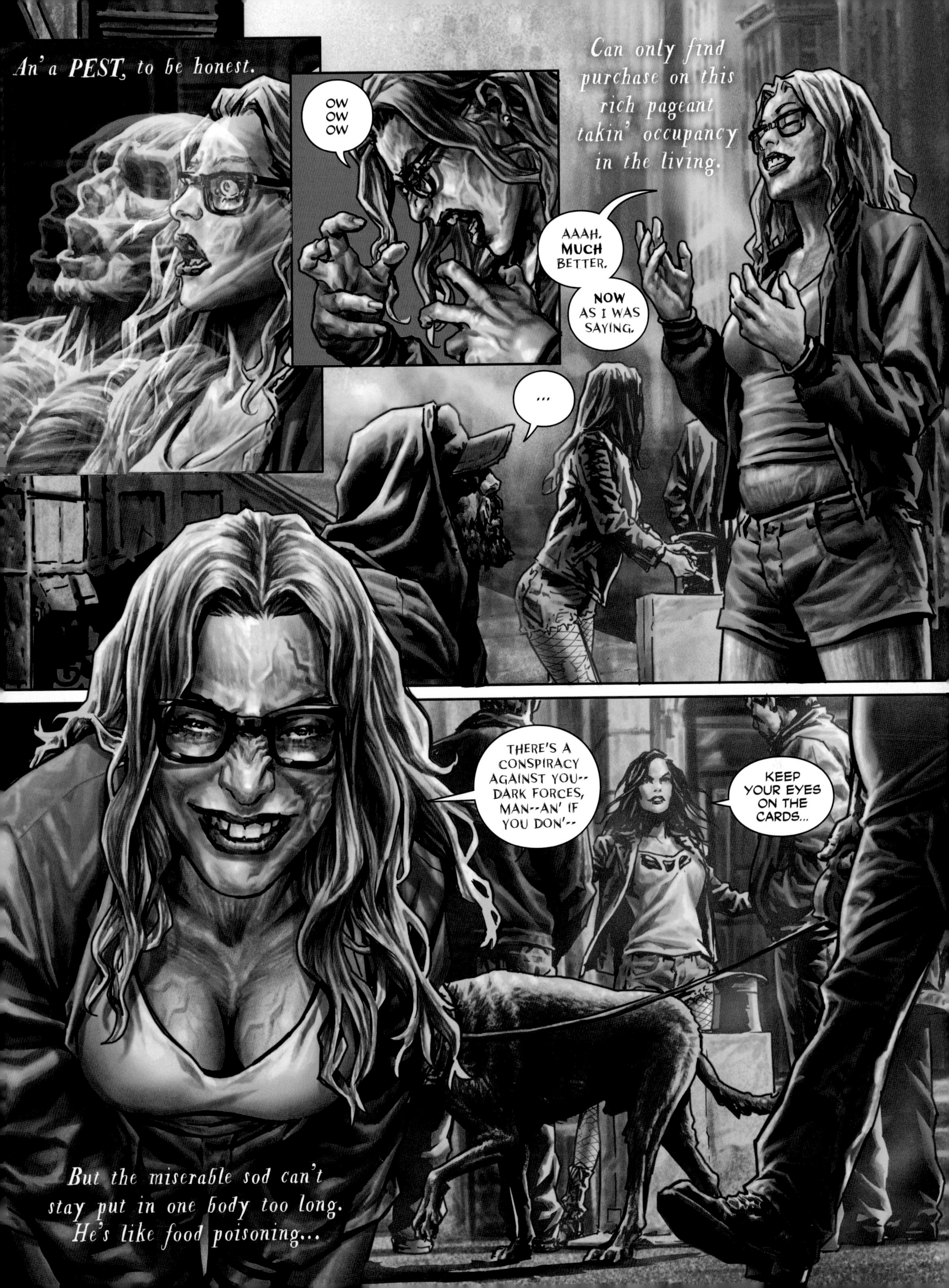
An' a PEST, to be honest.
OW OW OW
Can only find purchase on this rich pageant takin' occupancy in the living.
AAAH. MUCH BETTER.
NOW AS I WAS SAYING.
...
THERE'S A CONSPIRACY AGAINST YOU--DARK FORCES, MAN--AN' IF YOU DON'--
KEEP YOUR EYES ON THE CARDS...
But the miserable sod can't stay put in one body too long. He's like food poisoning...

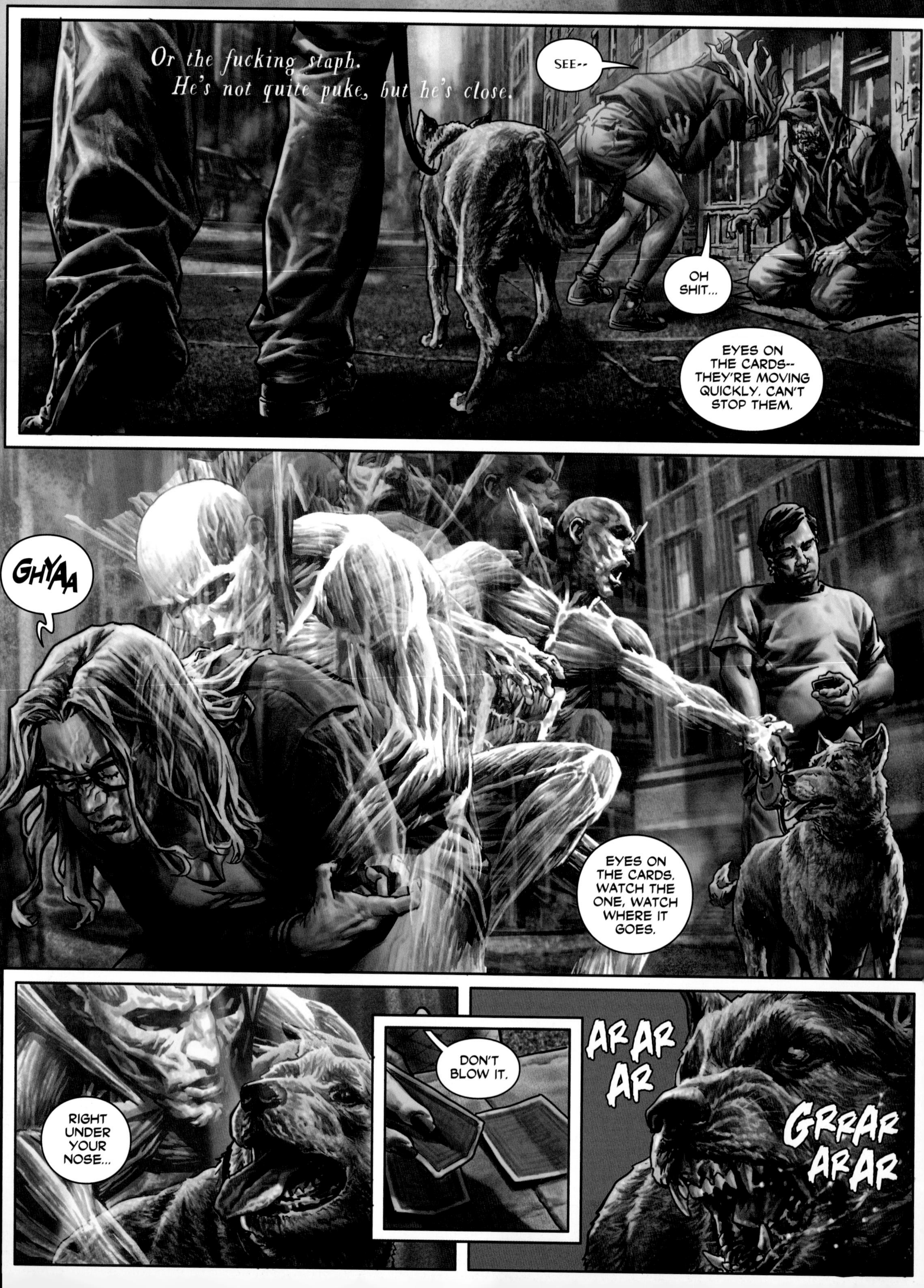
Or the fucking staph.
He's not quite puke, but he's close.
SEE--
OH SHIT...
EYES ON THE CARDS-- THEY'RE MOVING QUICKLY. CAN'T STOP THEM.
GHYAA
EYES ON THE CARDS. WATCH THE ONE, WATCH WHERE IT GOES.
RIGHT UNDER YOUR NOSE...
DON'T BLOW IT.
ARAR AR
GRRAR ARAR

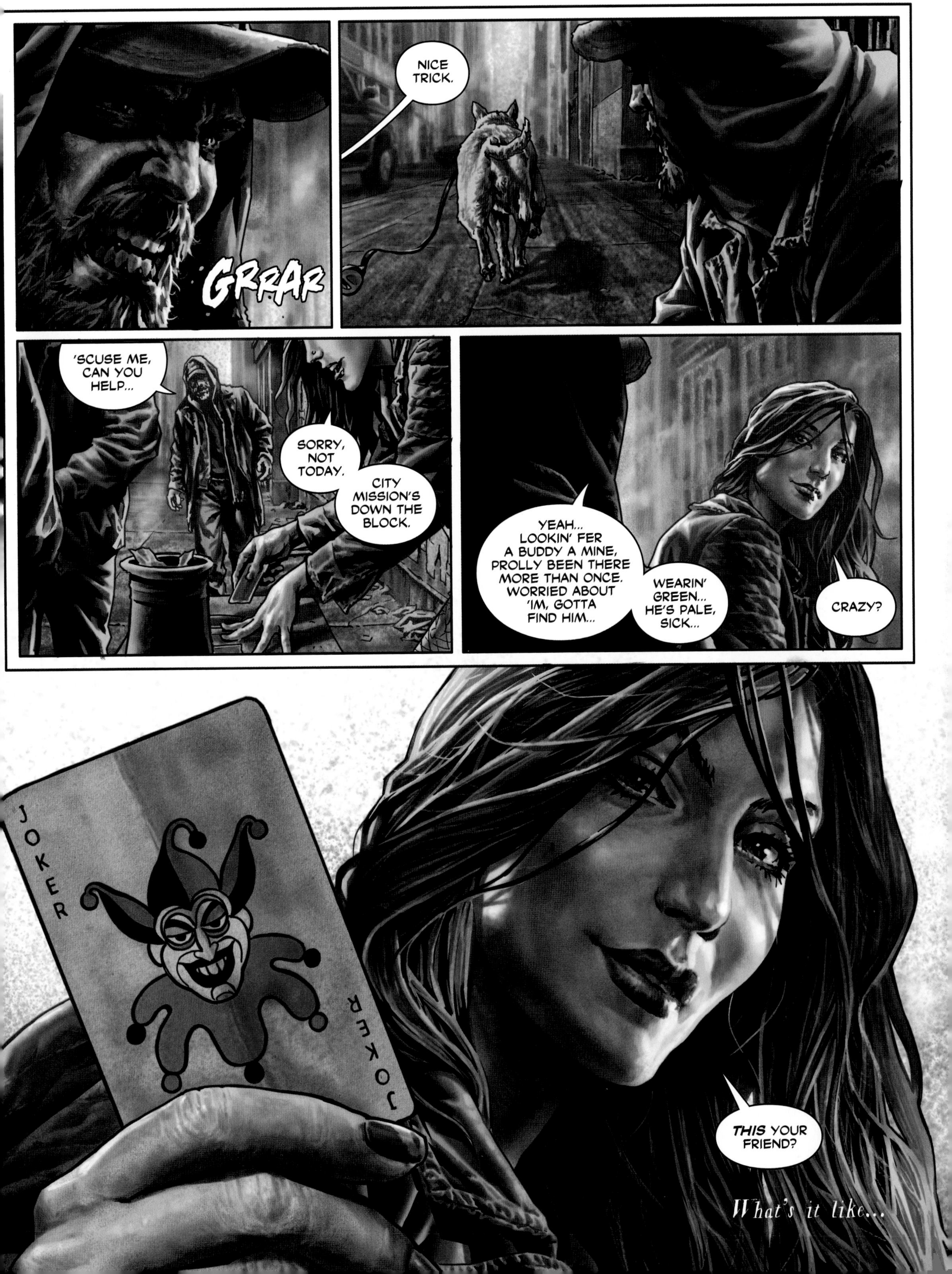
GRRAR
NICE TRICK.
'SCUSE ME, CAN YOU HELP...
SORRY, NOT TODAY.
CITY MISSION'S DOWN THE BLOCK.
YEAH... LOOKIN' FER A BUDDY A MINE, PROLLY BEEN THERE MORE THAN ONCE. WORRIED ABOUT 'IM, GOTTA FIND HIM...
WEARIN' GREEN... HE'S PALE, SICK...
CRAZY?
JOKER
JOKER
THIS YOUR FRIEND?
What's it like...

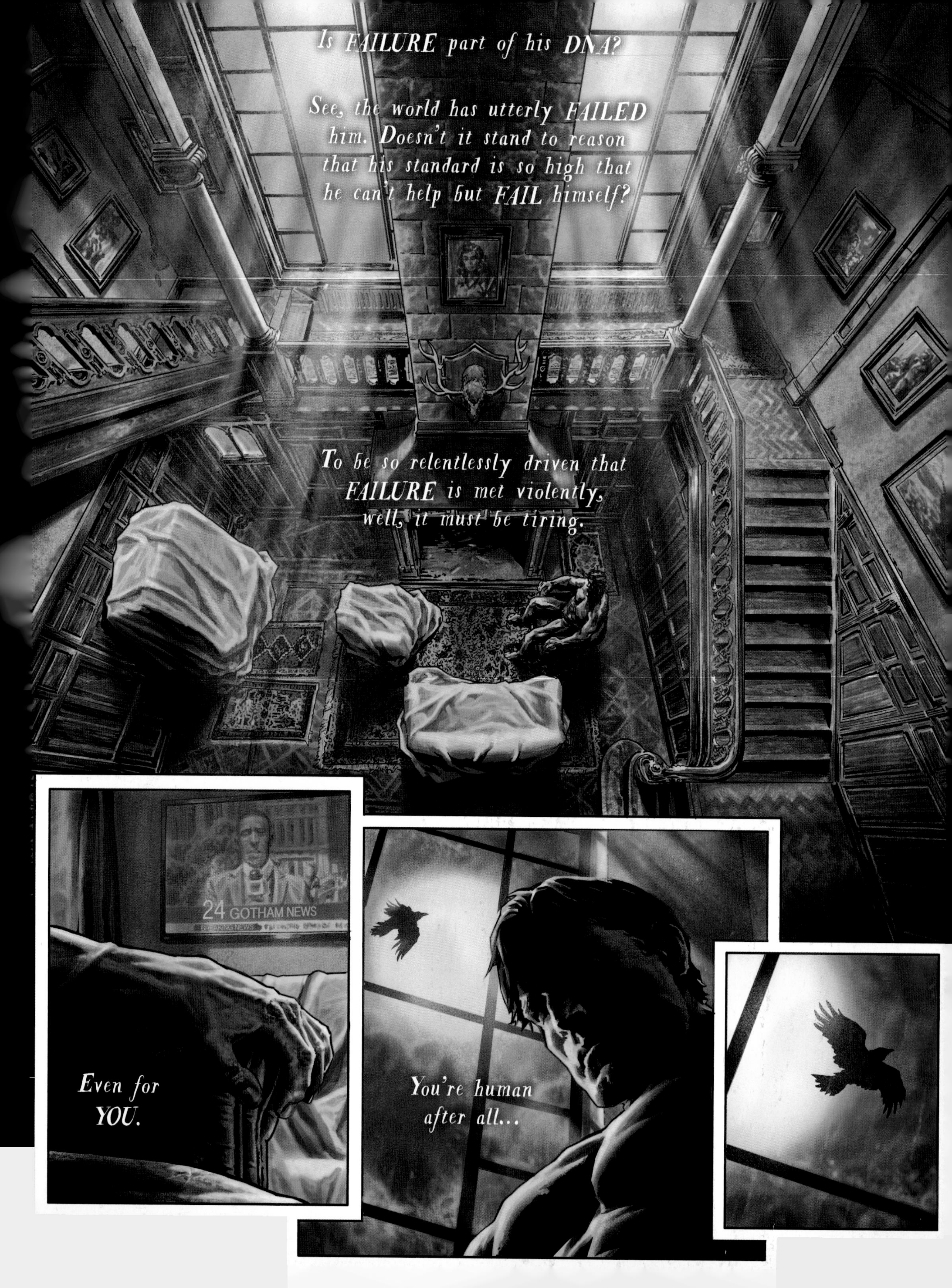
Is FAILURE part of his DNA?
See, the world has utterly FAILED him. Doesn't it stand to reason that his standard is so high that he can't help but FAIL himself?
To be so relentlessly driven that FAILURE is met violently, well, it must be tiring.
24 GOTHAM NEWS
Even for YOU.
You're human after all...

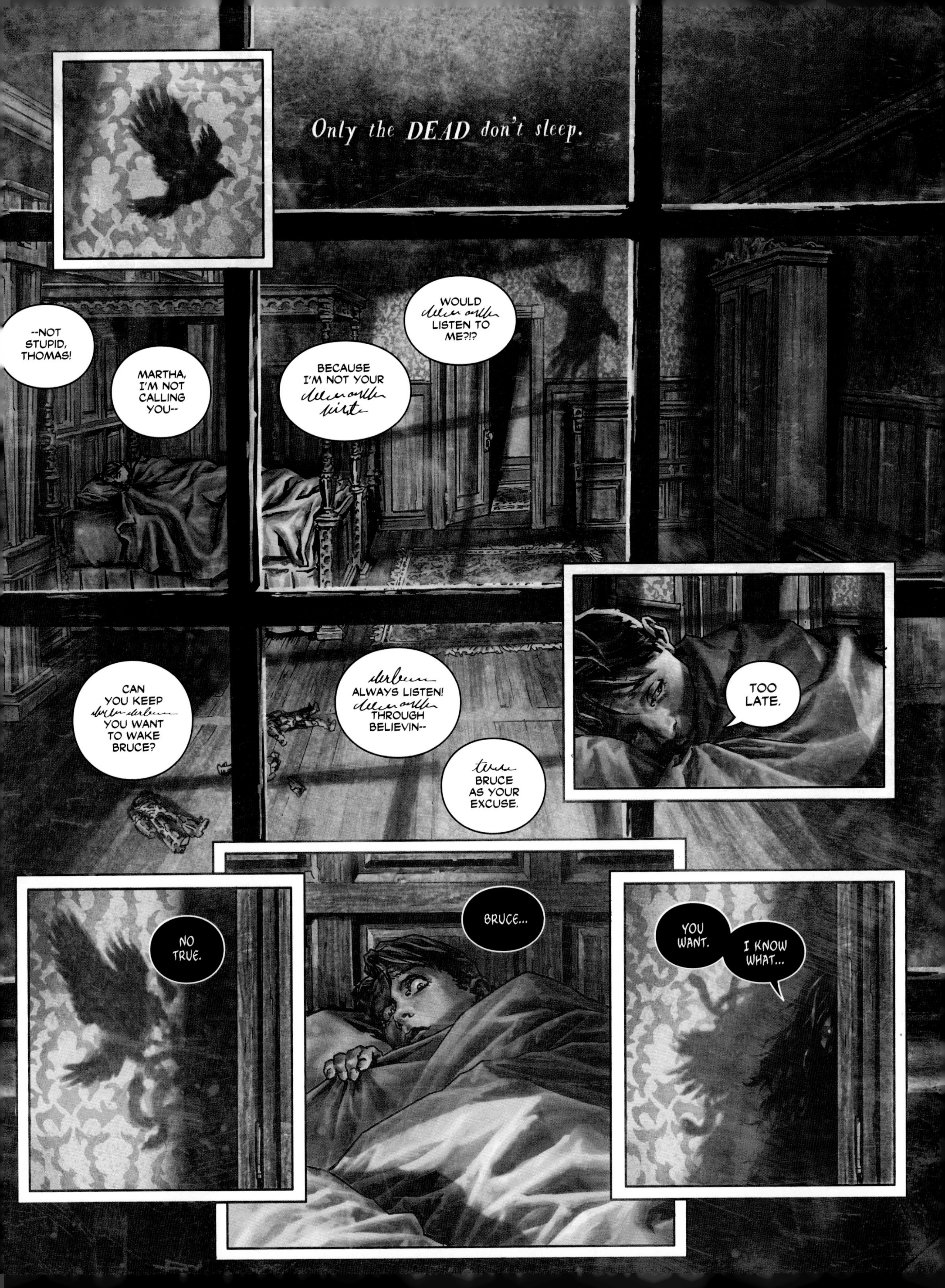

Only the DEAD don't sleep.
--NOT STUPID, THOMAS!
MARTHA, I'M NOT CALLING YOU--
BECAUSE I'M NOT YOUR
WOULD LISTEN TO ME?!?
CAN YOU KEEP YOU WANT TO WAKE BRUCE?
ALWAYS LISTEN! THROUGH BELIEVIN--
BRUCE AS YOUR EXCUSE.
TOO LATE.
NO TRUE.
BRUCE...
I KNOW WHAT...
YOU WANT.

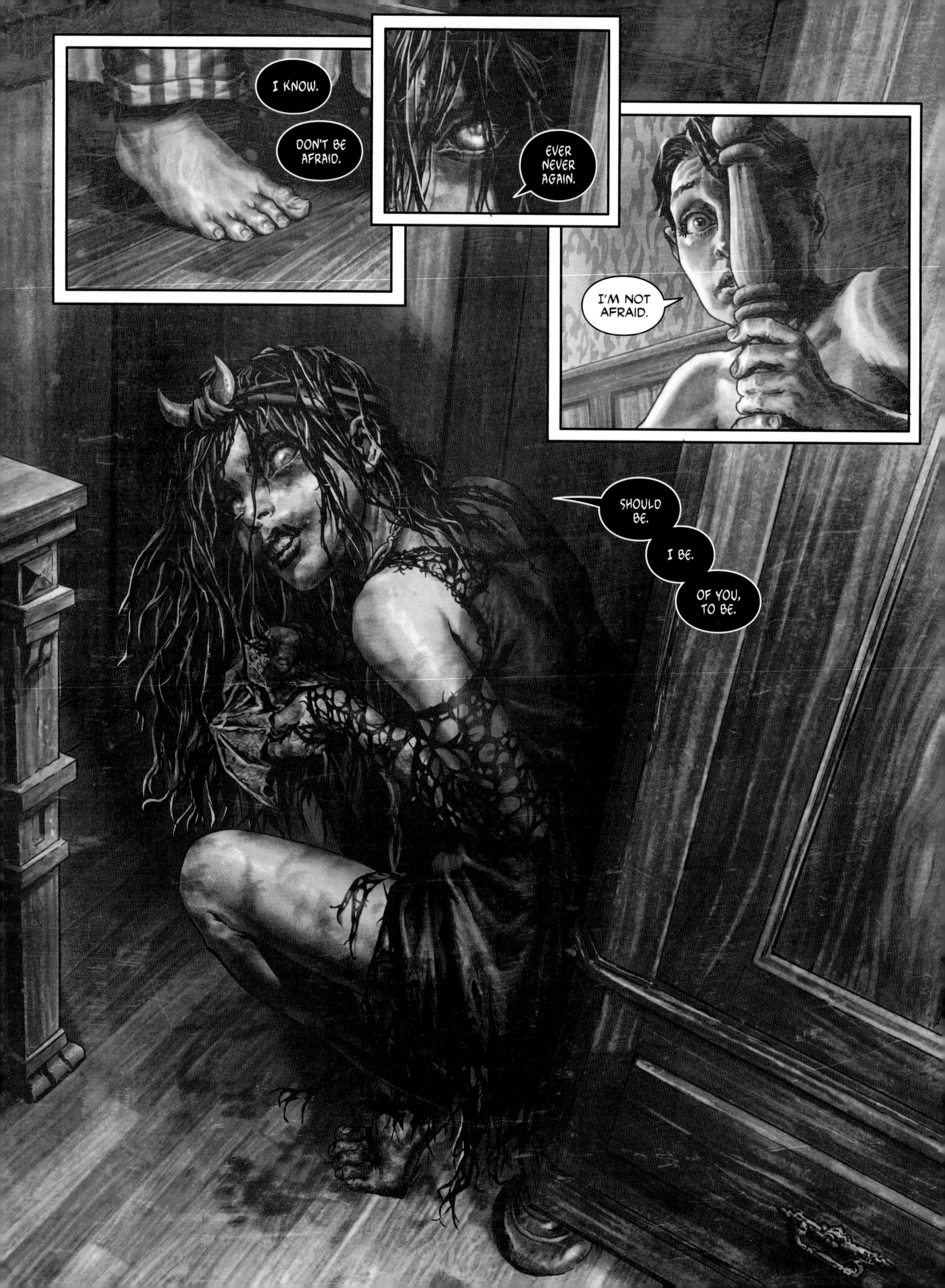
I KNOW.
DON'T BE AFRAID.
EVER NEVER AGAIN.
I'M NOT AFRAID.
SHOULD BE.
I BE.
OF YOU, TO BE.

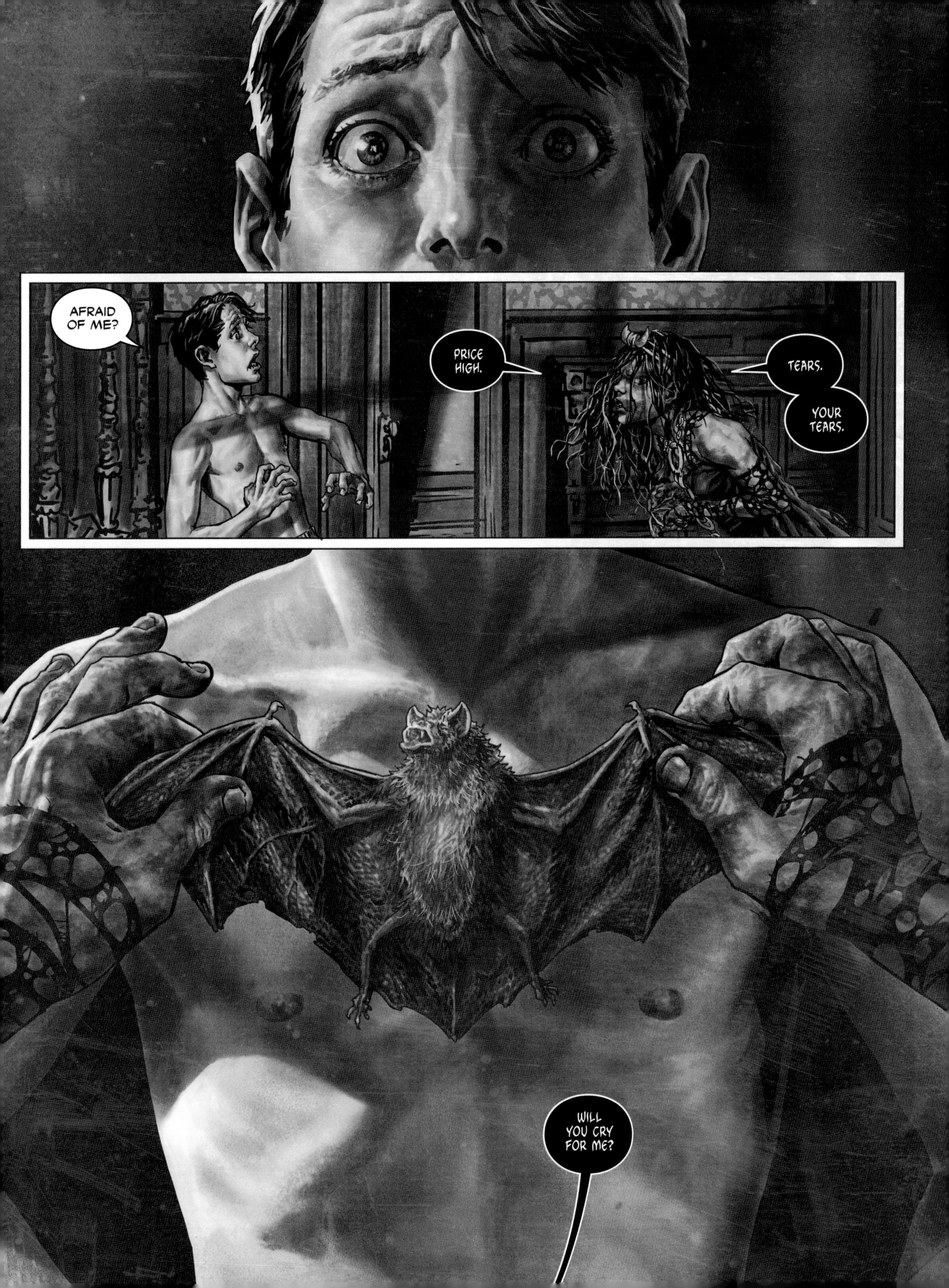
AFRAID OF ME?
PRICE HIGH.
TEARS.
YOUR TEARS.
WILL YOU CRY FOR ME?

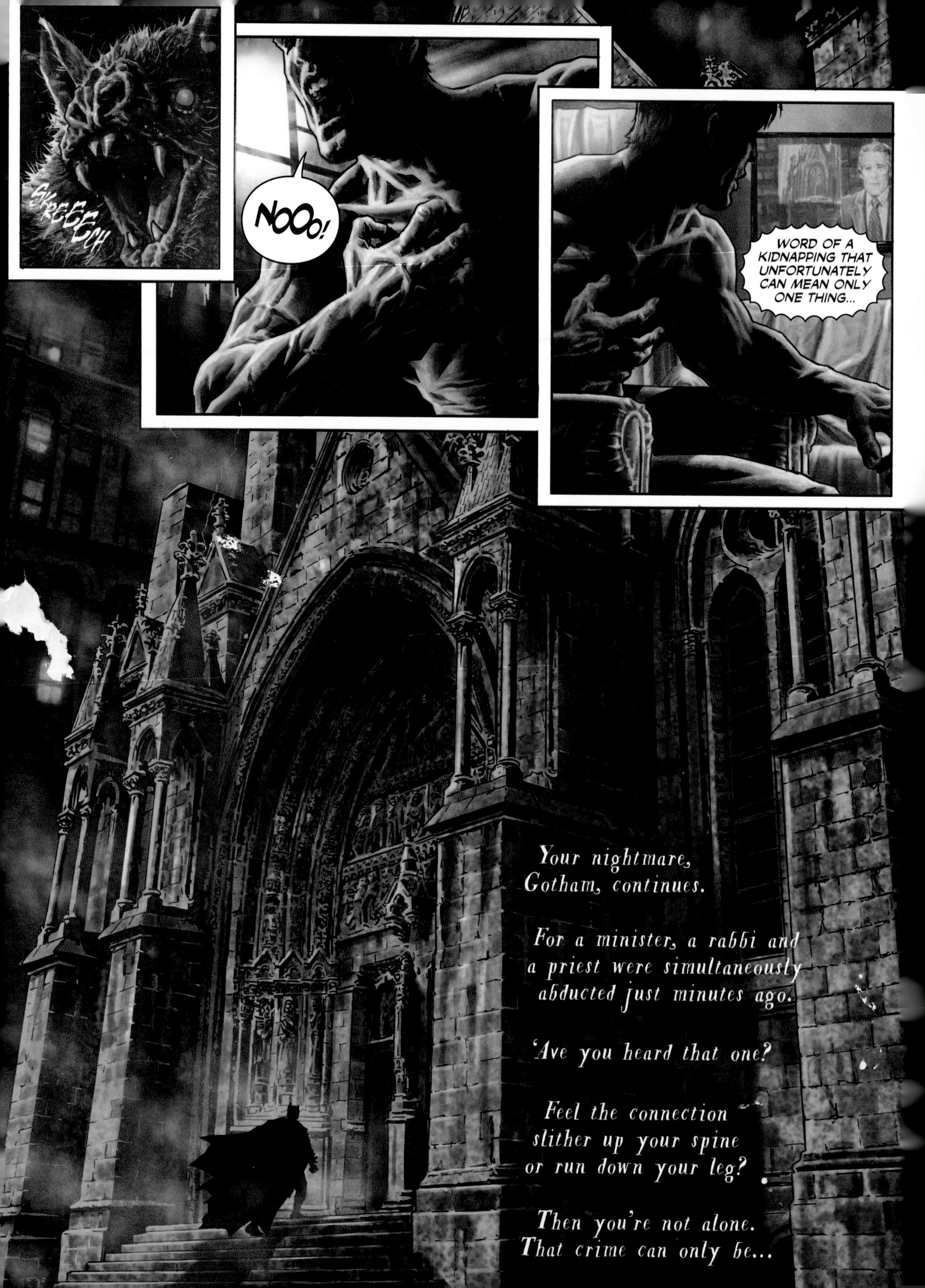
SKREEEECH
NOOo!
WORD OF A KIDNAPPING THAT UNFORTUNATELY CAN MEAN ONLY ONE THING...
Your nightmare, Gotham, continues.
For a minister, a rabbi and a priest were simultaneously abducted just minutes ago.
'Ave you heard that one?
Feel the connection slither up your spine or run down your leg?
Then you're not alone. That crime can only be...

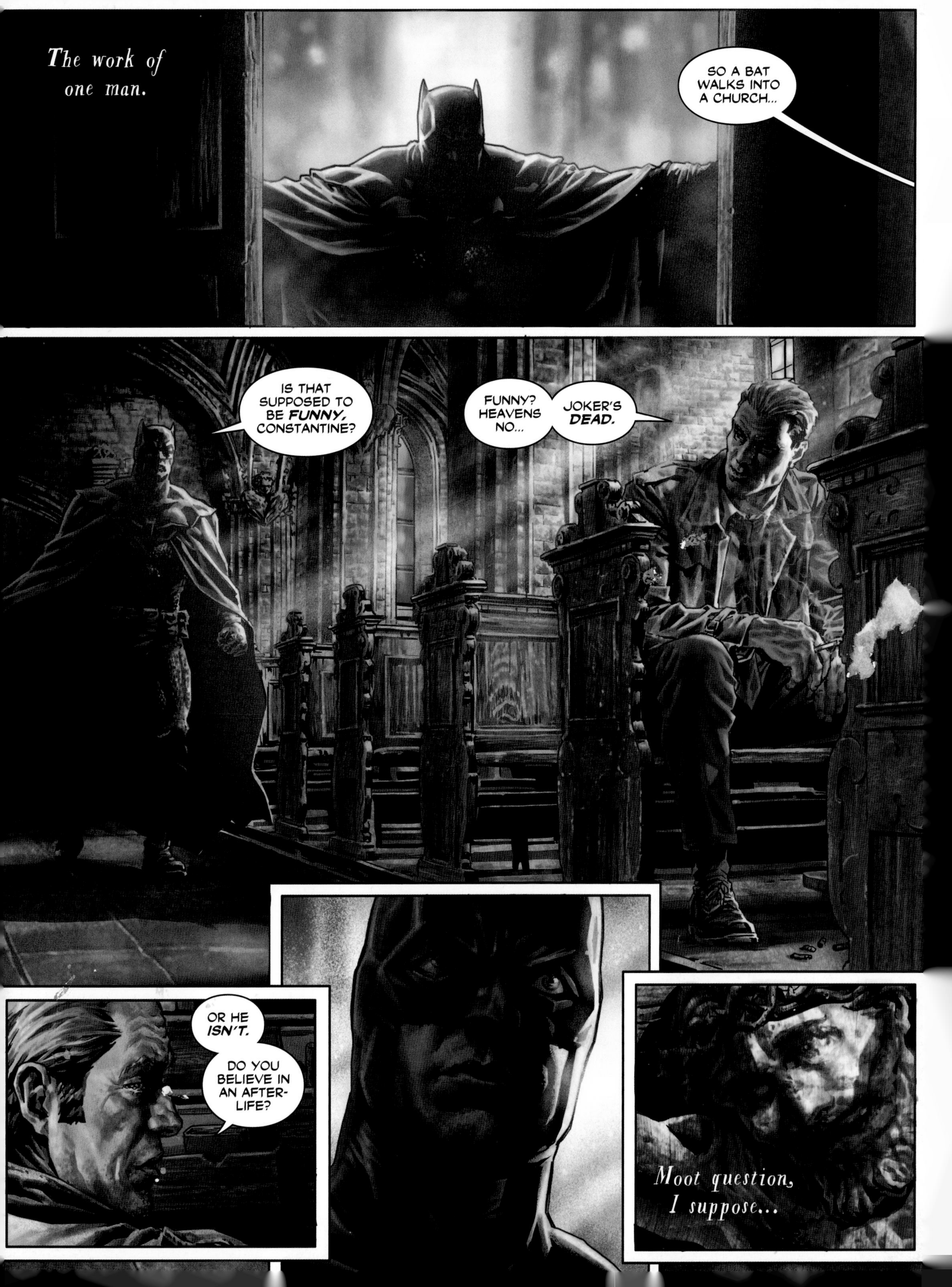
The work of one man.
SO A BAT WALKS INTO A CHURCH...
IS THAT SUPPOSED TO BE FUNNY, CONSTANTINE?
FUNNY? HEAVENS NO...
JOKER'S DEAD.
OR HE ISN'T.
DO YOU BELIEVE IN AN AFTER-LIFE?
Moot question, I suppose...

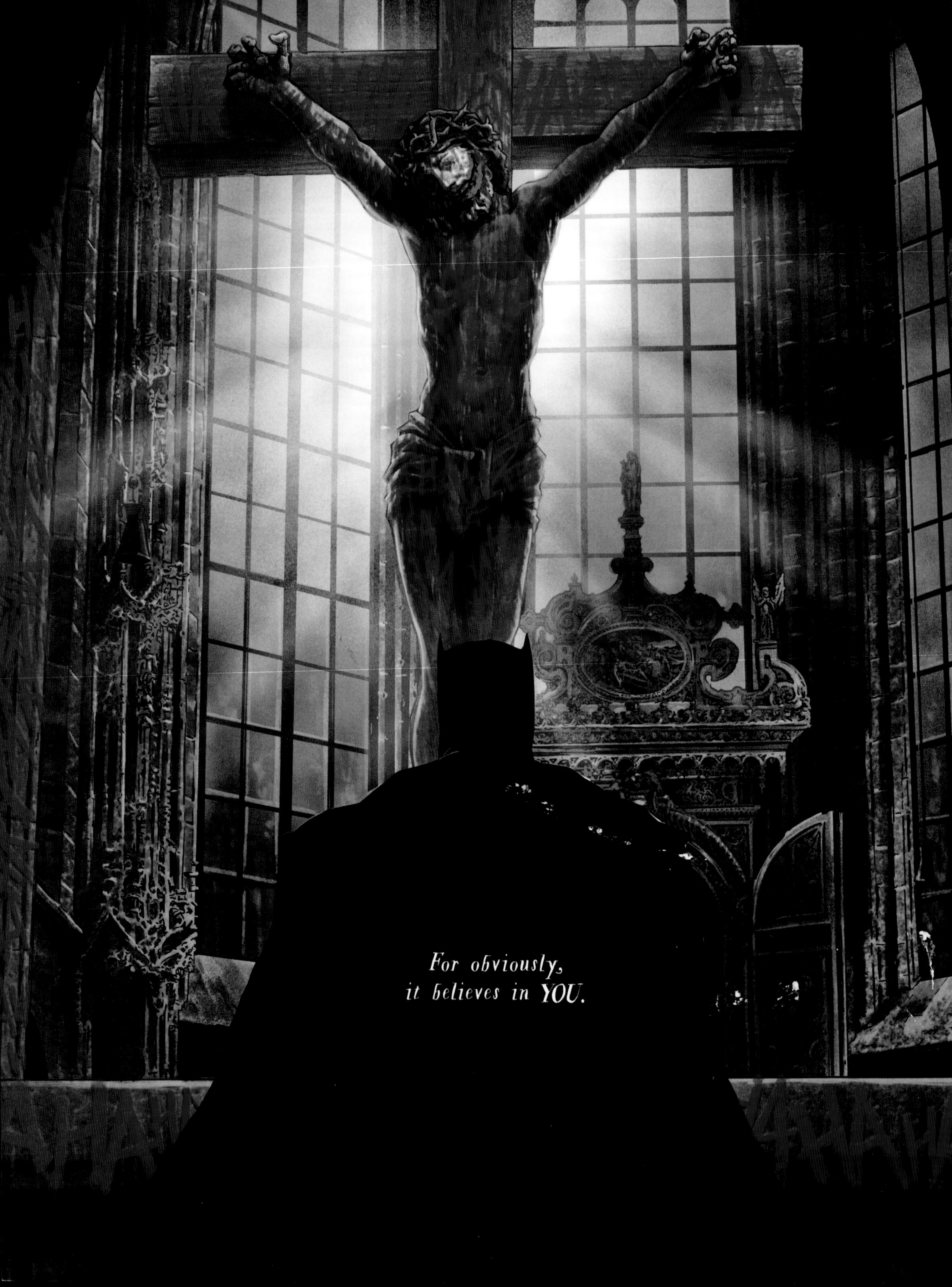
For obviously,
it believes in YOU.

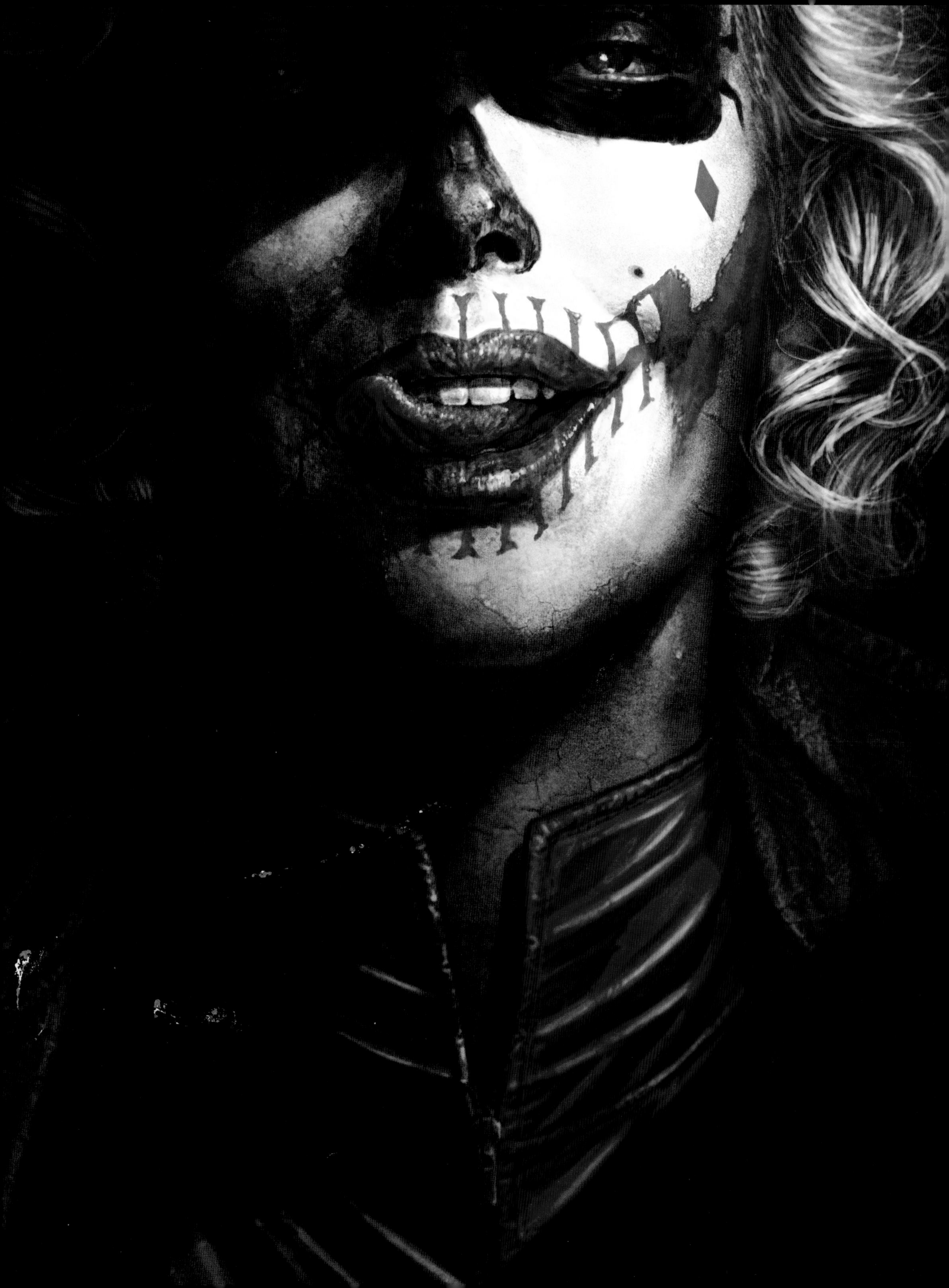

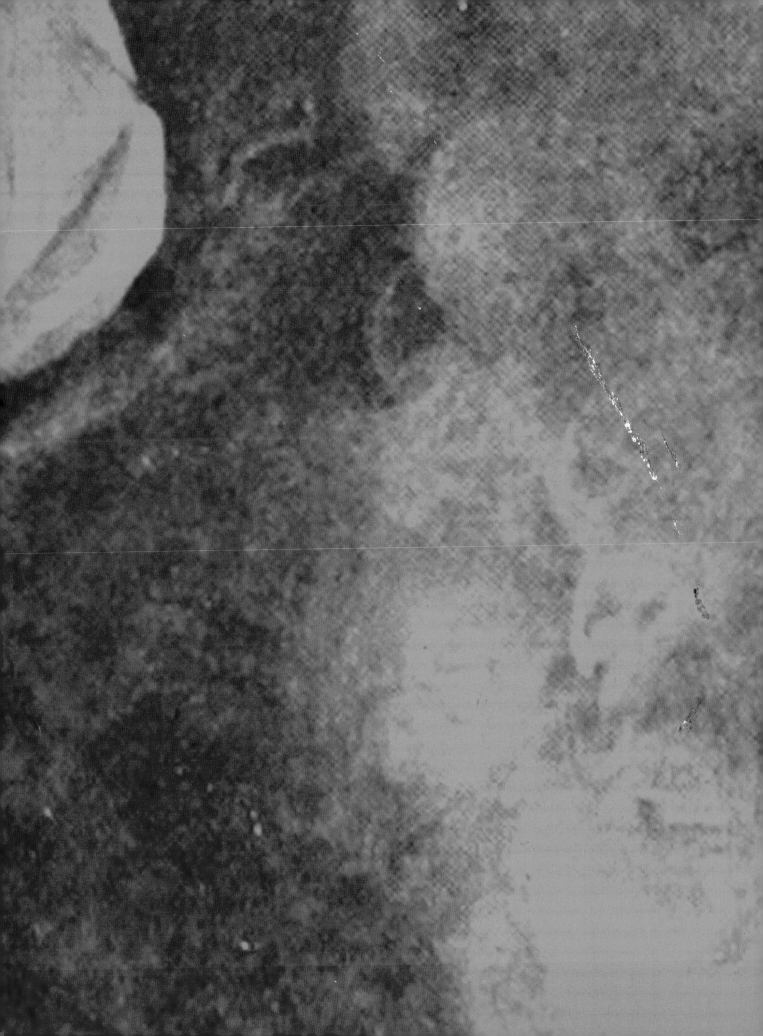

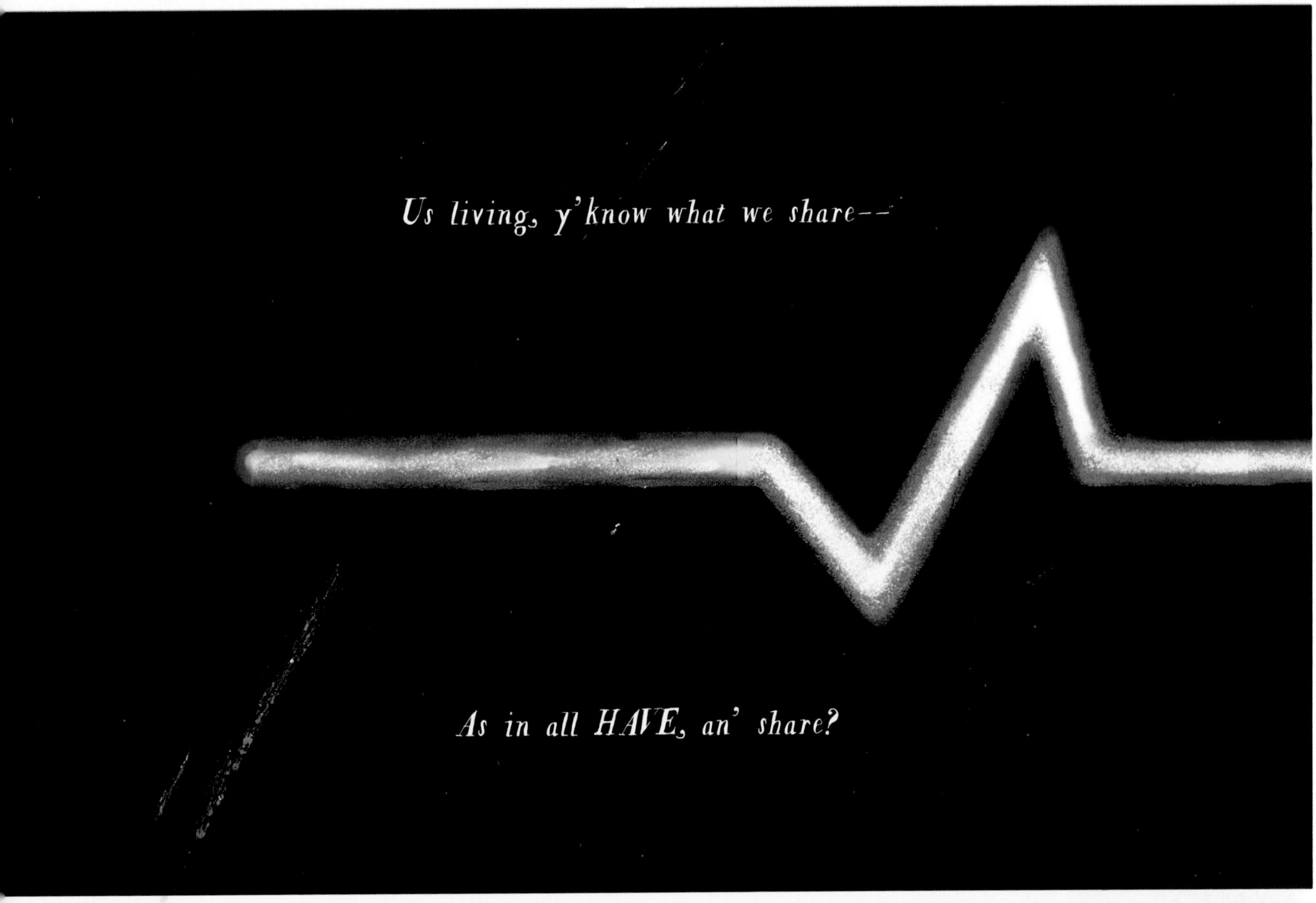
Us living, y'know what we share--
As in all HAVE, an' share?
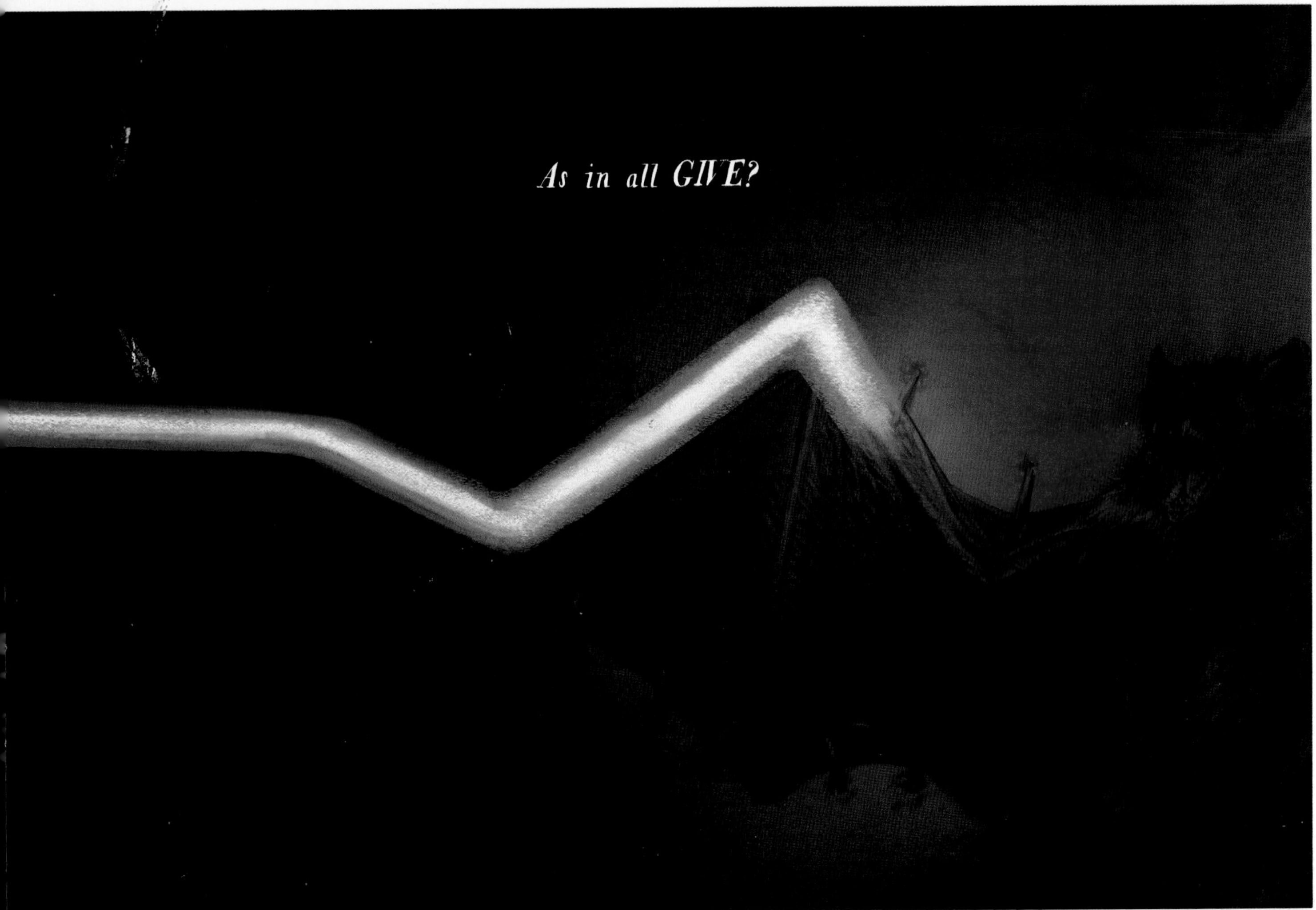
As in all GIVE?

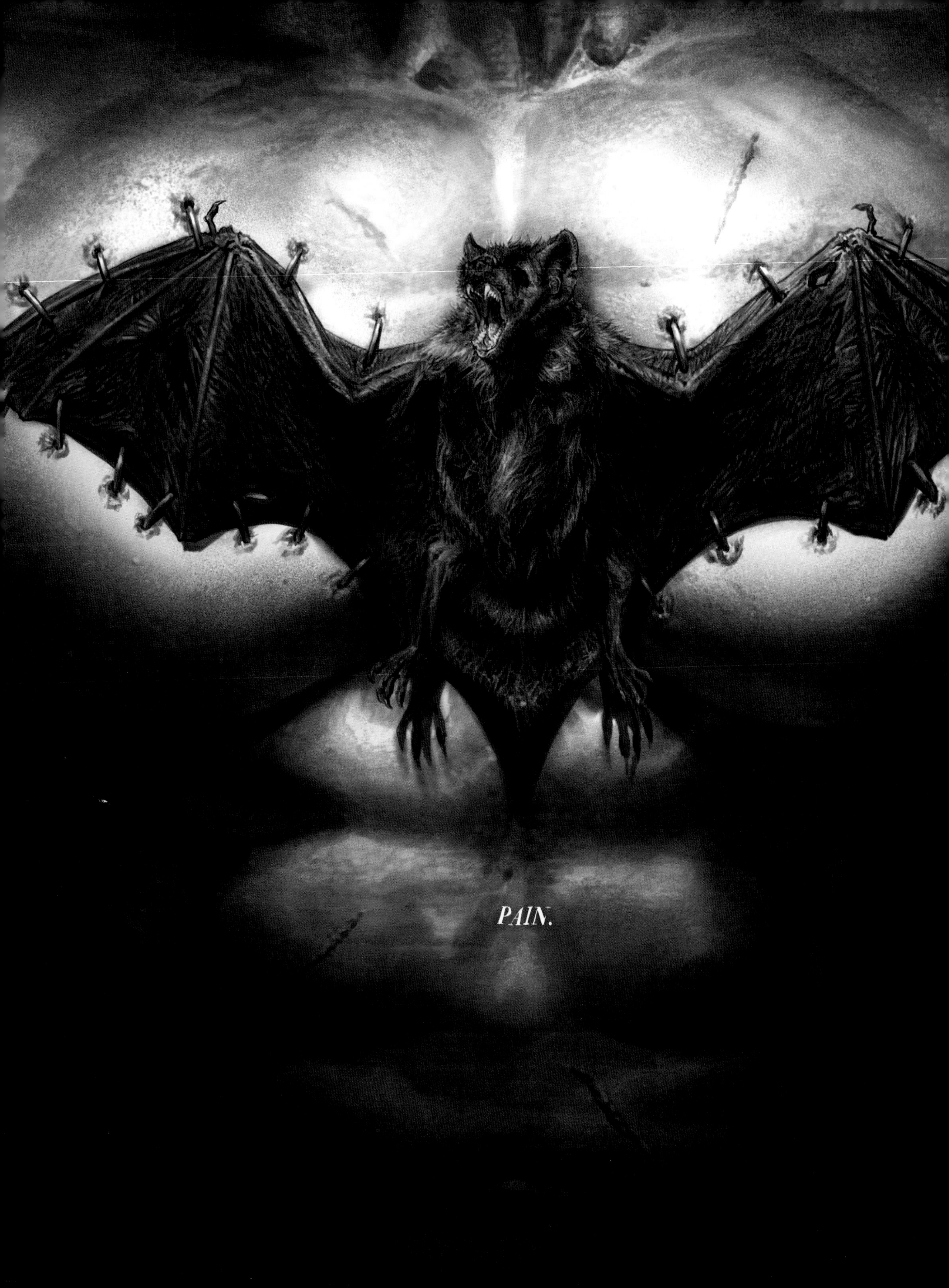
PAIN.

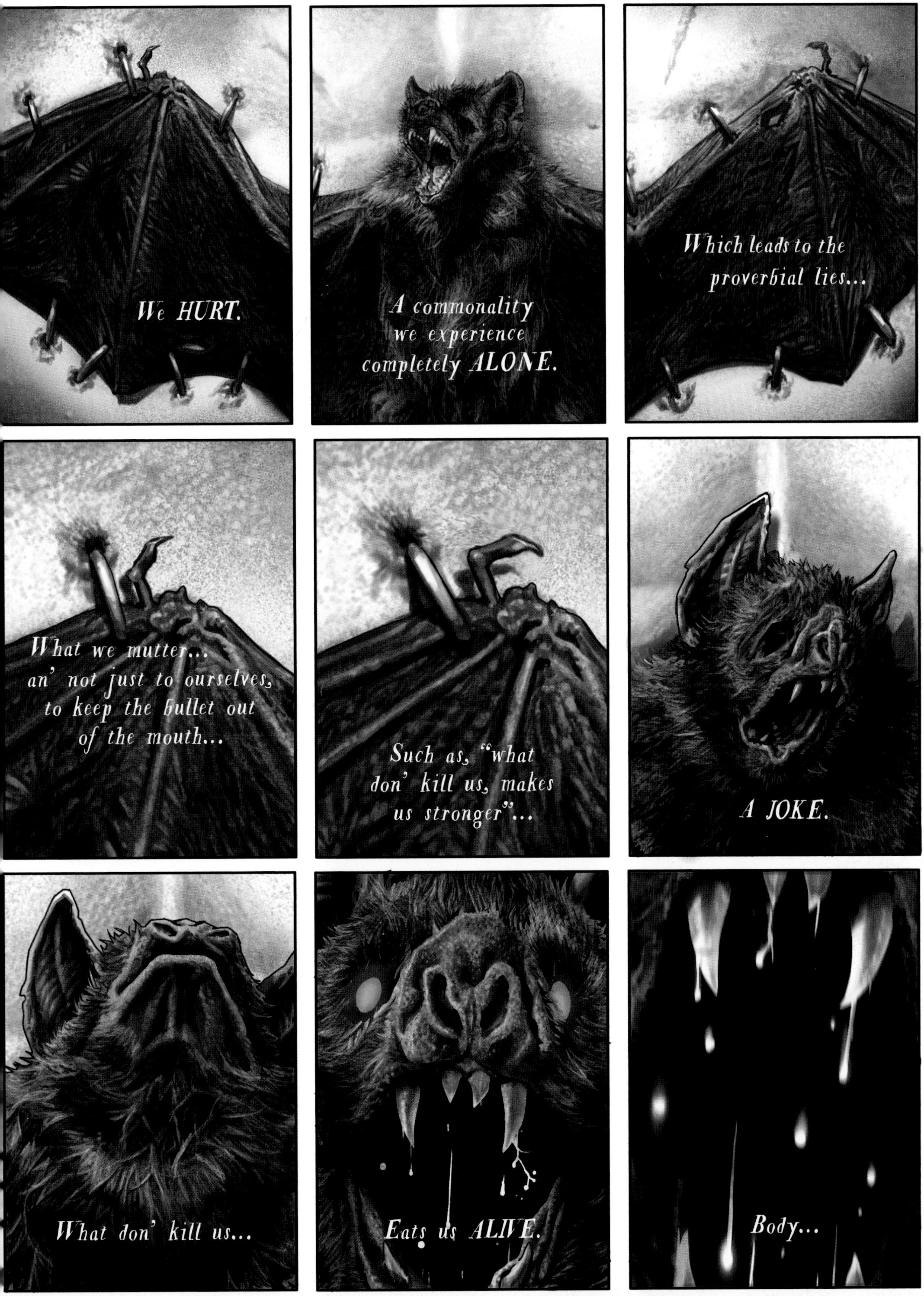
We HURT.
A commonality we experience completely ALONE.
Which leads to the proverbial lies...
What we mutter... an' not just to ourselves, to keep the bullet out of the mouth...
Such as, "what don' kill us, makes us stronger"...
A JOKE.
What don' kill us...
Eats us ALIVE.
Body...

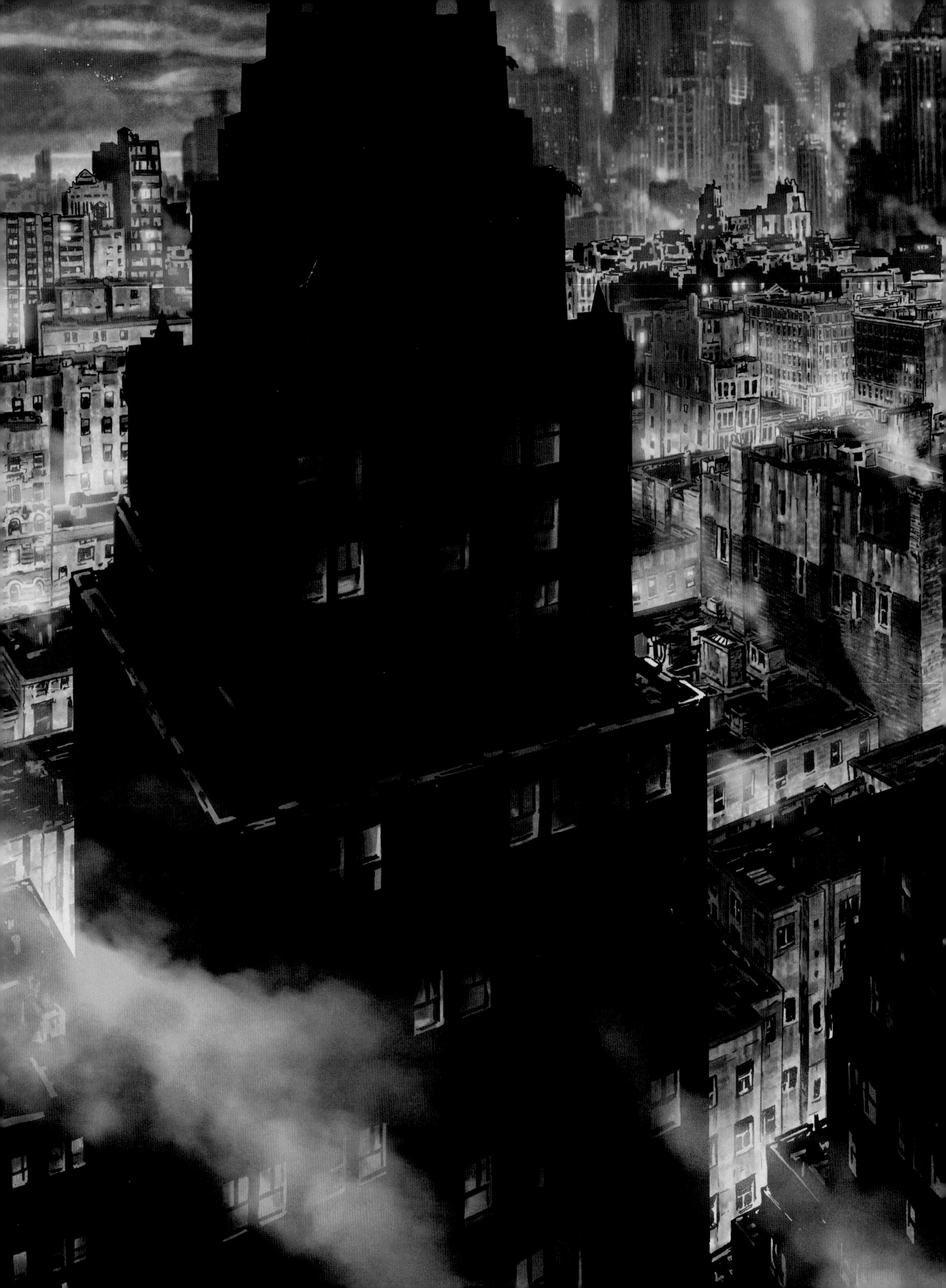

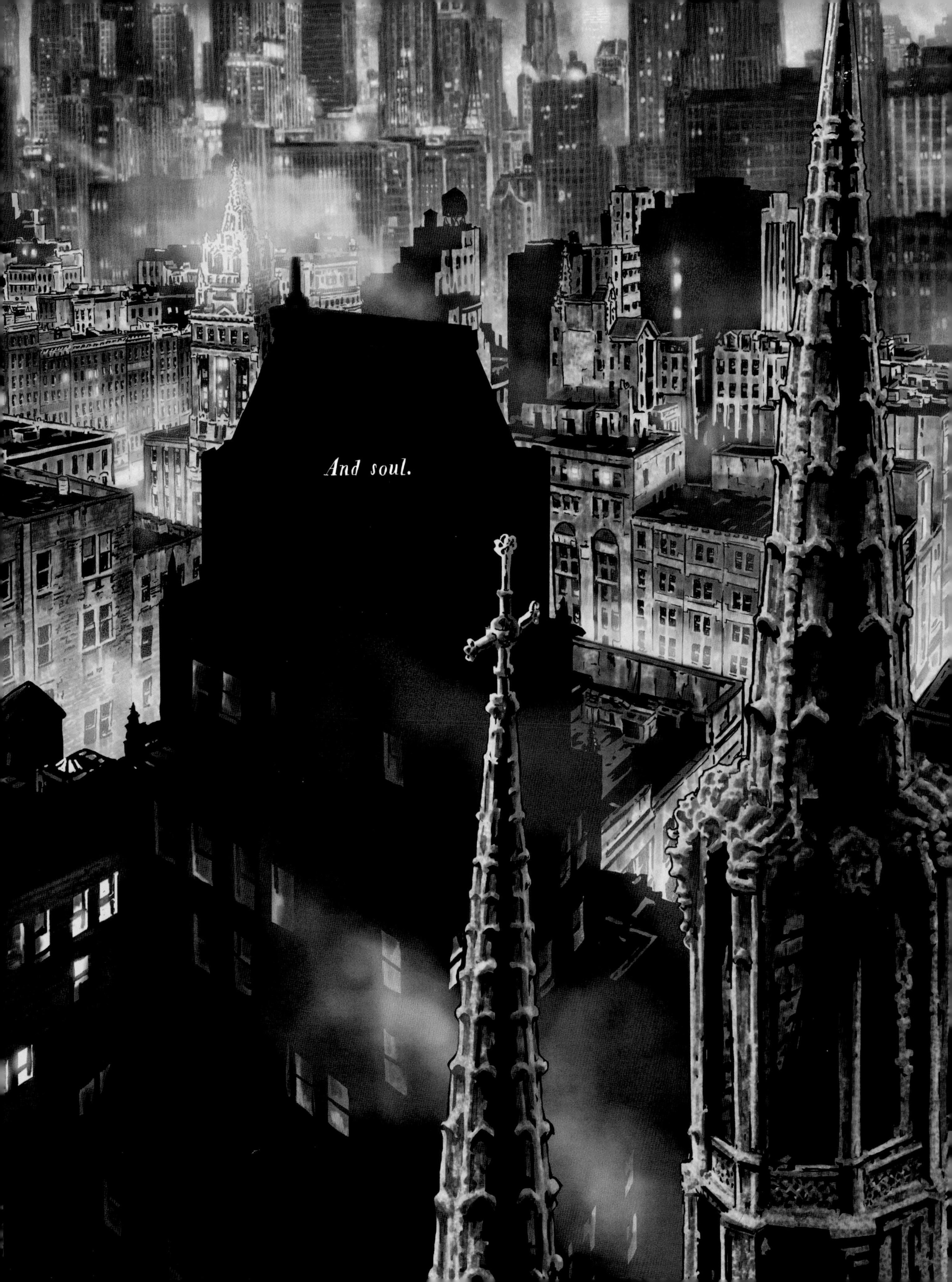
And soul.

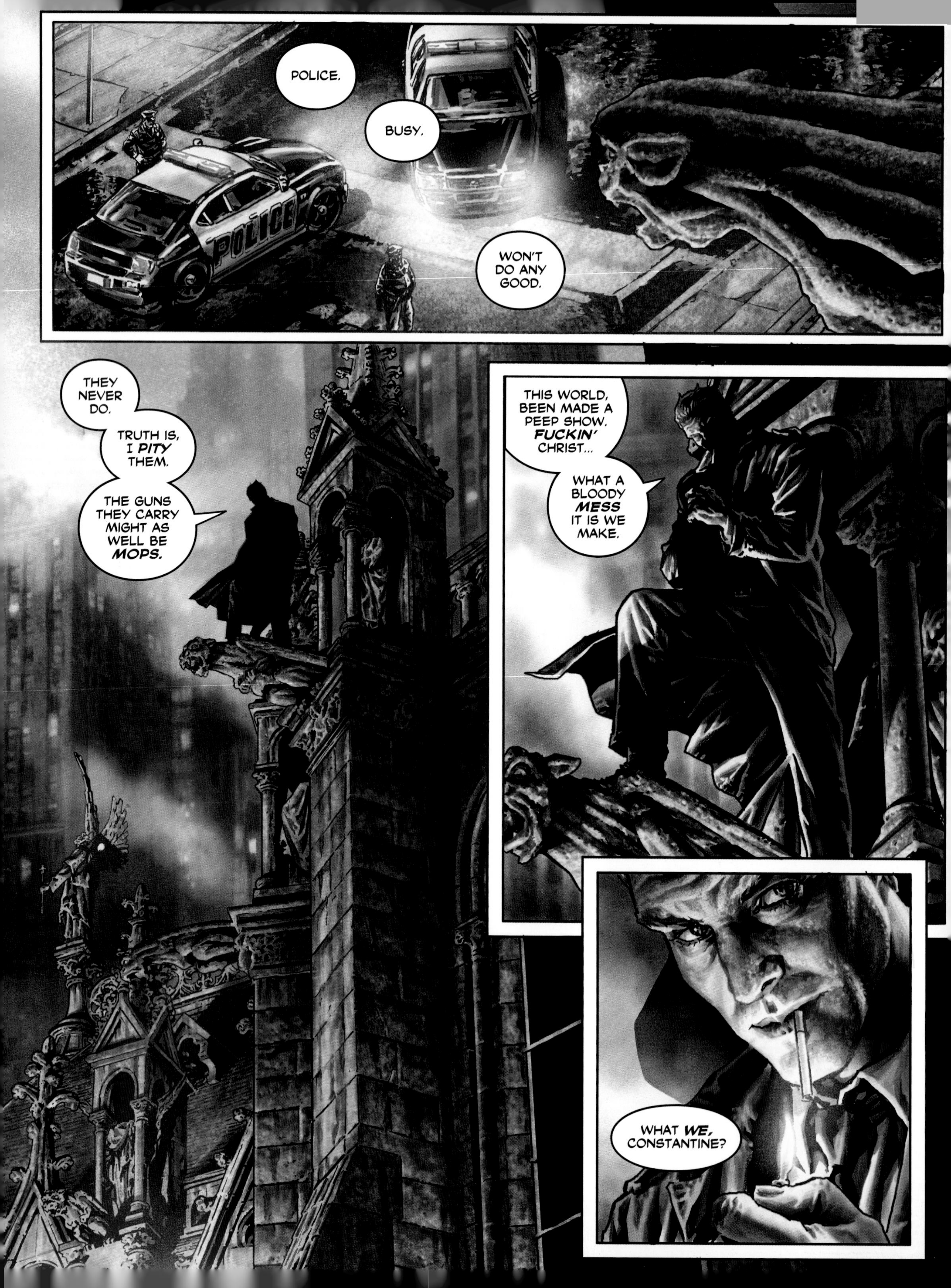
POLICE.
BUSY.
WON'T DO ANY GOOD.
THEY NEVER DO.
TRUTH IS, I *PITY* THEM.
THE GUNS THEY CARRY MIGHT AS WELL BE ***MOPS.***
THIS WORLD, BEEN MADE A PEEP SHOW. ***FUCKIN'*** CHRIST...
WHAT A BLOODY ***MESS*** IT IS WE MAKE.
WHAT ***WE,*** CONSTANTINE?

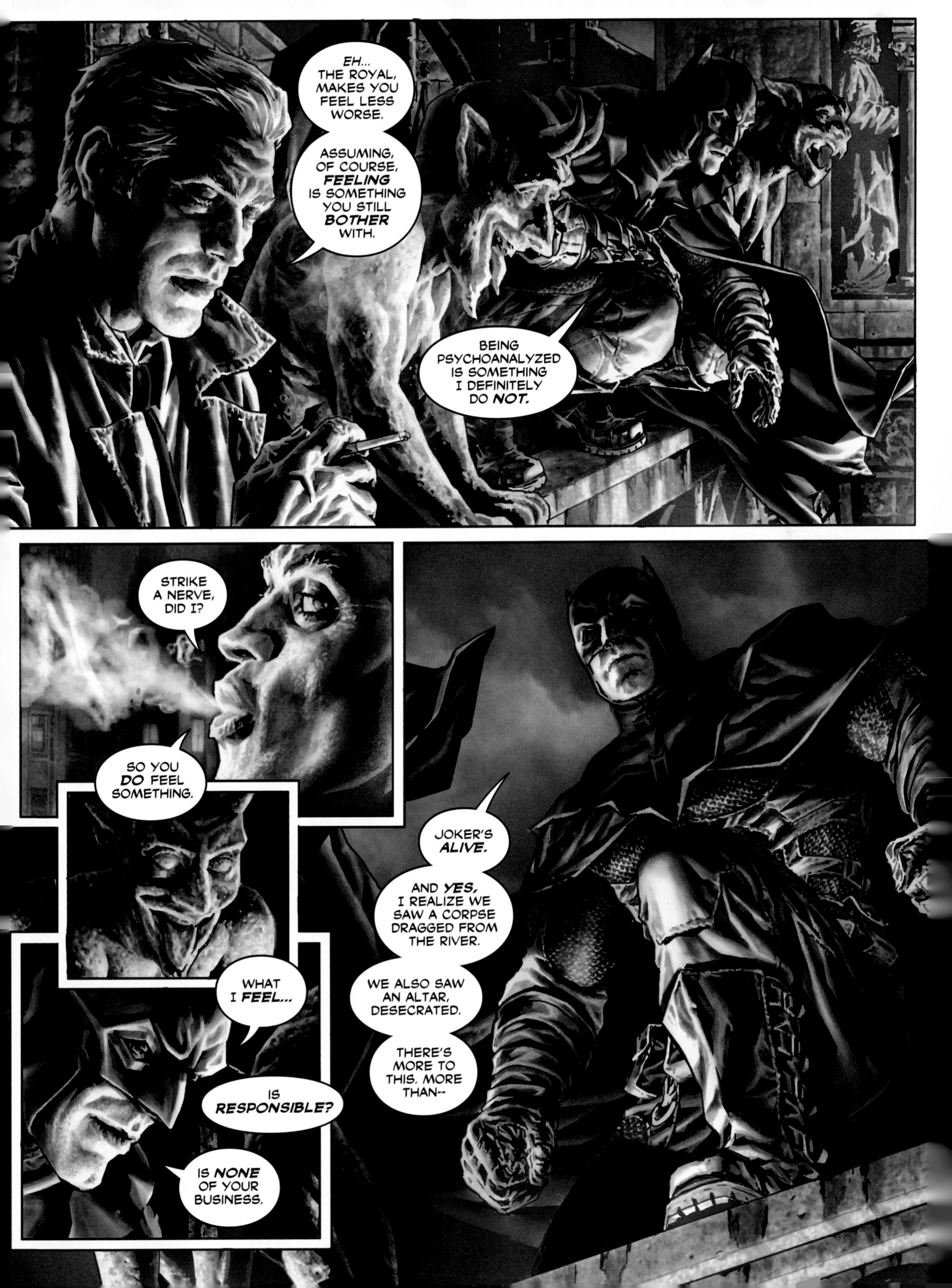
EH... THE ROYAL, MAKES YOU FEEL LESS WORSE.
ASSUMING, OF COURSE, FEELING IS SOMETHING YOU STILL BOTHER WITH.
BEING PSYCHOANALYZED IS SOMETHING I DEFINITELY DO NOT.
STRIKE A NERVE, DID I?
SO YOU DO FEEL SOMETHING.
WHAT I FEEL...
IS RESPONSIBLE?
IS NONE OF YOUR BUSINESS.
JOKER'S ALIVE.
AND YES, I REALIZE WE SAW A CORPSE DRAGGED FROM THE RIVER.
WE ALSO SAW AN ALTAR, DESECRATED.
THERE'S MORE TO THIS. MORE THAN--

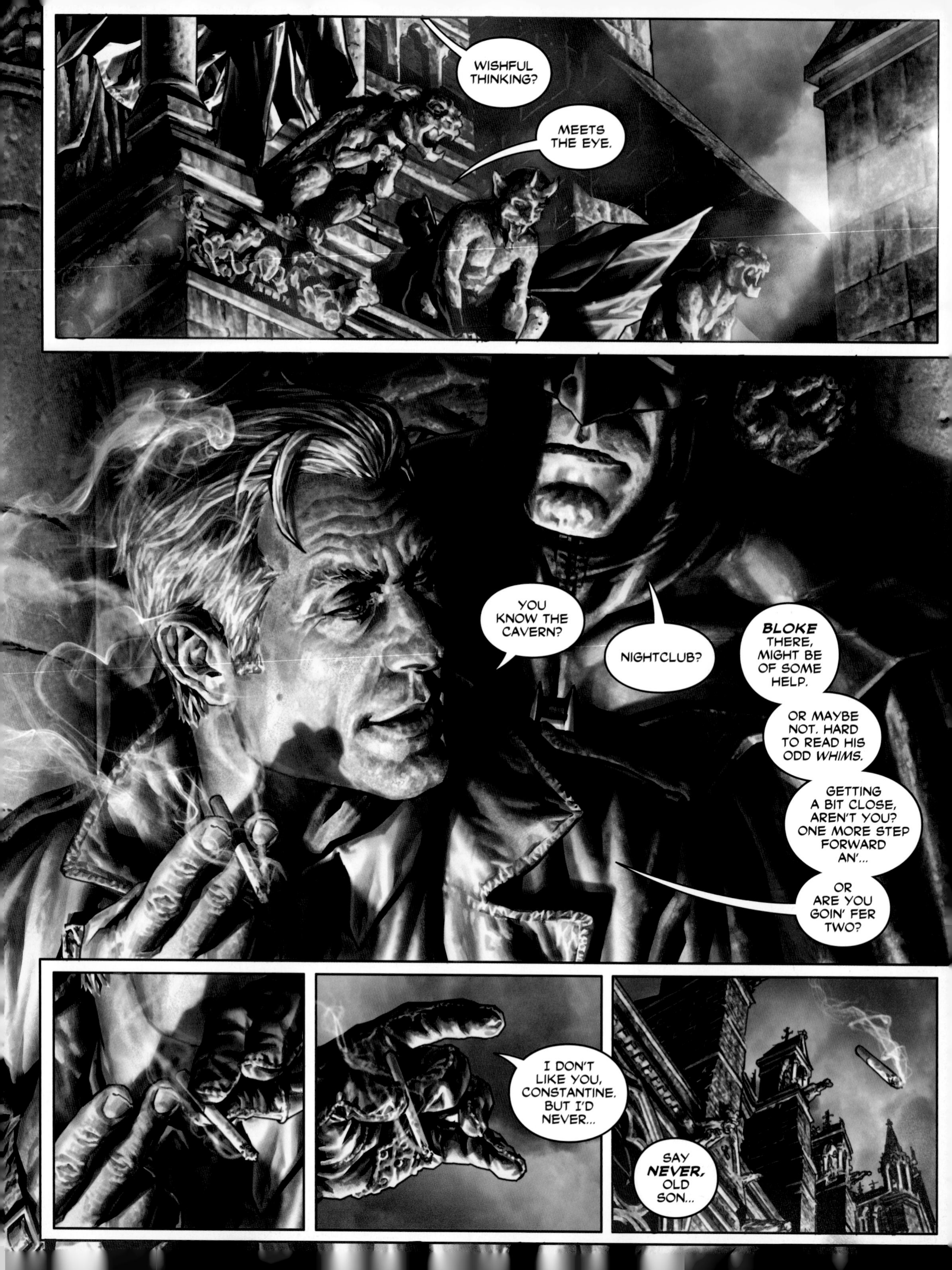
WISHFUL THINKING?
MEETS THE EYE.
YOU KNOW THE CAVERN?
NIGHTCLUB?
BLOKE THERE, MIGHT BE OF SOME HELP.
OR MAYBE NOT. HARD TO READ HIS ODD WHIMS.
GETTING A BIT CLOSE, AREN'T YOU? ONE MORE STEP FORWARD AN'...
OR ARE YOU GOIN' FER TWO?
I DON'T LIKE YOU, CONSTANTINE. BUT I'D NEVER...
SAY NEVER, OLD SON...

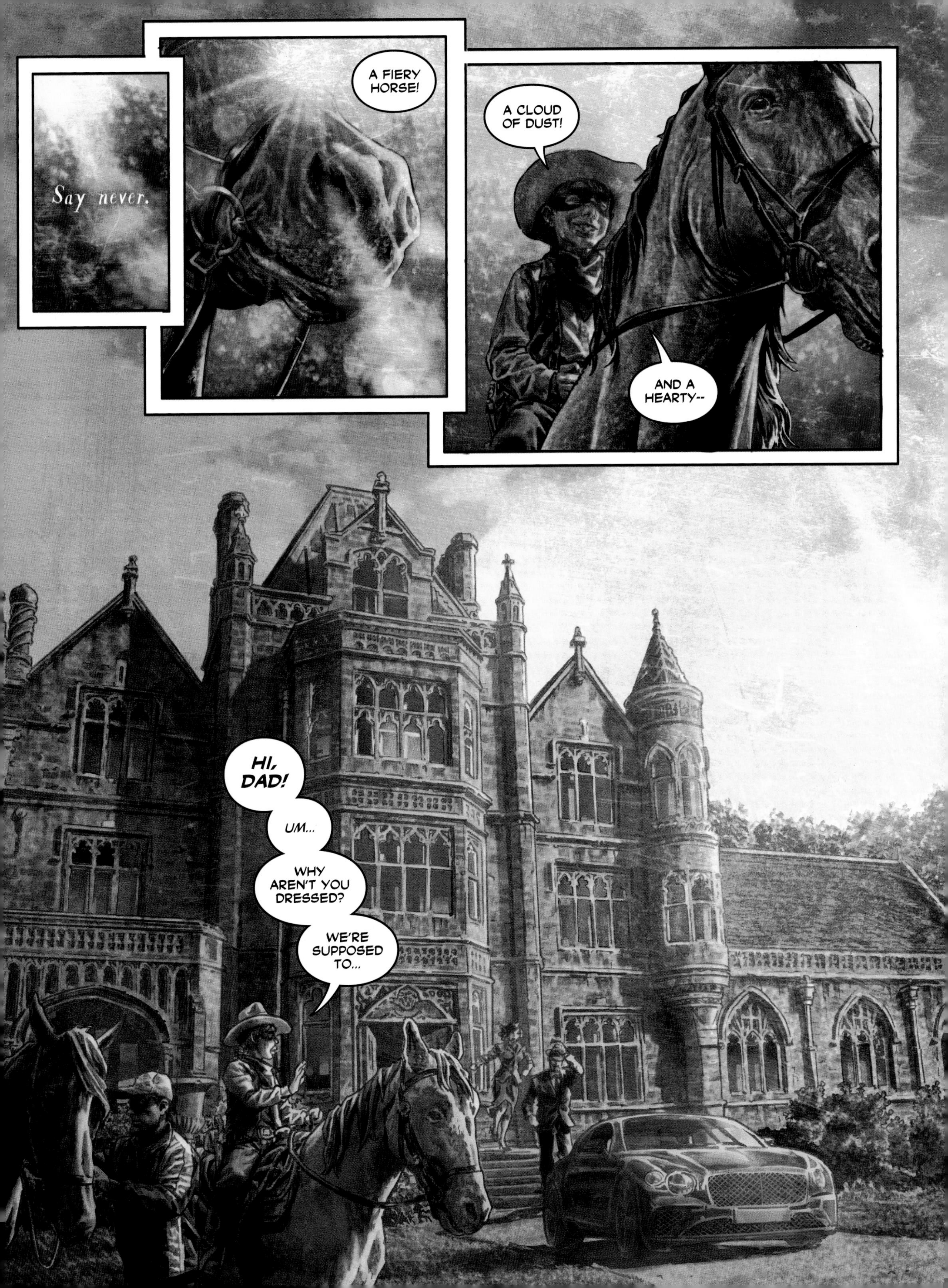
Say never.
A FIERY HORSE!
A CLOUD OF DUST!
AND A HEARTY--
HI, DAD!
UM...
WHY AREN'T YOU DRESSED?
WE'RE SUPPOSED TO...

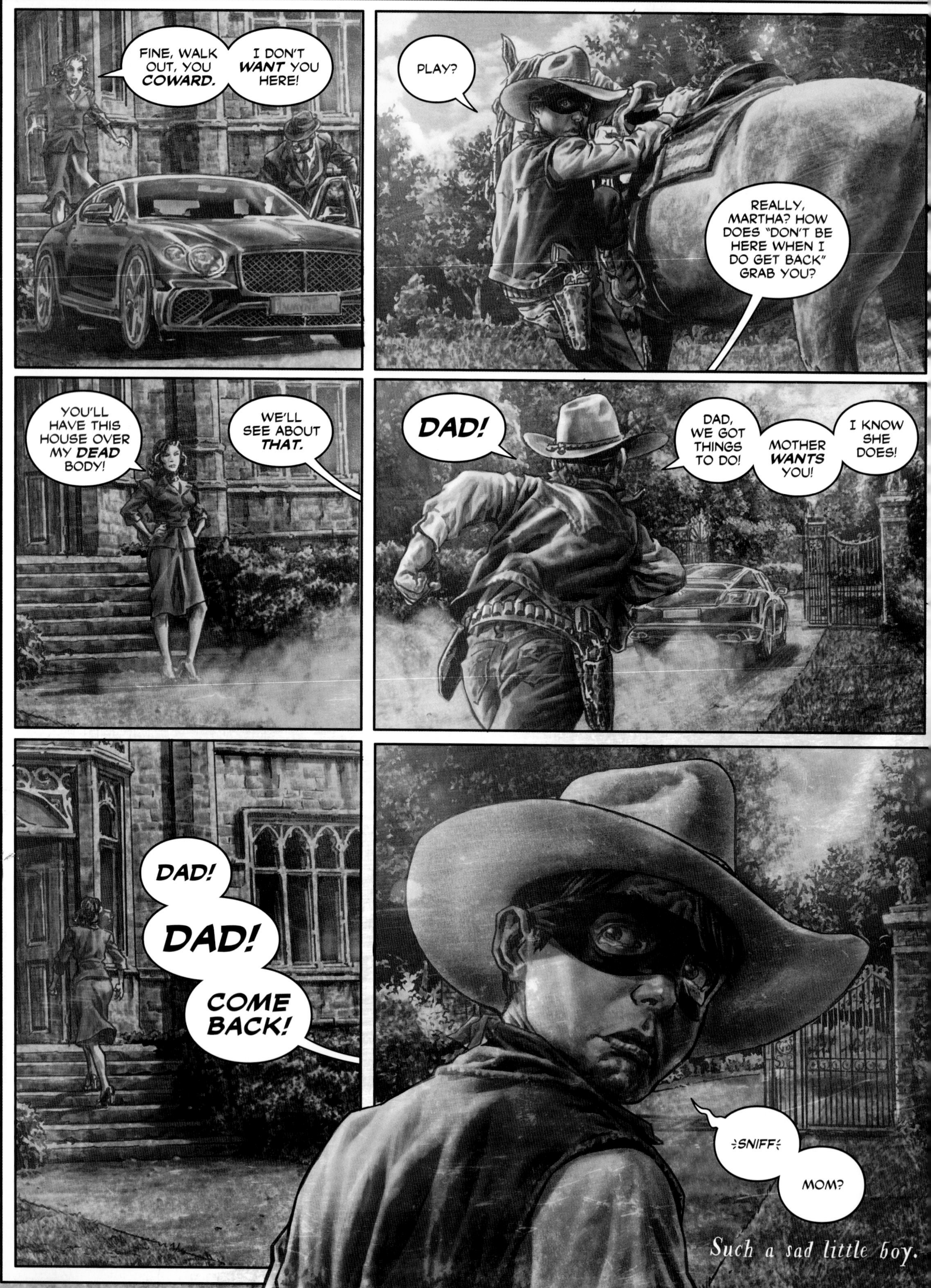
FINE, WALK OUT, YOU COWARD.
I DON'T WANT YOU HERE!
PLAY?
REALLY, MARTHA? HOW DOES "DON'T BE HERE WHEN I DO GET BACK" GRAB YOU?
YOU'LL HAVE THIS HOUSE OVER MY DEAD BODY!
WE'LL SEE ABOUT THAT.
DAD!
DAD, WE GOT THINGS TO DO!
MOTHER WANTS YOU!
I KNOW SHE DOES!
DAD!
DAD!
COME BACK!
SNIFF
MOM?
Such a sad little boy.

But sadness begets madness...

Right, *MAD* little boy?

Then badness.

Easier emotions to live with.

Such a *BAD* little boy.

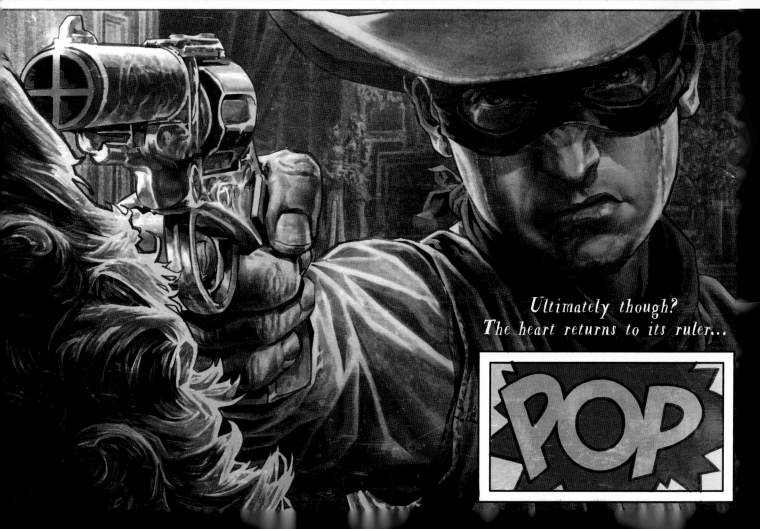

Ultimately though?
The heart returns to its ruler...

POP

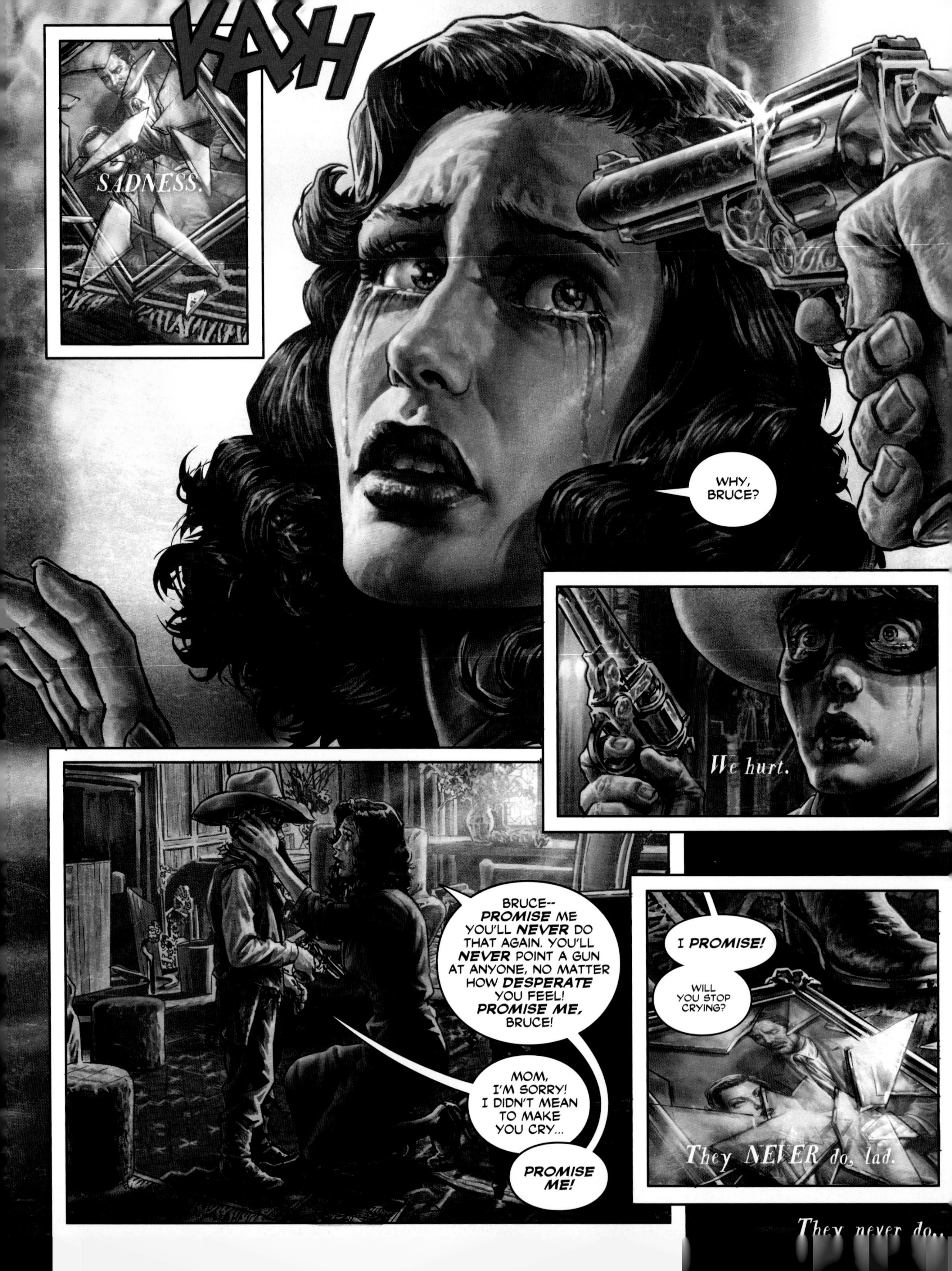
KASH
SADNESS.
WHY, BRUCE?
We hurt.
BRUCE-- PROMISE ME YOU'LL NEVER DO THAT AGAIN. YOU'LL NEVER POINT A GUN AT ANYONE, NO MATTER HOW DESPERATE YOU FEEL! PROMISE ME, BRUCE!
MOM, I'M SORRY! I DIDN'T MEAN TO MAKE YOU CRY...
PROMISE ME!
I PROMISE!
WILL YOU STOP CRYING?
They NEVER do, lad.
They never do..

SAD man.

MAD man.

BAD...

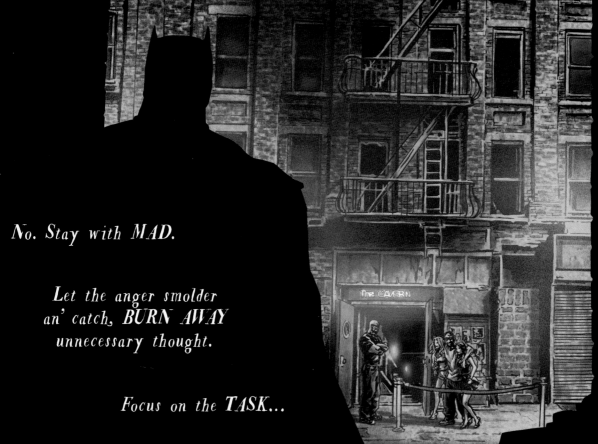

No. Stay with MAD.

Let the anger smolder
an' catch, BURN AWAY
unnecessary thought.

Focus on the TASK...

At fist.

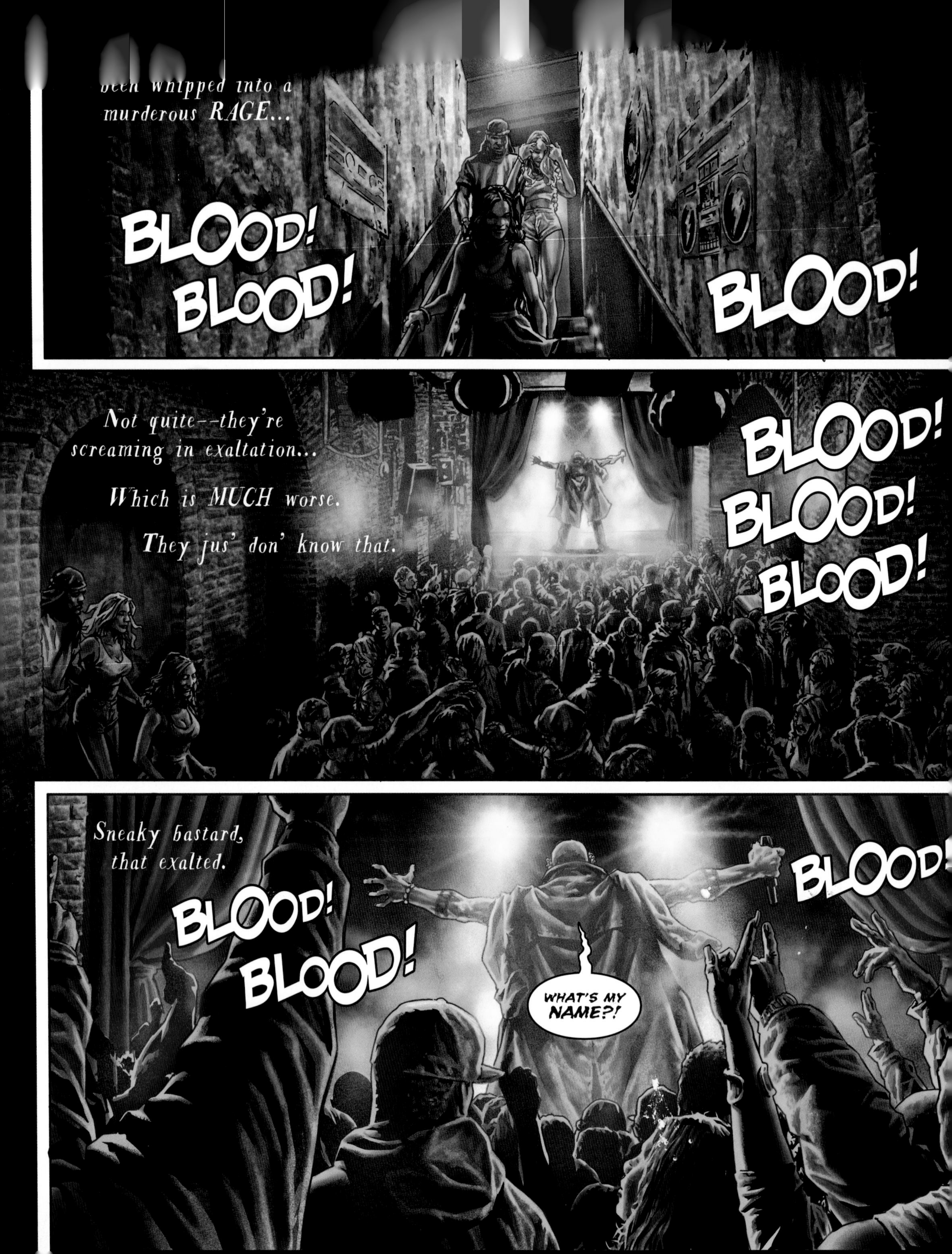

been whipped into a murderous RAGE...
BLOOD! BLOOD!
BLOOD!
Not quite--they're screaming in exaltation...
Which is MUCH worse.
They jus' don' know that.
BLOOD! BLOOD! BLOOD!
Sneaky bastard, that exalted.
BLOOD! BLOOD!
BLOOD!
WHAT'S MY NAME?!

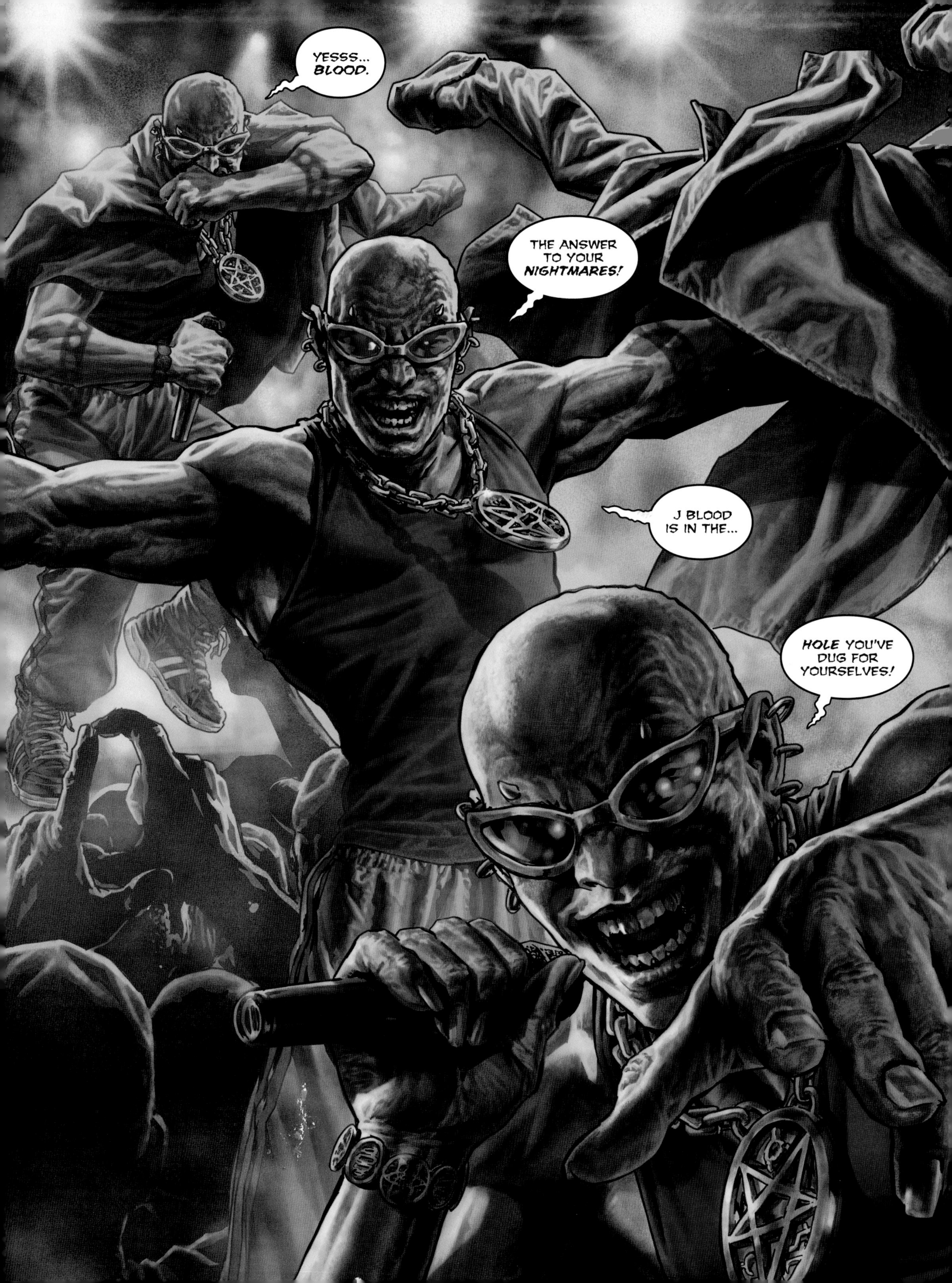
YESSS... BLOOD.
THE ANSWER TO YOUR NIGHTMARES!
J BLOOD IS IN THE...
HOLE YOU'VE DUG FOR YOURSELVES!

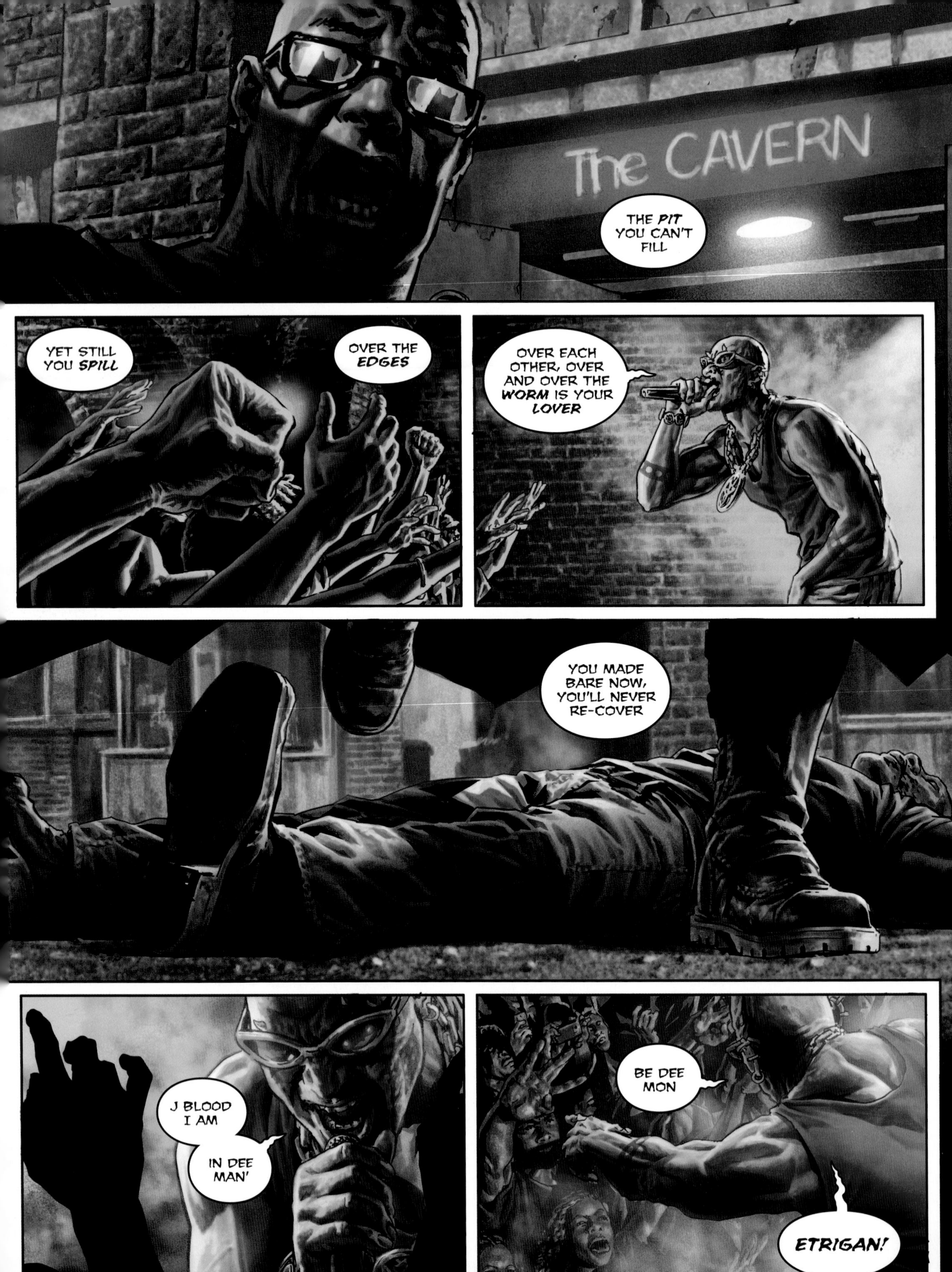
The CAVERN
THE PIT YOU CAN'T FILL
YET STILL YOU SPILL
OVER THE EDGES
OVER EACH OTHER, OVER AND OVER THE WORM IS YOUR LOVER
YOU MADE BARE NOW, YOU'LL NEVER RE-COVER
J BLOOD I AM
IN DEE MAN'
BE DEE MON
ETRIGAN!

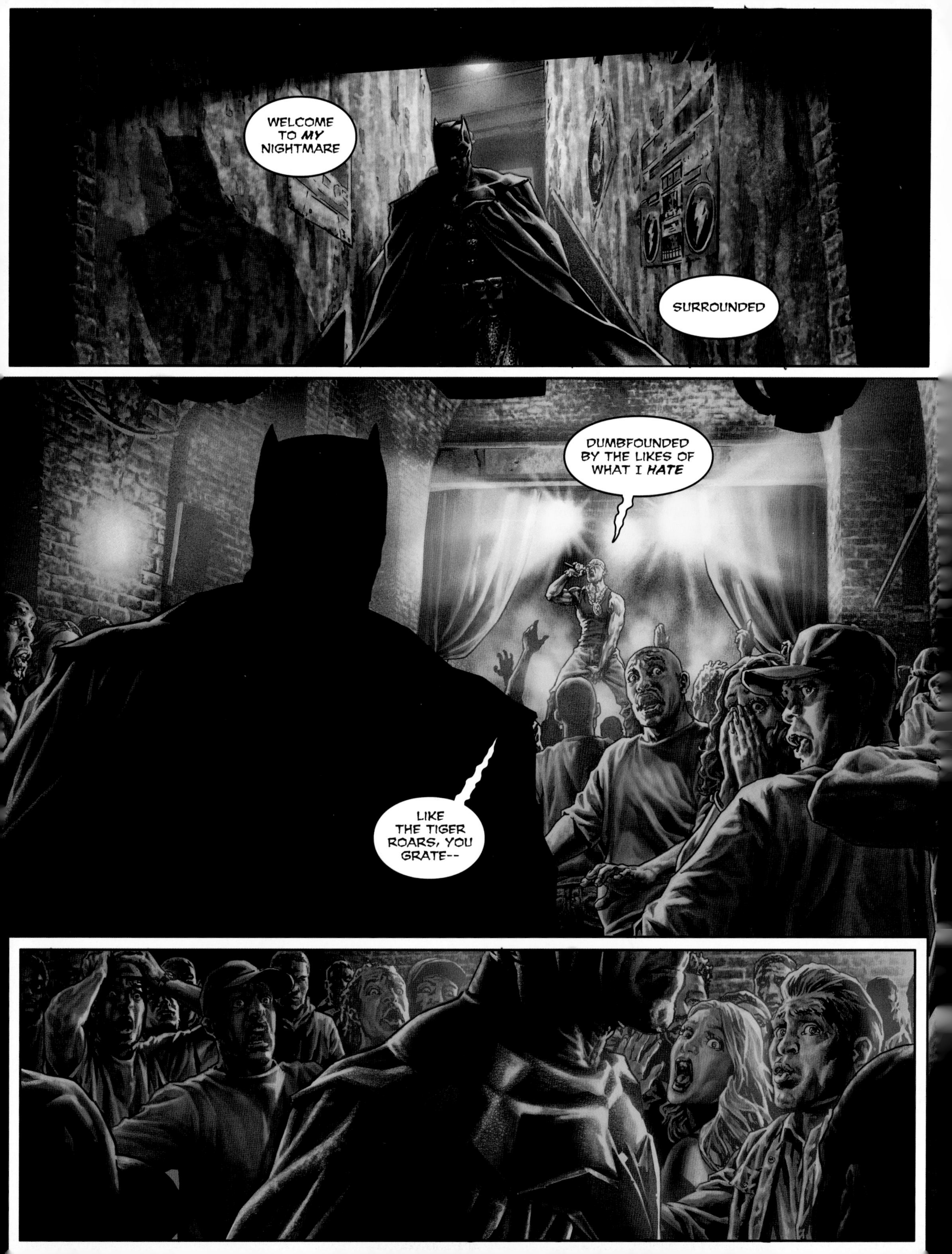
WELCOME TO MY NIGHTMARE
SURROUNDED
DUMBFOUNDED BY THE LIKES OF WHAT I HATE
LIKE THE TIGER ROARS, YOU GRATE--

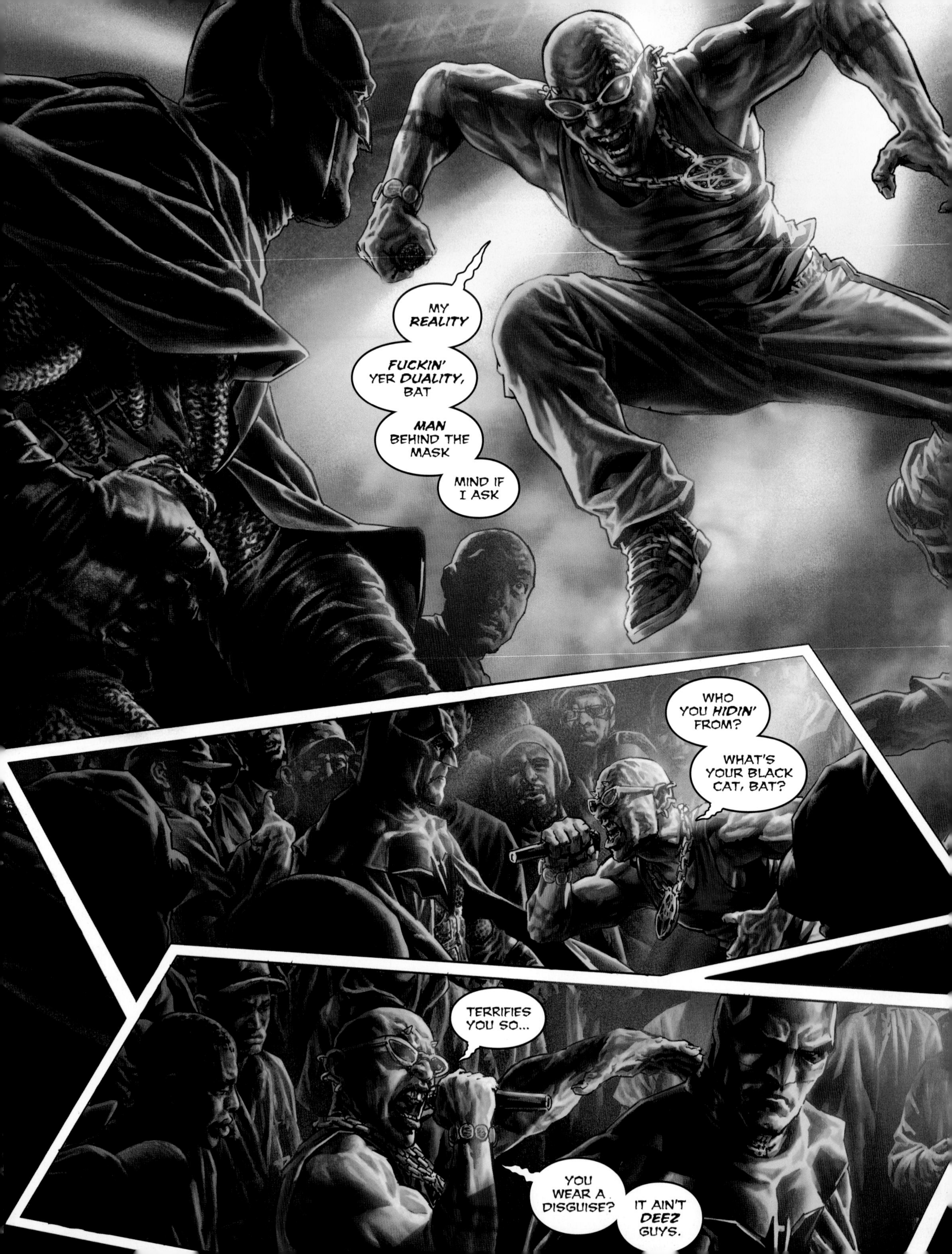

MY REALITY
FUCKIN' YER DUALITY, BAT
MAN BEHIND THE MASK
MIND IF I ASK
WHO YOU HIDIN' FROM?
WHAT'S YOUR BLACK CAT, BAT?
TERRIFIES YOU SO...
YOU WEAR A DISGUISE?
IT AIN'T DEEZ GUYS.

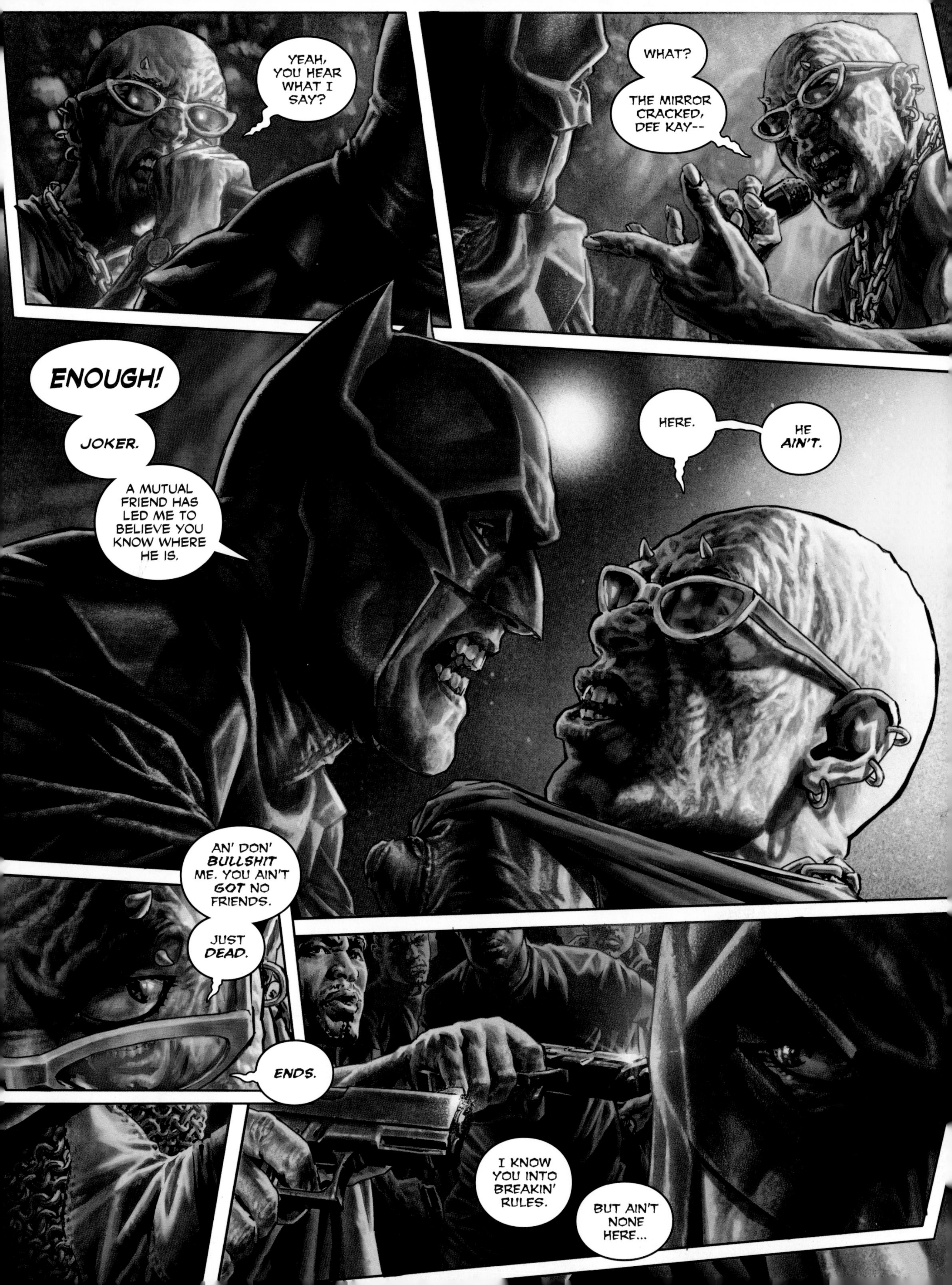
YEAH, YOU HEAR WHAT I SAY?
WHAT?
THE MIRROR CRACKED, DEE KAY--
ENOUGH!
JOKER.
A MUTUAL FRIEND HAS LED ME TO BELIEVE YOU KNOW WHERE HE IS.
HERE.
HE AIN'T.
AN' DON' BULLSHIT ME. YOU AIN'T GOT NO FRIENDS.
JUST DEAD.
ENDS.
I KNOW YOU INTO BREAKIN' RULES.
BUT AIN'T NONE HERE...

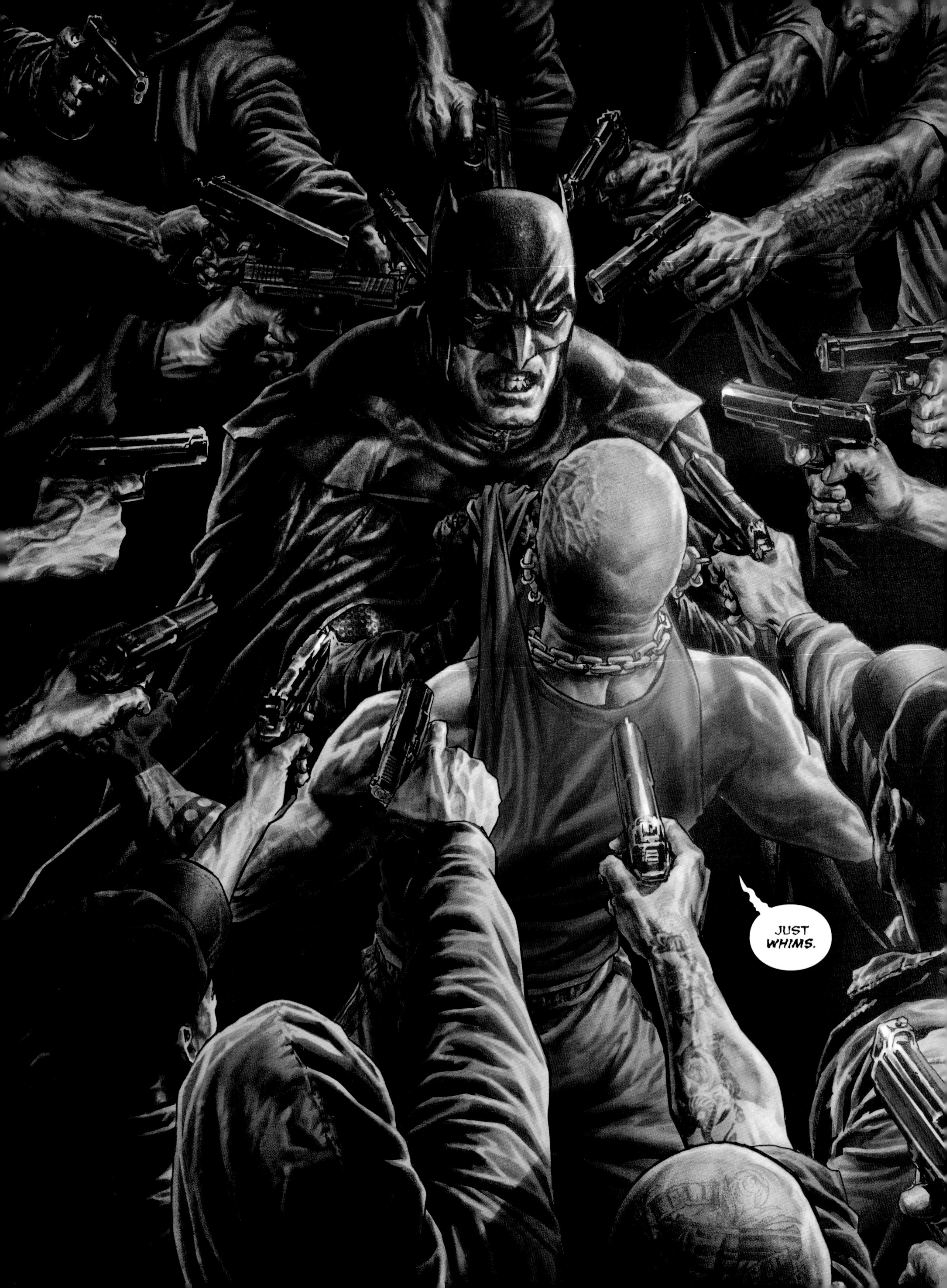
JUST WHIMS.

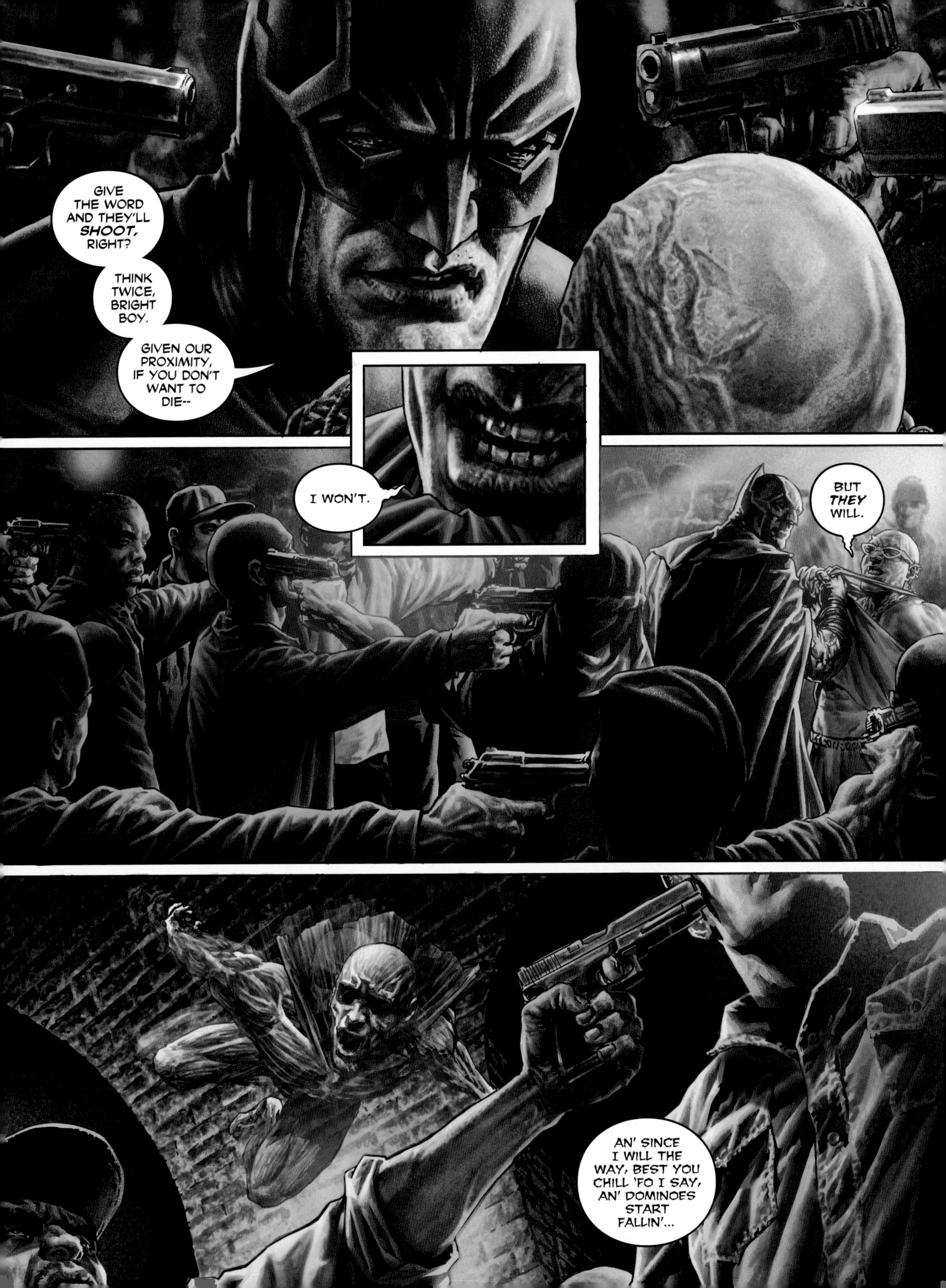
GIVE THE WORD AND THEY'LL *SHOOT,* RIGHT?
THINK TWICE, BRIGHT BOY.
GIVEN OUR PROXIMITY, IF YOU DON'T WANT TO DIE--
I WON'T.
BUT *THEY* WILL.
AN' SINCE I WILL THE WAY, BEST YOU CHILL 'FO I SAY, AN' DOMINOES START FALLIN'...

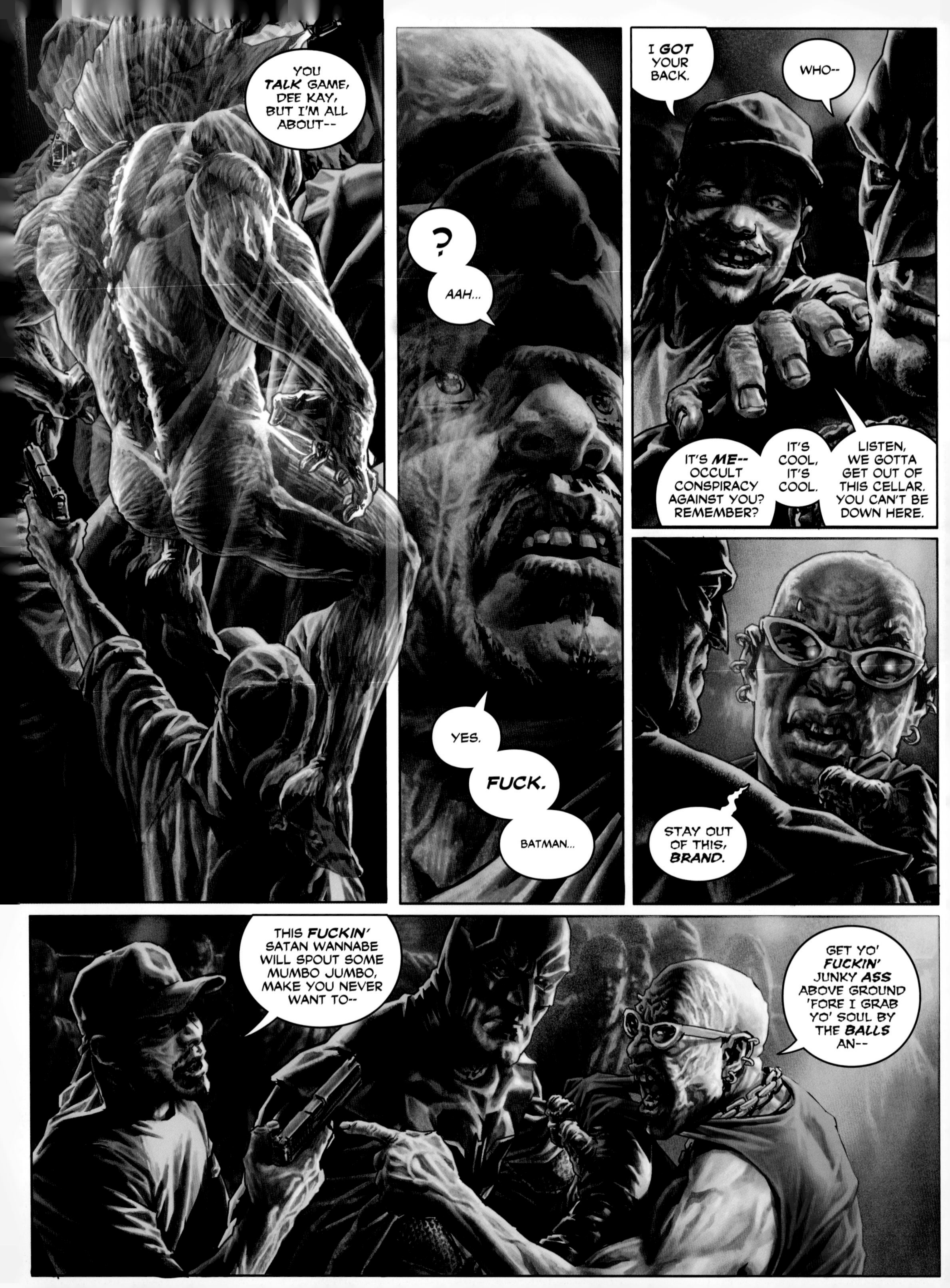
YOU TALK GAME, DEE KAY, BUT I'M ALL ABOUT--
?
AAH...
YES.
FUCK.
BATMAN...
I GOT YOUR BACK.
WHO--
LISTEN, WE GOTTA GET OUT OF THIS CELLAR. YOU CAN'T BE DOWN HERE.
IT'S COOL, IT'S COOL.
IT'S ME-- OCCULT CONSPIRACY AGAINST YOU? REMEMBER?
STAY OUT OF THIS, BRAND.
THIS FUCKIN' SATAN WANNABE WILL SPOUT SOME MUMBO JUMBO, MAKE YOU NEVER WANT TO--
GET YO' FUCKIN' JUNKY ASS ABOVE GROUND 'FORE I GRAB YO' SOUL BY THE BALLS AN--

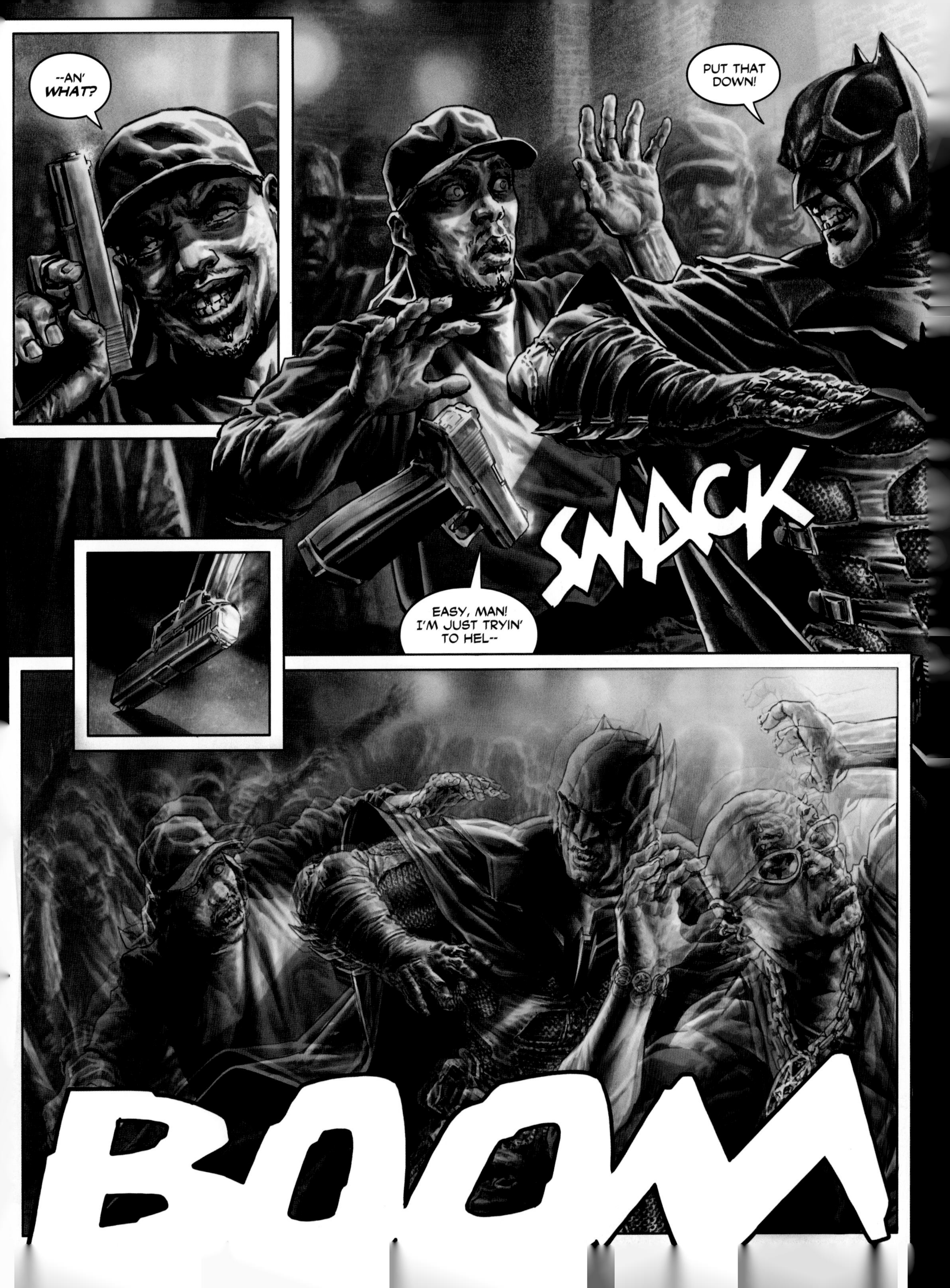
--AN' WHAT?
PUT THAT DOWN!
SMACK
EASY, MAN! I'M JUST TRYIN' TO HEL--
BOOM

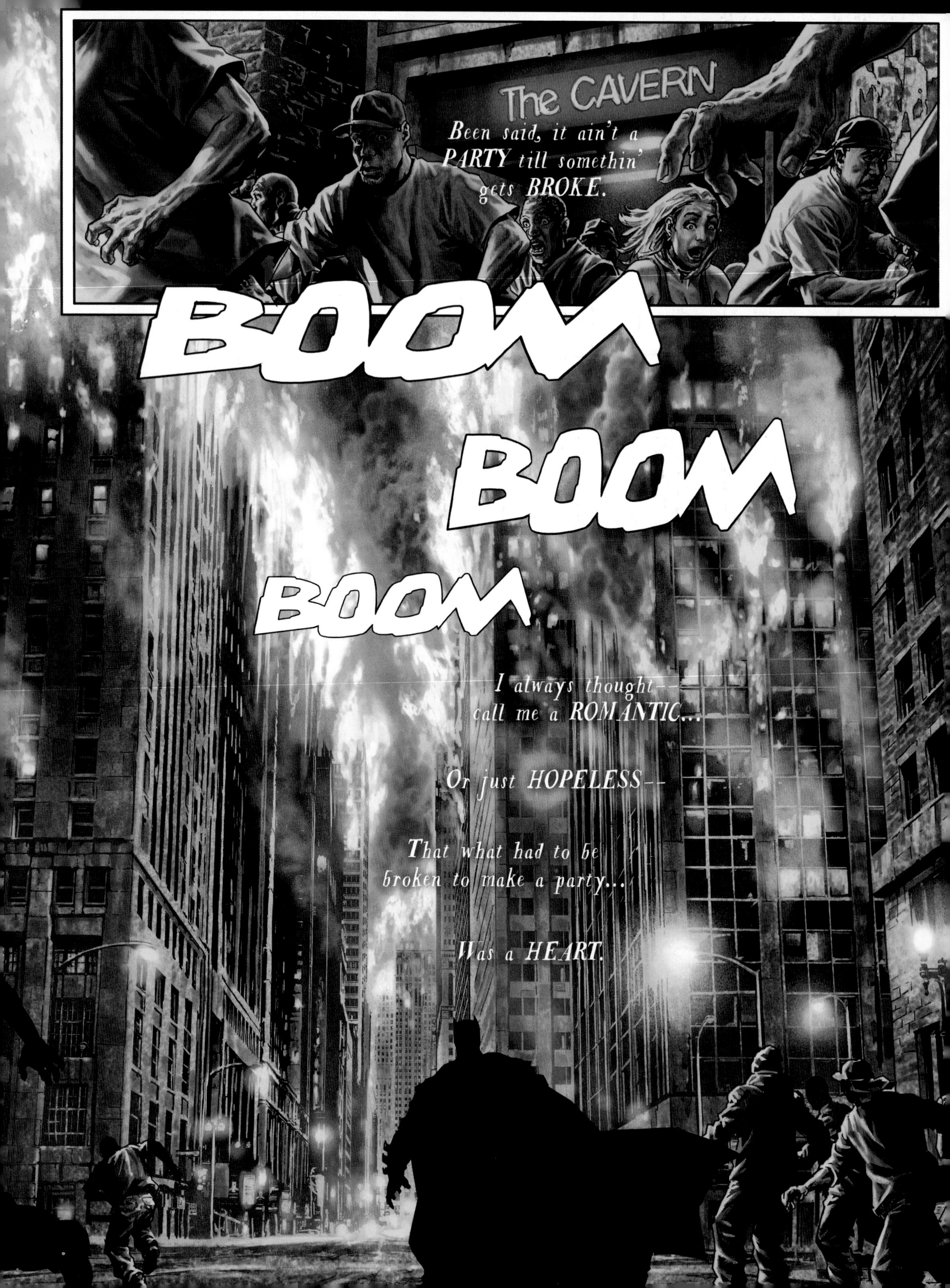
The CAVERN
Been said, it ain't a PARTY till somethin' gets BROKE.
BOOM
BOOM
BOOM
I always thought-- call me a ROMANTIC...
Or just HOPELESS--
That what had to be broken to make a party...
Was a HEART.

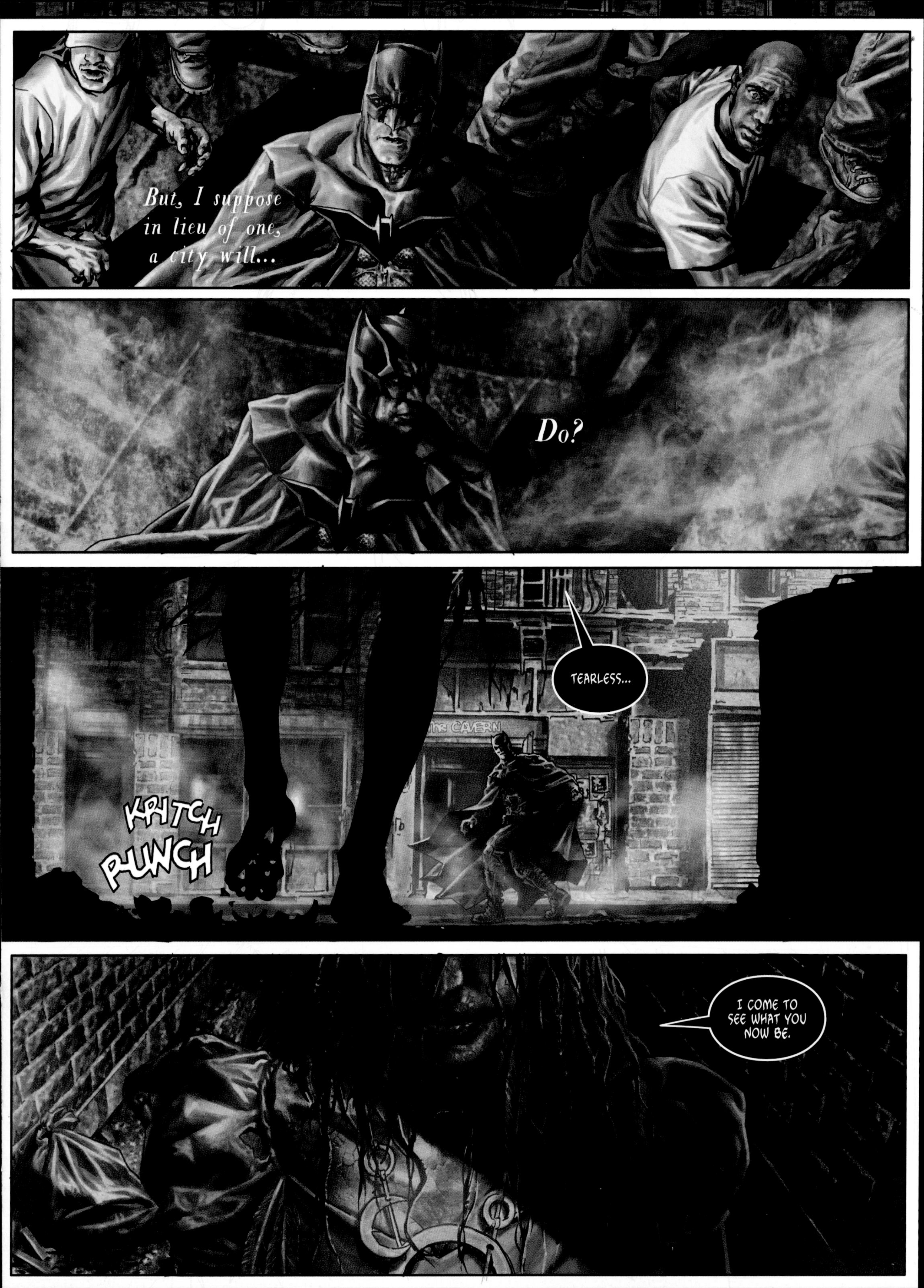

But, I suppose in lieu of one, a city will...
Do?
TEARLESS...
KRITCH
PUNCH
the CAVERN
I COME TO SEE WHAT YOU NOW BE.

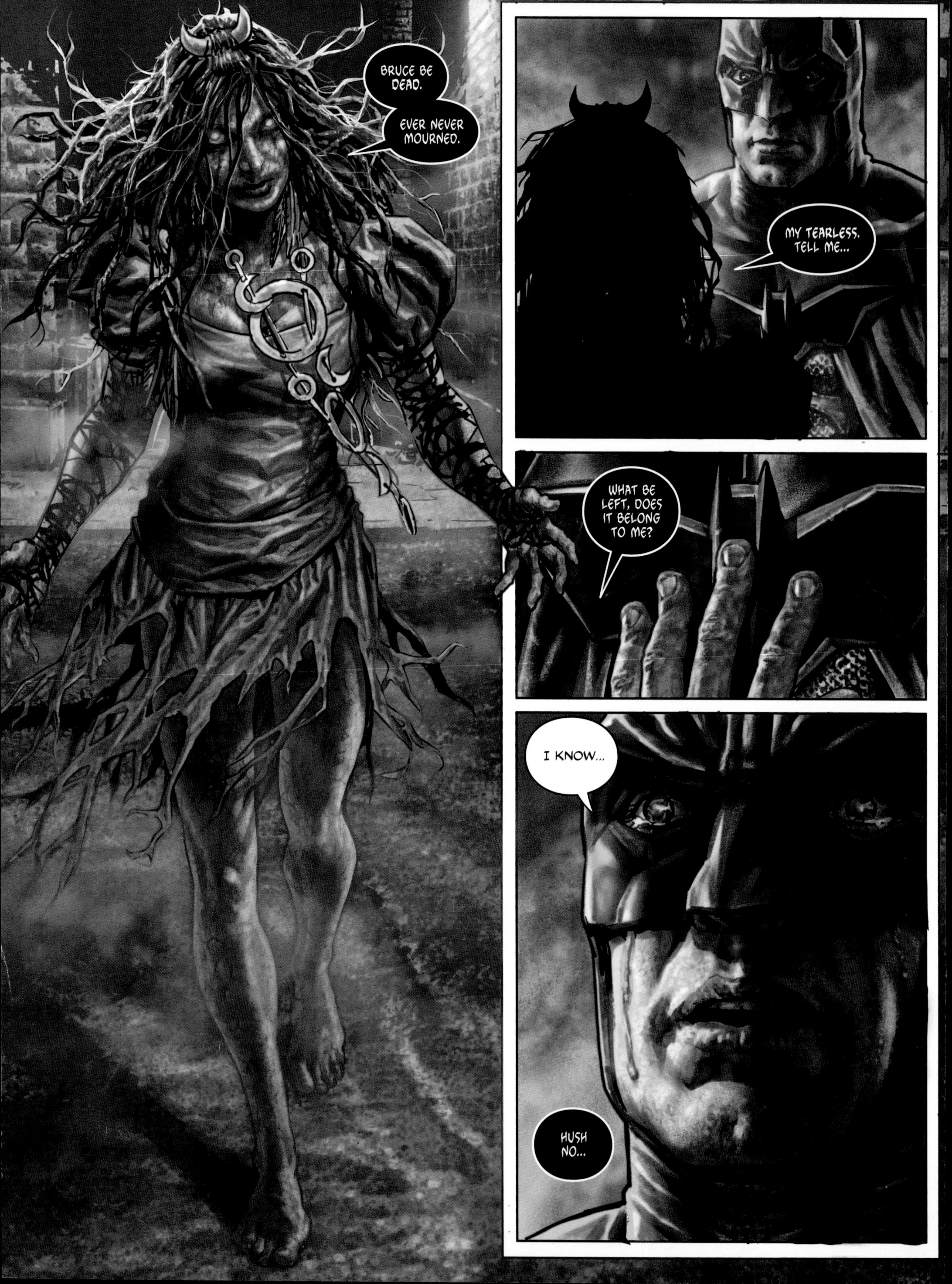
BRUCE BE DEAD.
EVER NEVER MOURNED.
MY TEARLESS. TELL ME...
WHAT BE LEFT, DOES IT BELONG TO ME?
I KNOW...
HUSH NO...

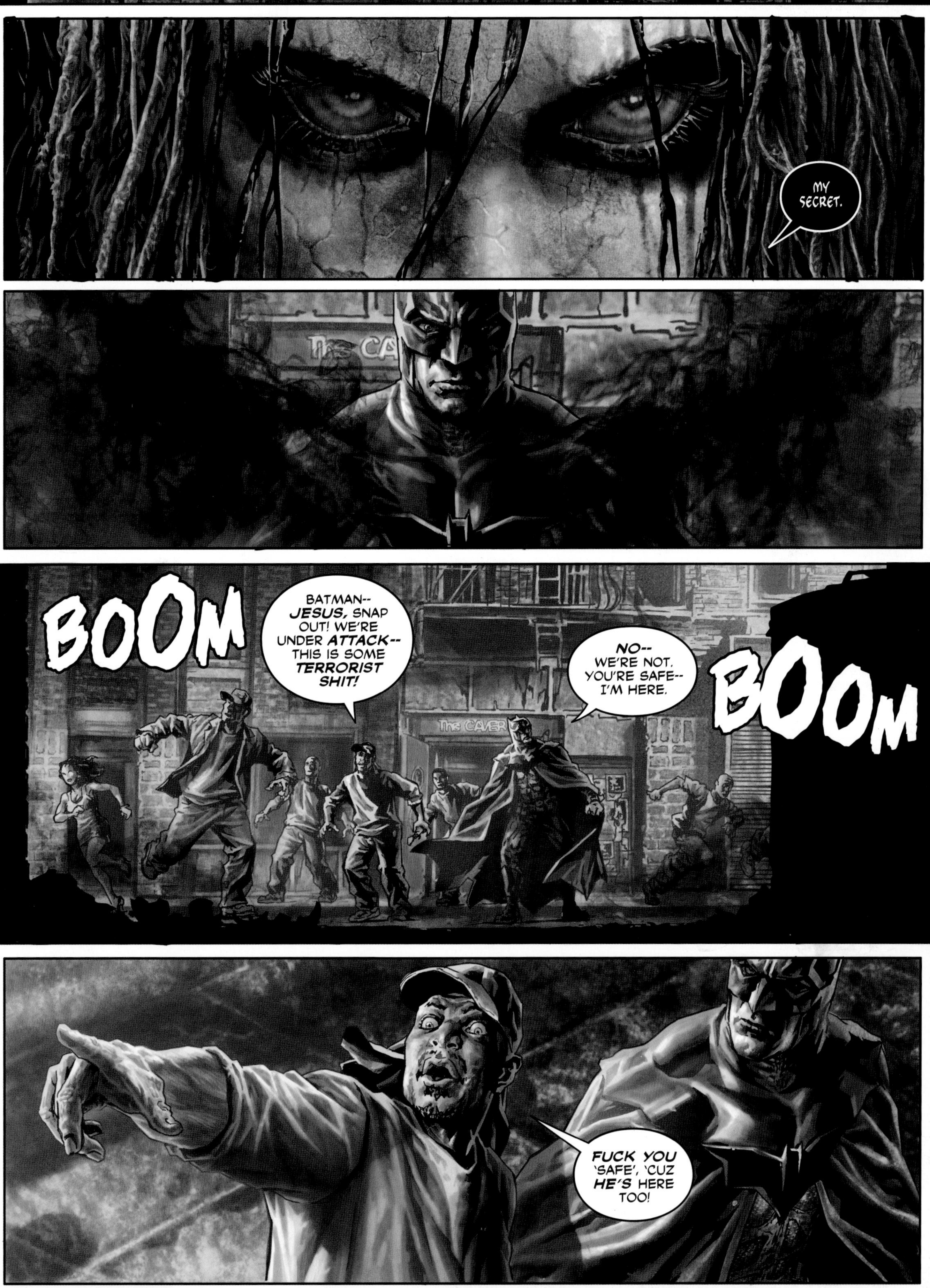
MY SECRET.
BOOM
BATMAN-- JESUS, SNAP OUT! WE'RE UNDER ATTACK-- THIS IS SOME TERRORIST SHIT!
NO-- WE'RE NOT. YOU'RE SAFE-- I'M HERE.
BOOM
FUCK YOU 'SAFE', 'CUZ HE'S HERE TOO!

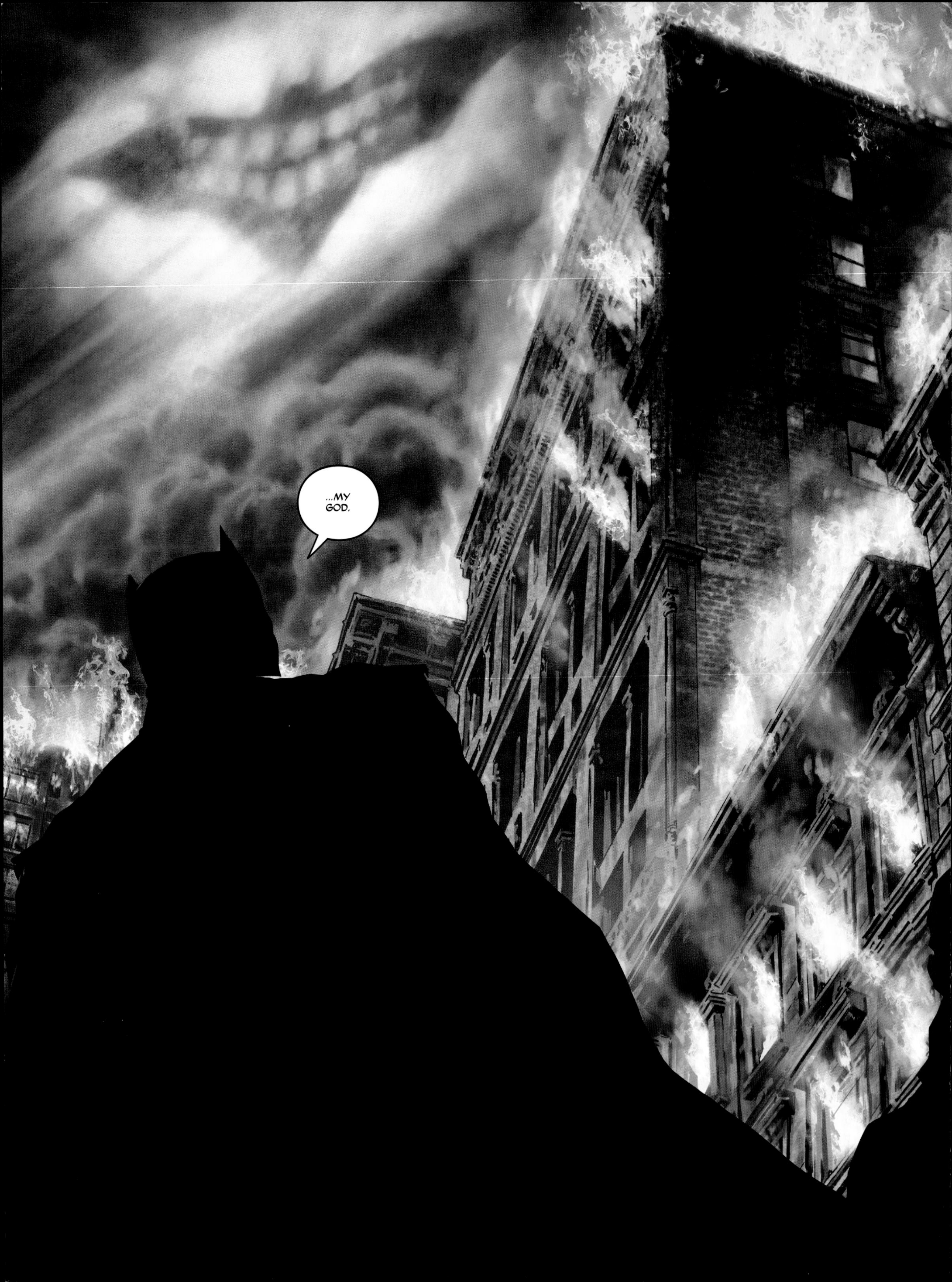
...MY GOD.

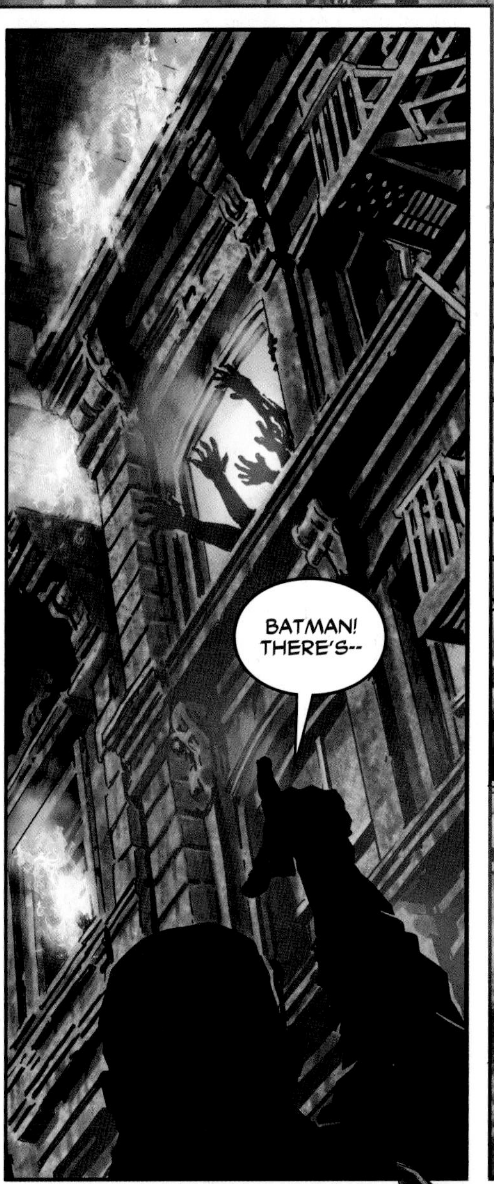
BATMAN! THERE'S--

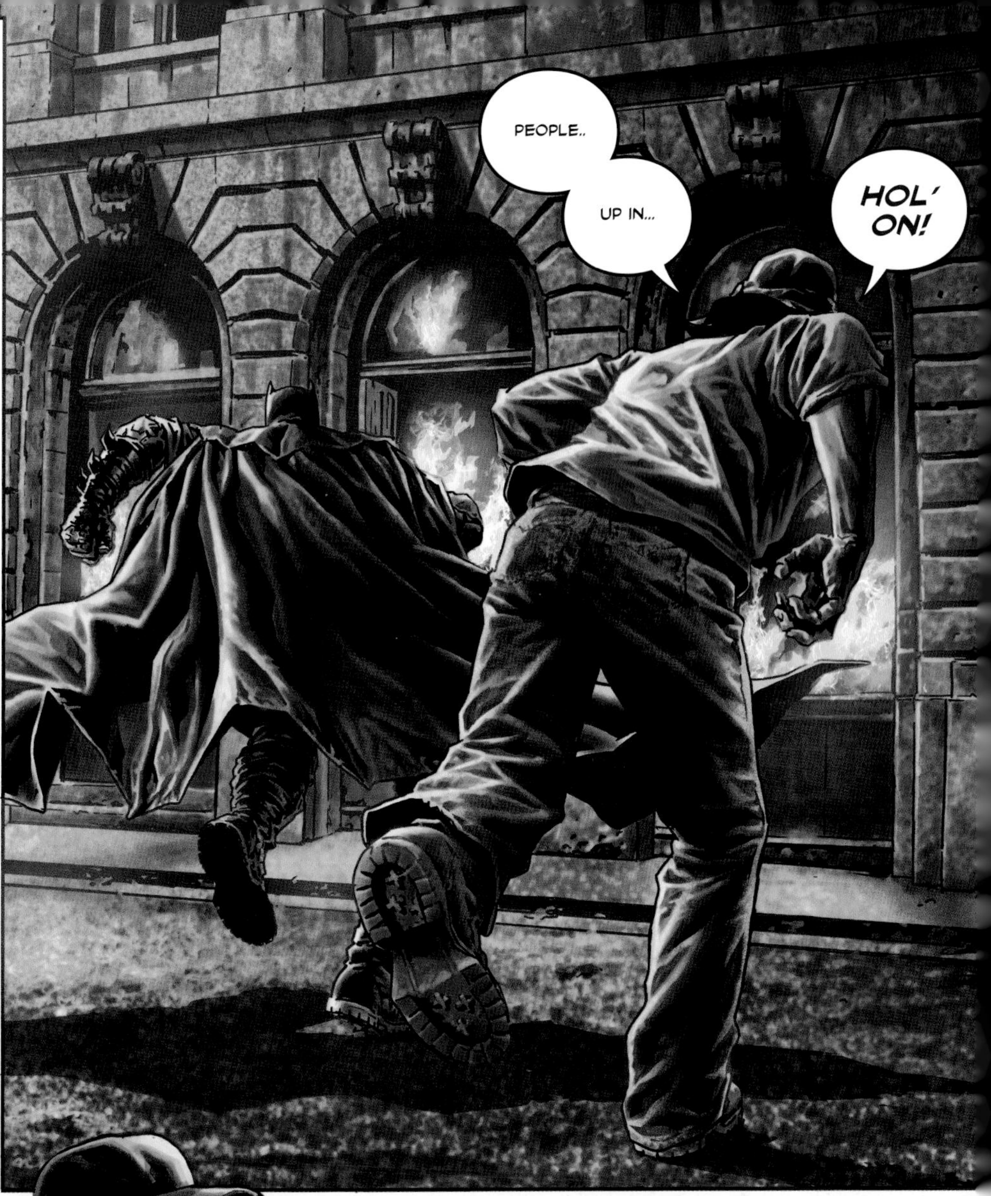
PEOPLE..
UP IN...
HOL' ON!

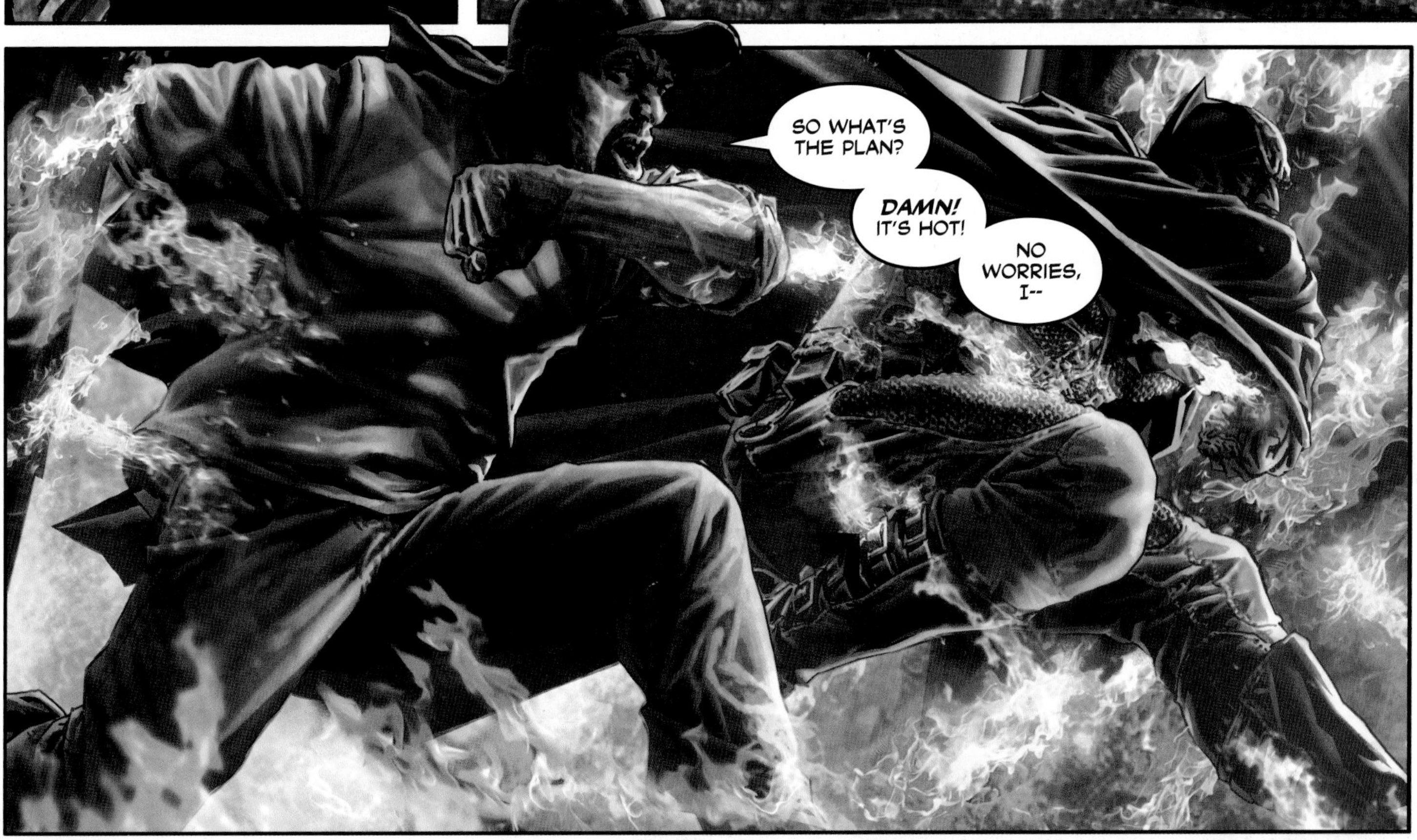
SO WHAT'S THE PLAN?
DAMN! IT'S HOT!
NO WORRIES, I--

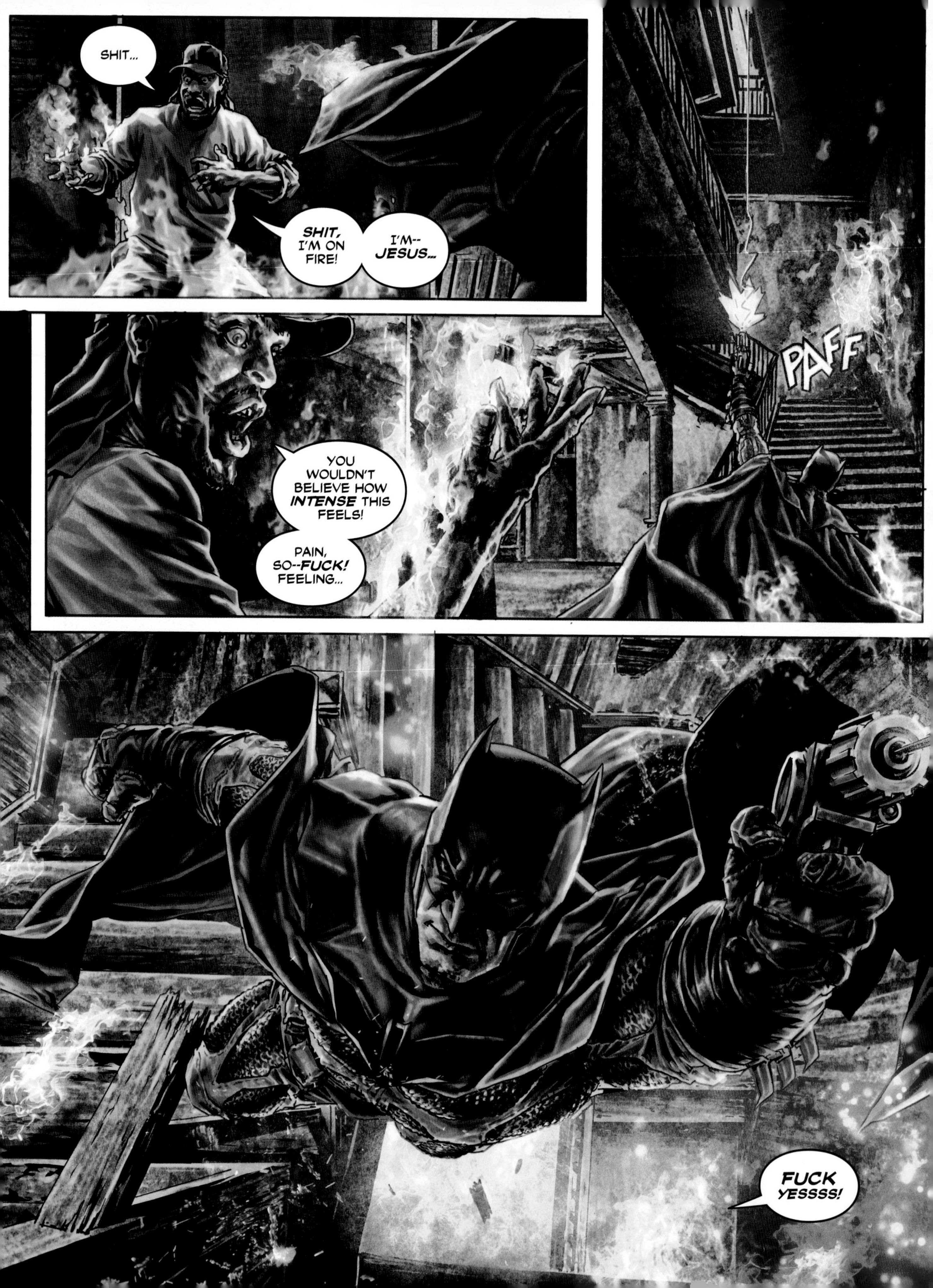

SHIT...
SHIT, I'M ON FIRE!
I'M-- JESUS...
YOU WOULDN'T BELIEVE HOW INTENSE THIS FEELS!
PAIN, SO--FUCK! FEELING...
PAFF
FUCK YESSSS!

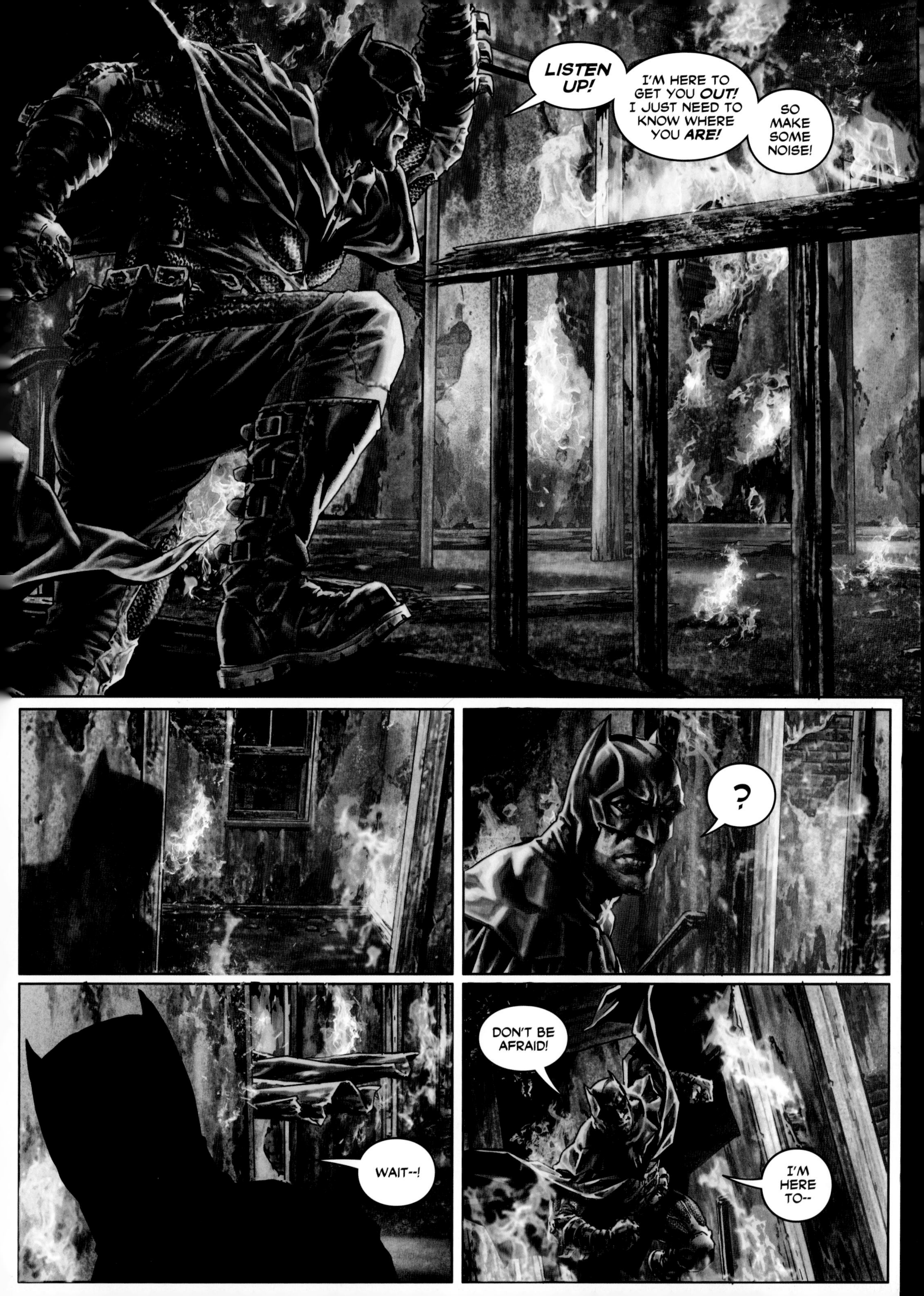
LISTEN UP!
I'M HERE TO GET YOU OUT! I JUST NEED TO KNOW WHERE YOU ARE!
SO MAKE SOME NOISE!
?
WAIT--!
DON'T BE AFRAID!
I'M HERE TO--

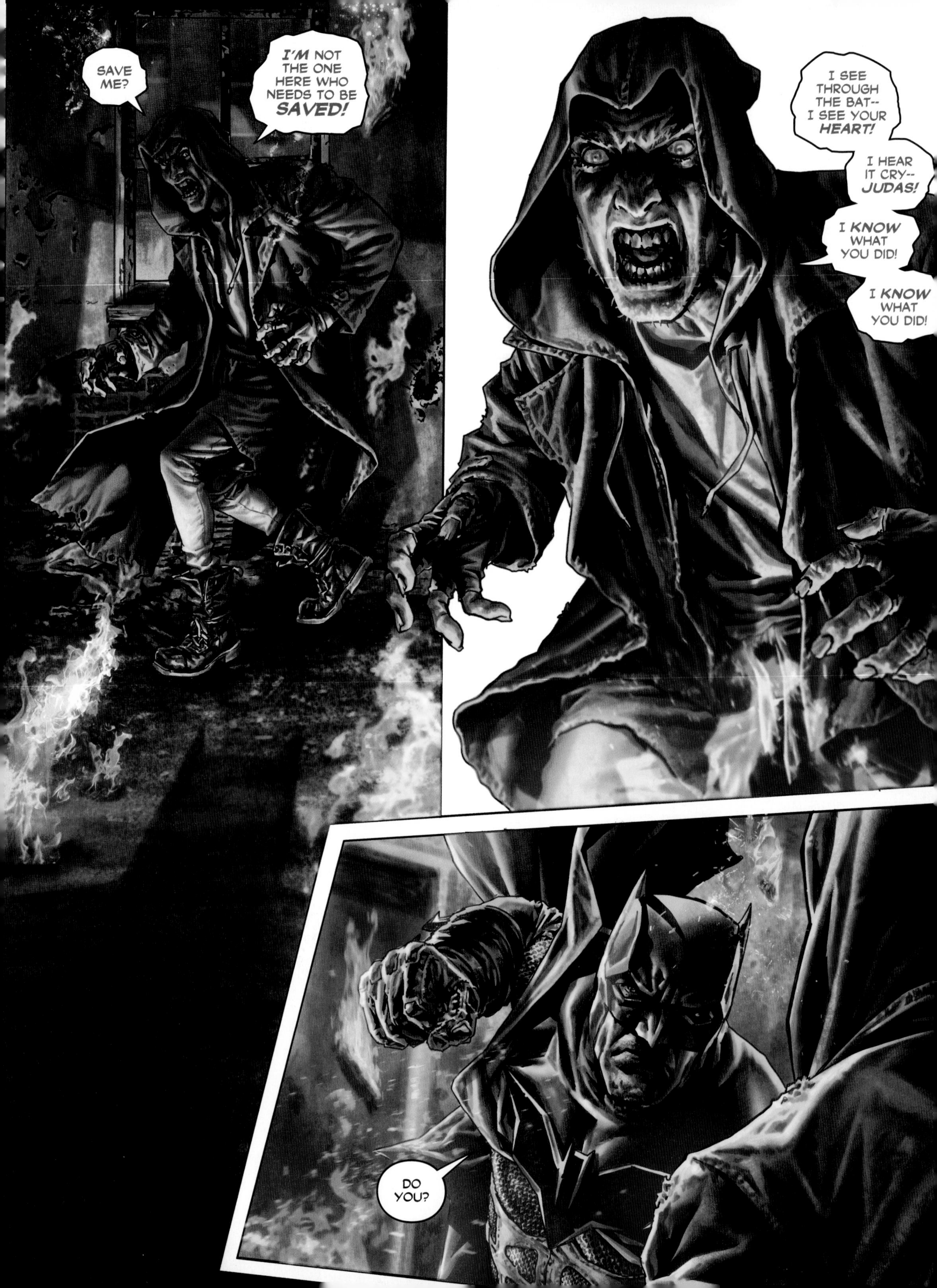
SAVE ME?
I'M NOT THE ONE HERE WHO NEEDS TO BE ***SAVED!***
I SEE THROUGH THE BAT-- I SEE YOUR ***HEART!***
I HEAR IT CRY-- ***JUDAS!***
I ***KNOW*** WHAT YOU DID!
I ***KNOW*** WHAT YOU DID!
DO YOU?

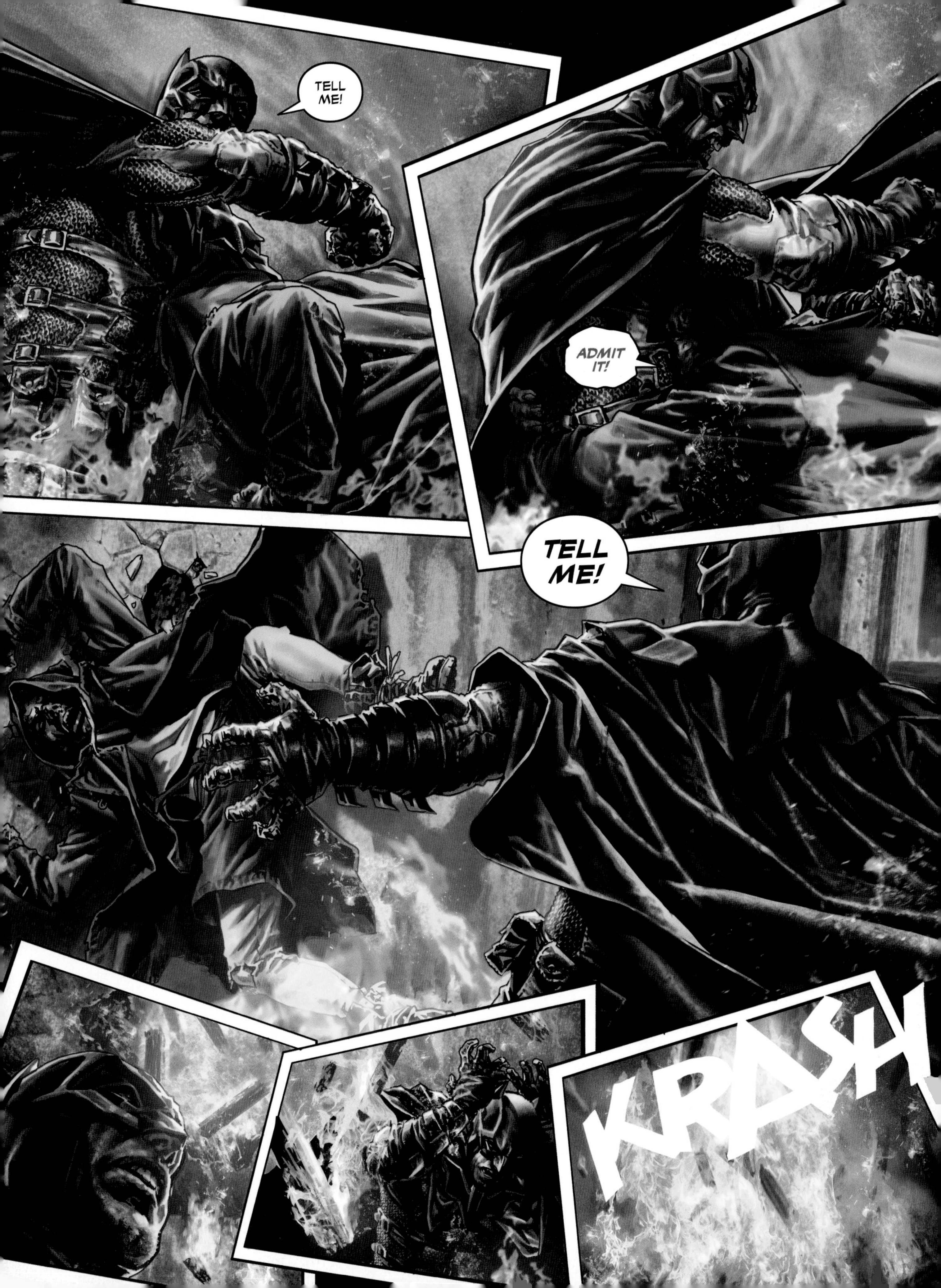
TELL ME!
ADMIT IT!
TELL ME!
KRASH

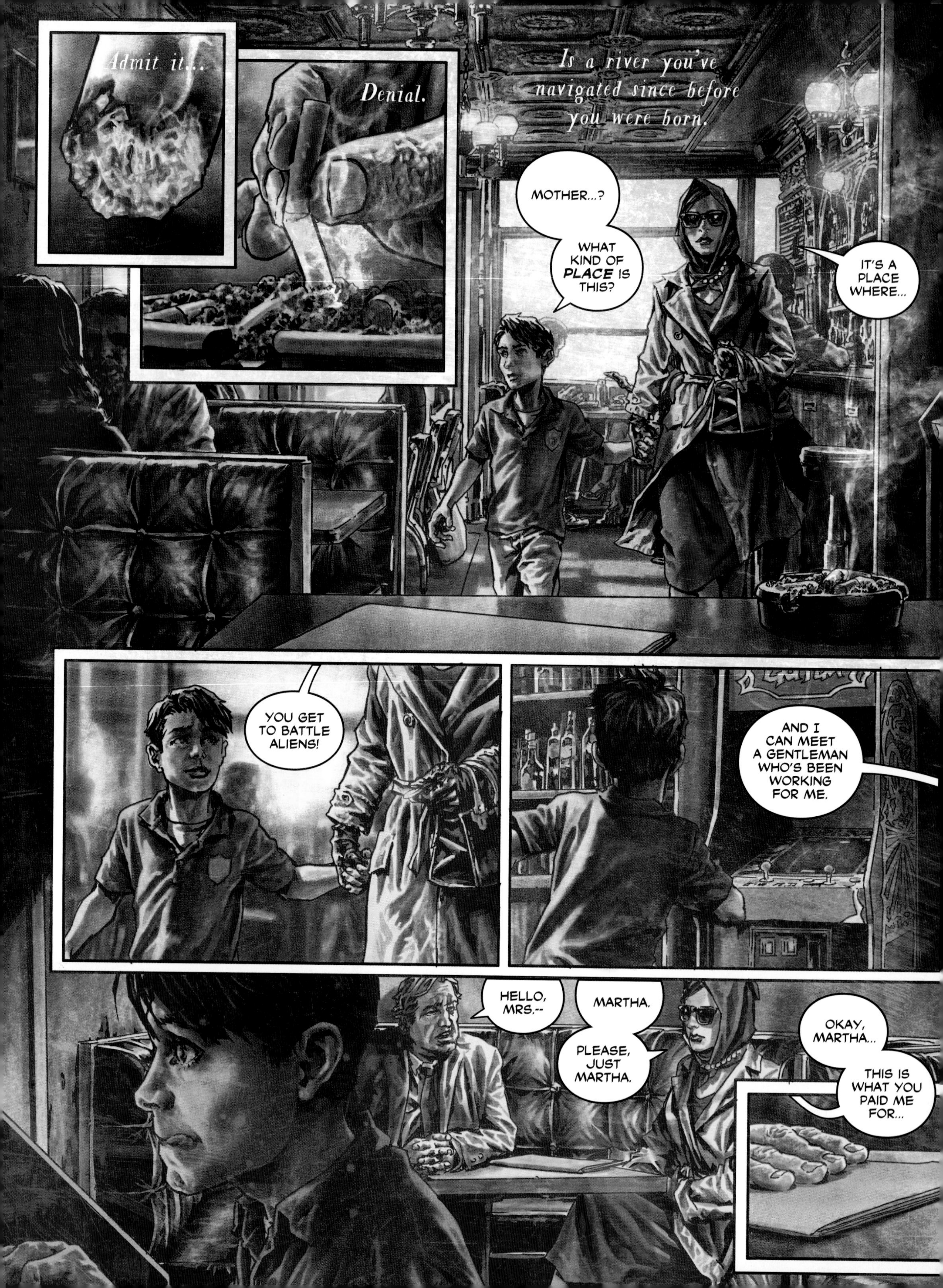
Admit it...
Denial.
Is a river you've navigated since before you were born.
MOTHER...?
WHAT KIND OF PLACE IS THIS?
IT'S A PLACE WHERE...
YOU GET TO BATTLE ALIENS!
AND I CAN MEET A GENTLEMAN WHO'S BEEN WORKING FOR ME.
HELLO, MRS.--
MARTHA.
PLEASE, JUST MARTHA.
OKAY, MARTHA...
THIS IS WHAT YOU PAID ME FOR...

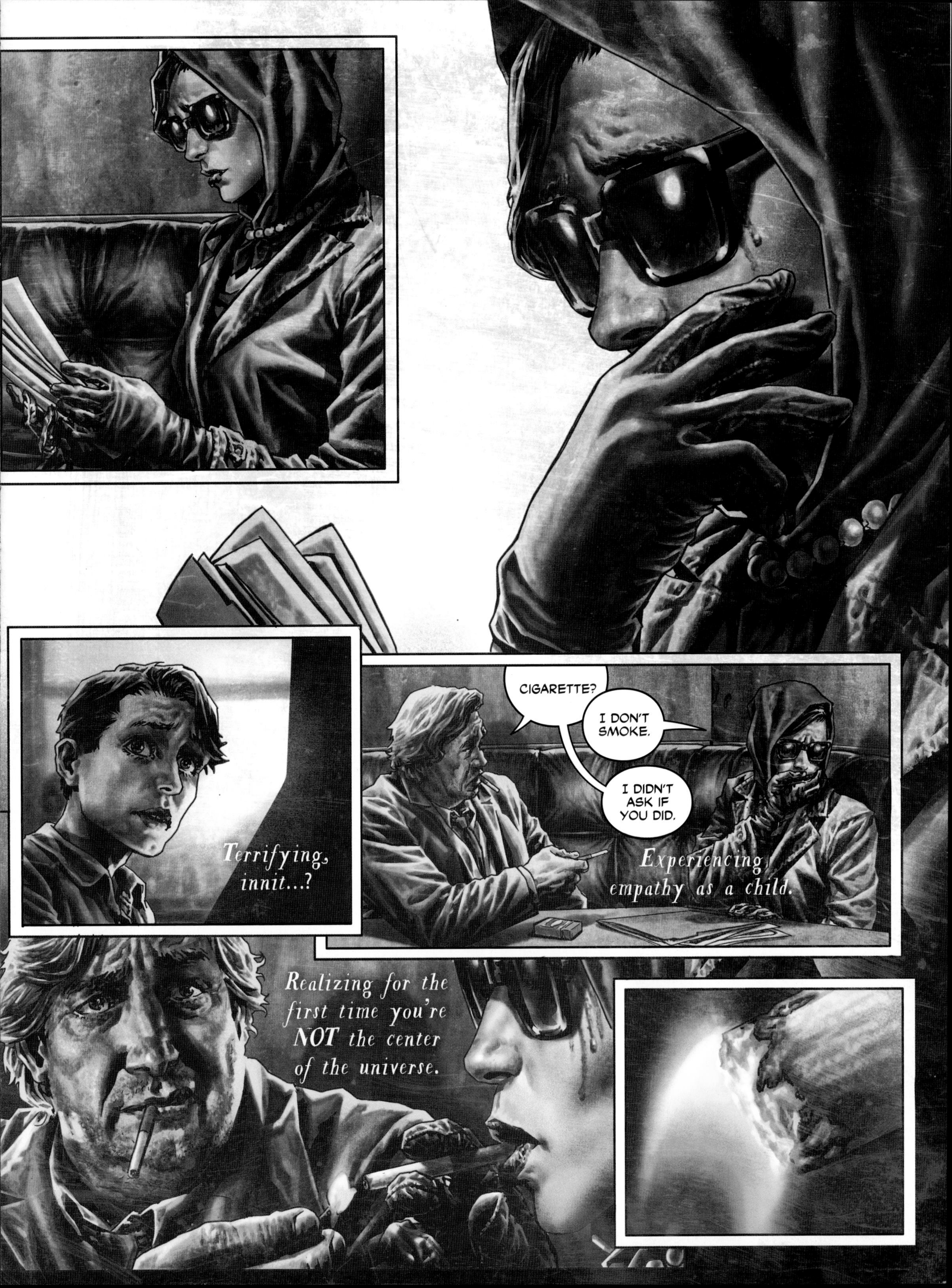
Terrifying, innit...?
CIGARETTE?
I DON'T SMOKE.
I DIDN'T ASK IF YOU DID.
Experiencing empathy as a child.
Realizing for the first time you're **NOT** the center of the universe.

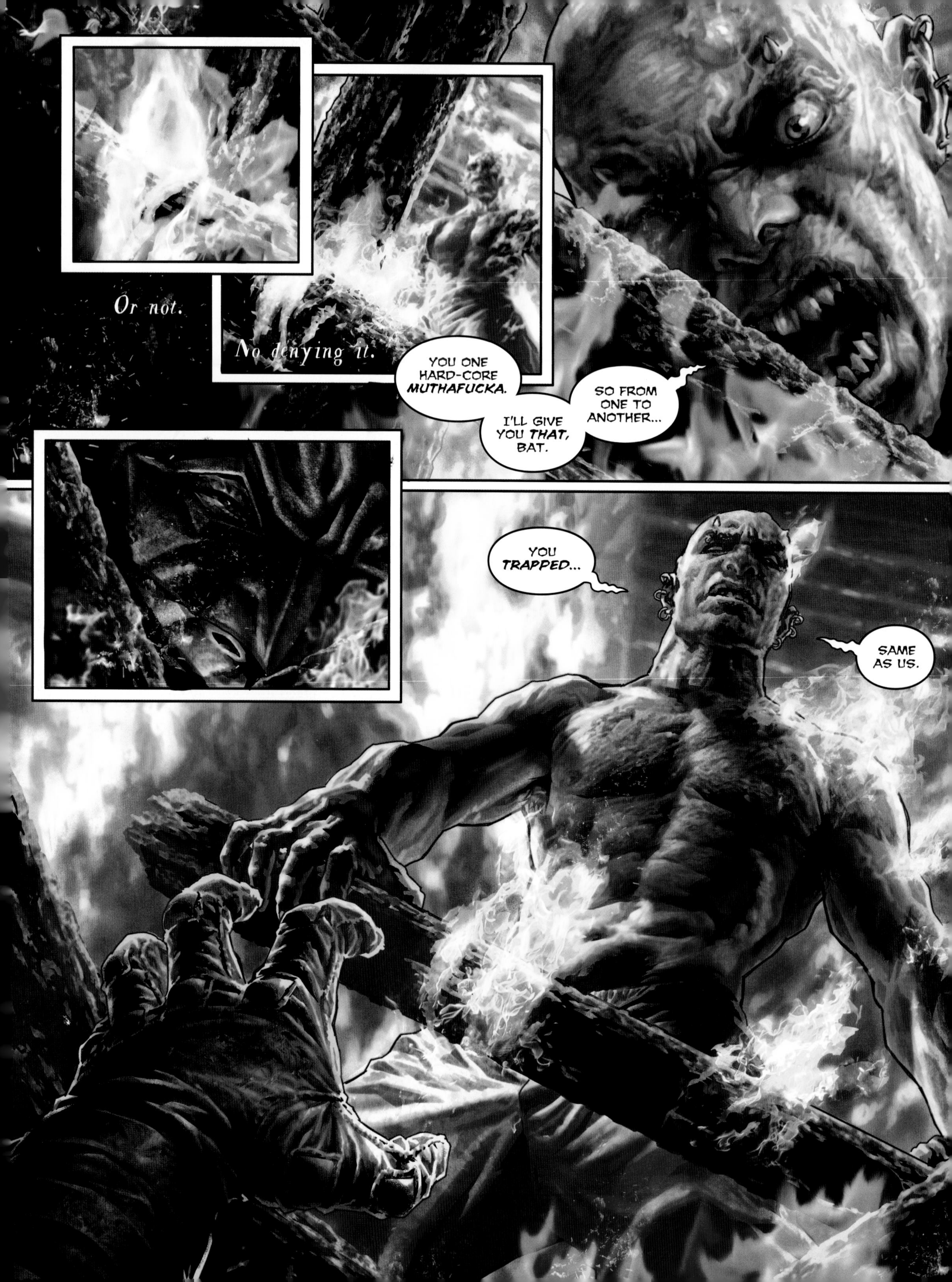

Or not.
No denying it.
YOU ONE HARD-CORE MUTHAFUCKA.
I'LL GIVE YOU THAT, BAT.
SO FROM ONE TO ANOTHER...
YOU TRAPPED...
SAME AS US.

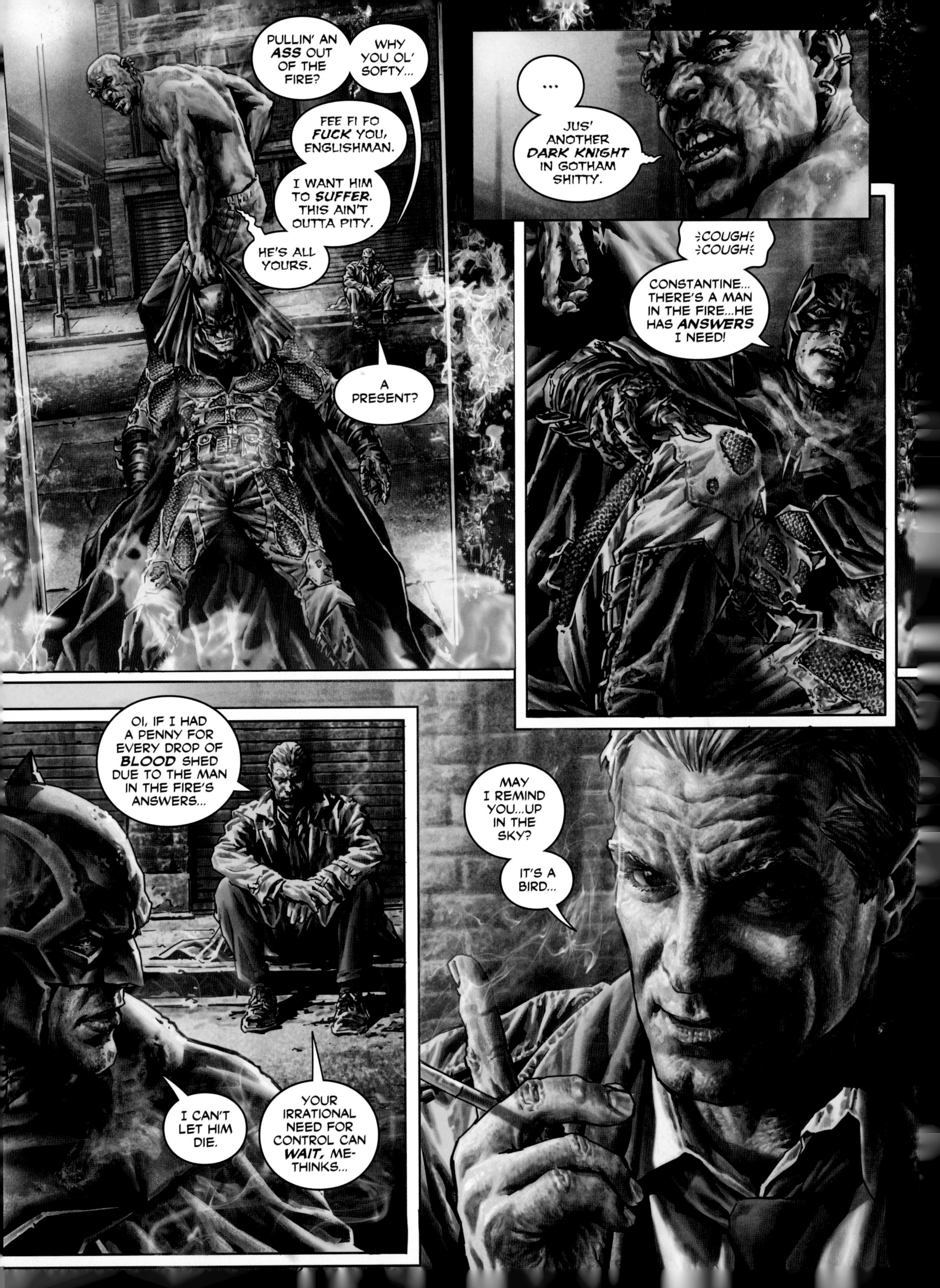
PULLIN' AN ASS OUT OF THE FIRE?
WHY YOU OL' SOFTY...
FEE FI FO FUCK YOU, ENGLISHMAN.
I WANT HIM TO SUFFER. THIS AIN'T OUTTA PITY.
HE'S ALL YOURS.
A PRESENT?
...
JUS' ANOTHER DARK KNIGHT IN GOTHAM SHITTY.
COUGH COUGH
CONSTANTINE... THERE'S A MAN IN THE FIRE...HE HAS ANSWERS I NEED!
OI, IF I HAD A PENNY FOR EVERY DROP OF BLOOD SHED DUE TO THE MAN IN THE FIRE'S ANSWERS...
I CAN'T LET HIM DIE.
YOUR IRRATIONAL NEED FOR CONTROL CAN WAIT, ME-THINKS...
MAY I REMIND YOU...UP IN THE SKY?
IT'S A BIRD...

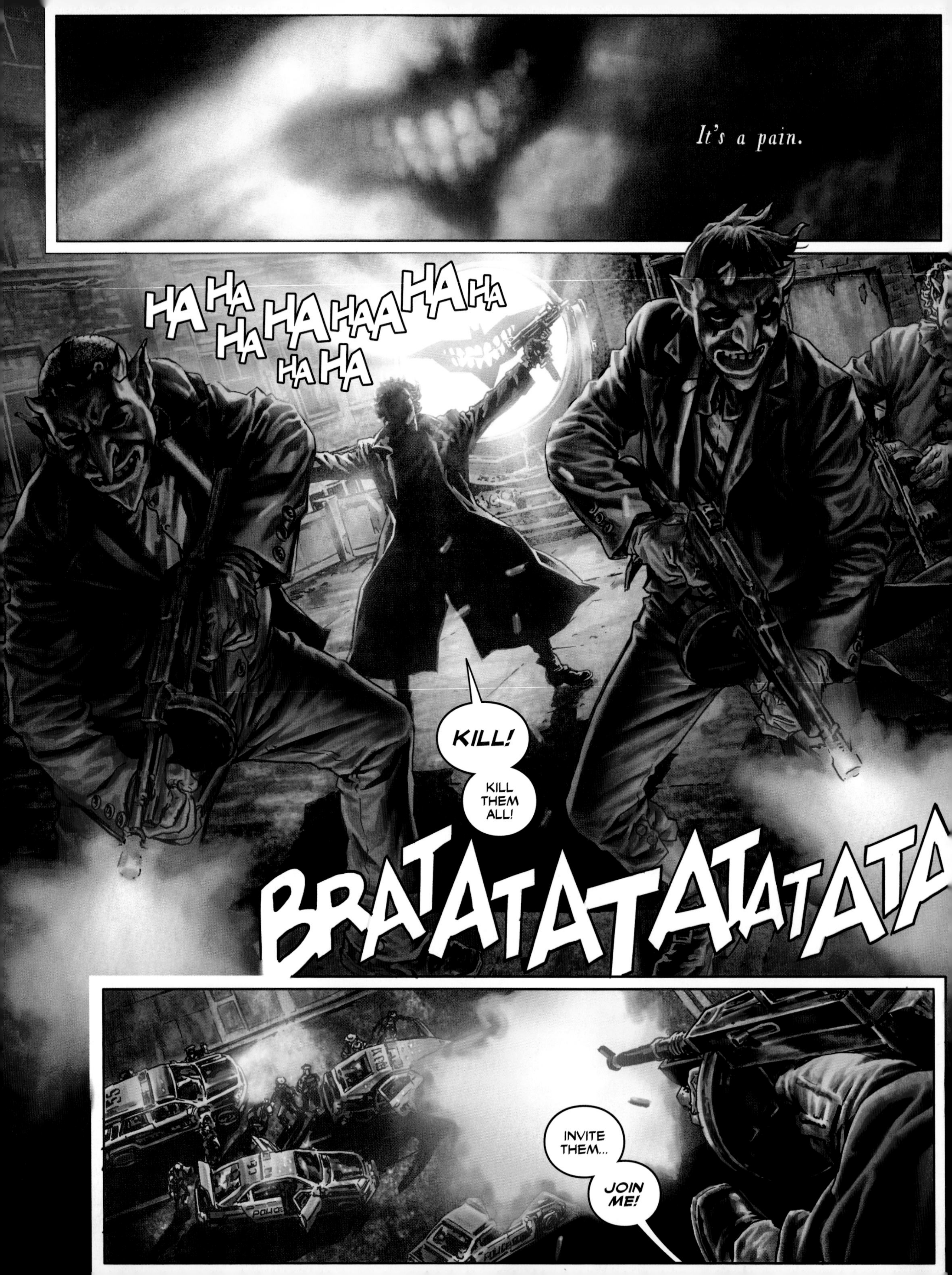
It's a pain.
HA HA HA HA HAA HA HA HA HA
KILL!
KILL THEM ALL!
BRATATATATATATA
INVITE THEM...
JOIN ME!

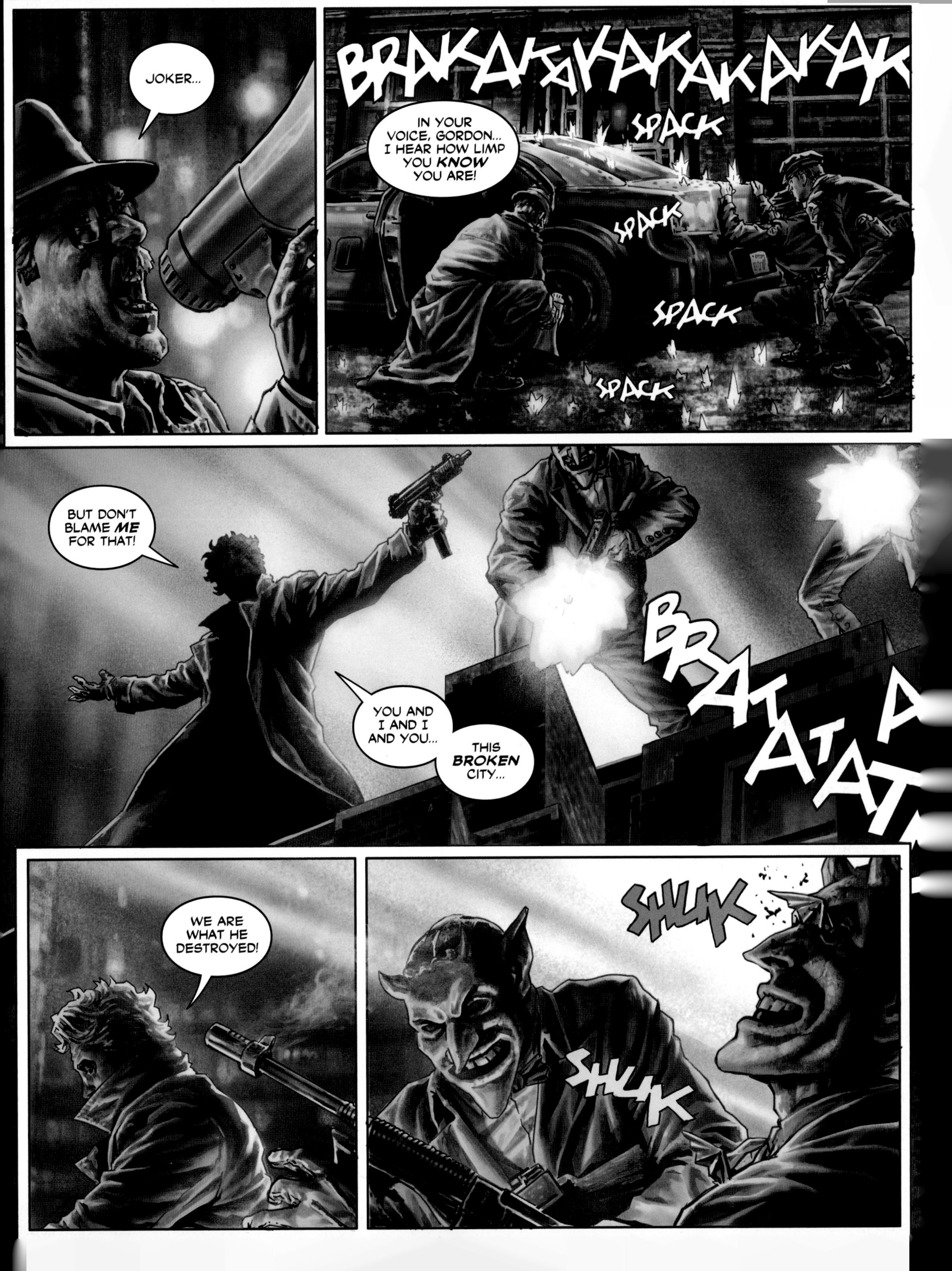
JOKER...
BRAKAKAKAKAKAKAKAK
IN YOUR VOICE, GORDON... I HEAR HOW LIMP YOU KNOW YOU ARE!
SPACK
SPACK
SPACK
SPACK
BUT DON'T BLAME ME FOR THAT!
YOU AND I AND I AND YOU...
THIS BROKEN CITY...
BRATATATA
WE ARE WHAT HE DESTROYED!
SHUK
SHUK

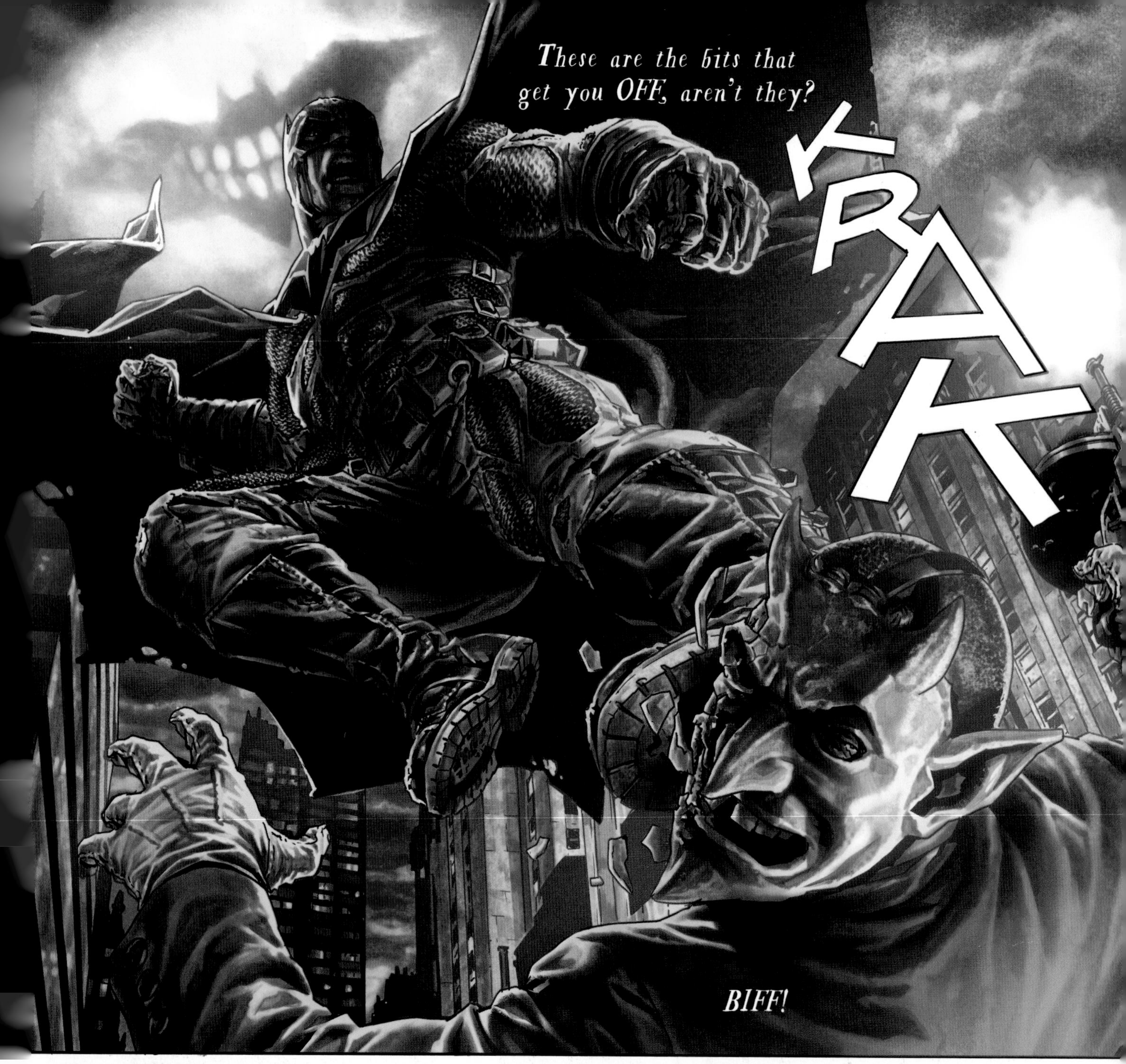
These are the bits that get you OFF, aren't they?
KRAK
BIFF!

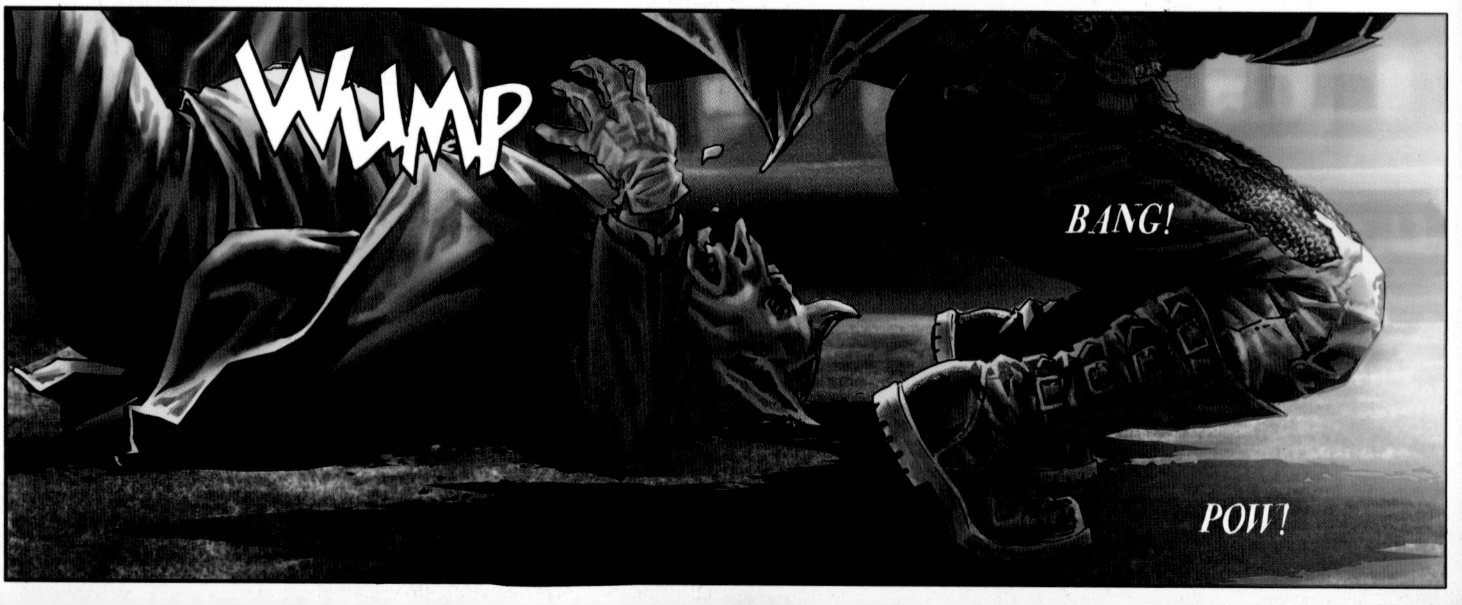
WUMP
BANG!
POW!

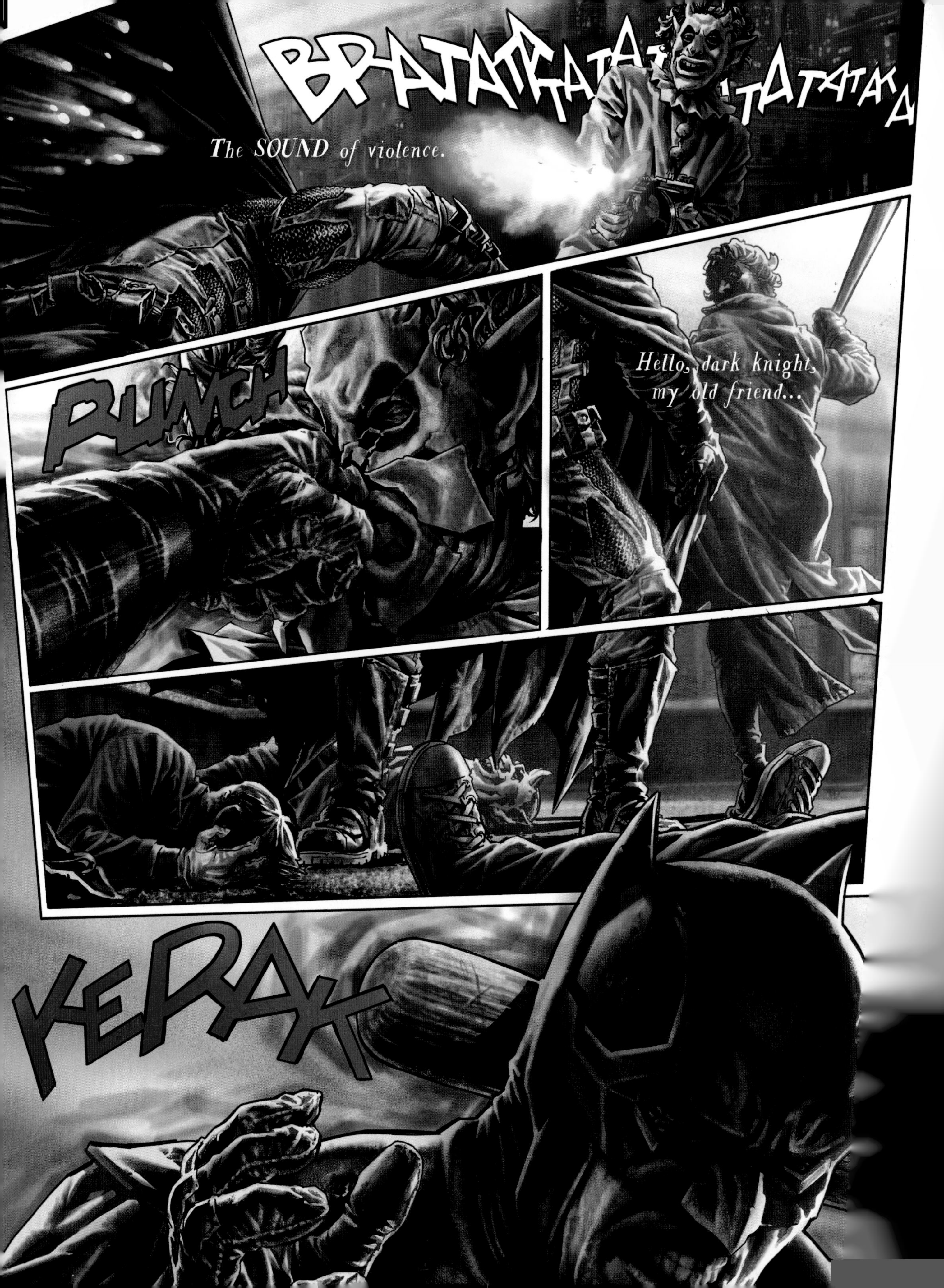
BRATATATATATATATATATATATATA
The SOUND of violence.
CRUNCH
Hello, dark knight, my old friend...
KERAK

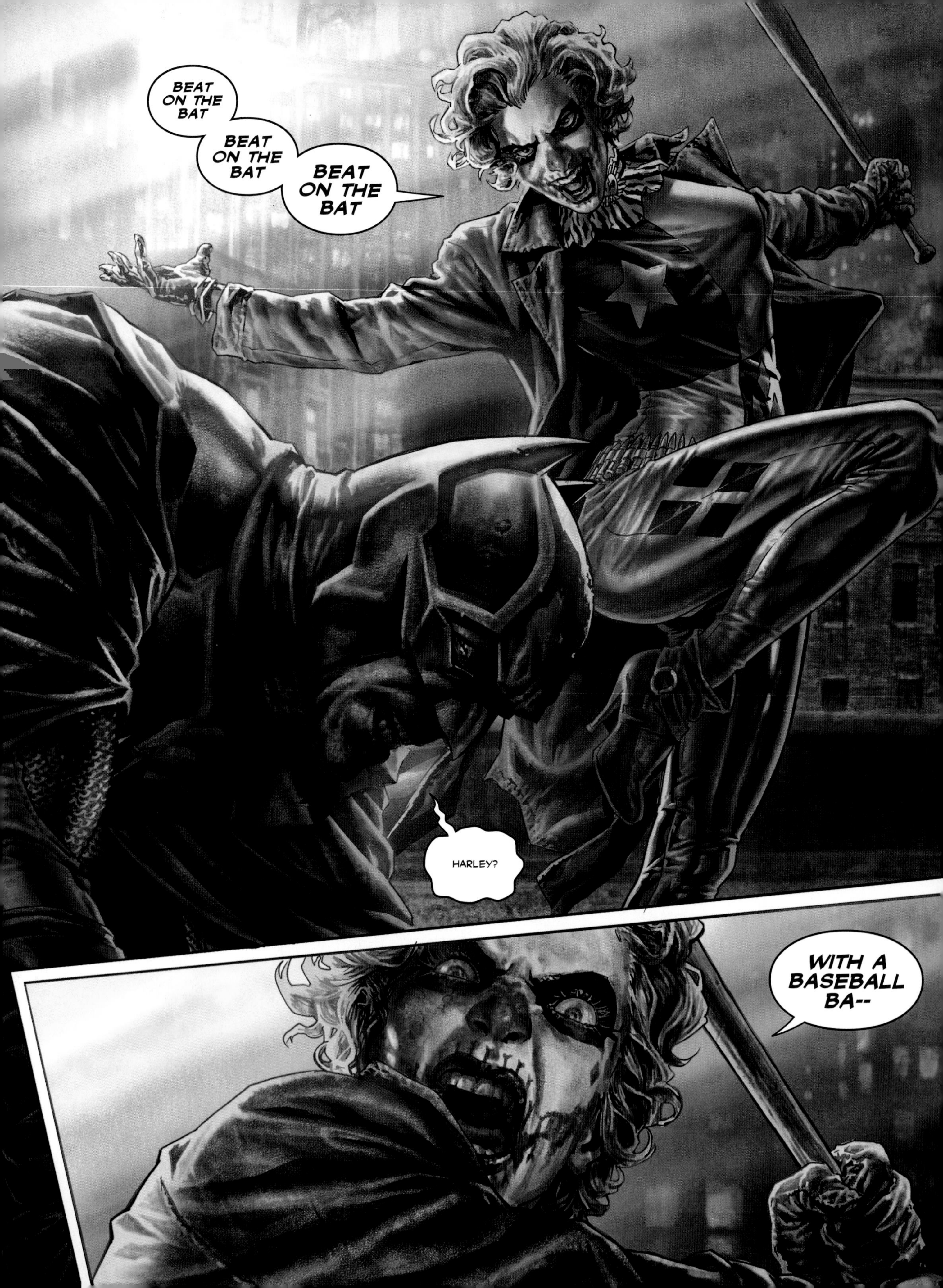
BEAT ON THE BAT
BEAT ON THE BAT
BEAT ON THE BAT
HARLEY?
WITH A BASEBALL BA--

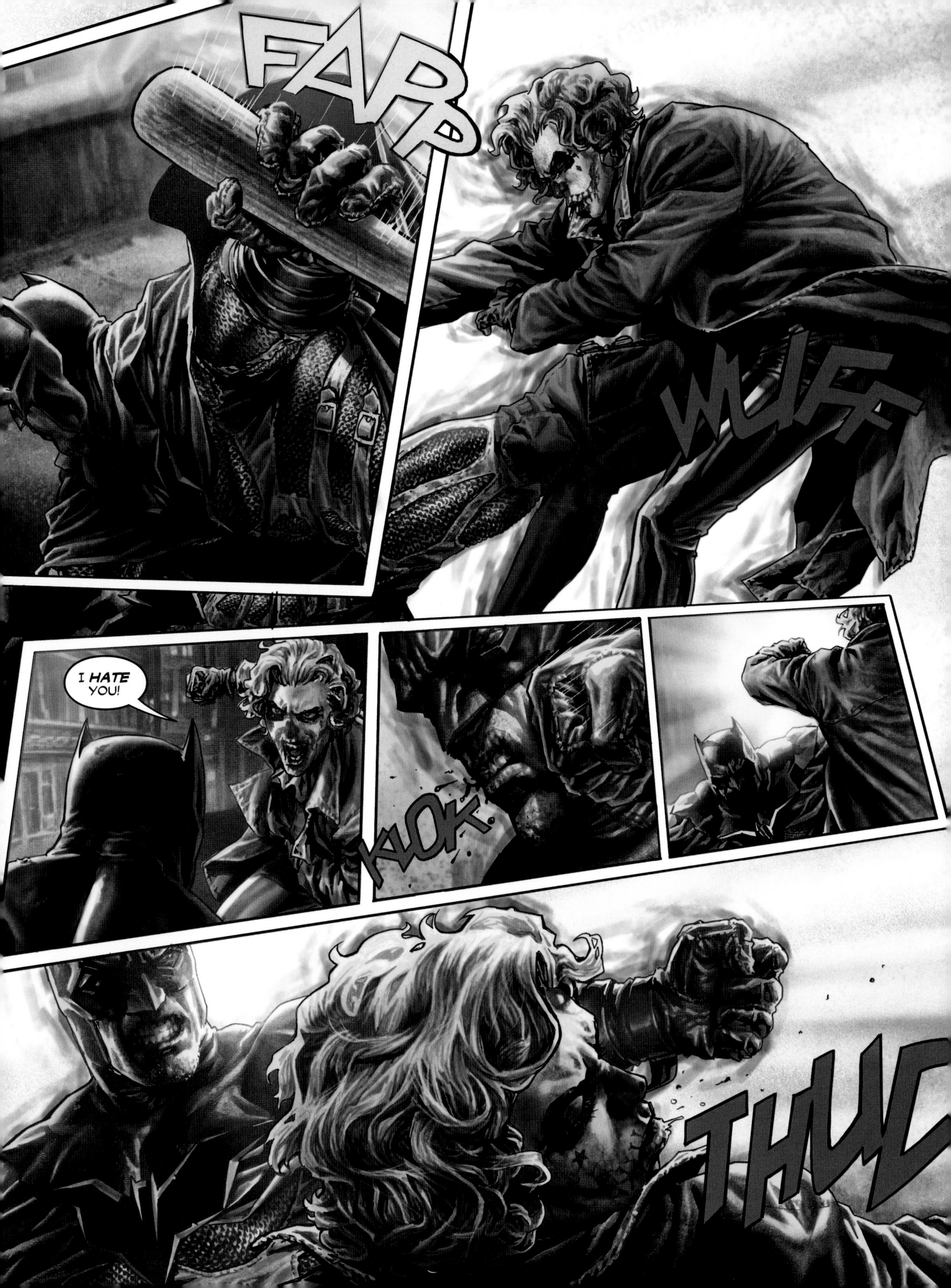
FAPP
WUFF
I HATE YOU!
KLOK
THUD

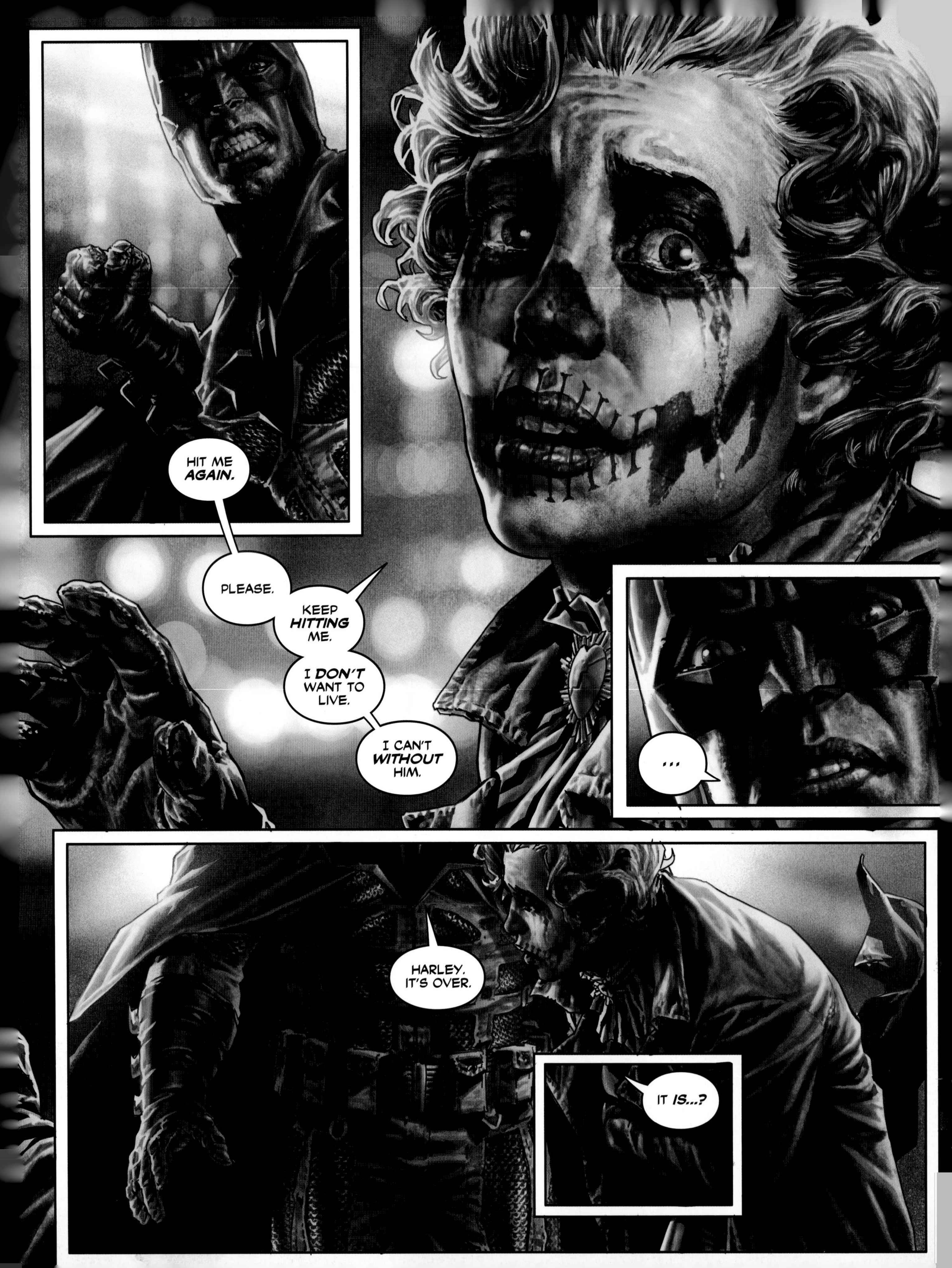
HIT ME AGAIN.
PLEASE.
KEEP HITTING ME.
I DON'T WANT TO LIVE.
I CAN'T WITHOUT HIM.
...
HARLEY. IT'S OVER.
IT IS...?

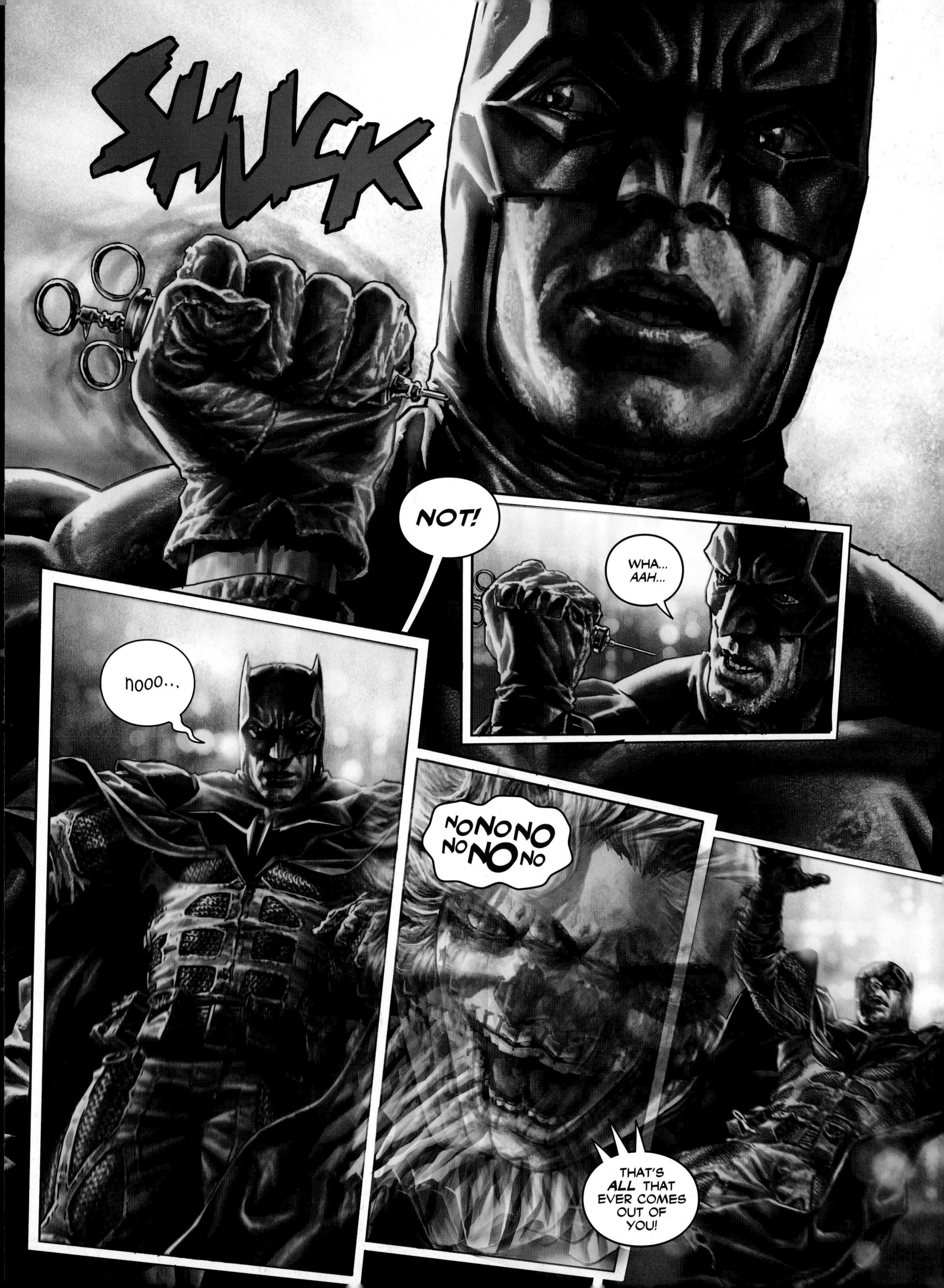

SHUCK
NOT!
WHA... AAH...
nooo...
NONONO NONONO
THAT'S ALL THAT EVER COMES OUT OF YOU!

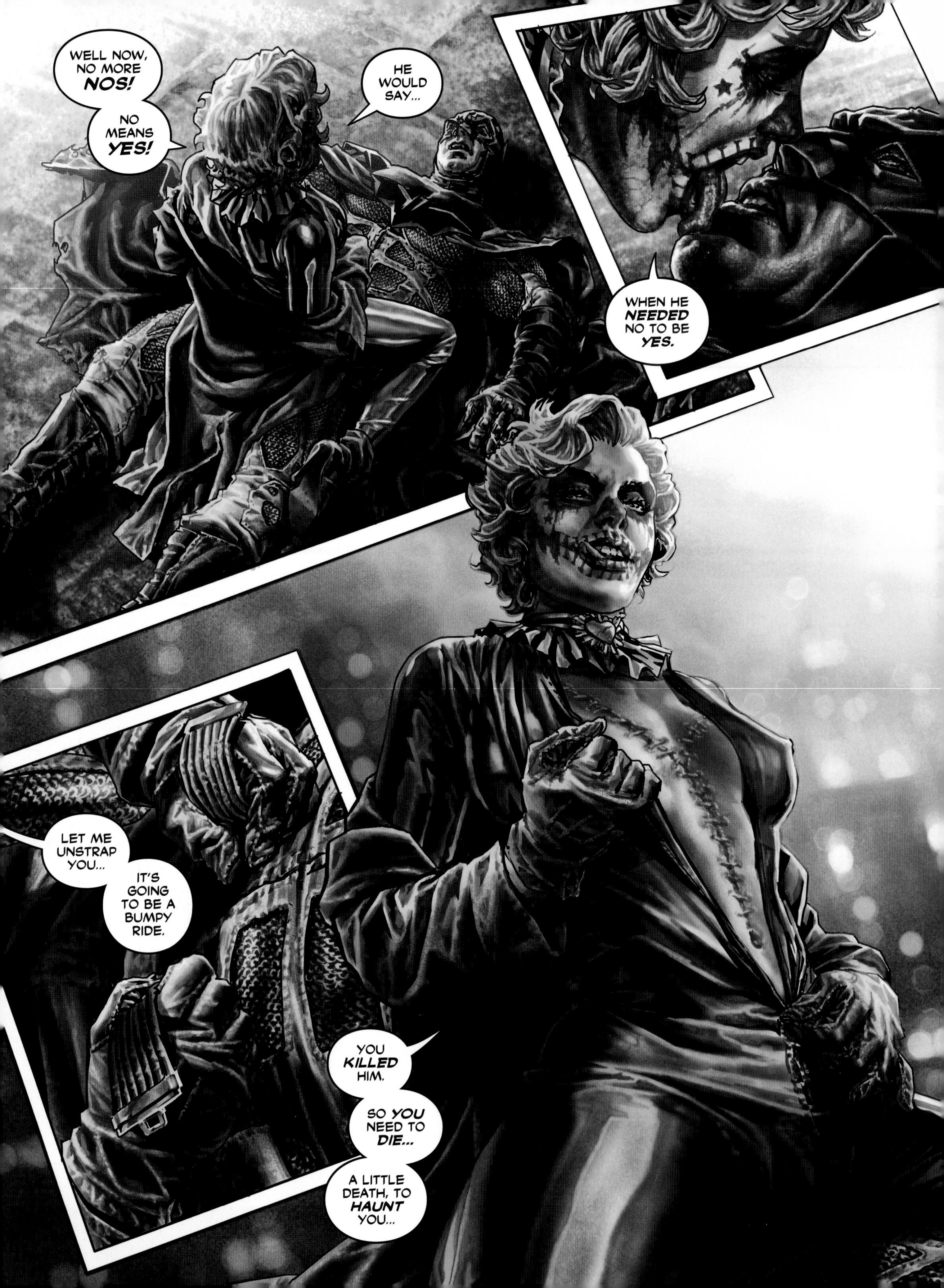
WELL NOW, NO MORE **NOS!**
NO MEANS ***YES!***
HE WOULD SAY...
WHEN HE ***NEEDED*** NO TO BE ***YES.***
LET ME UNSTRAP YOU...
IT'S GOING TO BE A BUMPY RIDE.
YOU ***KILLED*** HIM.
SO ***YOU*** NEED TO ***DIE...***
A LITTLE DEATH, TO ***HAUNT*** YOU...

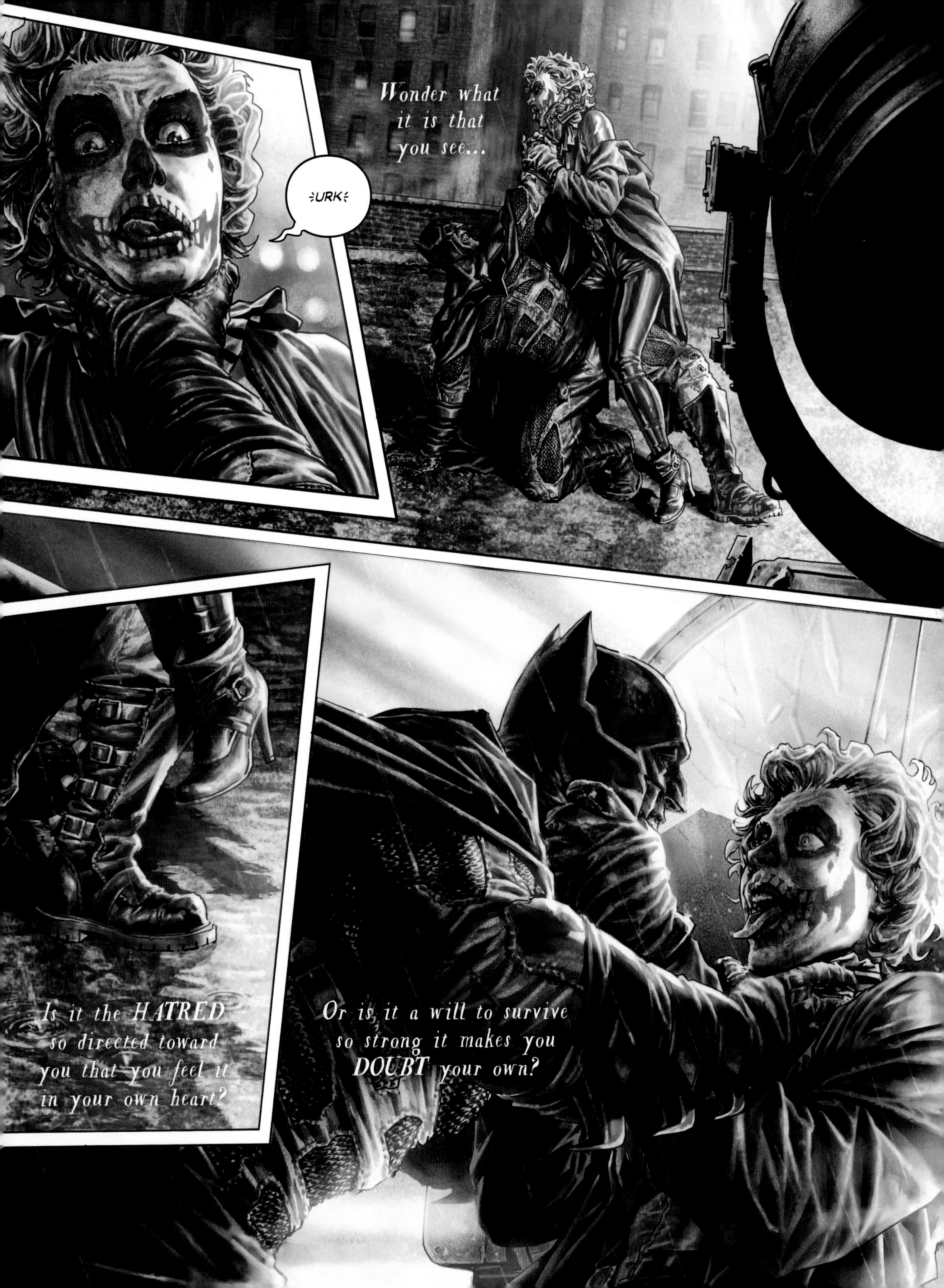
Wonder what it is that you see...
URK
Is it the HATRED so directed toward you that you feel it in your own heart?
Or is it a will to survive so strong it makes you DOUBT your own?

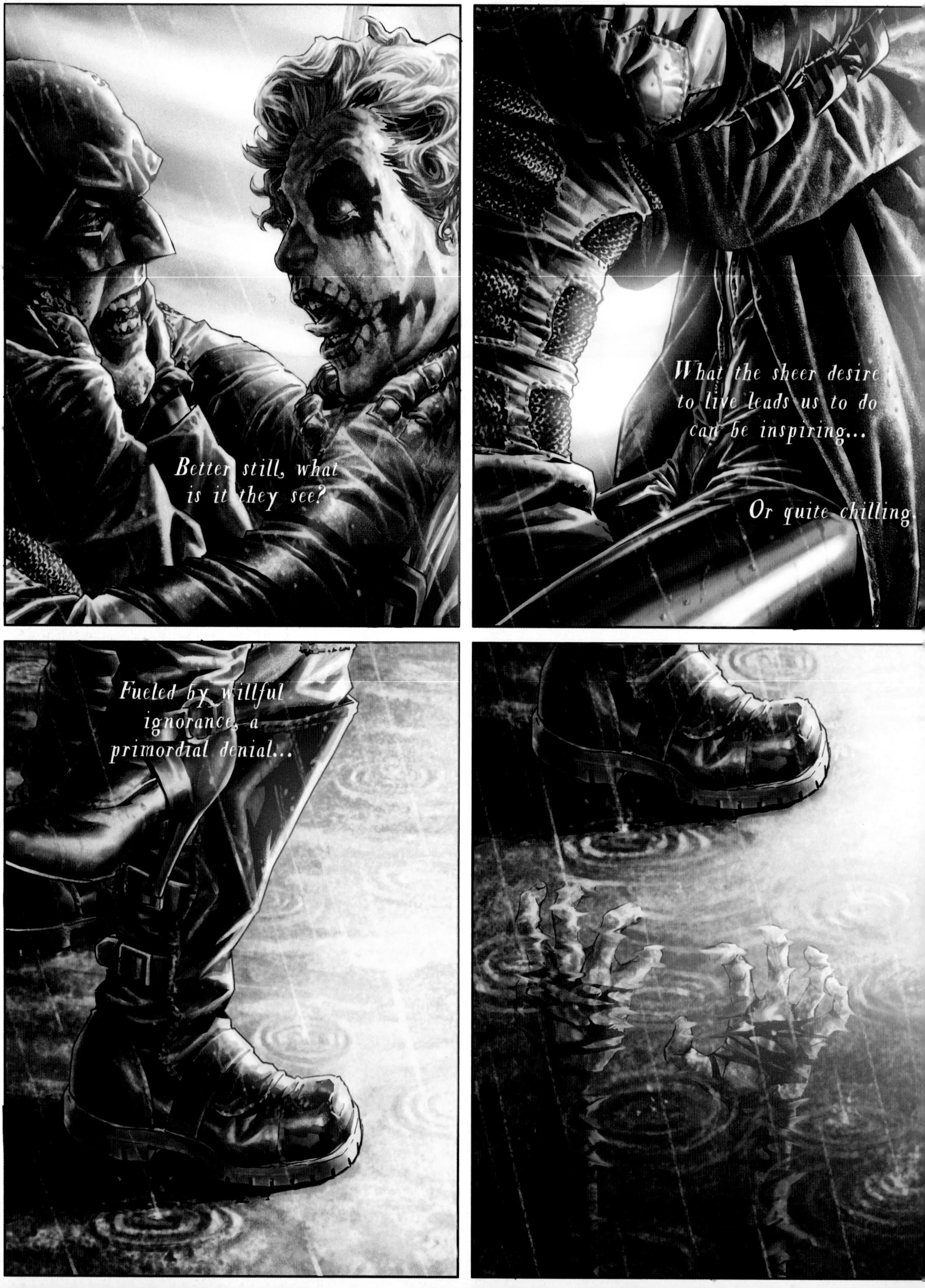
Better still, what is it they see?
What the sheer desire to live leads us to do can be inspiring...
Or quite chilling.
Fueled by willful ignorance, a primordial denial...

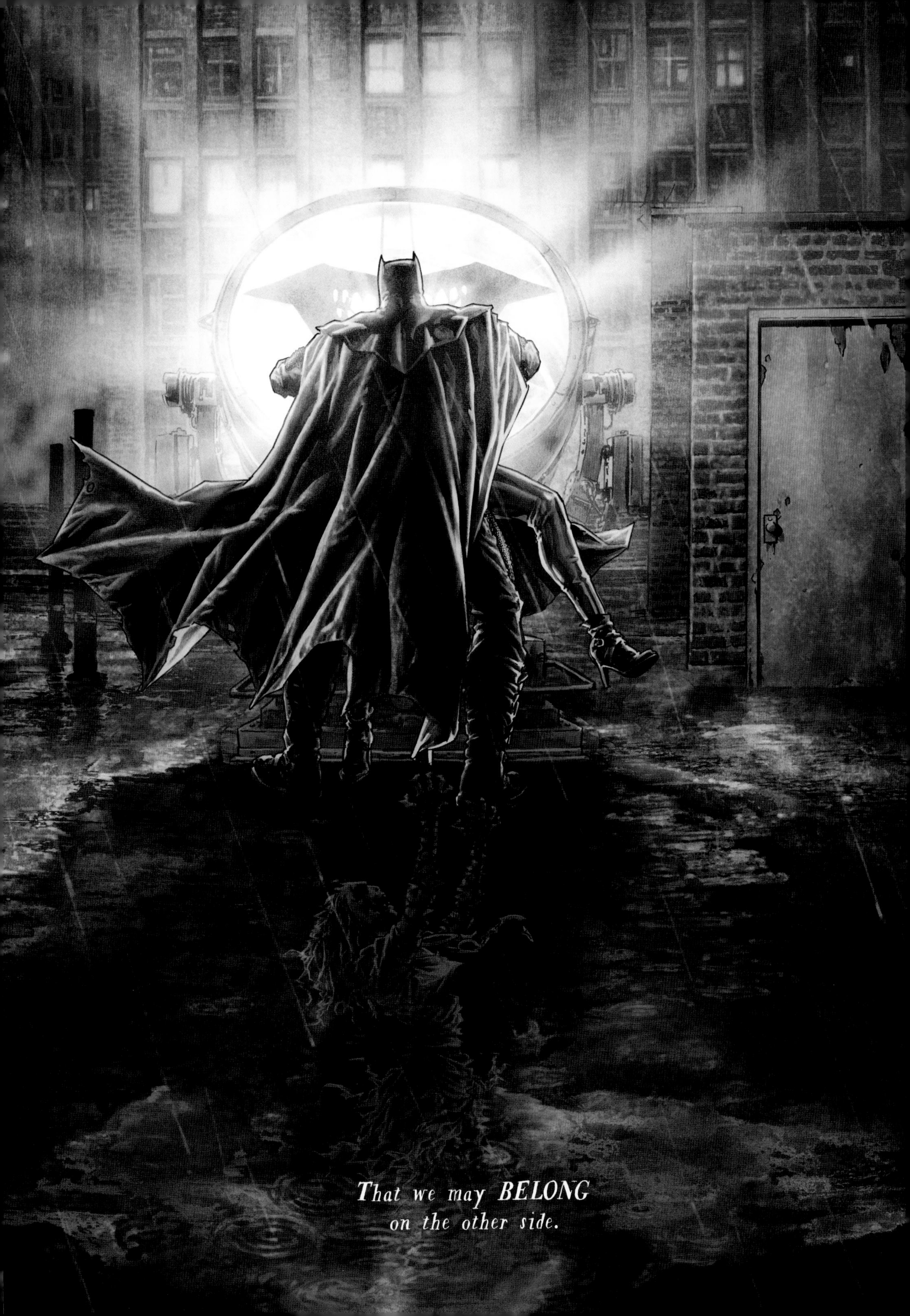
That we may BELONG
on the other side.

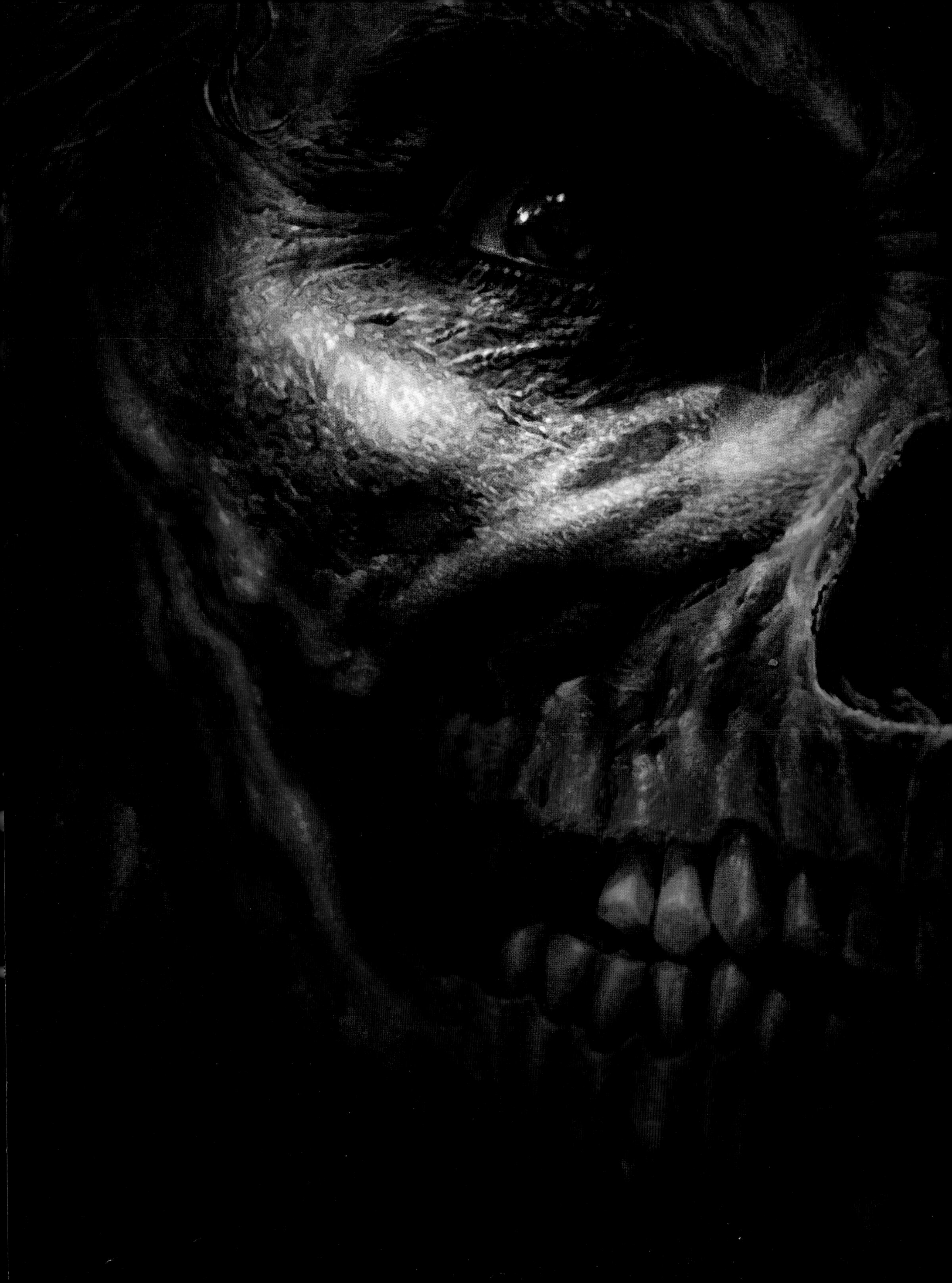

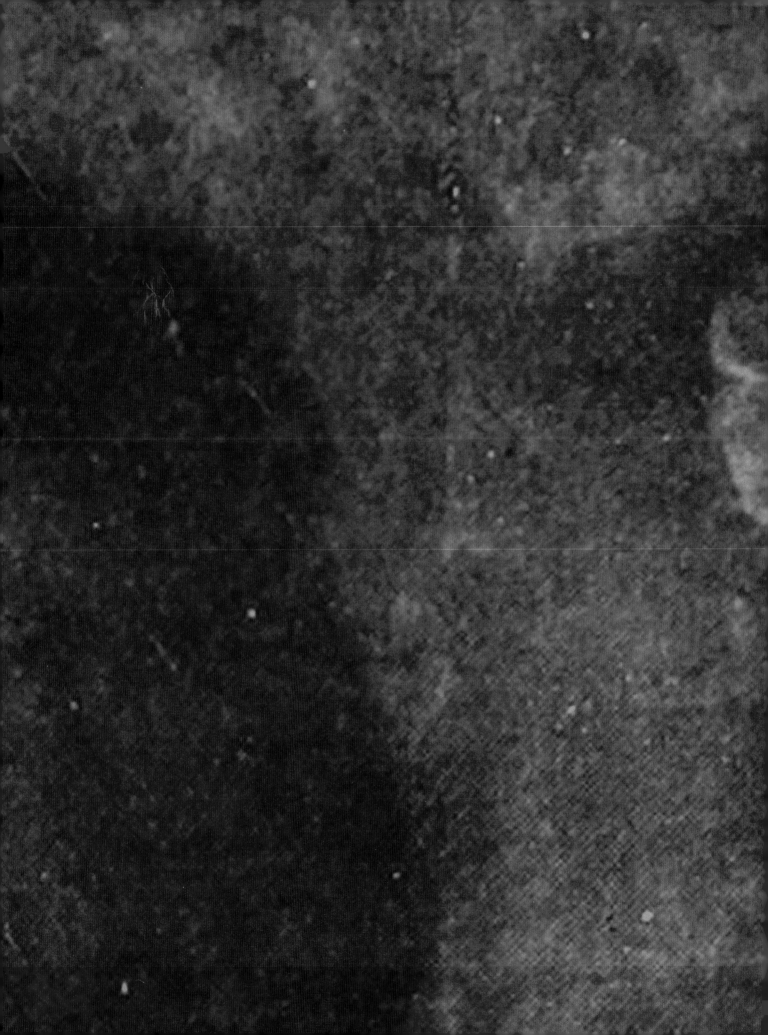

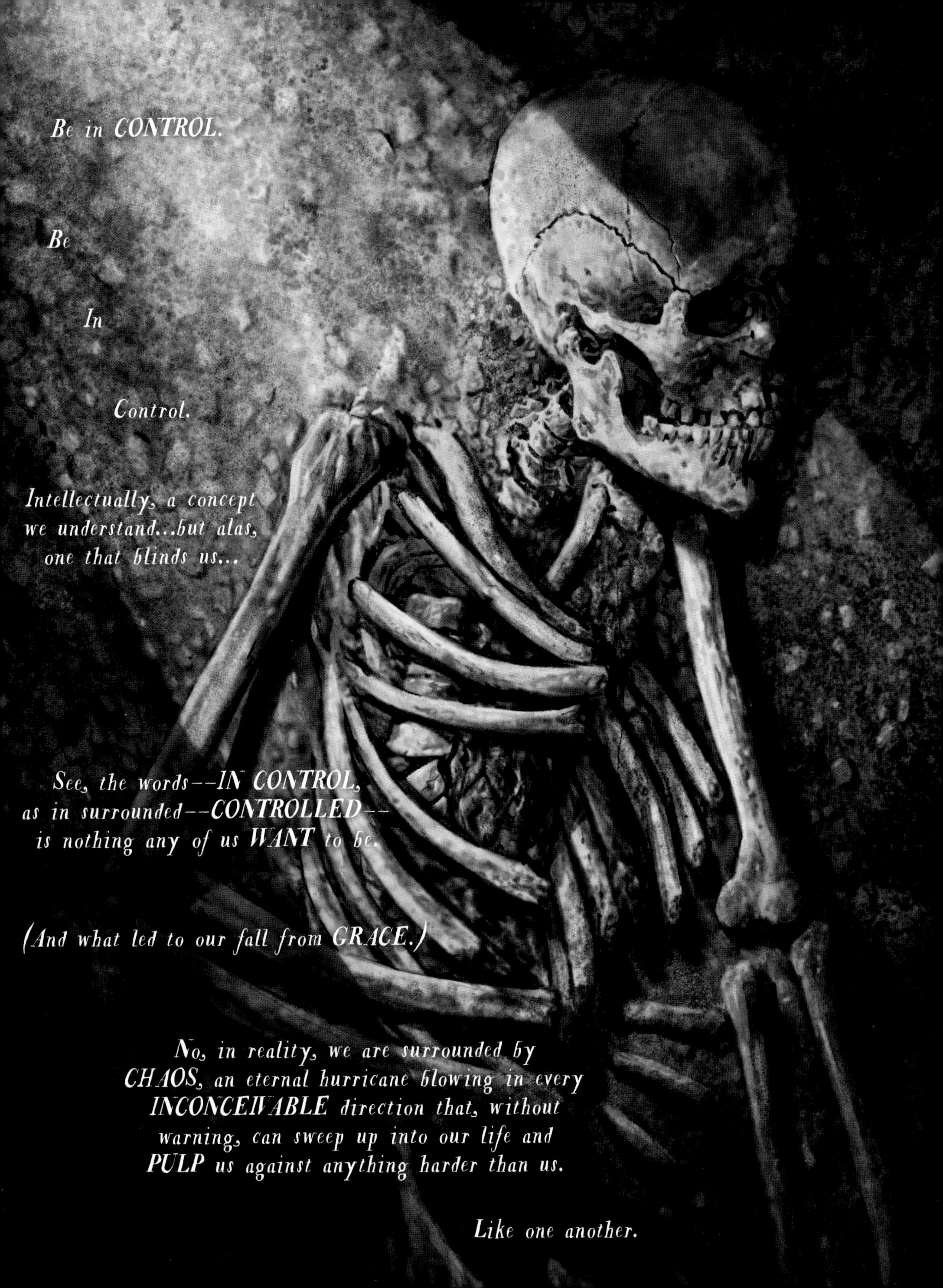
Be in CONTROL.
Be
In
Control.
Intellectually, a concept we understand...but alas, one that blinds us...
See, the words--IN CONTROL, as in surrounded--CONTROLLED--is nothing any of us WANT to be.
(And what led to our fall from GRACE.)
No, in reality, we are surrounded by CHAOS, an eternal hurricane blowing in every INCONCEIVABLE direction that, without warning, can sweep up into our life and PULP us against anything harder than us.
Like one another.

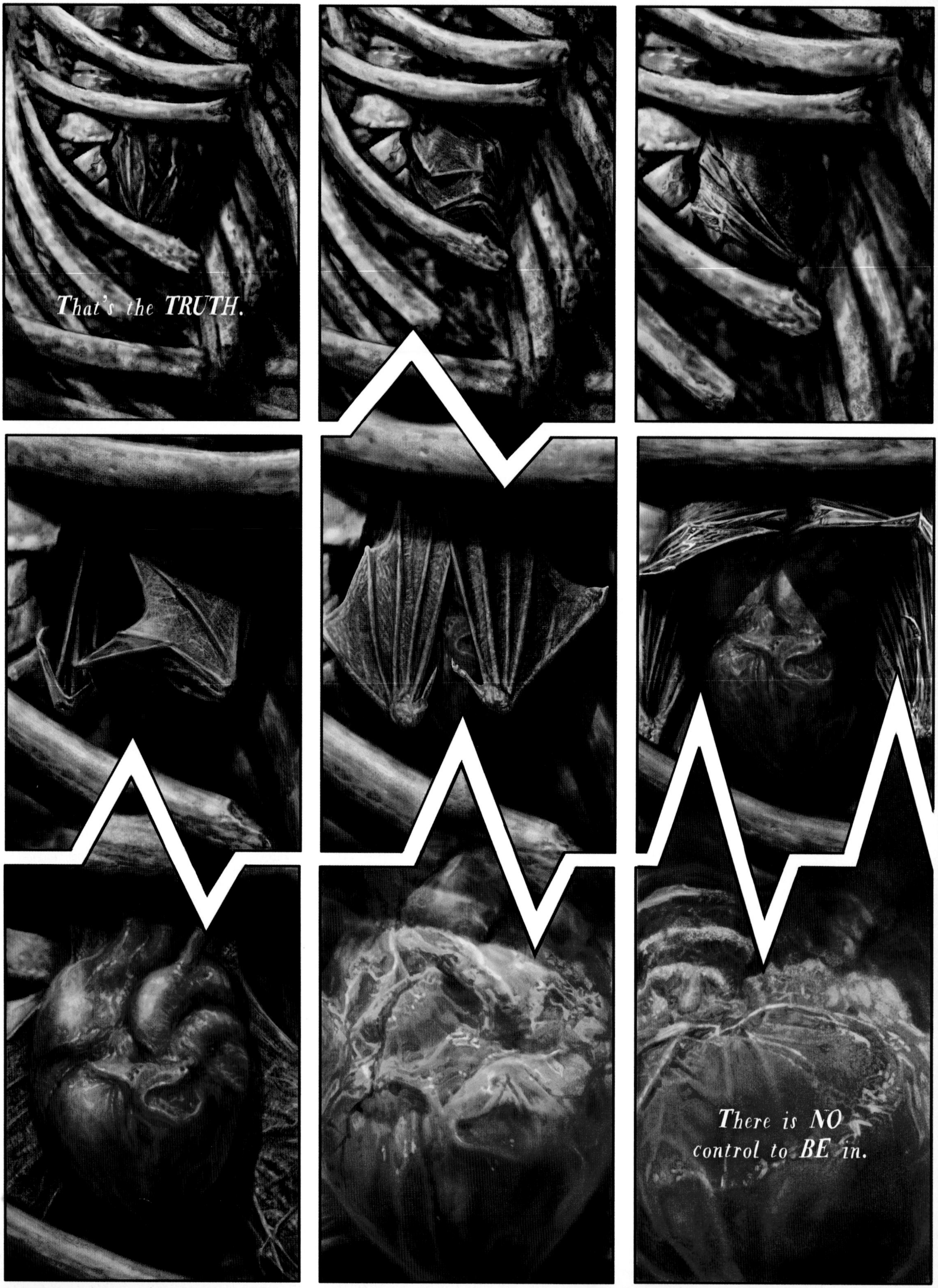
That's the TRUTH.
There is NO control to BE in.

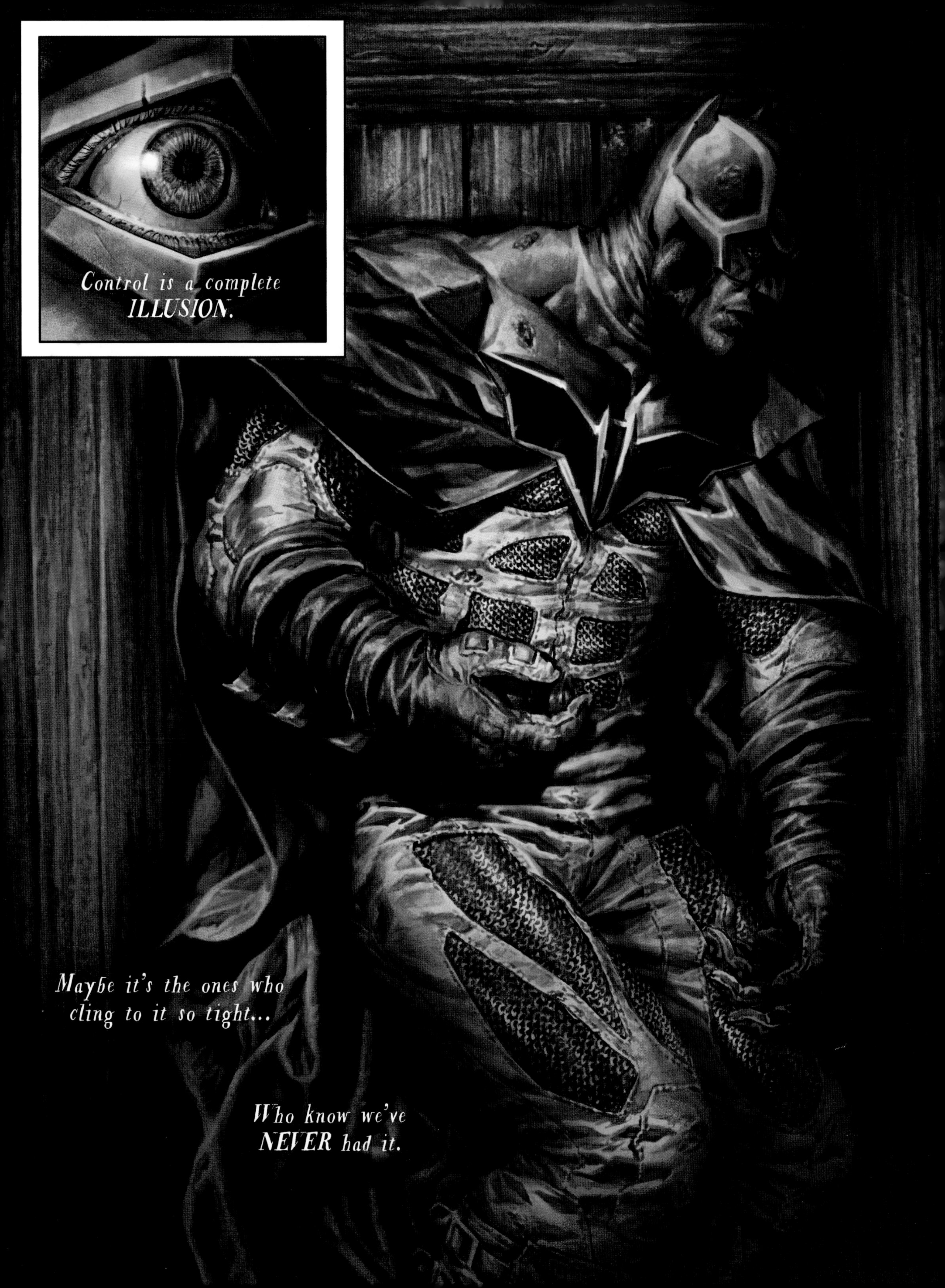
Control is a complete ILLUSION.
Maybe it's the ones who cling to it so tight...
Who know we've NEVER had it.

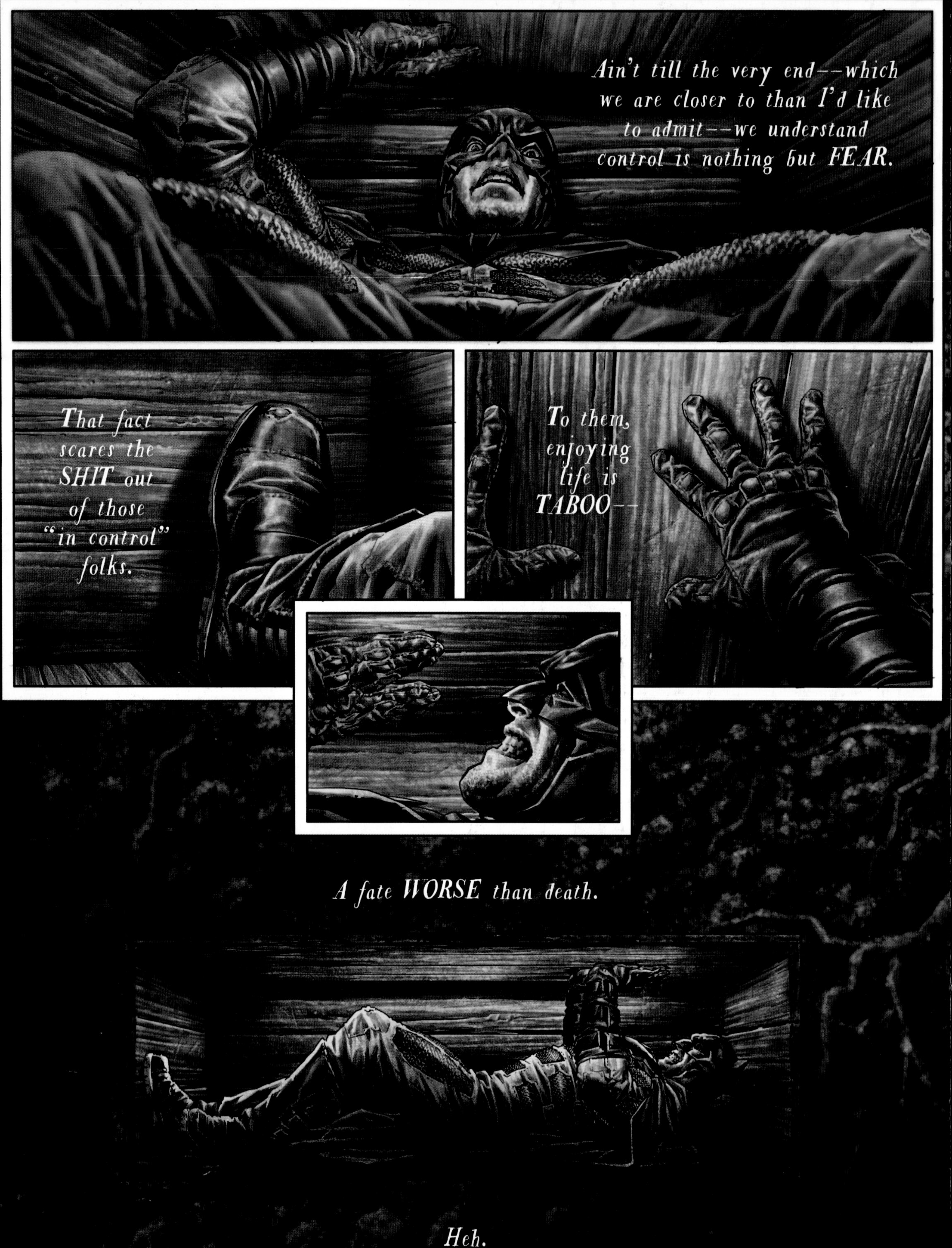
Ain't till the very end--which we are closer to than I'd like to admit--we understand control is nothing but FEAR.
That fact scares the SHIT out of those "in control" folks.
To them, enjoying life is TABOO--
A fate WORSE than death.
Heh.

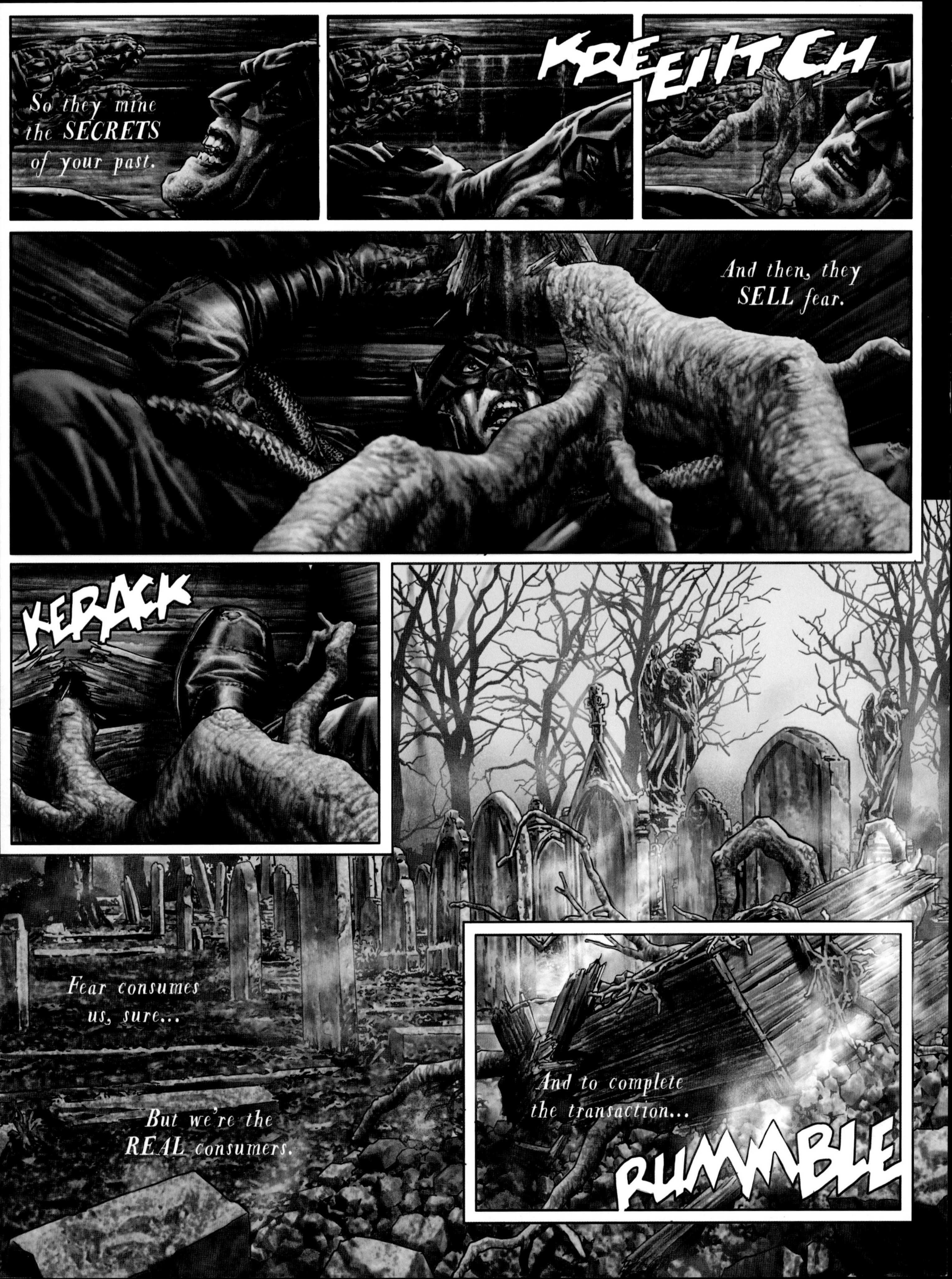
So they mine the SECRETS of your past.
KREEIITCH
And then, they SELL fear.
KERACK
Fear consumes us, sure...
But we're the REAL consumers.
And to complete the transaction...
RUMMBLE

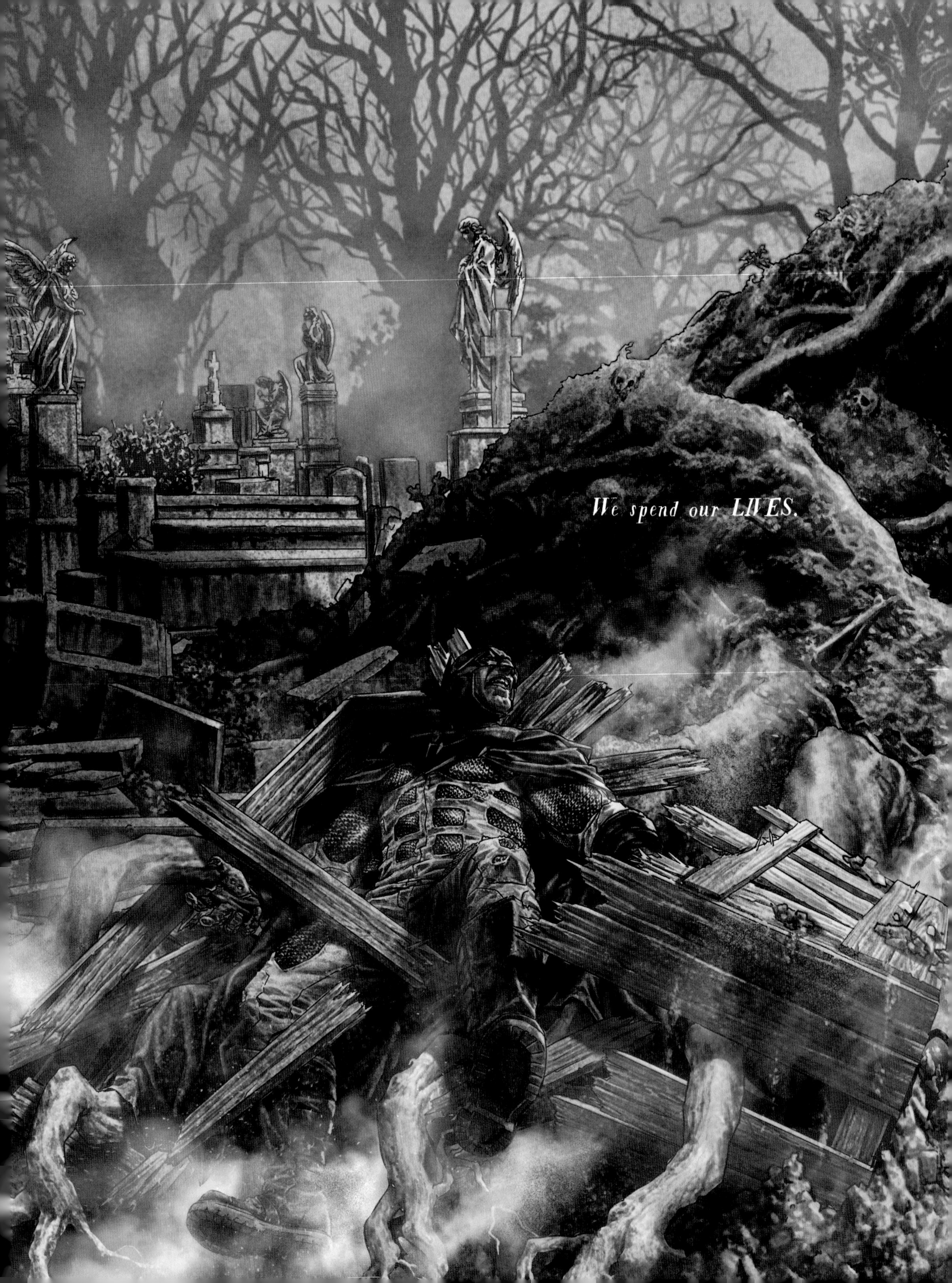
We spend our LIVES.

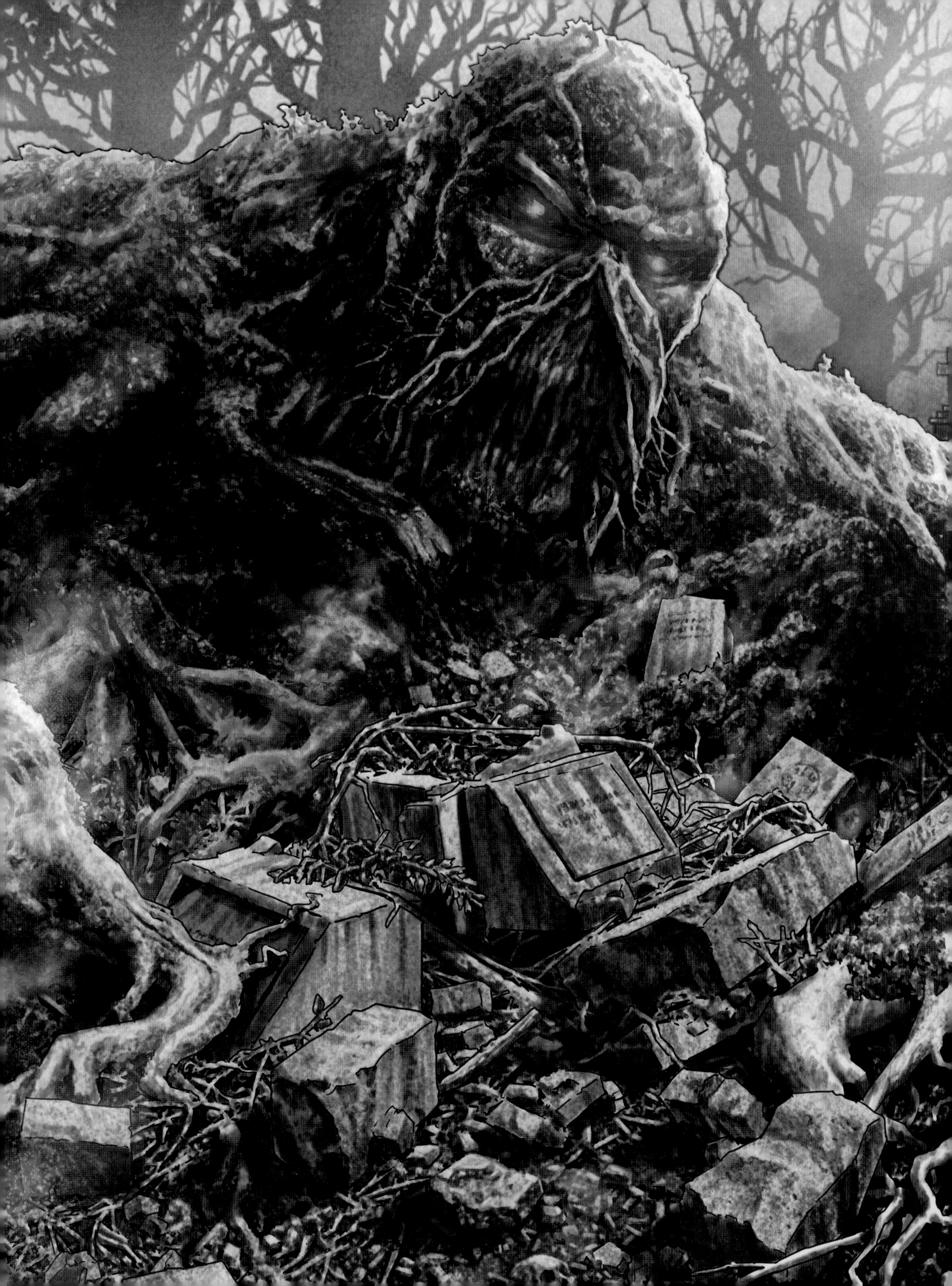

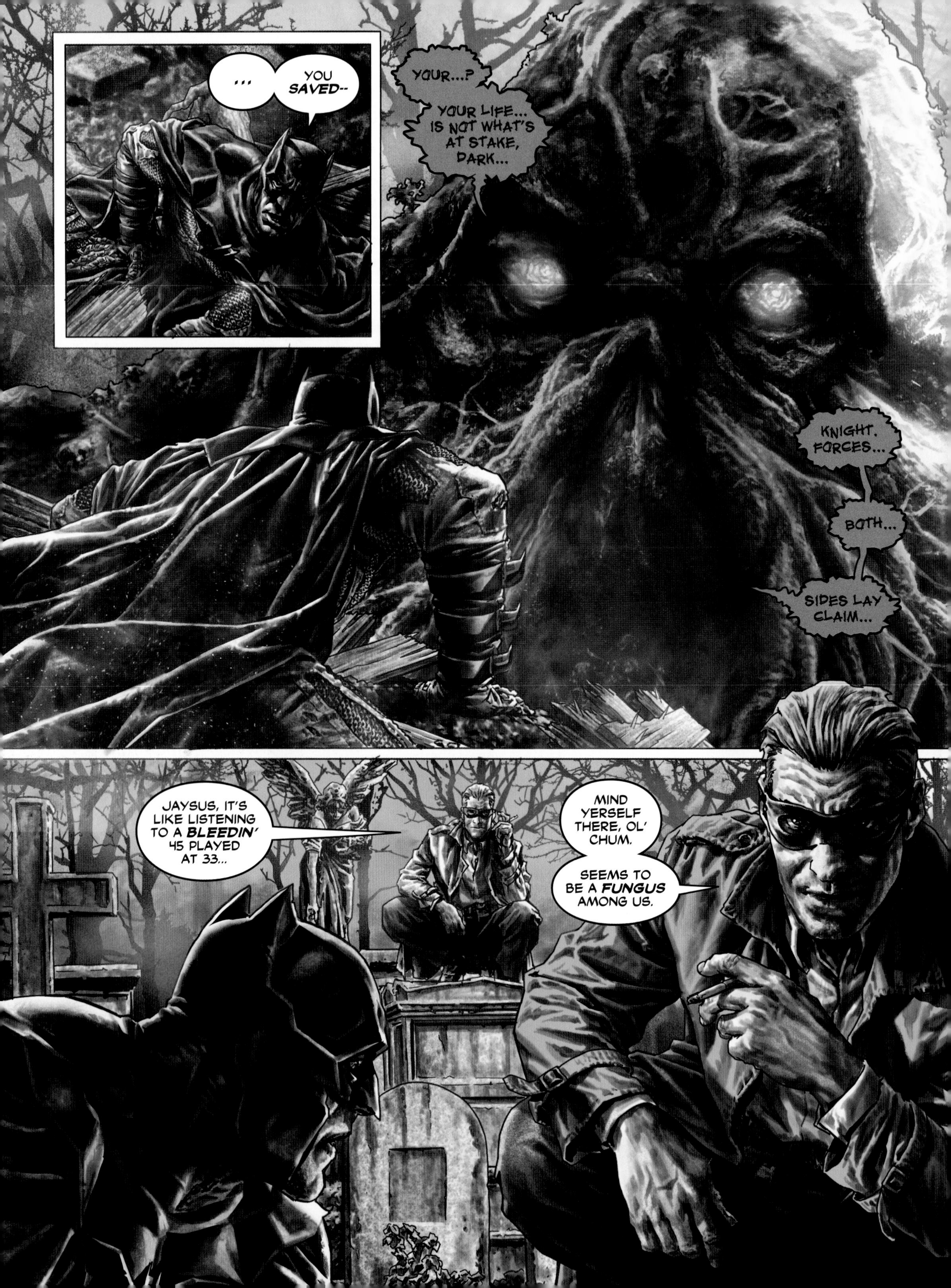
...
YOU SAVED--
YOUR...?
YOUR LIFE... IS NOT WHAT'S AT STAKE, DARK...
KNIGHT. FORCES...
BOTH...
SIDES LAY CLAIM...
JAYSUS, IT'S LIKE LISTENING TO A BLEEDIN' 45 PLAYED AT 33...
MIND YERSELF THERE, OL' CHUM.
SEEMS TO BE A FUNGUS AMONG US.

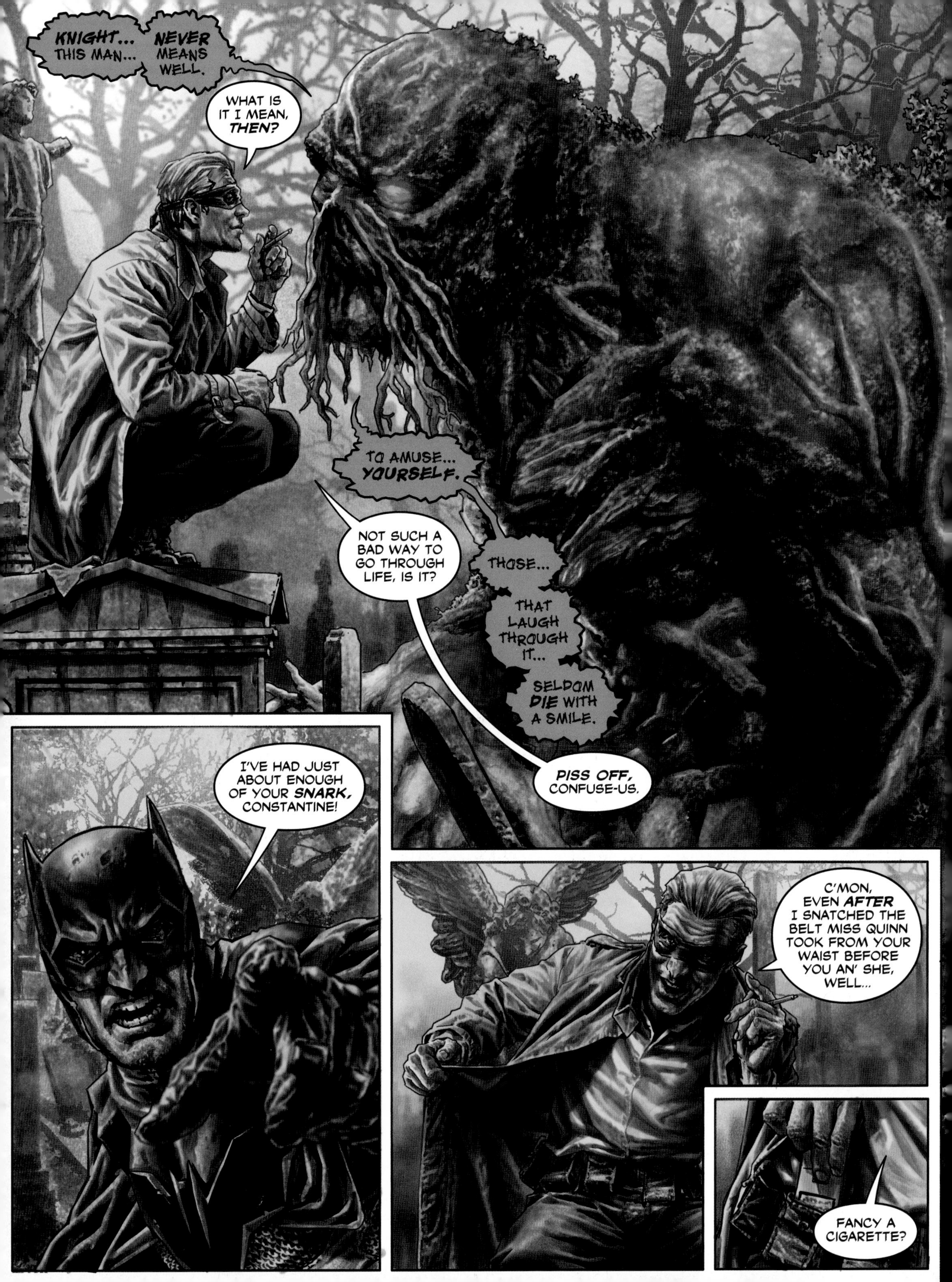
KNIGHT... THIS MAN...
NEVER MEANS WELL.
WHAT IS IT I MEAN, THEN?
TO AMUSE... YOURSELF.
NOT SUCH A BAD WAY TO GO THROUGH LIFE, IS IT?
THOSE...
THAT LAUGH THROUGH IT...
SELDOM DIE WITH A SMILE.
PISS OFF, CONFUSE-US.
I'VE HAD JUST ABOUT ENOUGH OF YOUR SNARK, CONSTANTINE!
C'MON, EVEN AFTER I SNATCHED THE BELT MISS QUINN TOOK FROM YOUR WAIST BEFORE YOU AN' SHE, WELL...
FANCY A CIGARETTE?

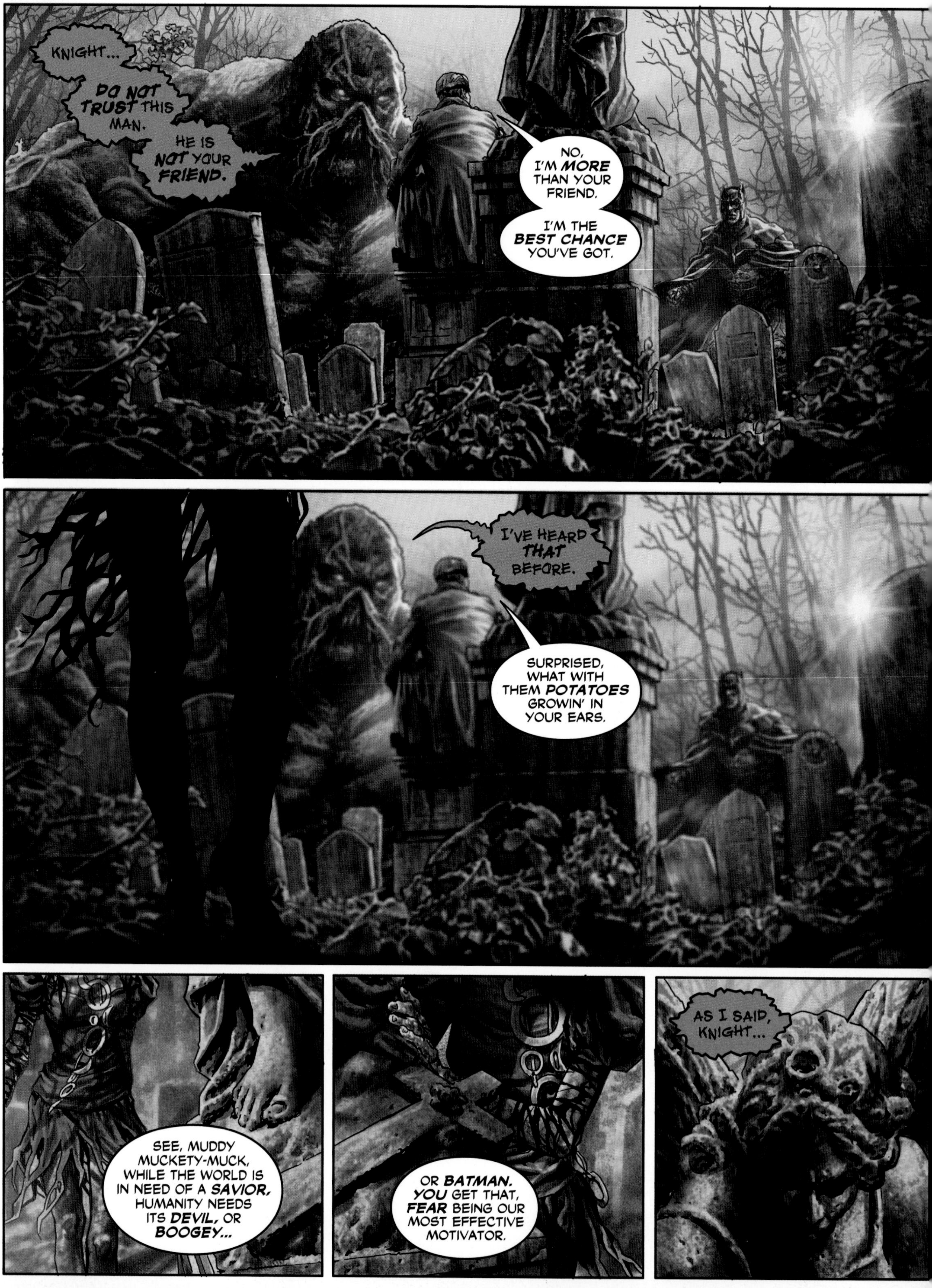
KNIGHT...
DO NOT TRUST THIS MAN.
HE IS NOT YOUR FRIEND.
NO, I'M MORE THAN YOUR FRIEND.
I'M THE BEST CHANCE YOU'VE GOT.
I'VE HEARD THAT BEFORE.
SURPRISED, WHAT WITH THEM POTATOES GROWIN' IN YOUR EARS.
SEE, MUDDY MUCKETY-MUCK, WHILE THE WORLD IS IN NEED OF A SAVIOR, HUMANITY NEEDS ITS DEVIL, OR BOOGEY...
OR BATMAN. YOU GET THAT, FEAR BEING OUR MOST EFFECTIVE MOTIVATOR.
AS I SAID, KNIGHT...

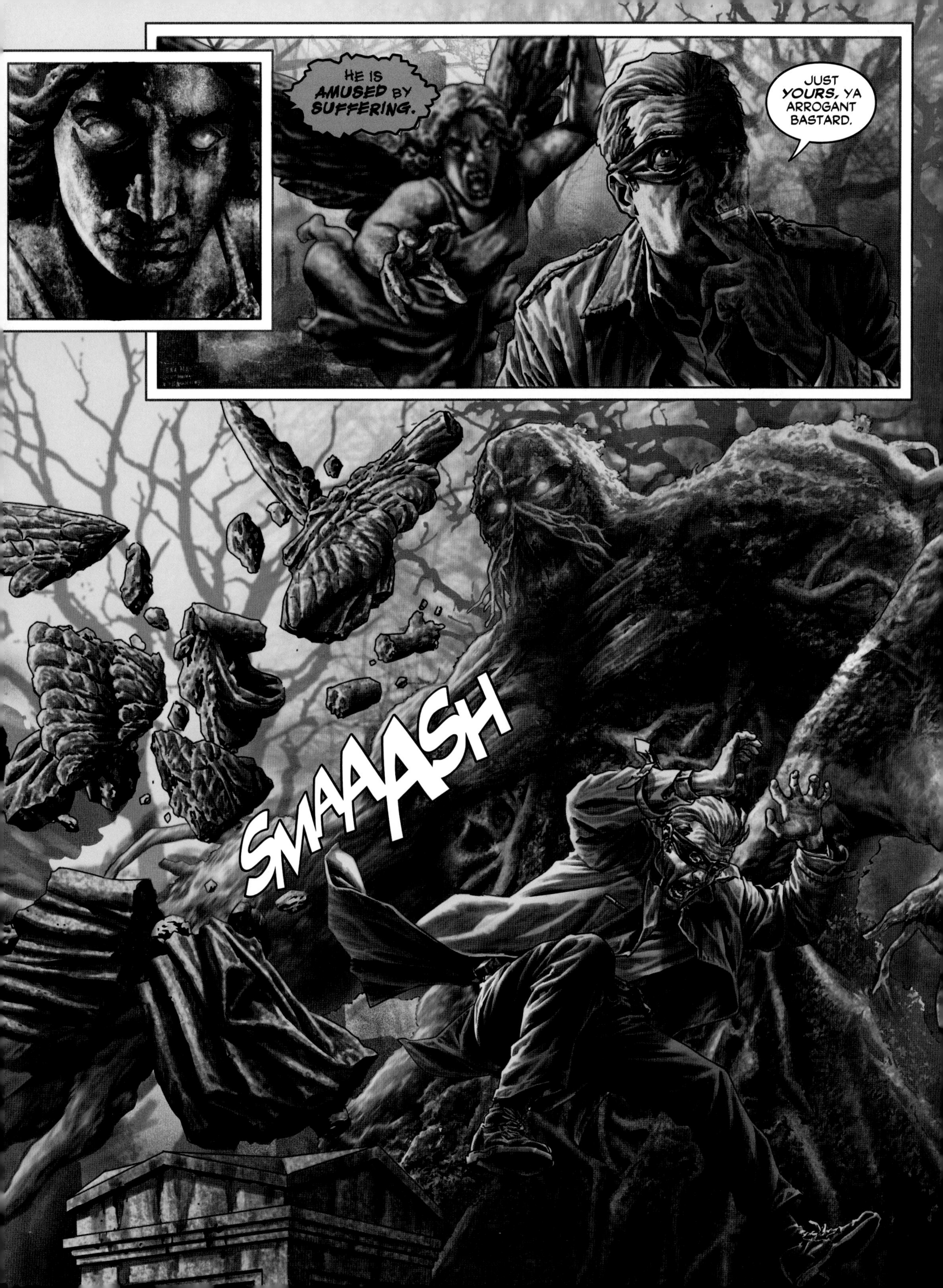
HE IS AMUSED BY SUFFERING.
JUST YOURS, YA ARROGANT BASTARD.
SMAAASH

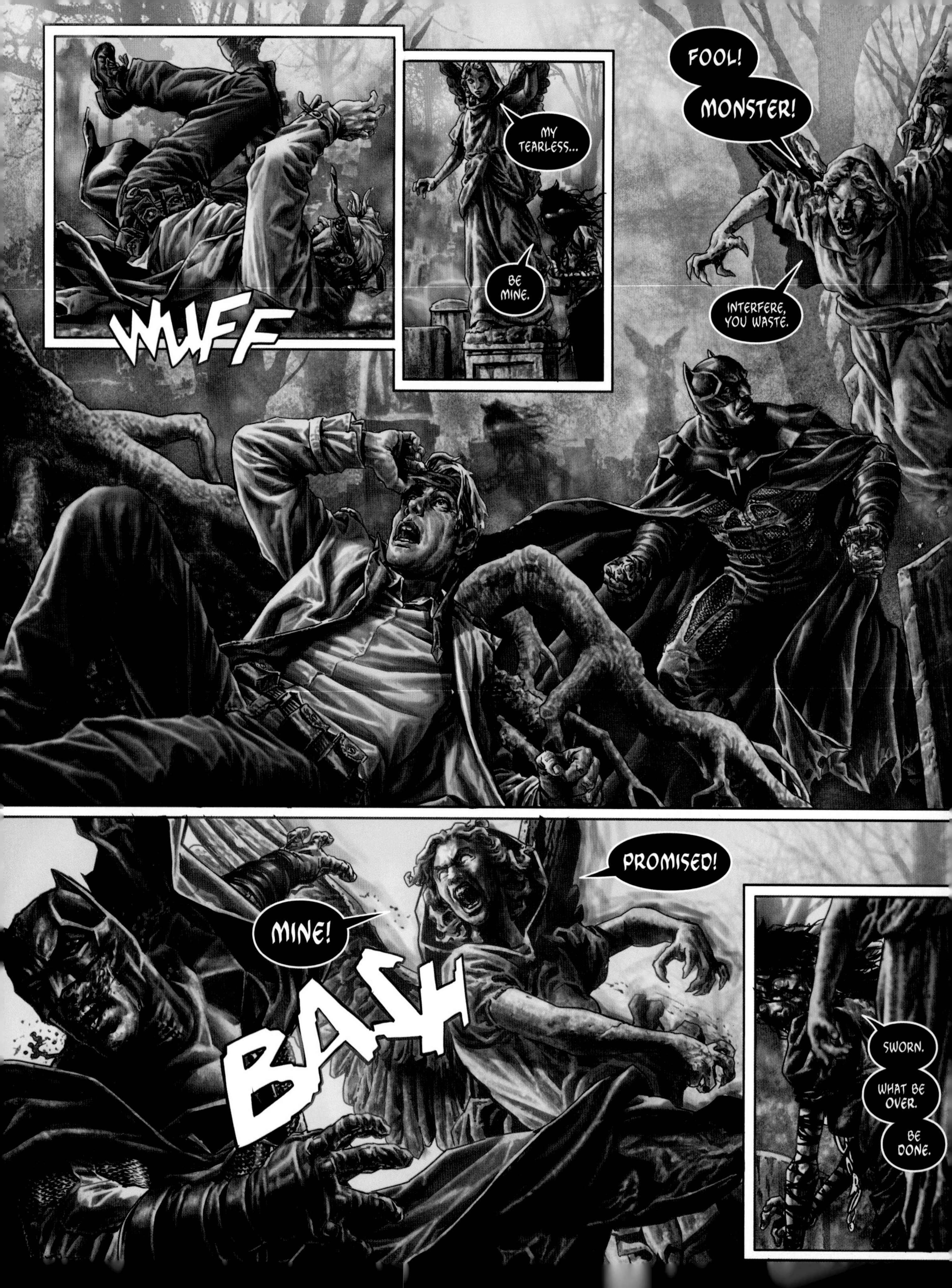
WUFF
MY TEARLESS...
BE MINE.
FOOL!
MONSTER!
INTERFERE, YOU WASTE.
PROMISED!
MINE!
BAM
SWORN.
WHAT BE OVER.
BE DONE.

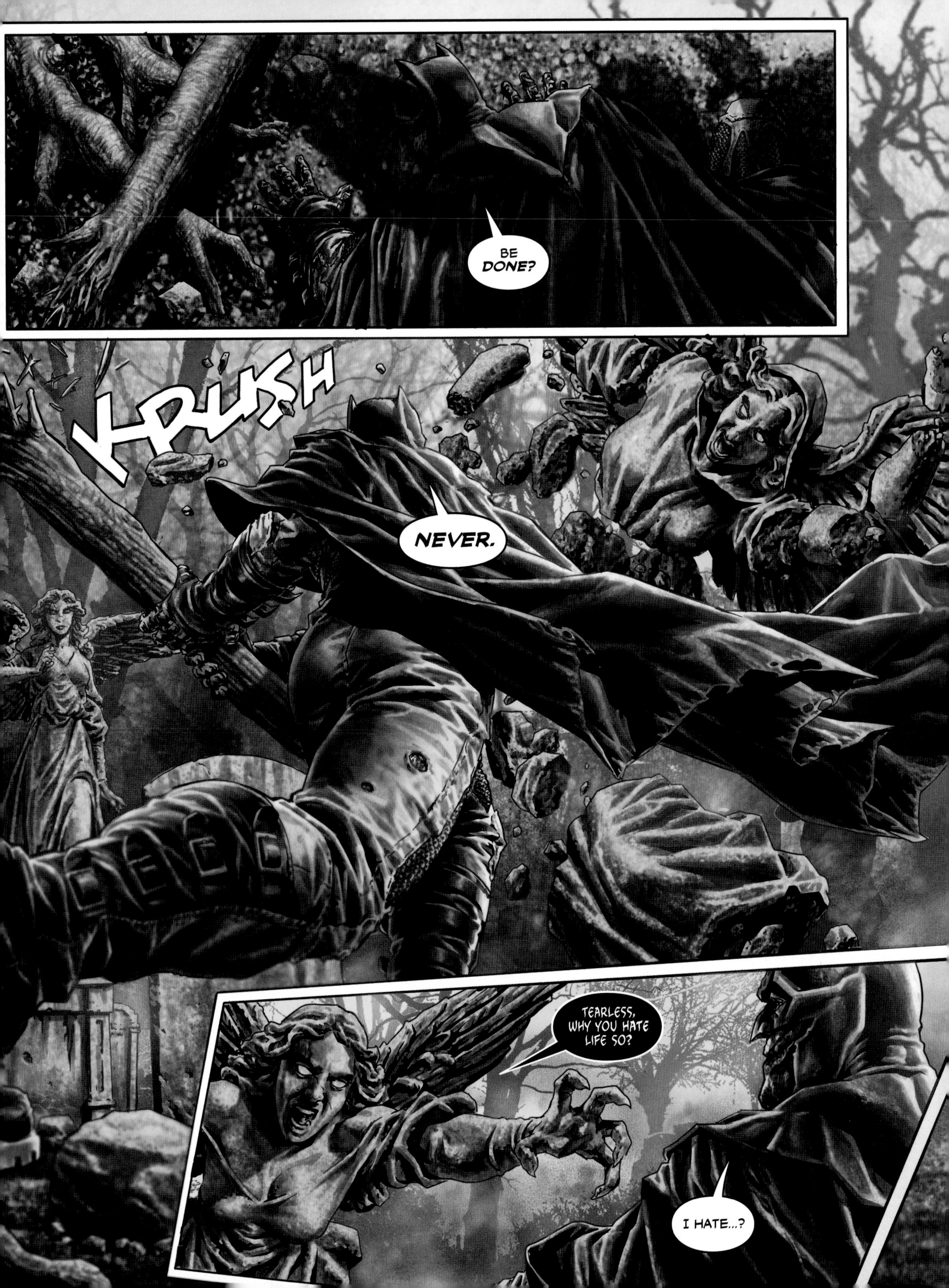
BE DONE?
KRUSH
NEVER.
TEARLESS, WHY YOU HATE LIFE SO?
I HATE...?

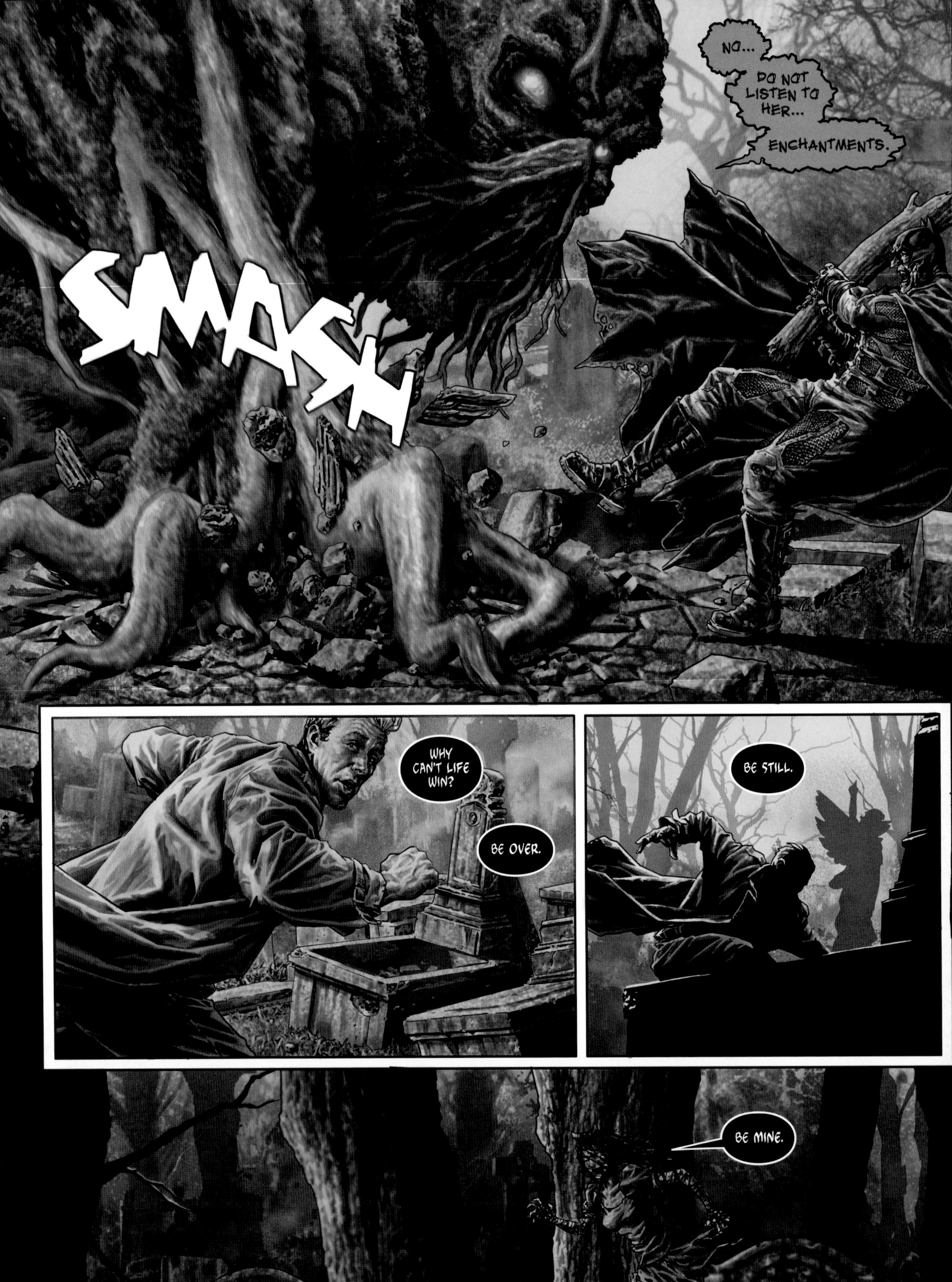
NO...
DO NOT LISTEN TO HER...
ENCHANTMENTS.
SMASH
WHY CAN'T LIFE WIN?
BE OVER.
BE STILL.
BE MINE.

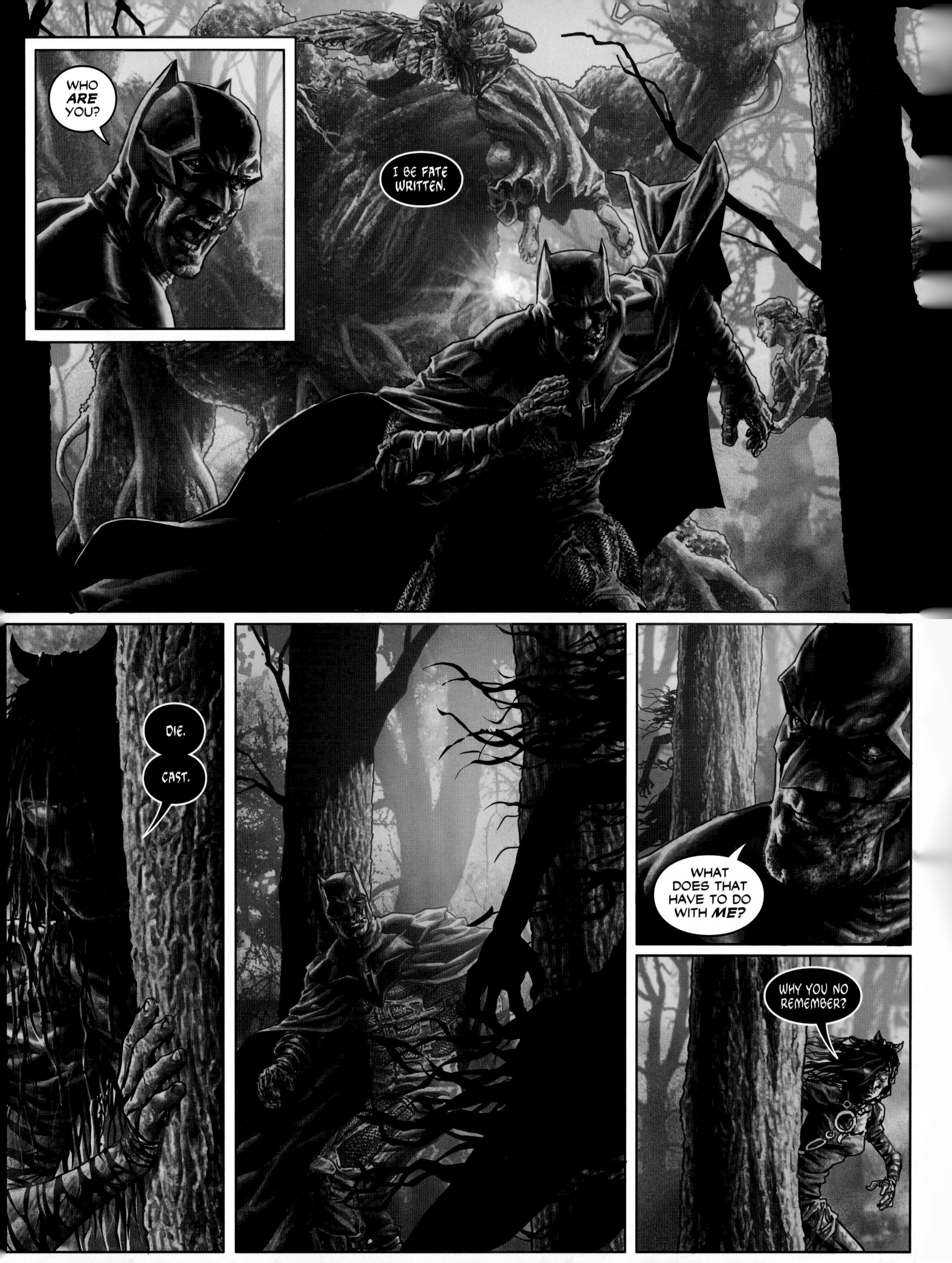
WHO ARE YOU?
I BE FATE WRITTEN.
DIE.
CAST.
WHAT DOES THAT HAVE TO DO WITH ME?
WHY YOU NO REMEMBER?

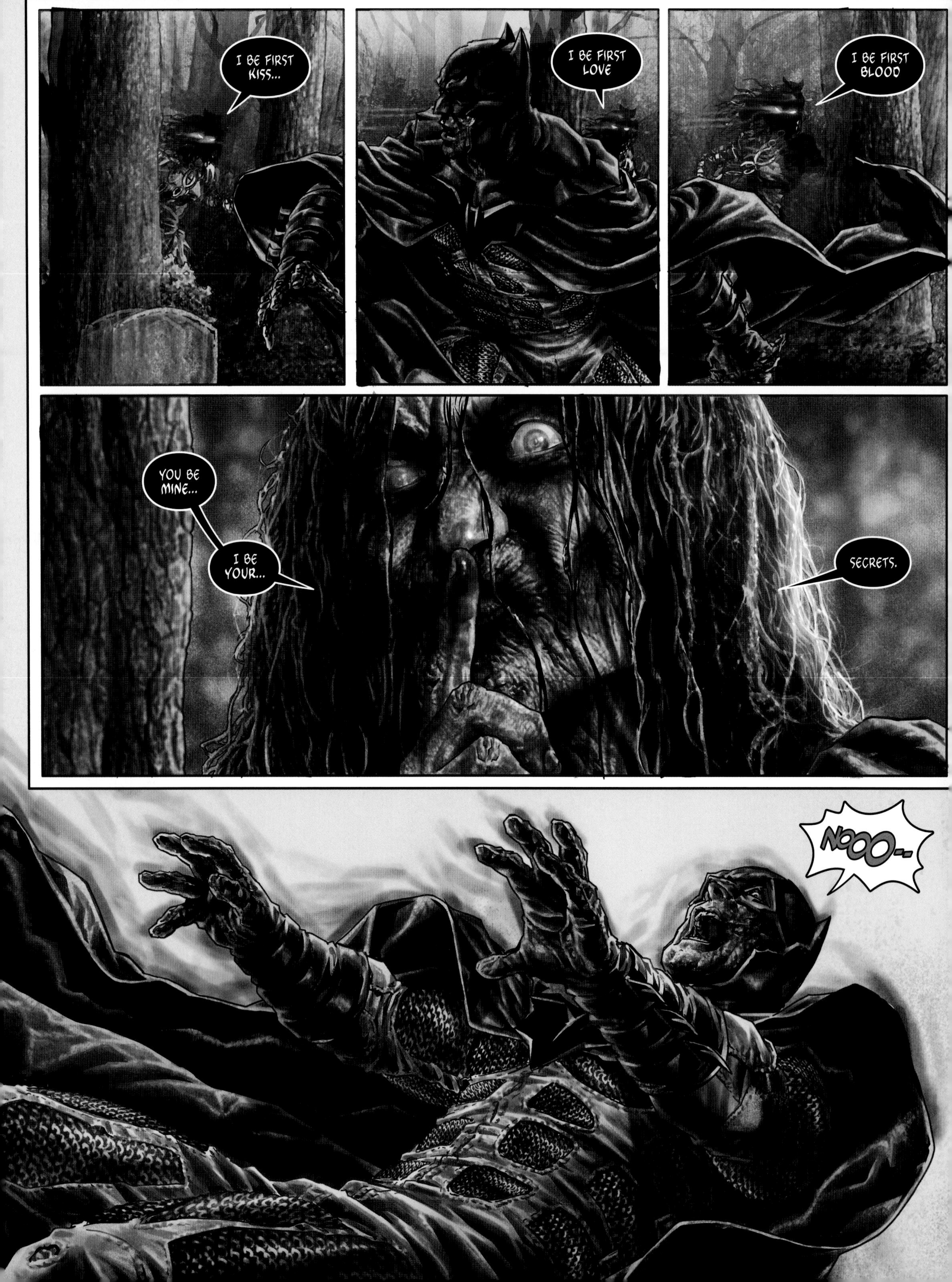
I BE FIRST KISS...
I BE FIRST LOVE
I BE FIRST BLOOD
YOU BE MINE...
I BE YOUR...
SECRETS.
NOOO--

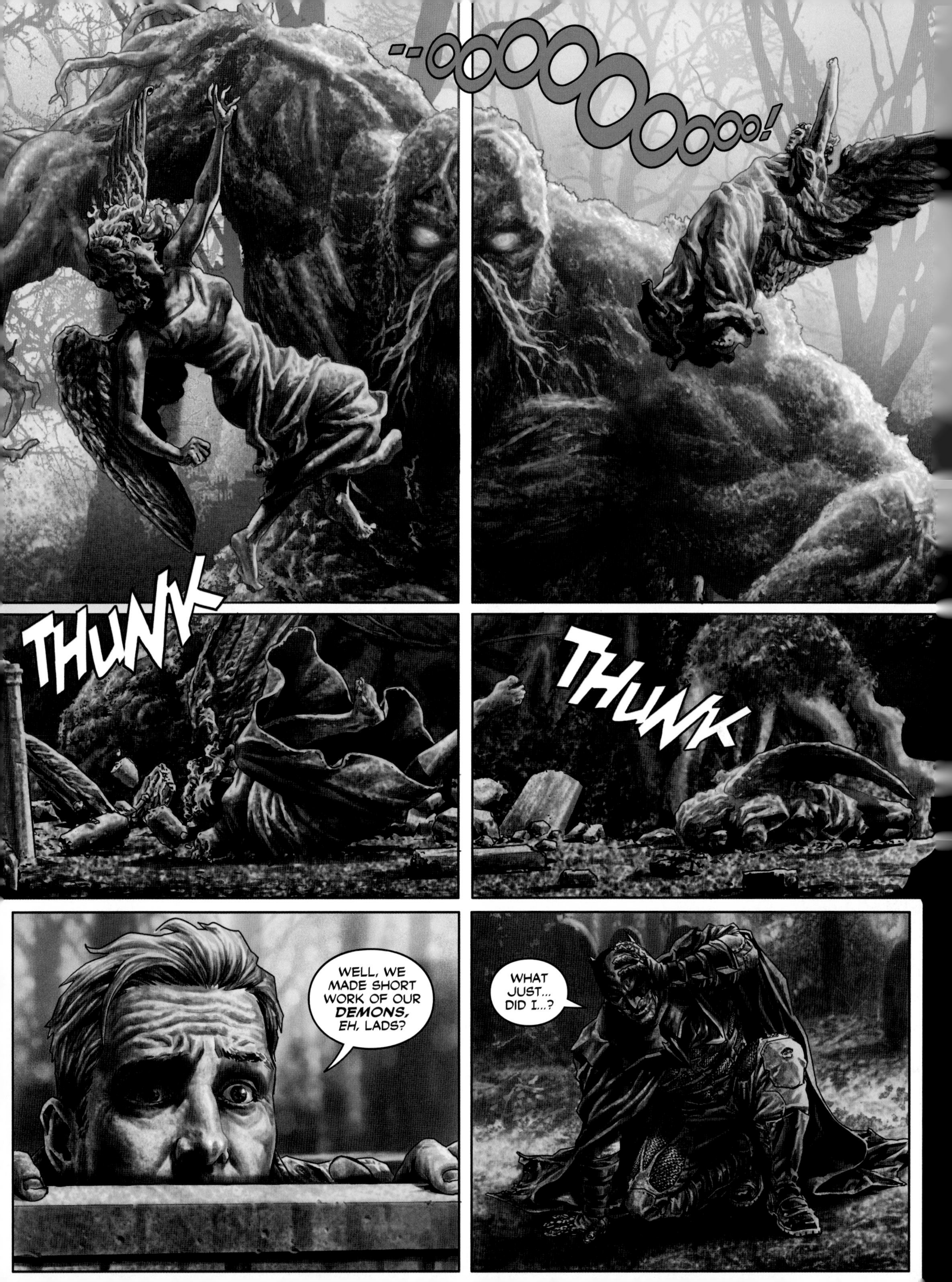
--OOOOOOOOooo!
THUNK
THUNK
WELL, WE MADE SHORT WORK OF OUR *DEMONS*, EH, LADS?
WHAT JUST... DID I...?

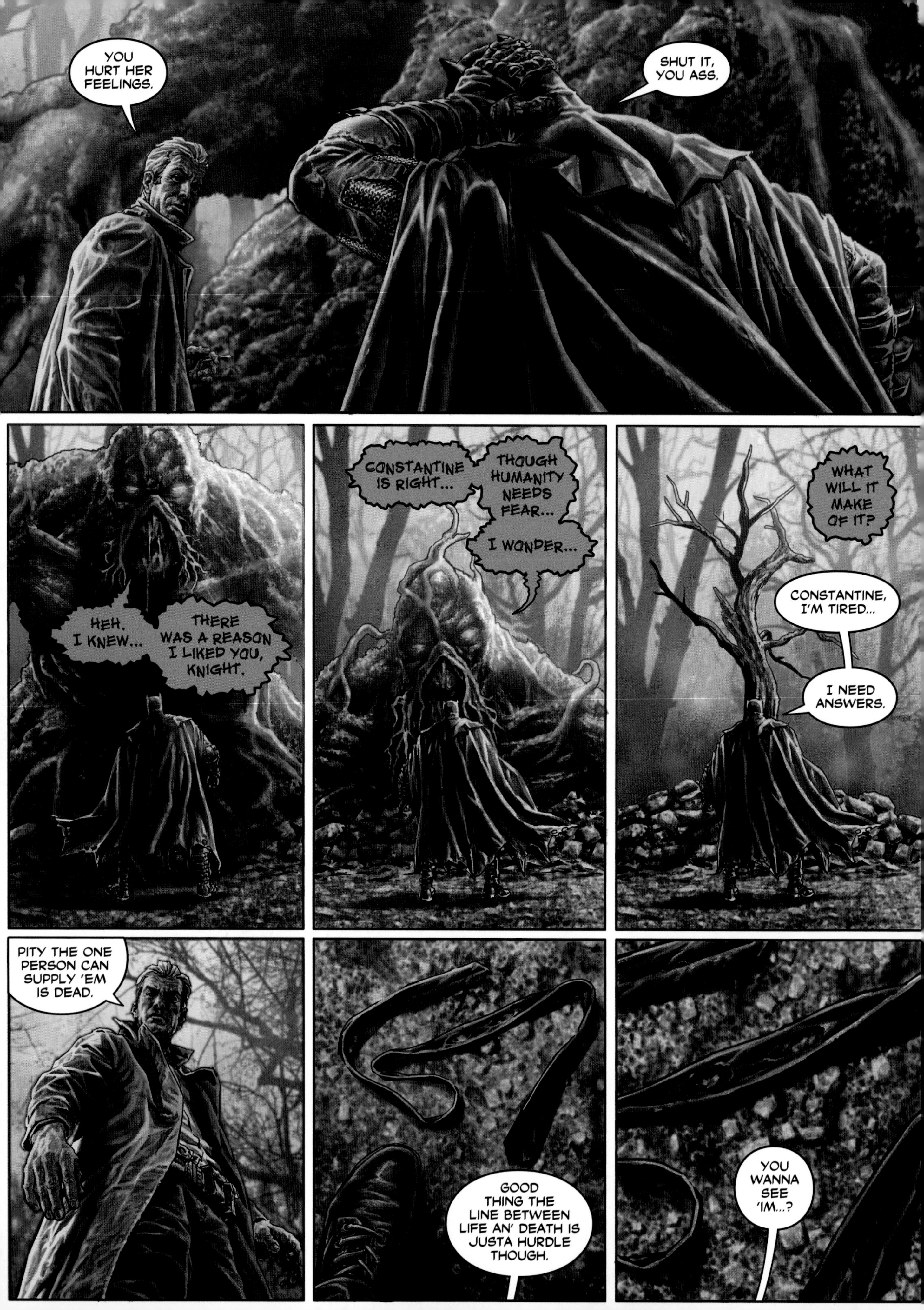
YOU HURT HER FEELINGS.
SHUT IT, YOU ASS.
HEH. I KNEW...
THERE WAS A REASON I LIKED YOU, KNIGHT.
CONSTANTINE IS RIGHT...
THOUGH HUMANITY NEEDS FEAR...
I WONDER...
WHAT WILL IT MAKE OF IT?
CONSTANTINE, I'M TIRED...
I NEED ANSWERS.
PITY THE ONE PERSON CAN SUPPLY 'EM IS DEAD.
GOOD THING THE LINE BETWEEN LIFE AN' DEATH IS JUSTA HURDLE THOUGH.
YOU WANNA SEE 'IM...?

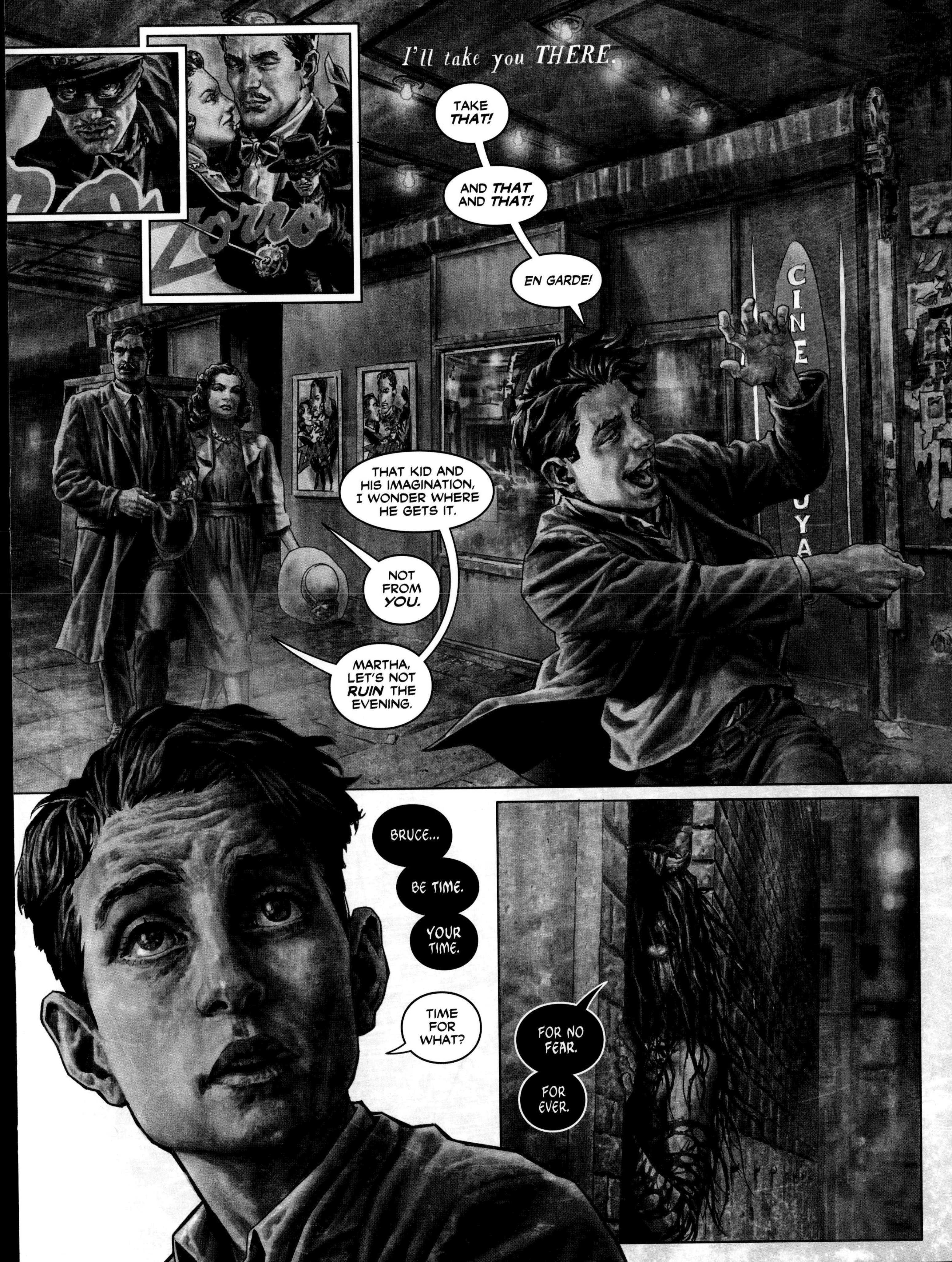
I'll take you THERE.
TAKE THAT!
AND THAT AND THAT!
EN GARDE!
THAT KID AND HIS IMAGINATION, I WONDER WHERE HE GETS IT.
NOT FROM YOU.
MARTHA, LET'S NOT RUIN THE EVENING.
BRUCE...
BE TIME.
YOUR TIME.
TIME FOR WHAT?
FOR NO FEAR.
FOR EVER.

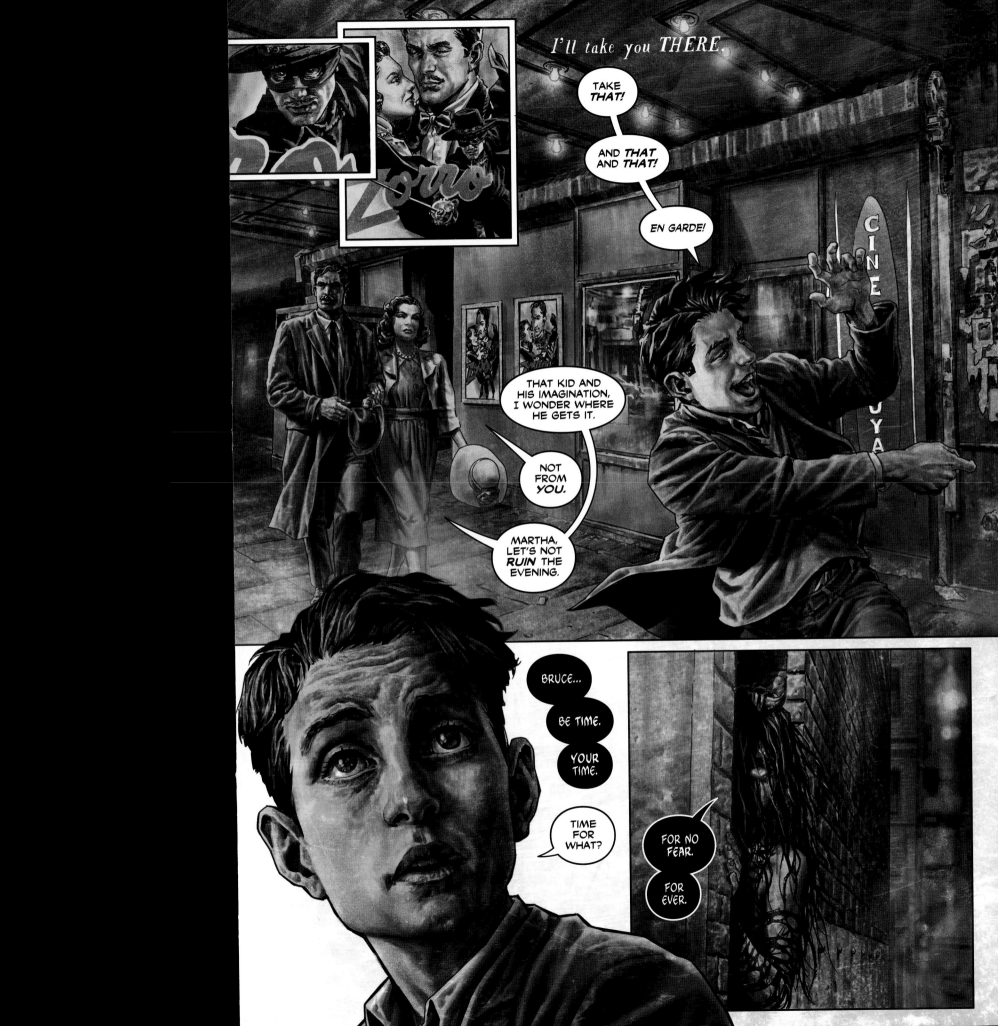

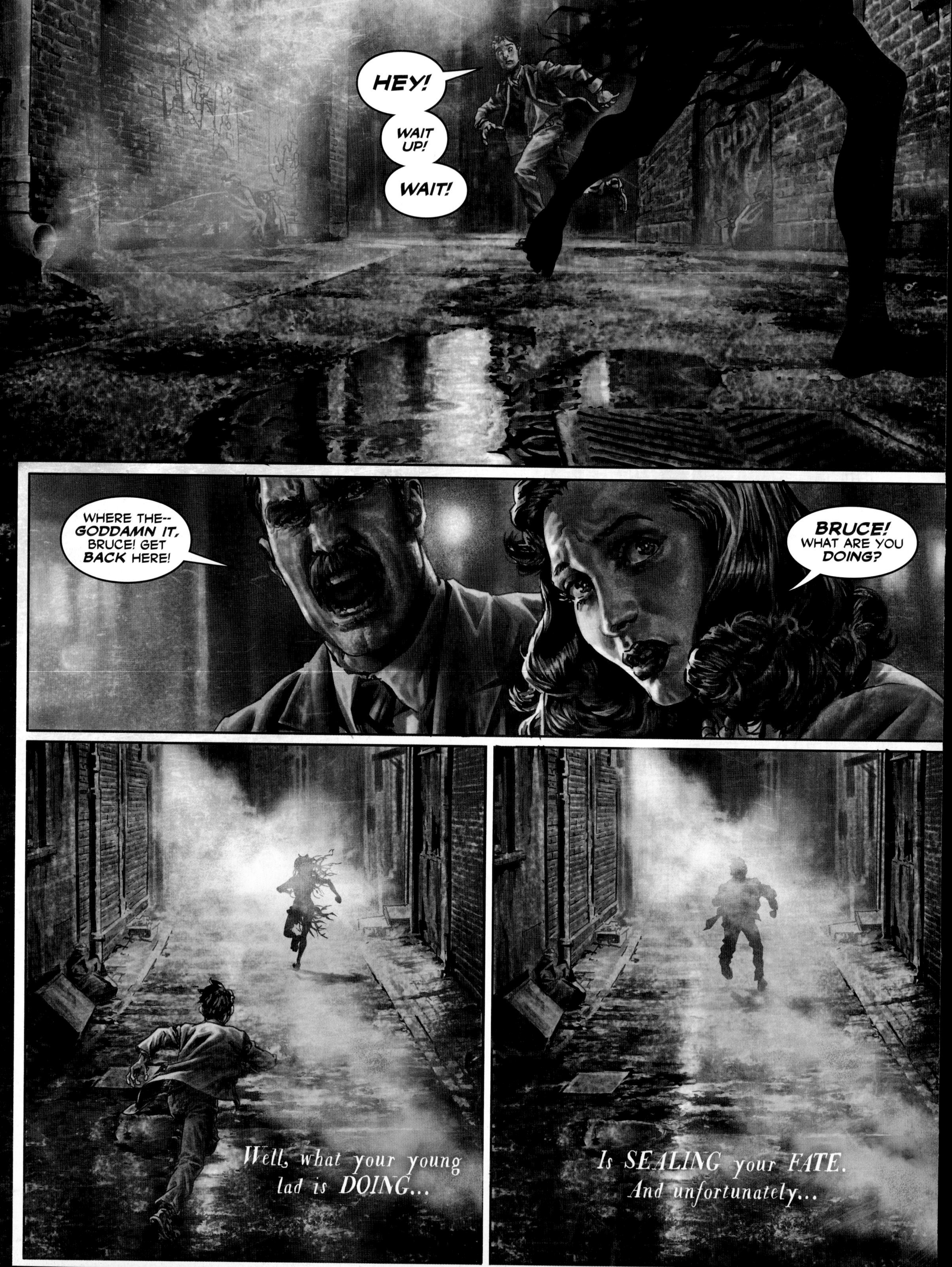
HEY!
WAIT UP!
WAIT!
WHERE THE-- GODDAMN IT, BRUCE! GET BACK HERE!
BRUCE! WHAT ARE YOU DOING?
Well, what your young lad is DOING...
Is SEALING your FATE. And unfortunately...

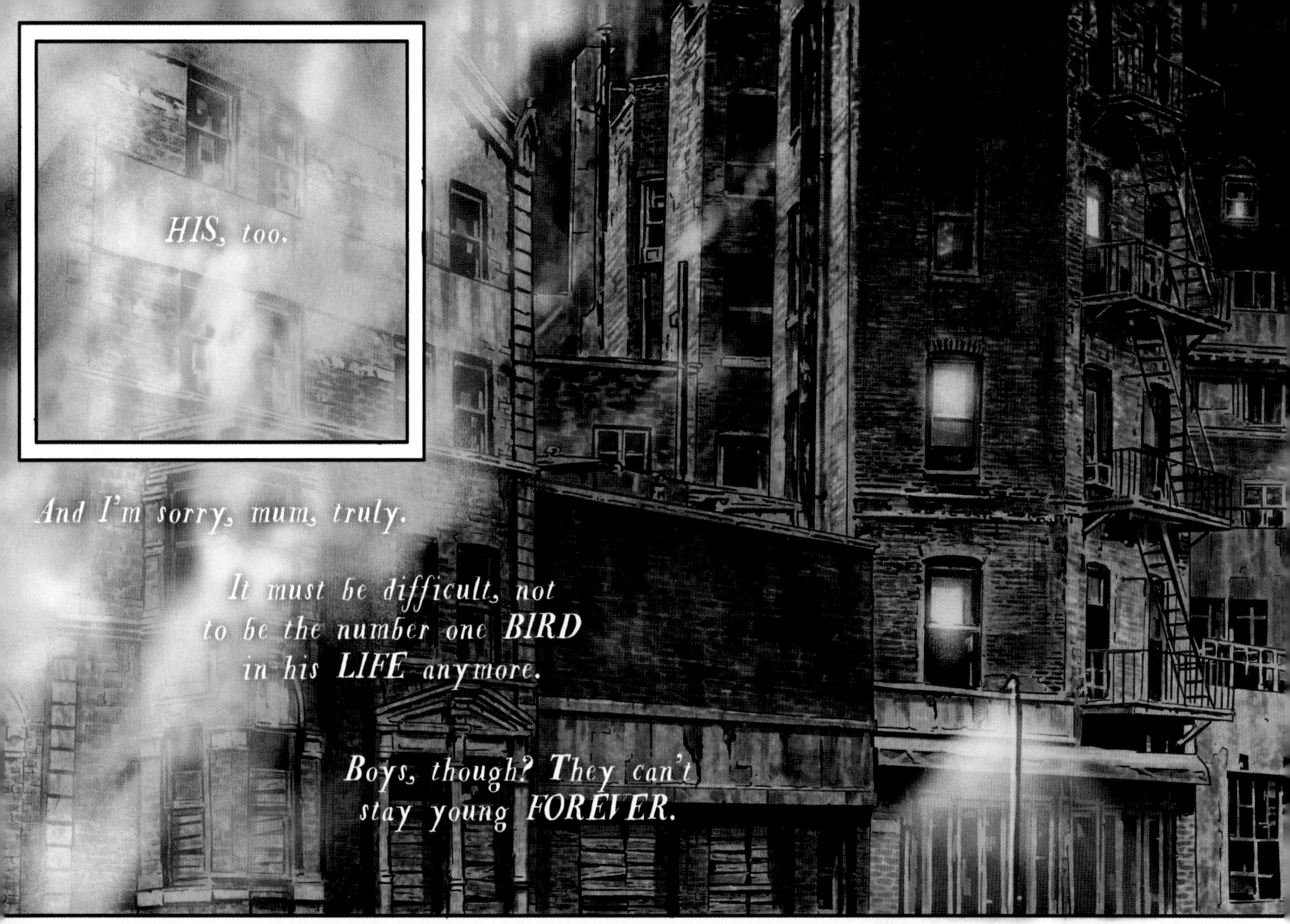
HIS, too.
And I'm sorry, mum, truly.
It must be difficult, not to be the number one BIRD in his LIFE anymore.
Boys, though? They can't stay young FOREVER.

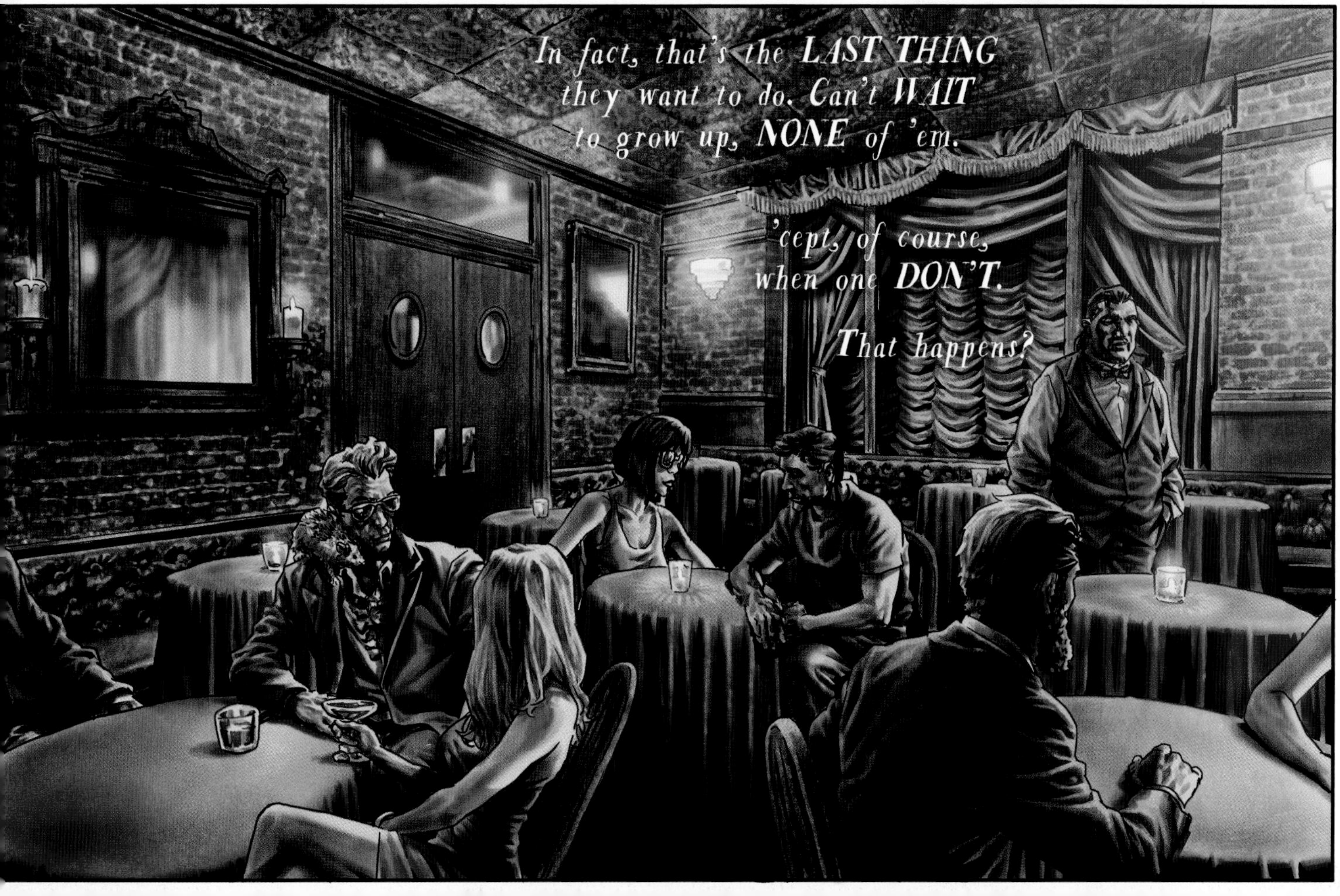
In fact, that's the LAST THING they want to do. Can't WAIT to grow up, NONE of 'em.
'cept, of course, when one DON'T.
That happens?

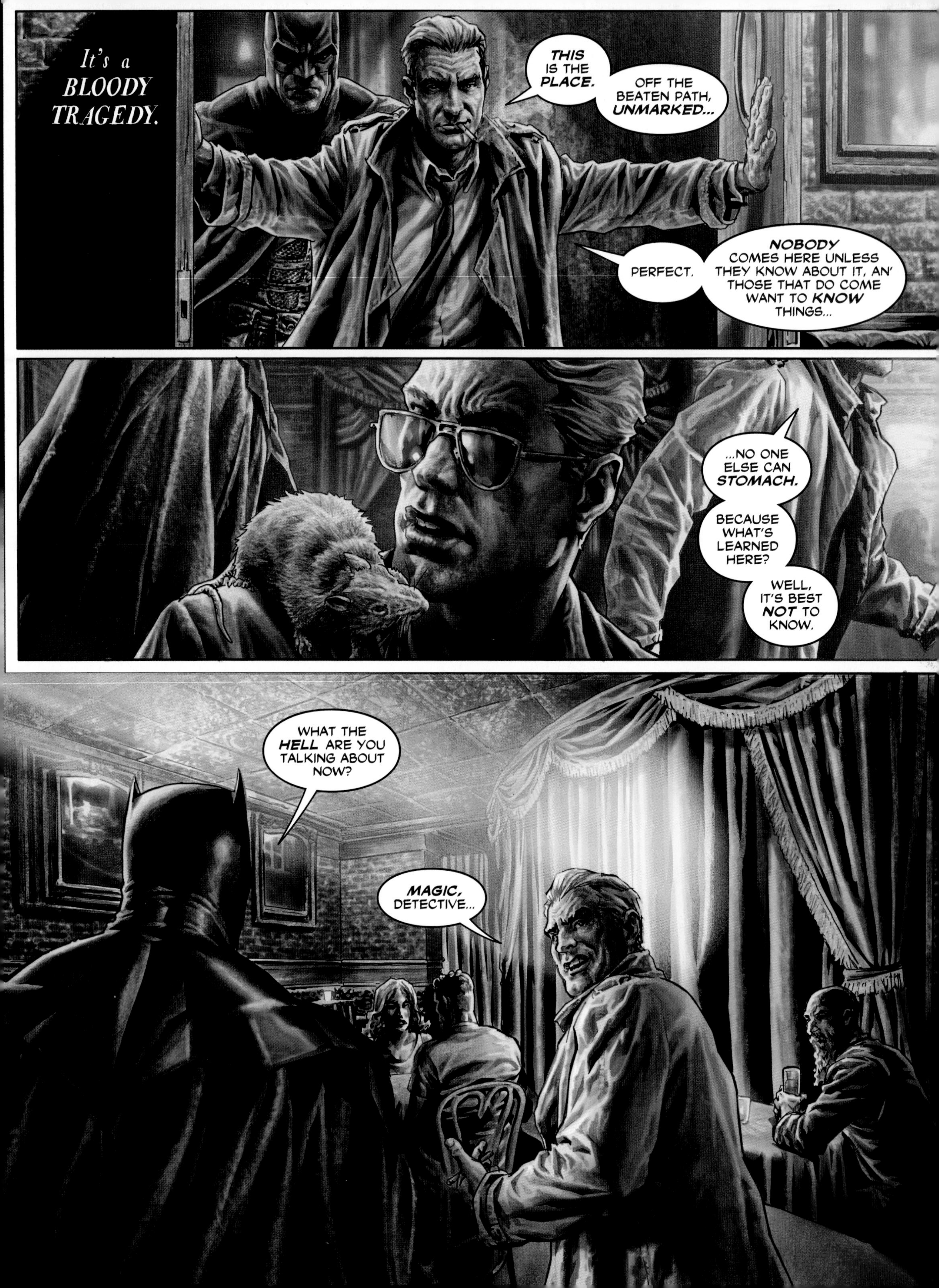
It's a BLOODY TRAGEDY.
THIS IS THE PLACE.
OFF THE BEATEN PATH, UNMARKED...
PERFECT.
NOBODY COMES HERE UNLESS THEY KNOW ABOUT IT, AN' THOSE THAT DO COME WANT TO KNOW THINGS...
...NO ONE ELSE CAN STOMACH.
BECAUSE WHAT'S LEARNED HERE?
WELL, IT'S BEST NOT TO KNOW.
WHAT THE HELL ARE YOU TALKING ABOUT NOW?
MAGIC, DETECTIVE...

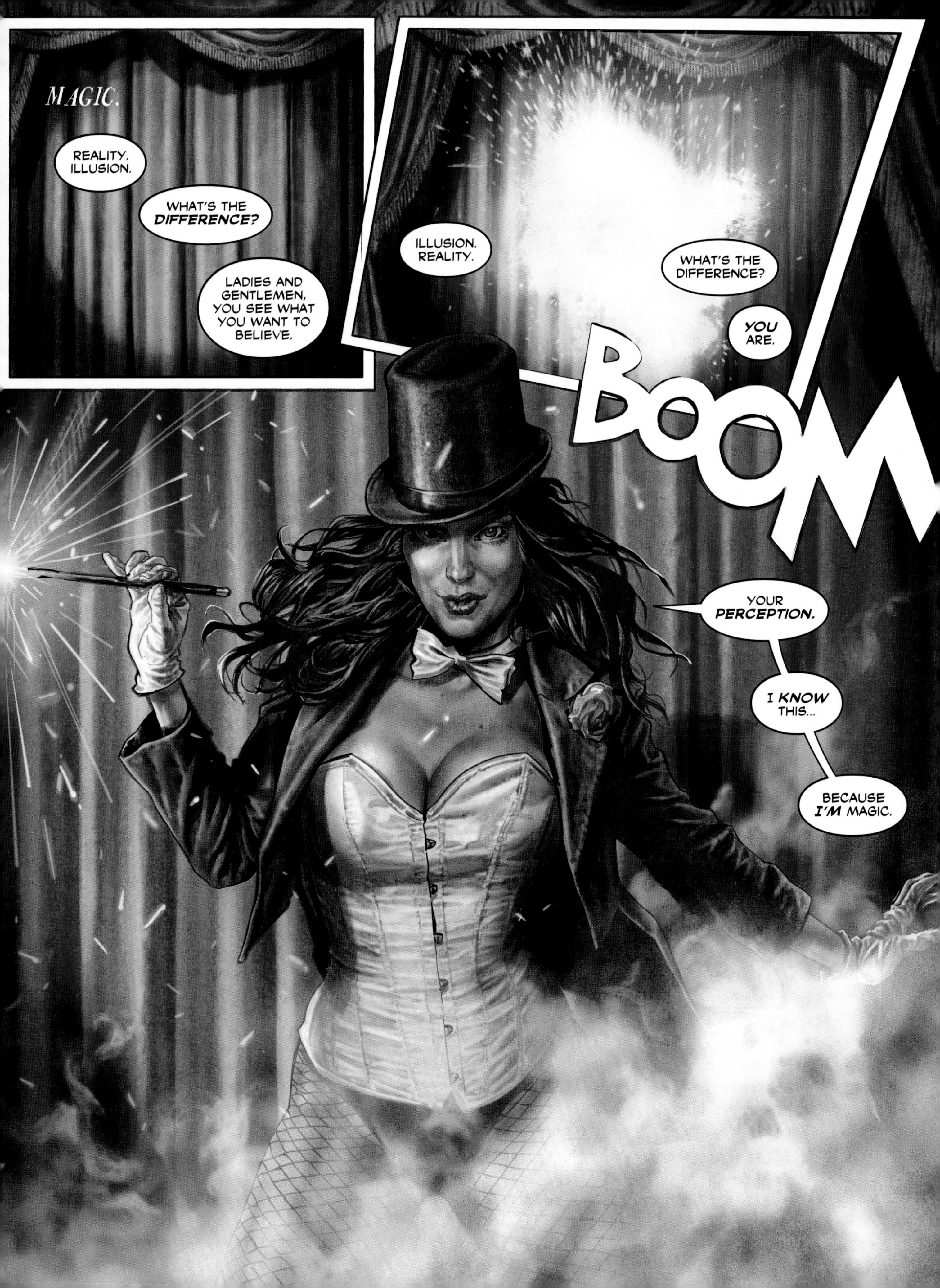
MAGIC.
REALITY. ILLUSION.
WHAT'S THE DIFFERENCE?
LADIES AND GENTLEMEN, YOU SEE WHAT YOU WANT TO BELIEVE.
ILLUSION. REALITY.
WHAT'S THE DIFFERENCE?
YOU ARE.
BOOM
YOUR PERCEPTION.
I KNOW THIS...
BECAUSE I'M MAGIC.

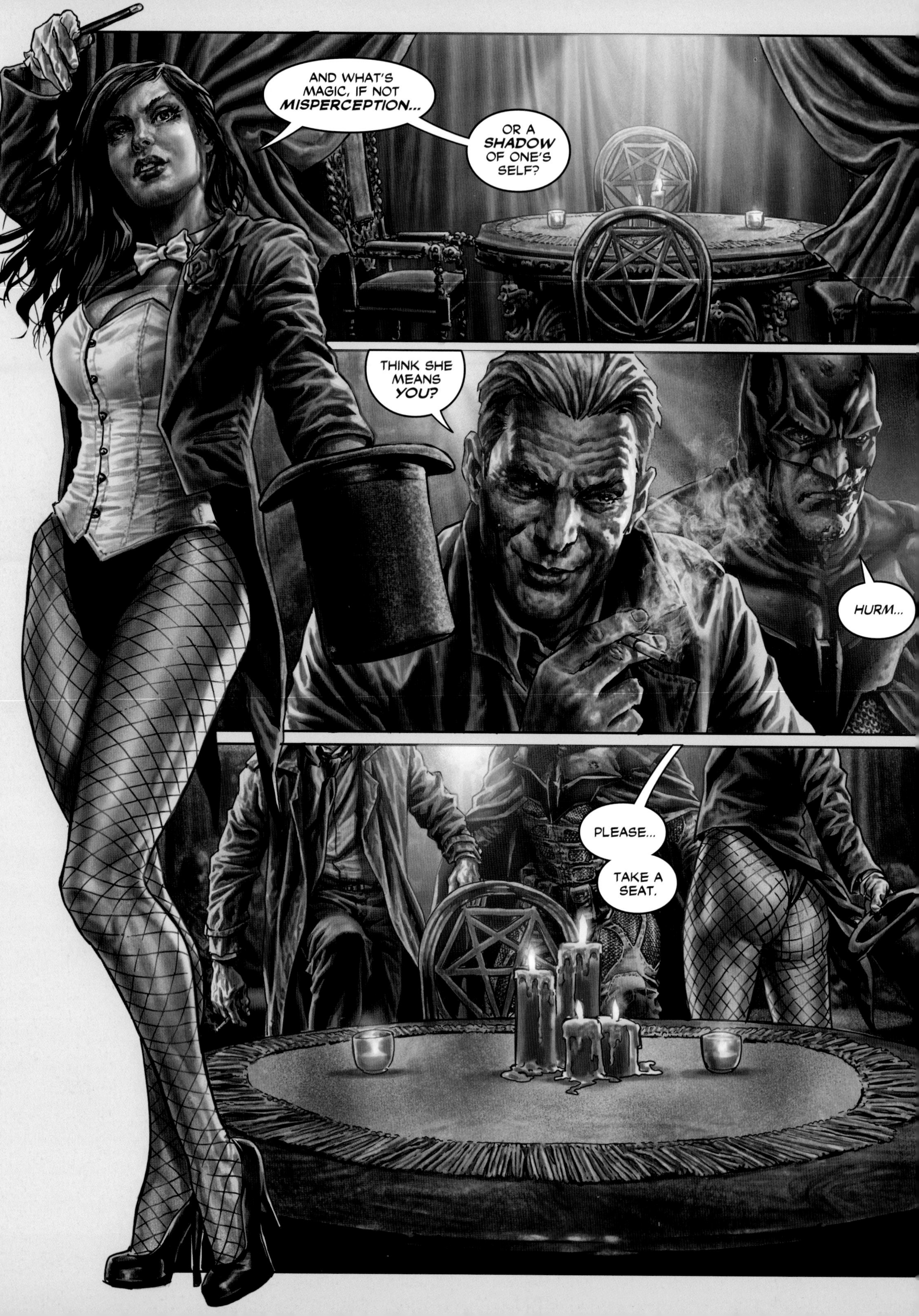
AND WHAT'S MAGIC, IF NOT MISPERCEPTION...
OR A SHADOW OF ONE'S SELF?
THINK SHE MEANS YOU?
HURM...
PLEASE...
TAKE A SEAT.

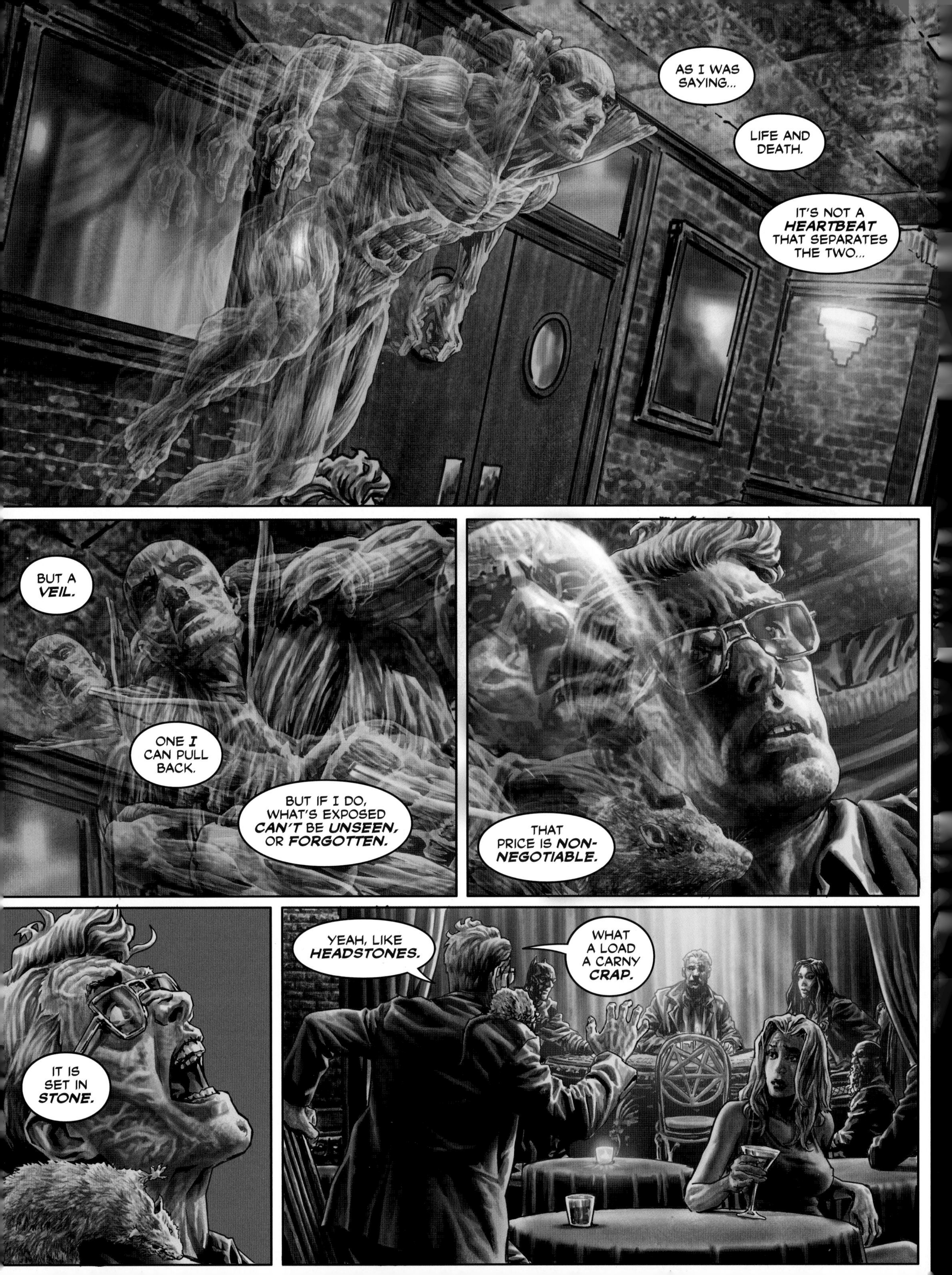

AS I WAS SAYING...
LIFE AND DEATH.
IT'S NOT A HEARTBEAT THAT SEPARATES THE TWO...
BUT A VEIL.
ONE I CAN PULL BACK.
BUT IF I DO, WHAT'S EXPOSED CAN'T BE UNSEEN, OR FORGOTTEN.
THAT PRICE IS NON-NEGOTIABLE.
IT IS SET IN STONE.
YEAH, LIKE HEADSTONES.
WHAT A LOAD A CARNY CRAP.

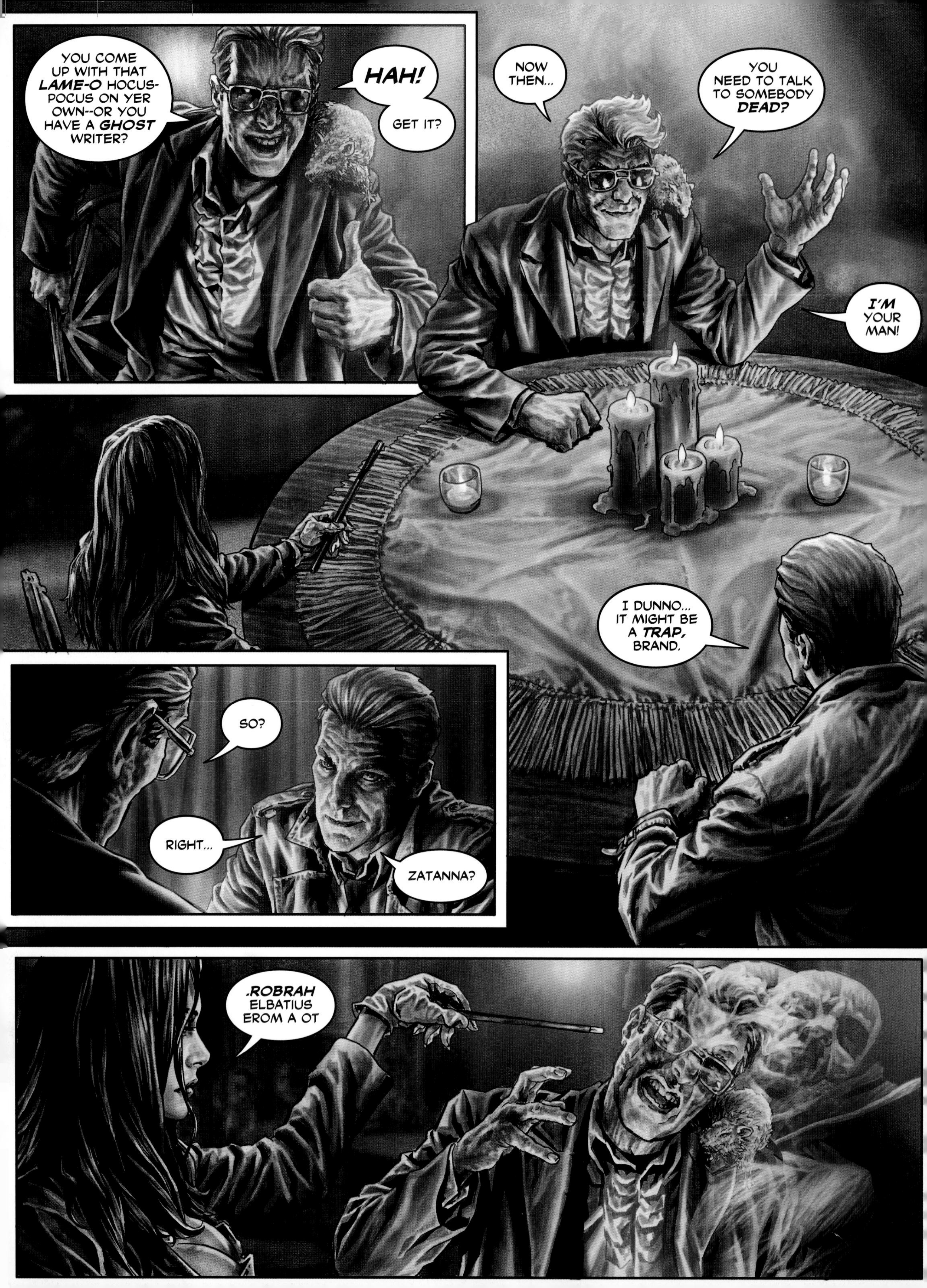
YOU COME UP WITH THAT LAME-O HOCUS-POCUS ON YER OWN--OR YOU HAVE A GHOST WRITER?
HAH!
GET IT?
NOW THEN...
YOU NEED TO TALK TO SOMEBODY DEAD?
I'M YOUR MAN!
I DUNNO... IT MIGHT BE A TRAP, BRAND.
SO?
RIGHT...
ZATANNA?
.ROBRAH ELBATIUS EROM A OT

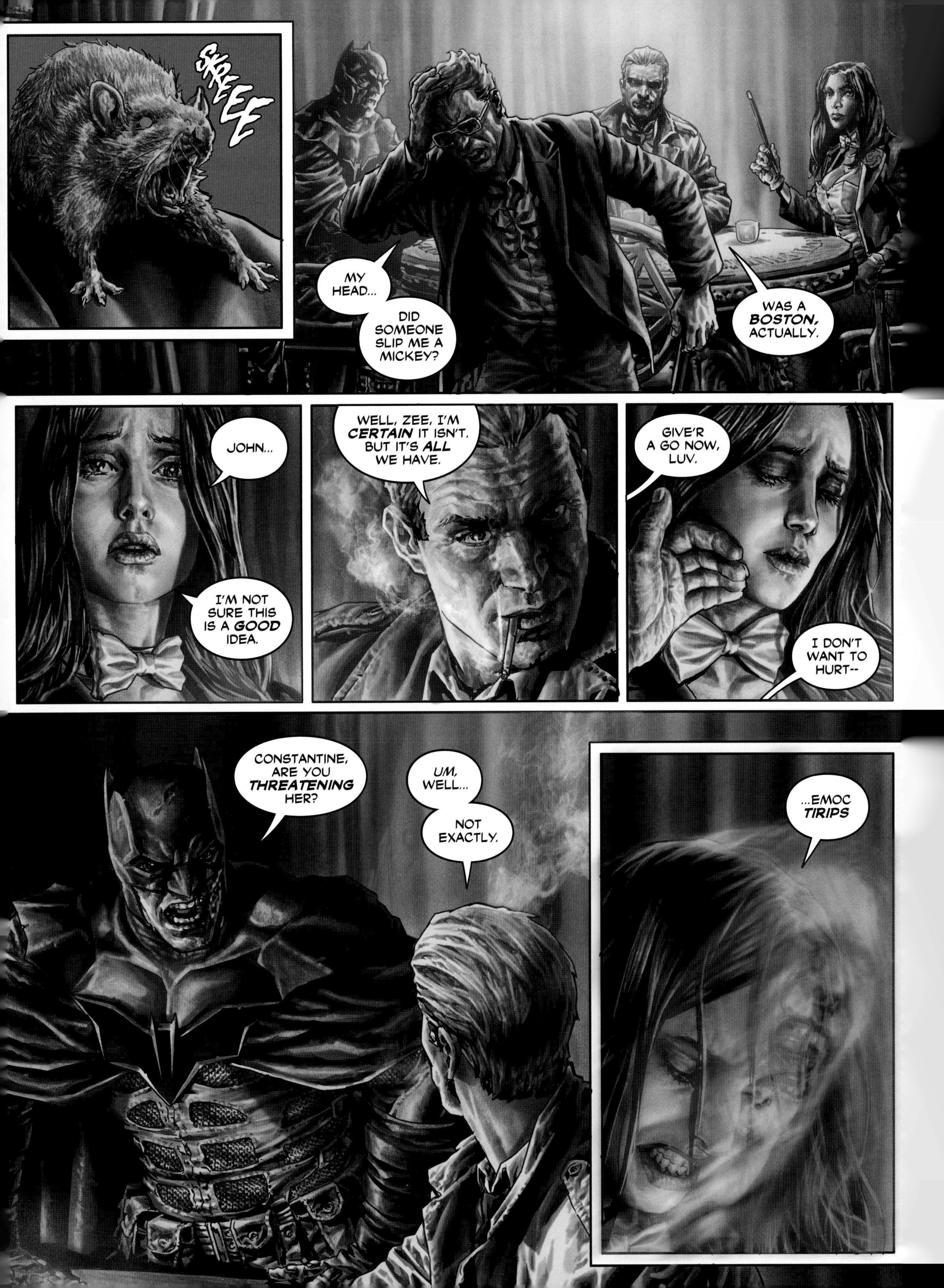

SKREEEE
MY HEAD...
DID SOMEONE SLIP ME A MICKEY?
WAS A BOSTON, ACTUALLY.
JOHN...
I'M NOT SURE THIS IS A GOOD IDEA.
WELL, ZEE, I'M CERTAIN IT ISN'T. BUT IT'S ALL WE HAVE.
GIVE'R A GO NOW, LUV.
I DON'T WANT TO HURT--
CONSTANTINE, ARE YOU THREATENING HER?
UM, WELL...
NOT EXACTLY.
...EMOC TIRIPS

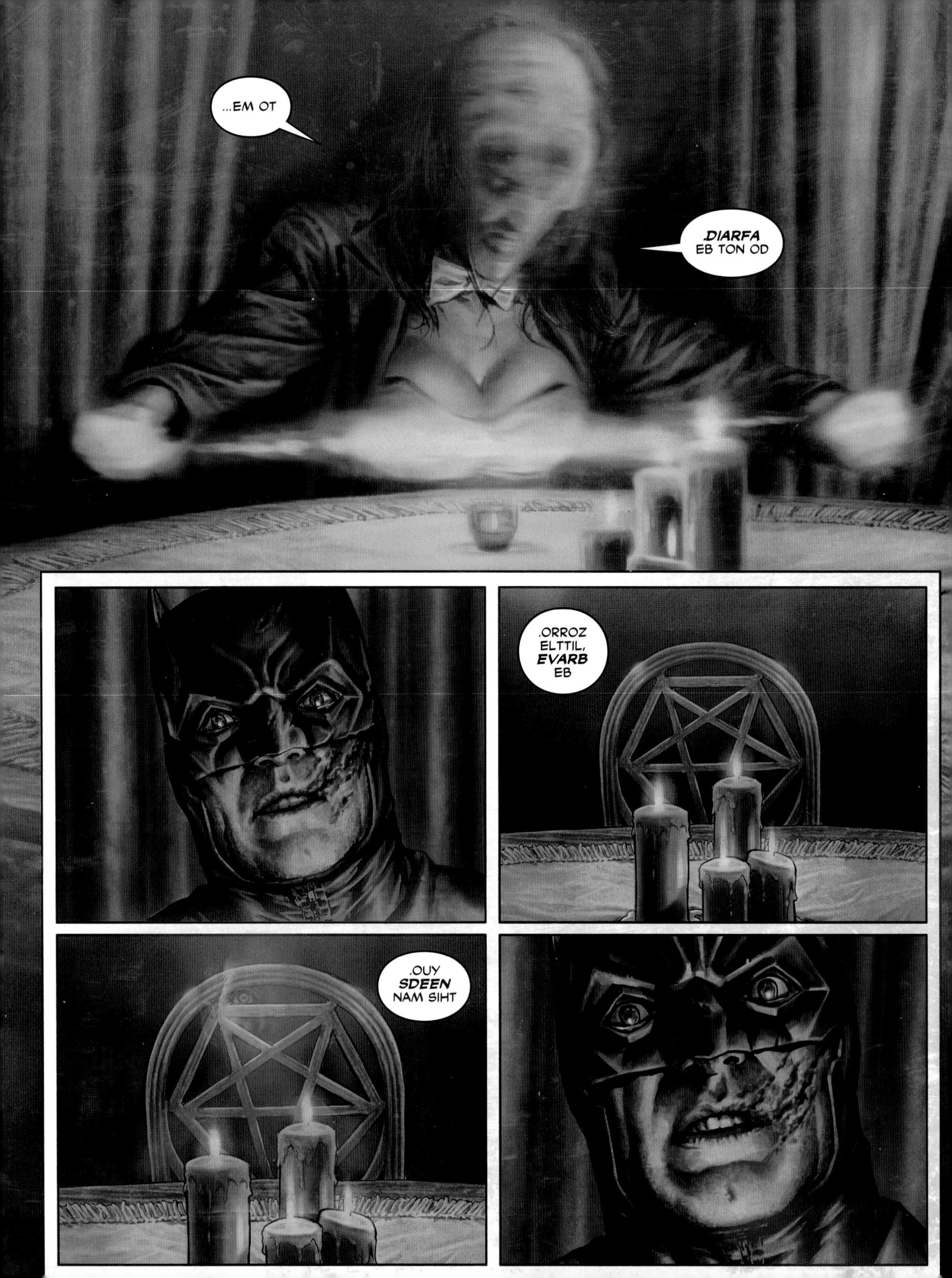
...EM OT
DIARFA EB TON OD
.ORROZ ELTTIL, EVARB EB
.OUY SDEEN NAM SIHT

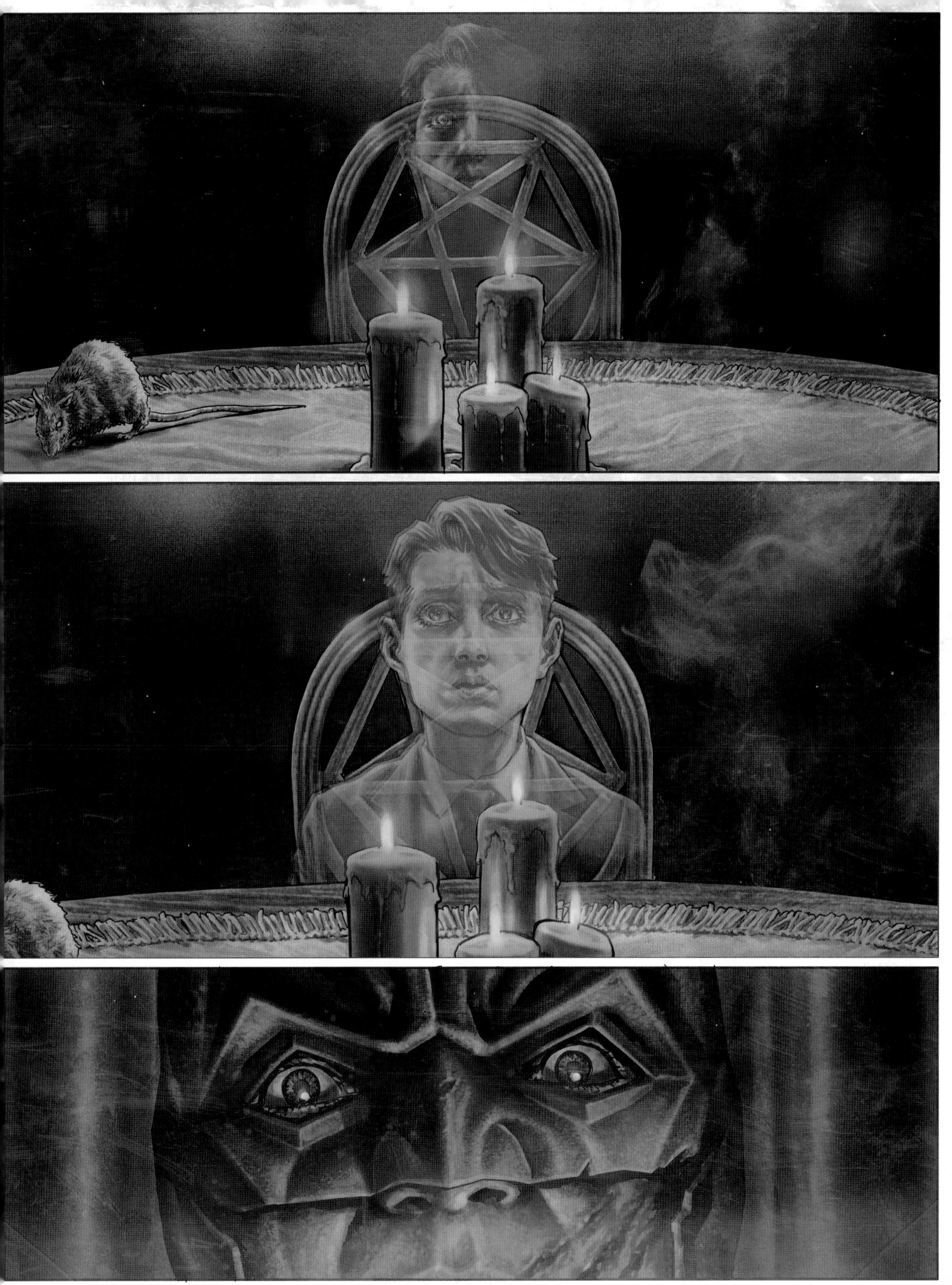

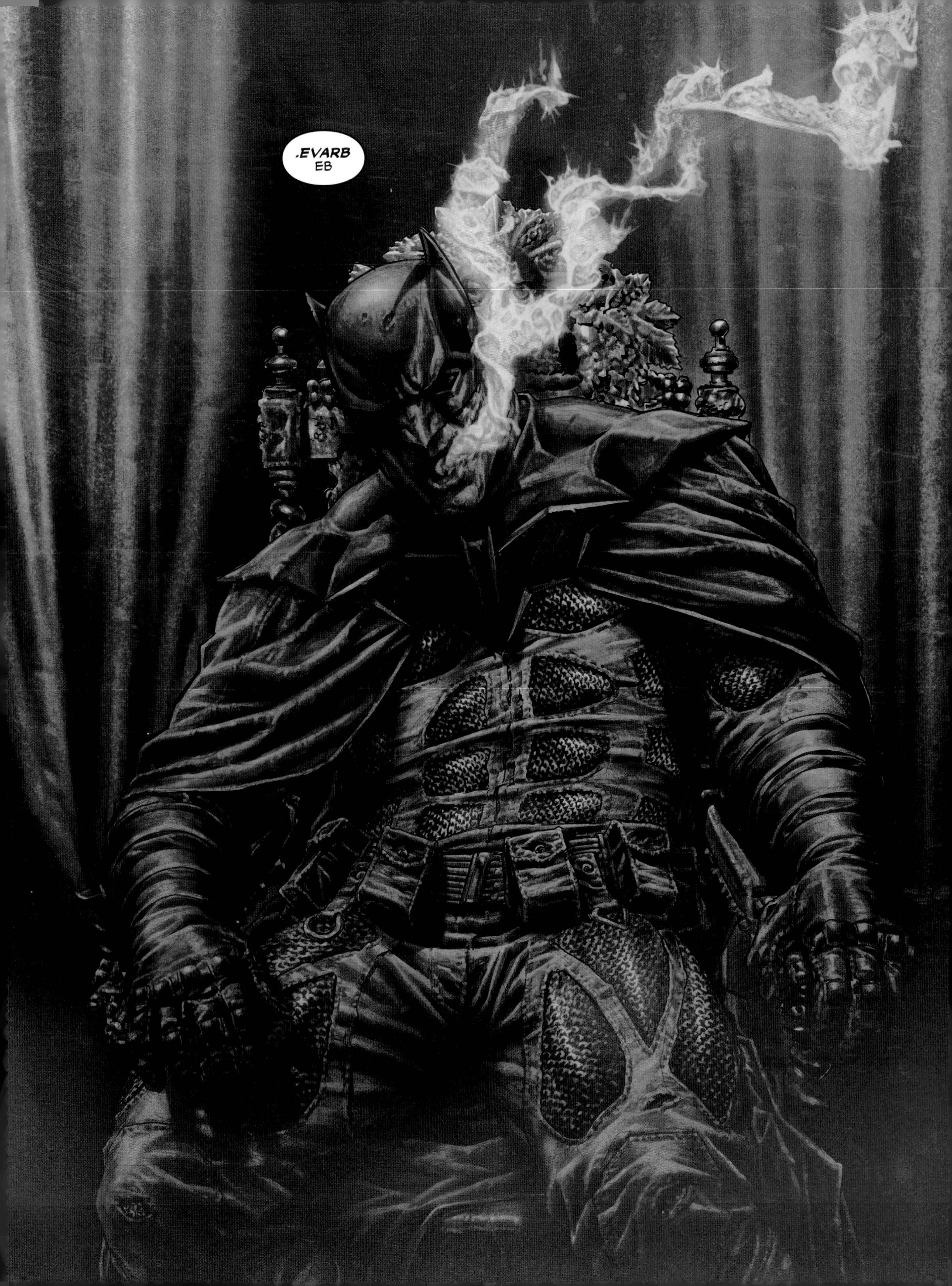
.EVARB EB

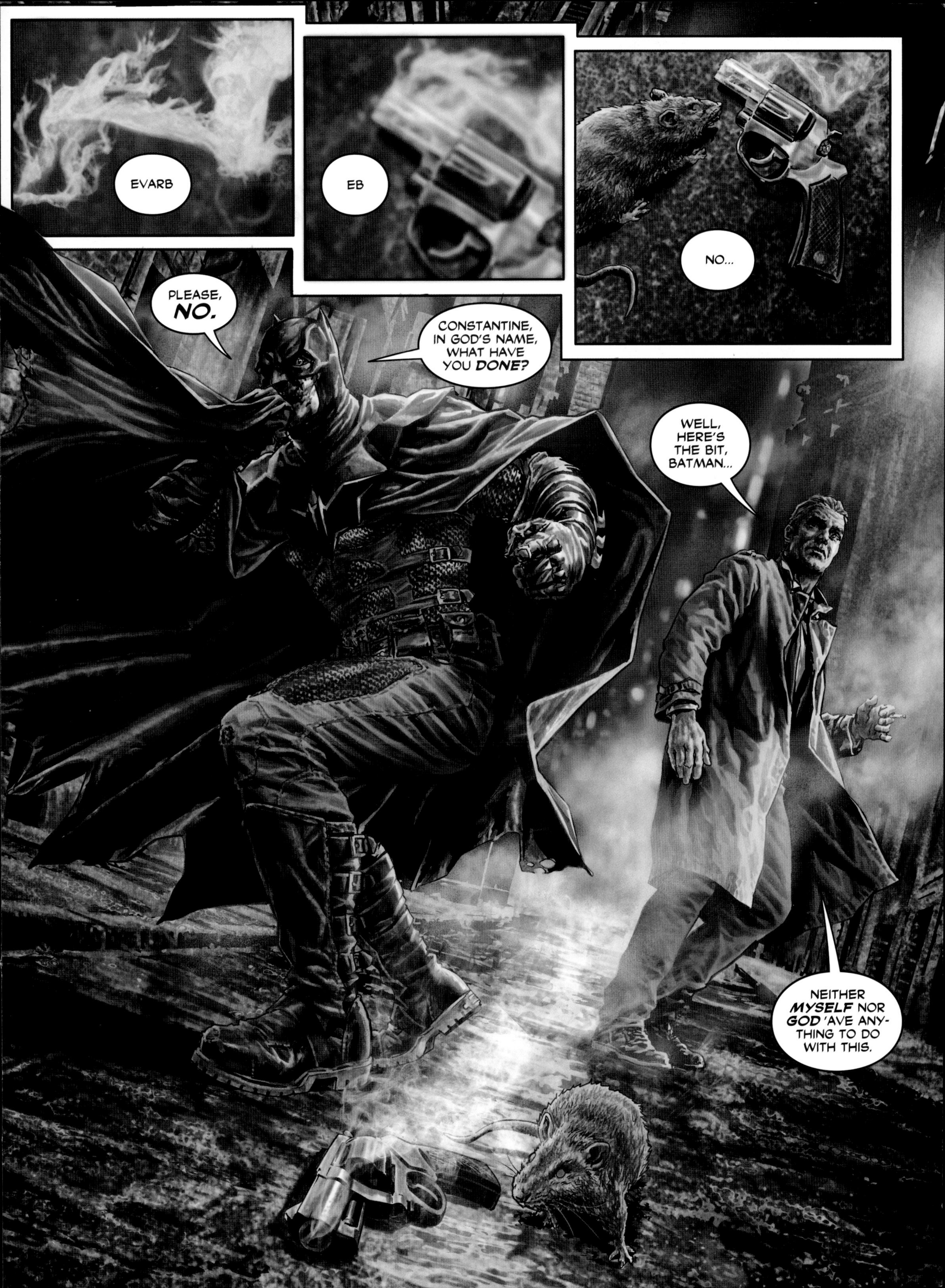
EVARB
EB
NO...
PLEASE, NO.
CONSTANTINE, IN GOD'S NAME, WHAT HAVE YOU DONE?
WELL, HERE'S THE BIT, BATMAN...
NEITHER MYSELF NOR GOD 'AVE ANY-THING TO DO WITH THIS.

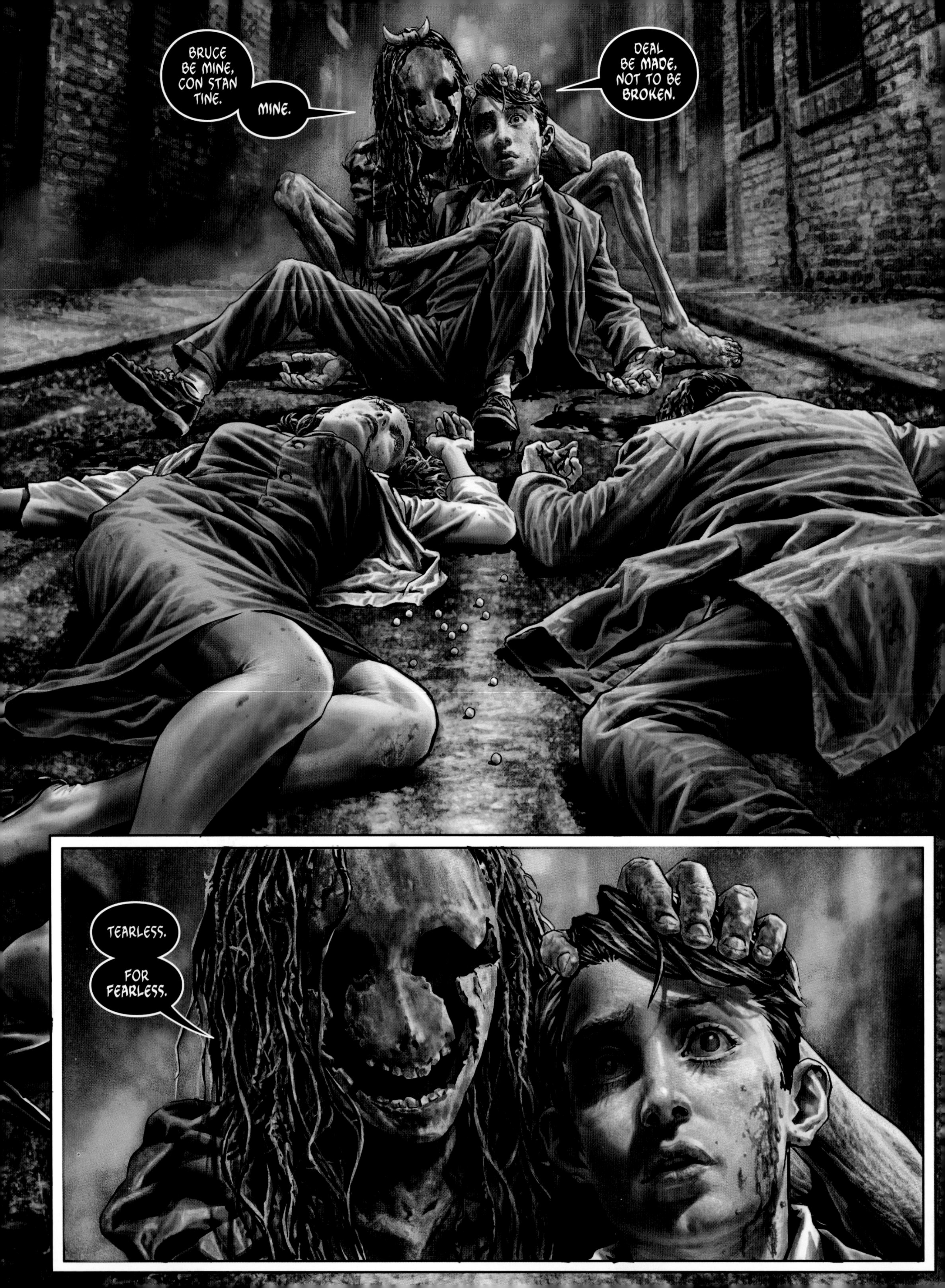
BRUCE BE MINE, CON STAN TINE.
MINE.
DEAL BE MADE, NOT TO BE BROKEN.
TEARLESS.
FOR FEARLESS.

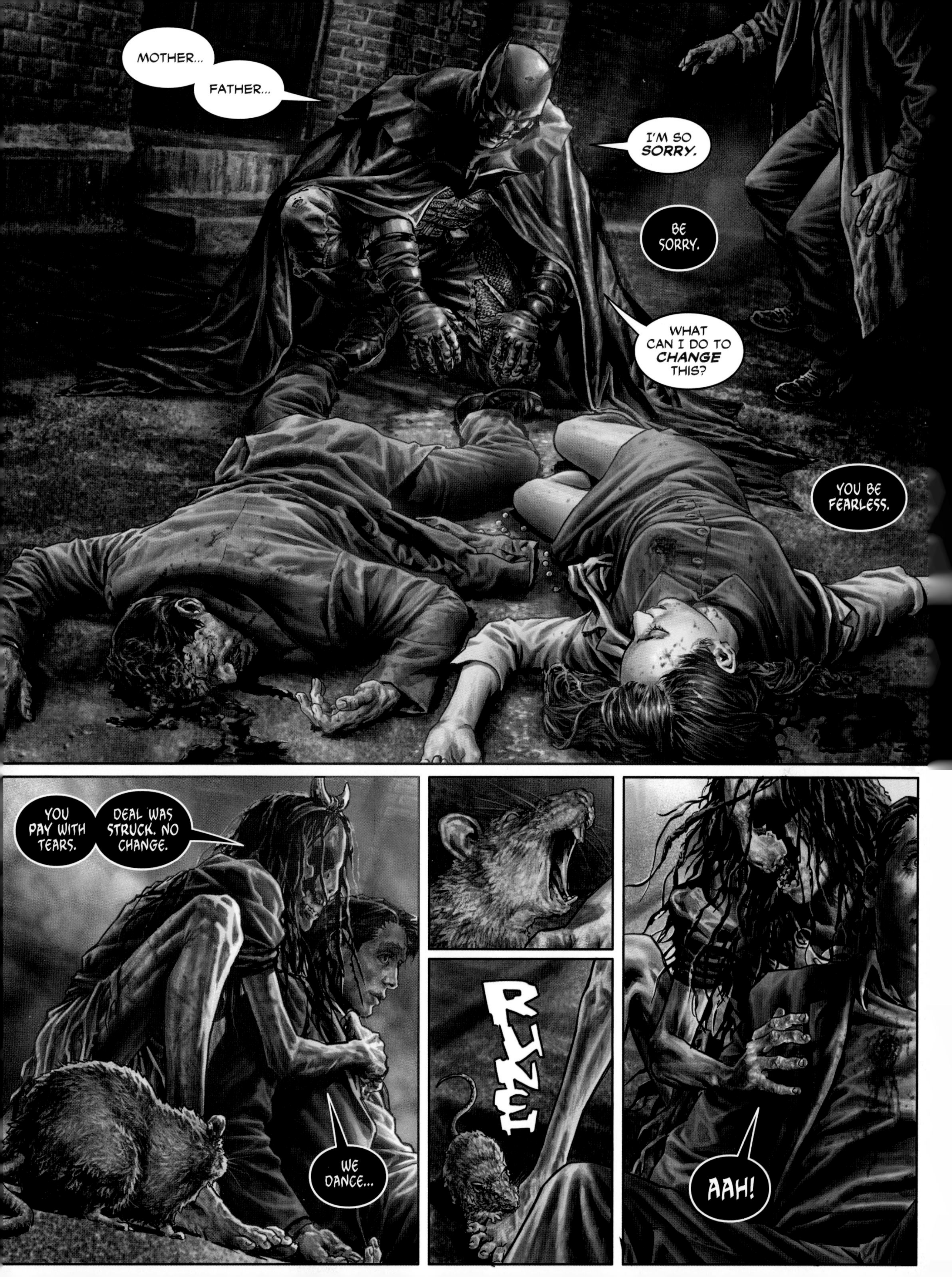

MOTHER...
FATHER...
I'M SO SORRY.
BE SORRY.
WHAT CAN I DO TO CHANGE THIS?
YOU BE FEARLESS.
YOU PAY WITH TEARS.
DEAL WAS STRUCK. NO CHANGE.
WE DANCE...
RUNE!
AAH!

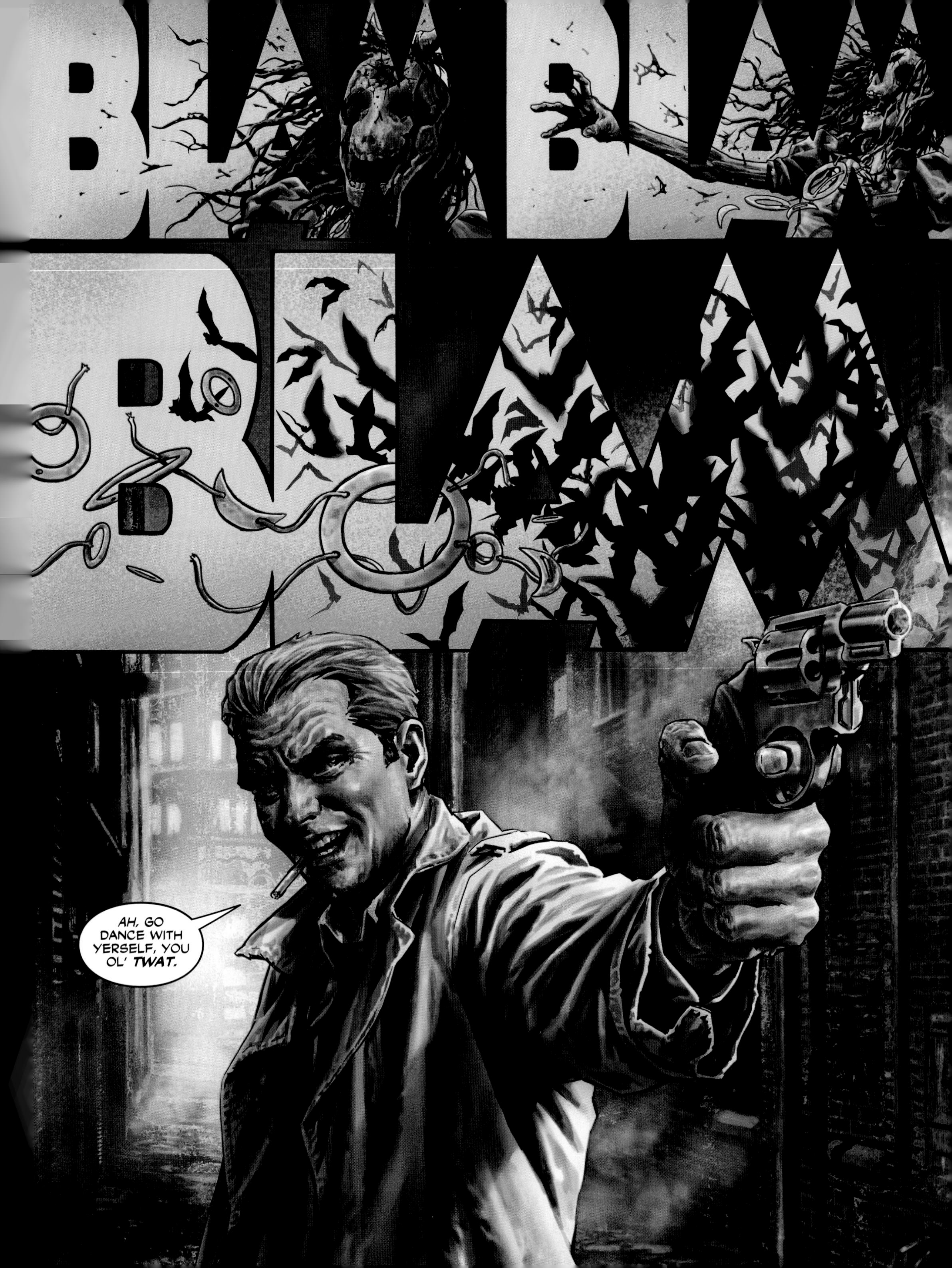

BLAM BLAM
BLAM
AH, GO DANCE WITH YERSELF, YOU OL' *TWAT.*

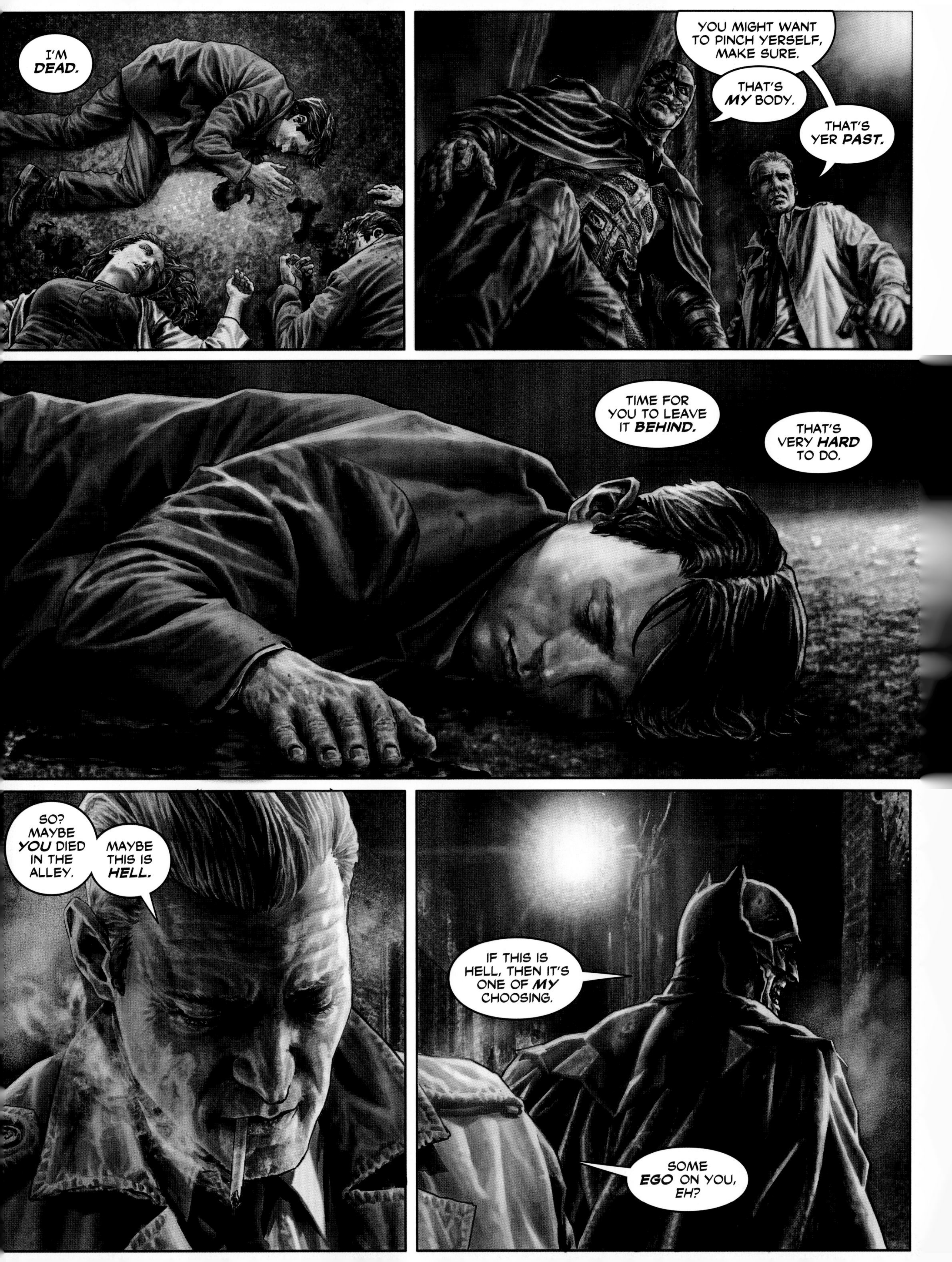
I'M DEAD.
YOU MIGHT WANT TO PINCH YERSELF, MAKE SURE.
THAT'S MY BODY.
THAT'S YER PAST.
TIME FOR YOU TO LEAVE IT BEHIND.
THAT'S VERY HARD TO DO.
SO? MAYBE YOU DIED IN THE ALLEY.
MAYBE THIS IS HELL.
IF THIS IS HELL, THEN IT'S ONE OF MY CHOOSING.
SOME EGO ON YOU, EH?

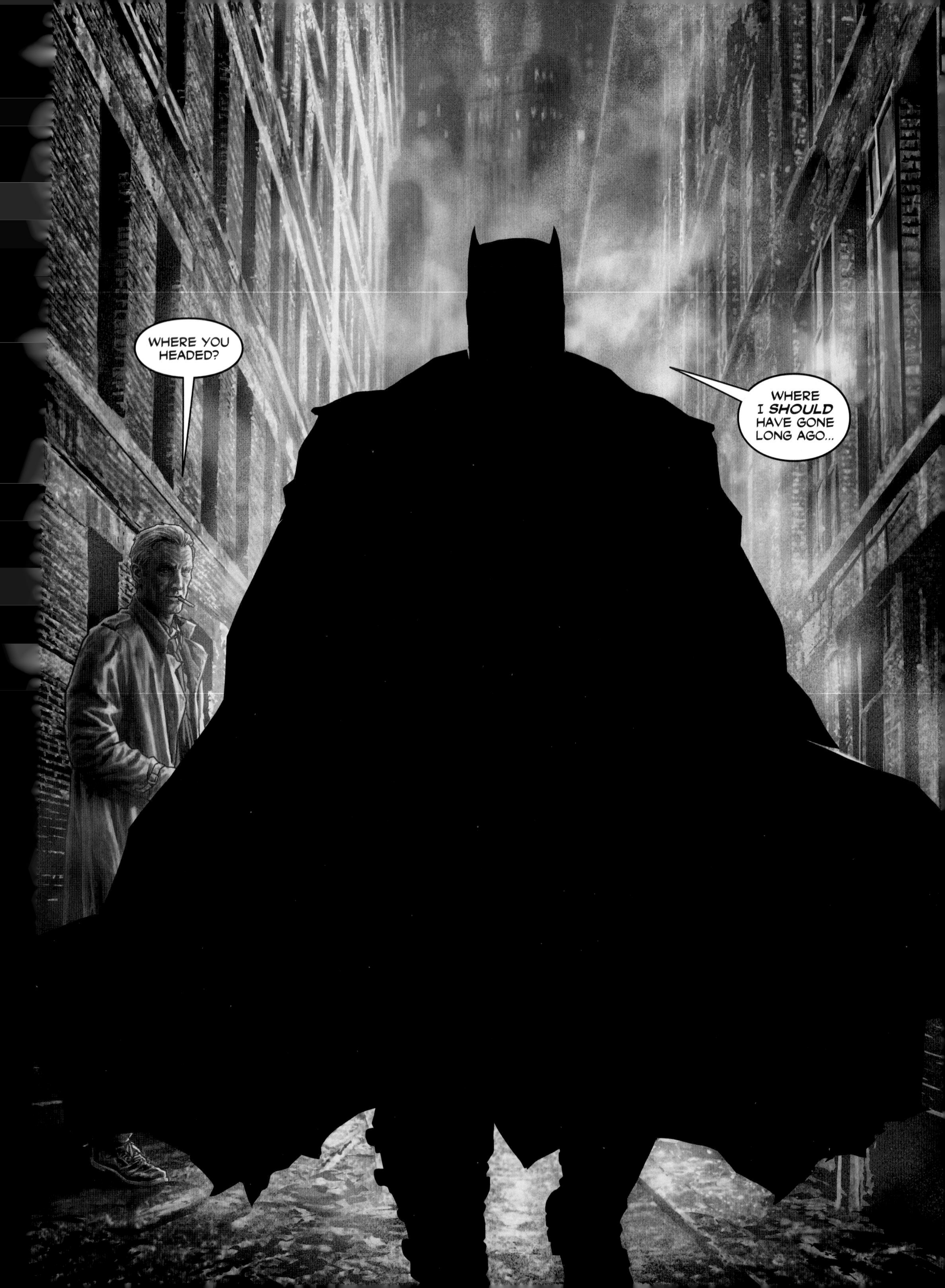
WHERE YOU HEADED?
WHERE I *SHOULD* HAVE GONE LONG AGO...

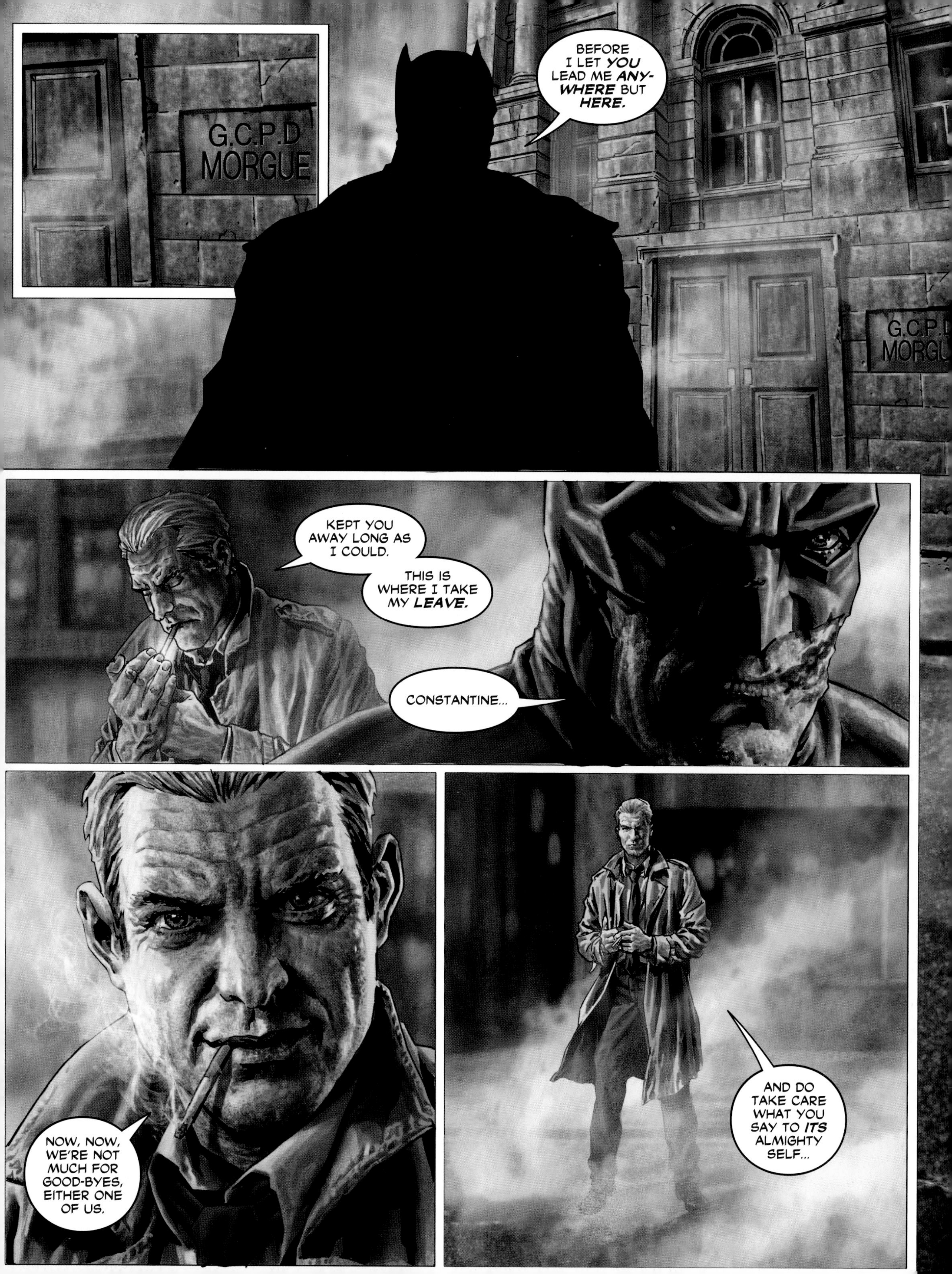
G.C.P.D MORGUE
BEFORE I LET *YOU* LEAD ME *ANY-WHERE* BUT *HERE.*
KEPT YOU AWAY LONG AS I COULD.
THIS IS WHERE I TAKE MY *LEAVE.*
CONSTANTINE...
NOW, NOW, WE'RE NOT MUCH FOR GOOD-BYES, EITHER ONE OF US.
AND DO TAKE CARE WHAT YOU SAY TO *ITS* ALMIGHTY SELF...

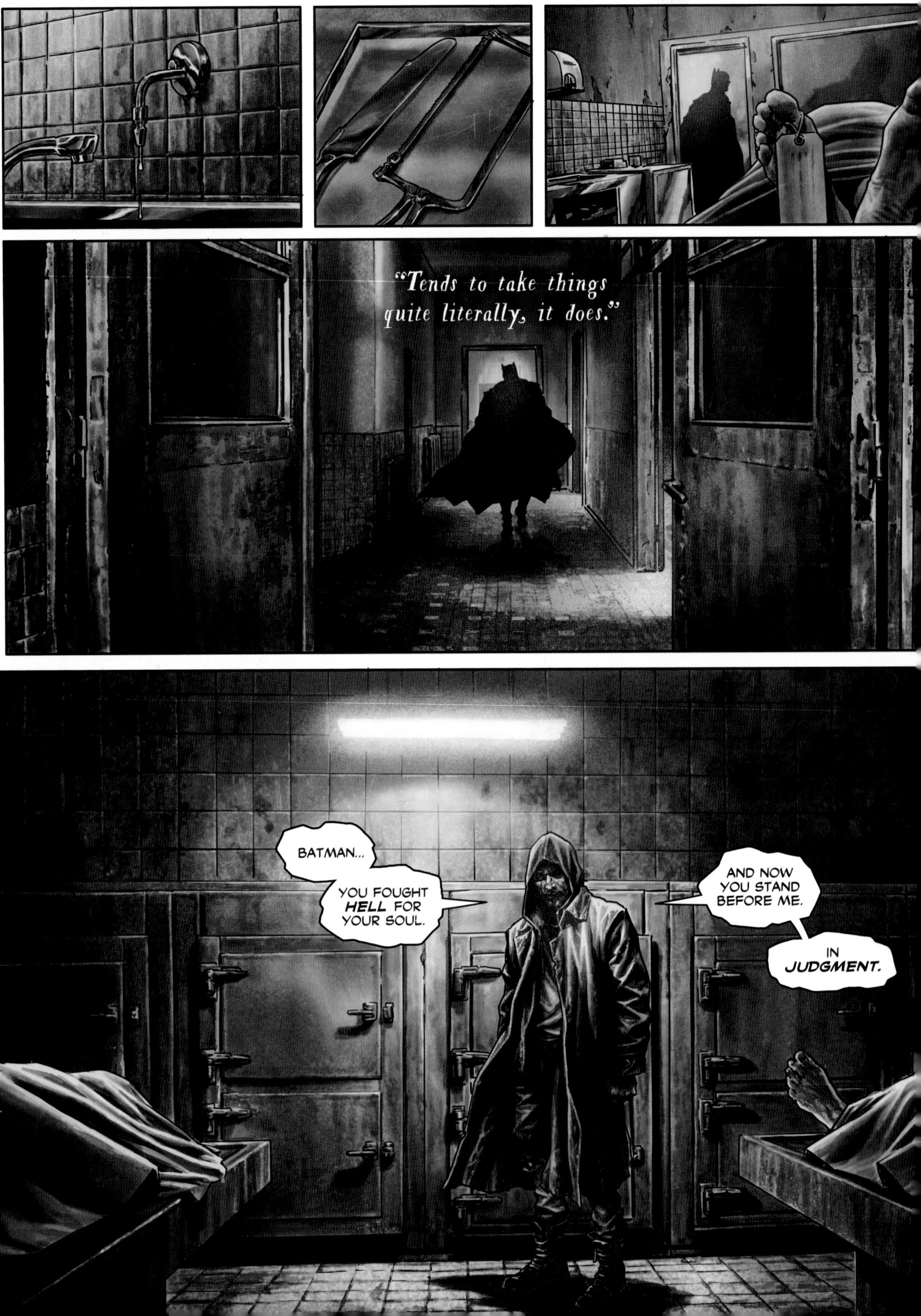
"Tends to take things quite literally, it does."
BATMAN...
YOU FOUGHT HELL FOR YOUR SOUL.
AND NOW YOU STAND BEFORE ME.
IN JUDGMENT.

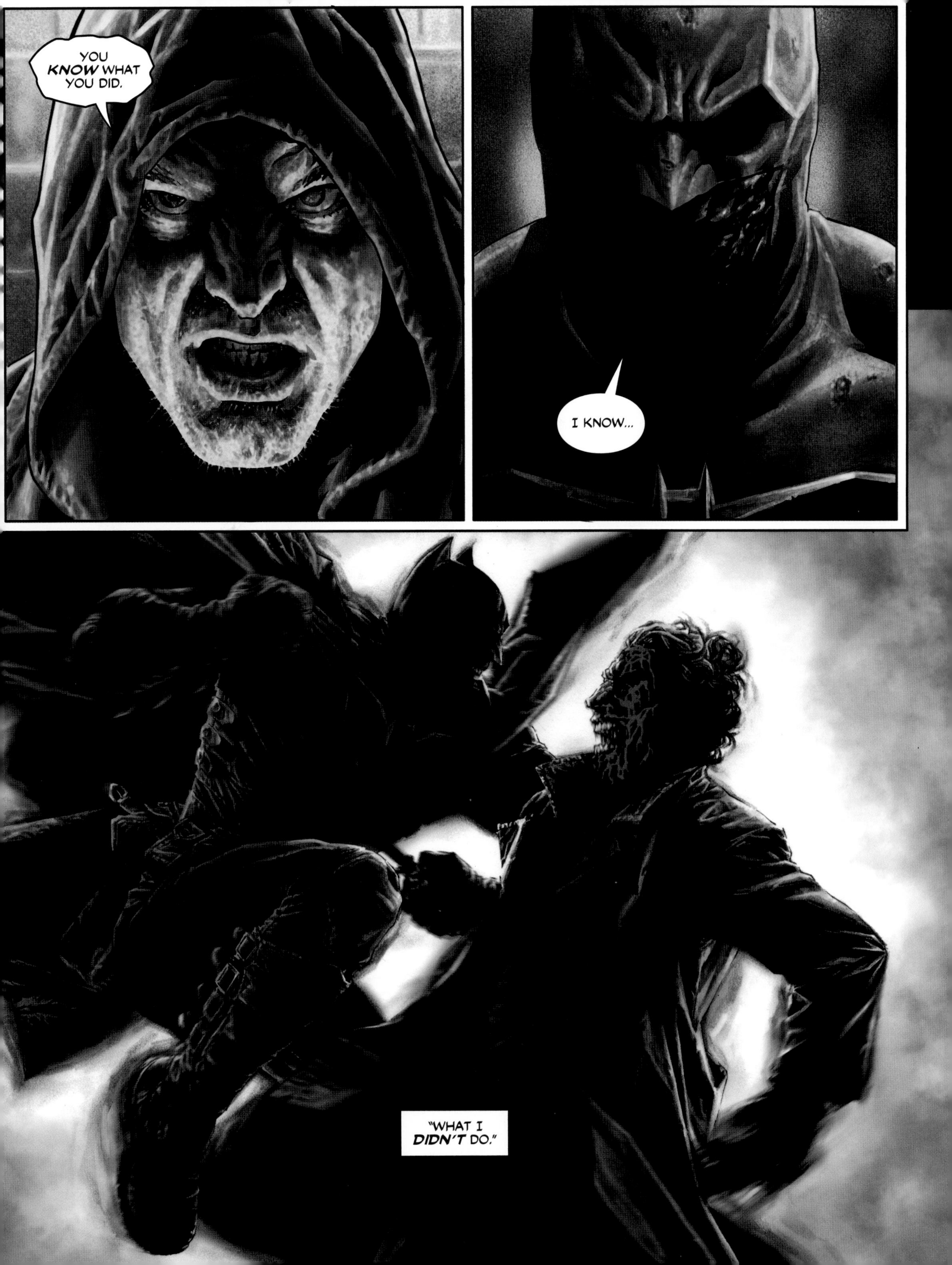
YOU KNOW WHAT YOU DID.
I KNOW...
"WHAT I DIDN'T DO."

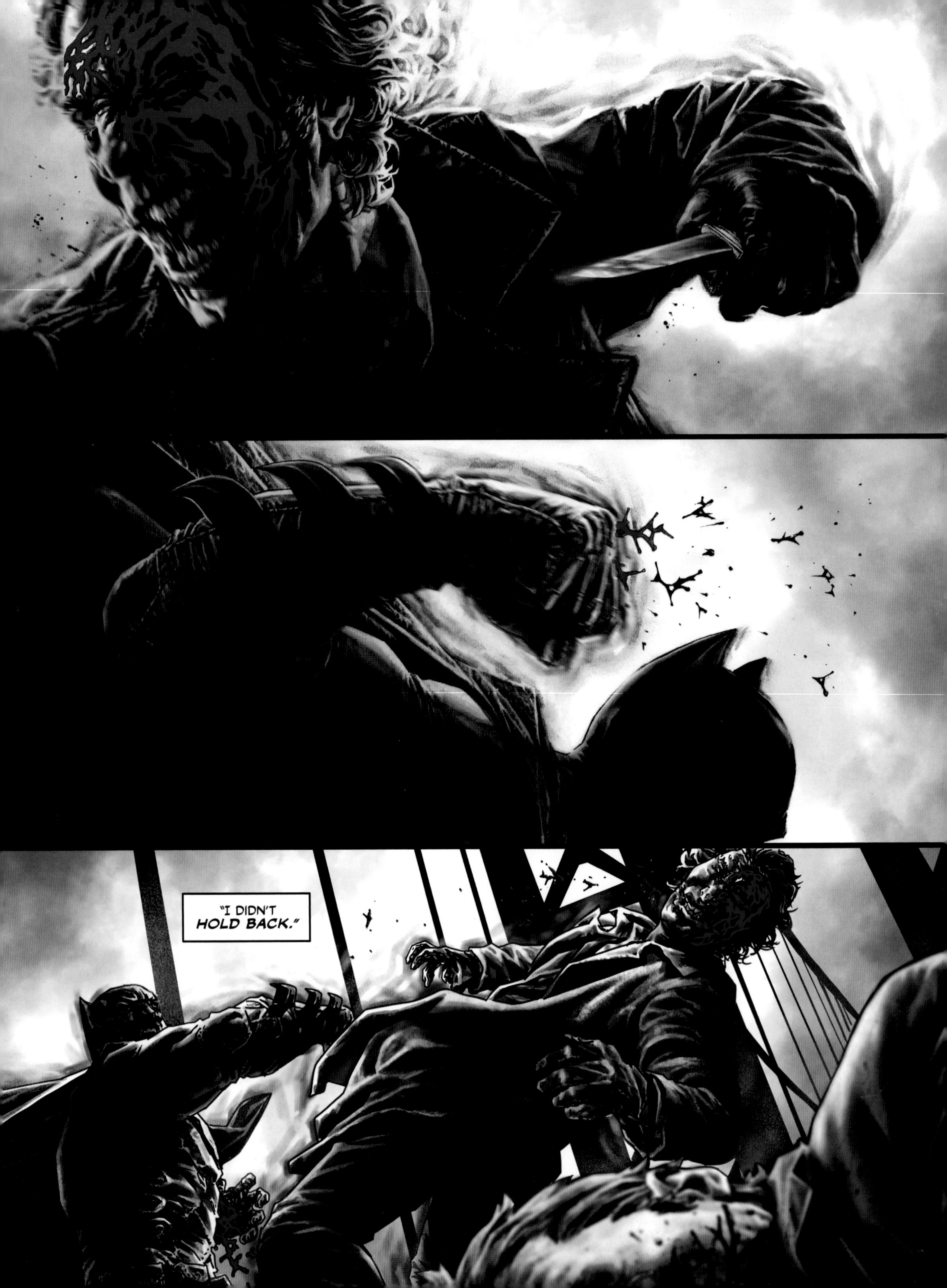
"I DIDN'T HOLD BACK."

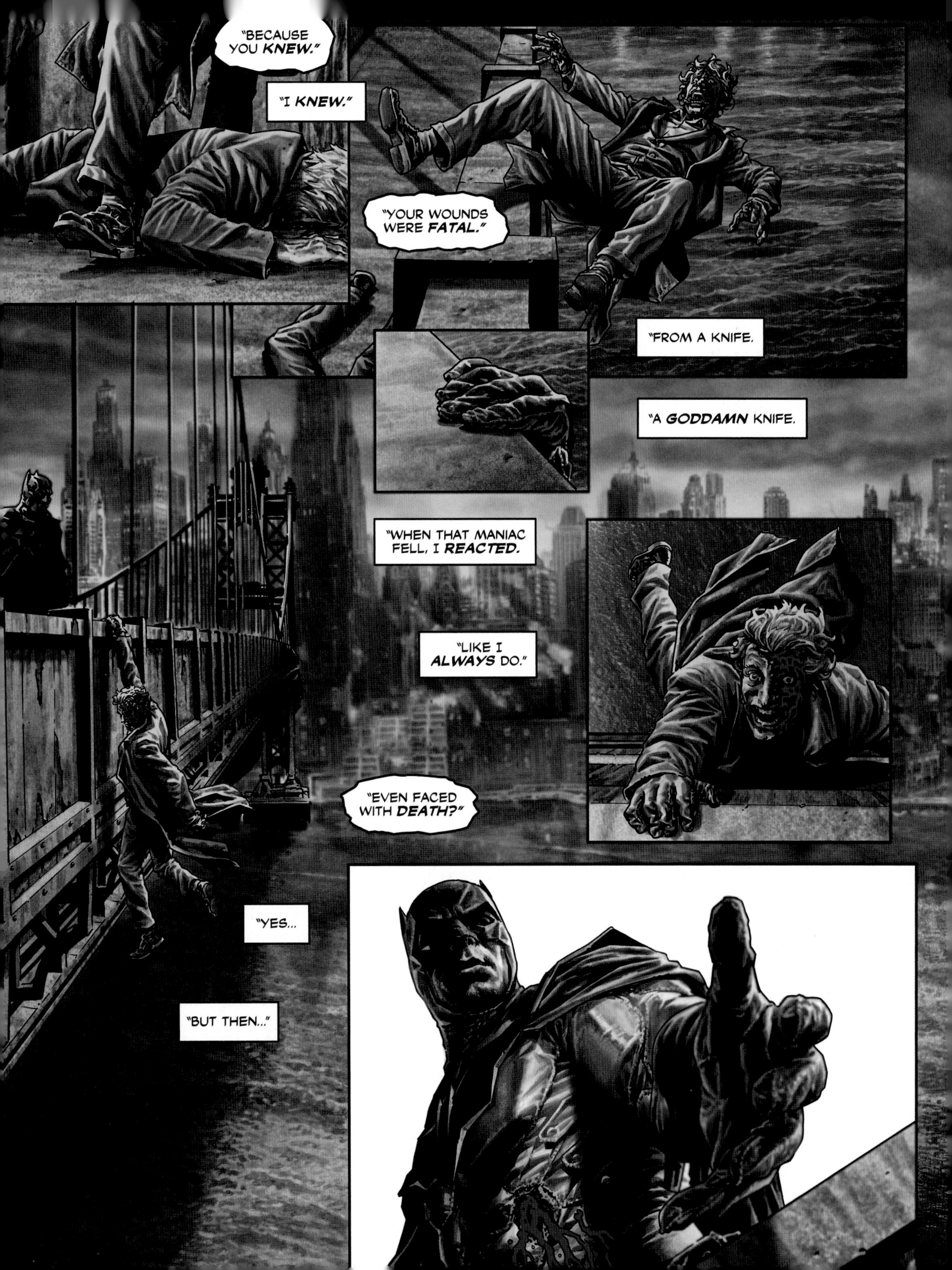
"BECAUSE YOU KNEW."
"I KNEW."
"YOUR WOUNDS WERE FATAL."
"FROM A KNIFE.
"A GODDAMN KNIFE.
"WHEN THAT MANIAC FELL, I REACTED.
"LIKE I ALWAYS DO."
"EVEN FACED WITH DEATH?"
"YES...
"BUT THEN..."

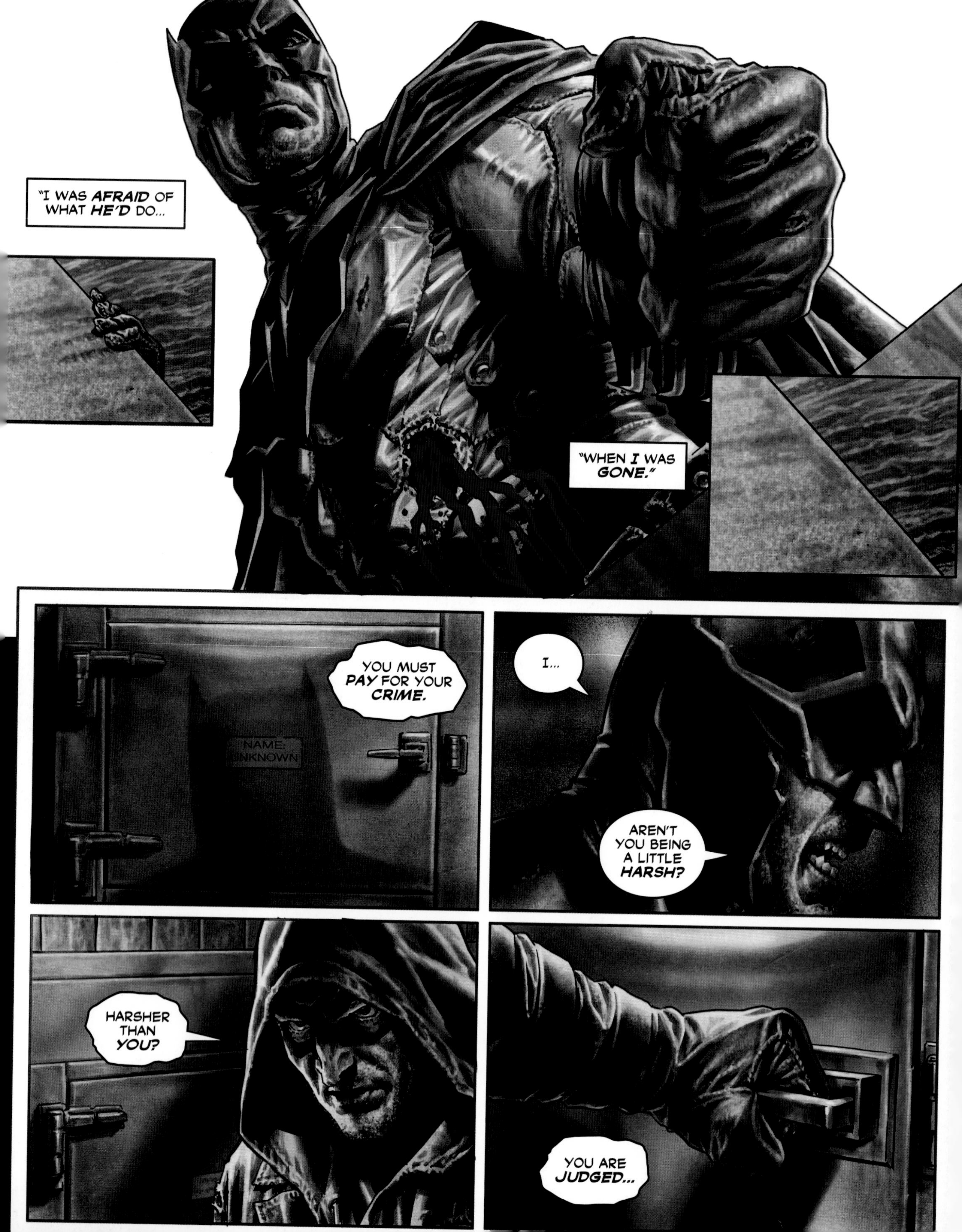
"I WAS AFRAID OF WHAT HE'D DO...
"WHEN I WAS GONE."
YOU MUST PAY FOR YOUR CRIME.
NAME: UNKNOWN
I...
AREN'T YOU BEING A LITTLE HARSH?
HARSHER THAN YOU?
YOU ARE JUDGED...

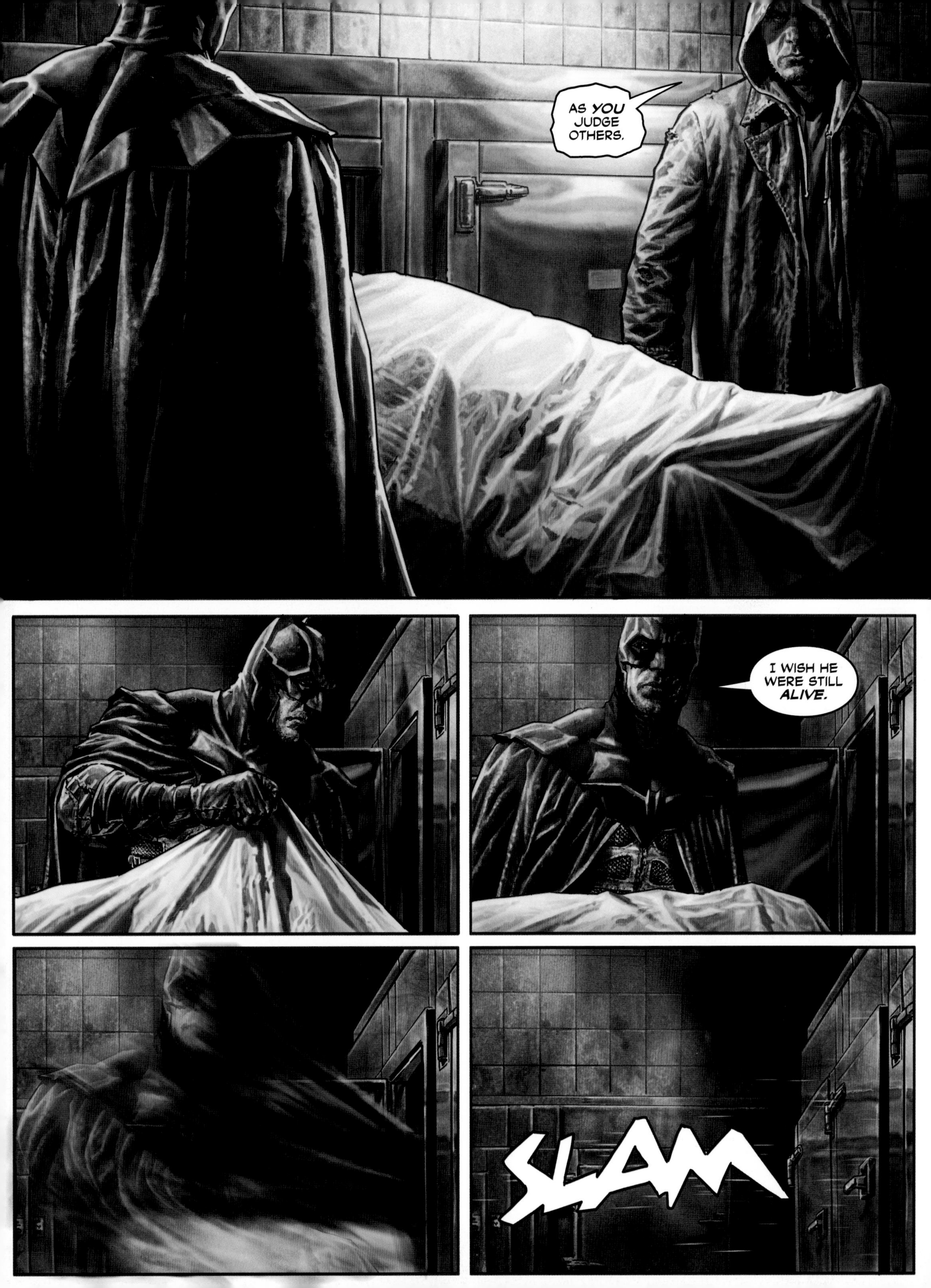
AS YOU JUDGE OTHERS.
I WISH HE WERE STILL ALIVE.
SLAM

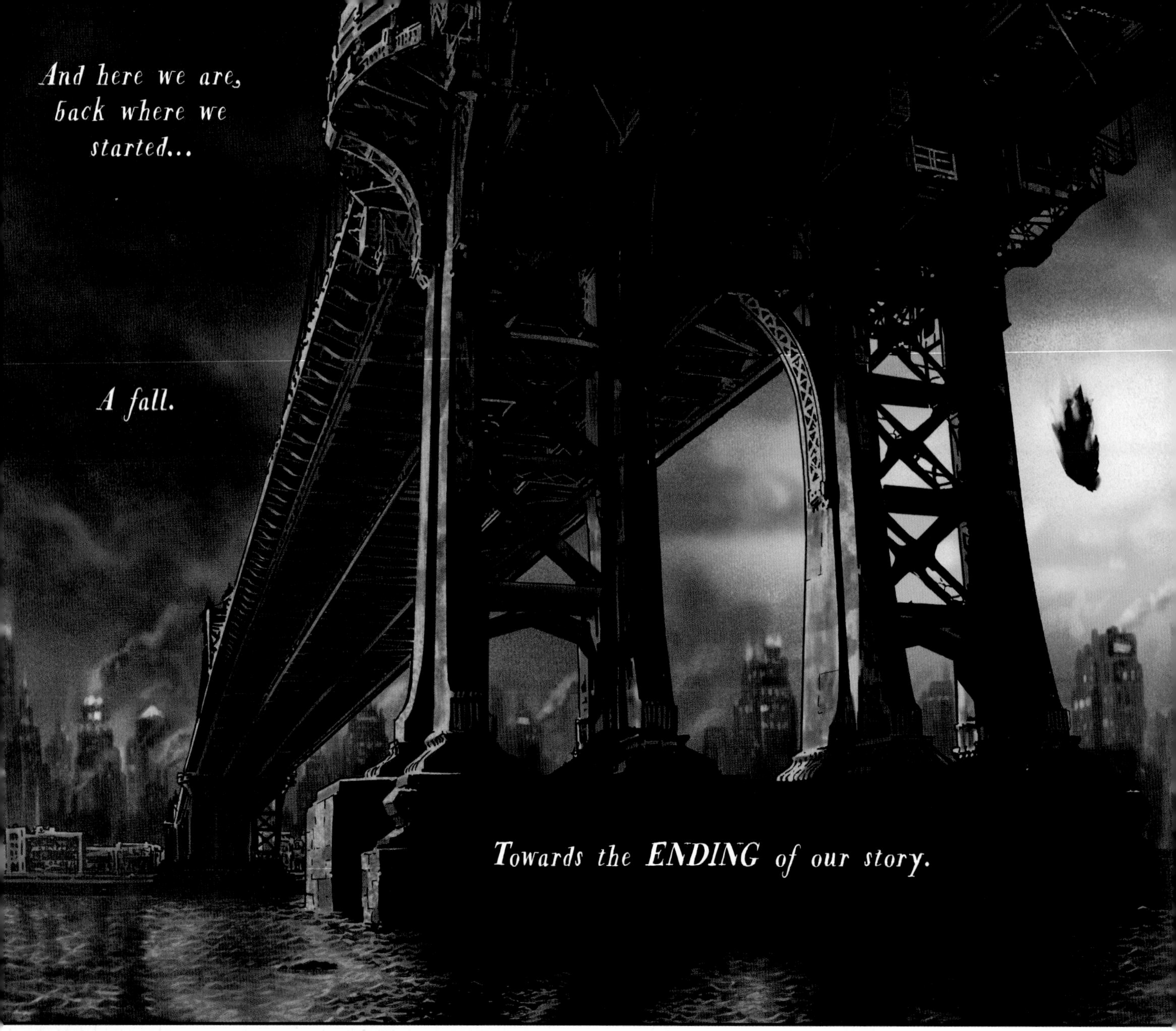
And here we are, back where we started...
A fall.
Towards the ENDING of our story.
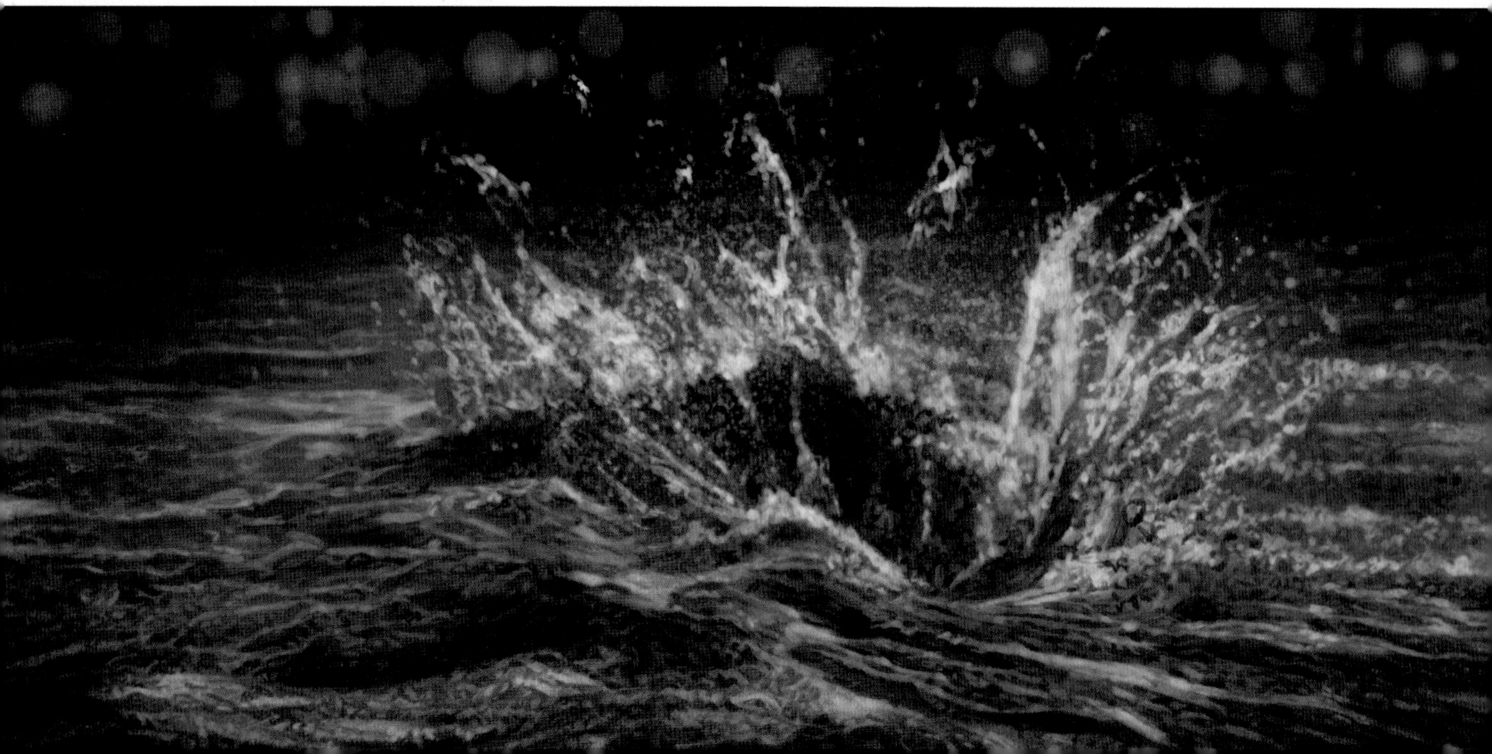

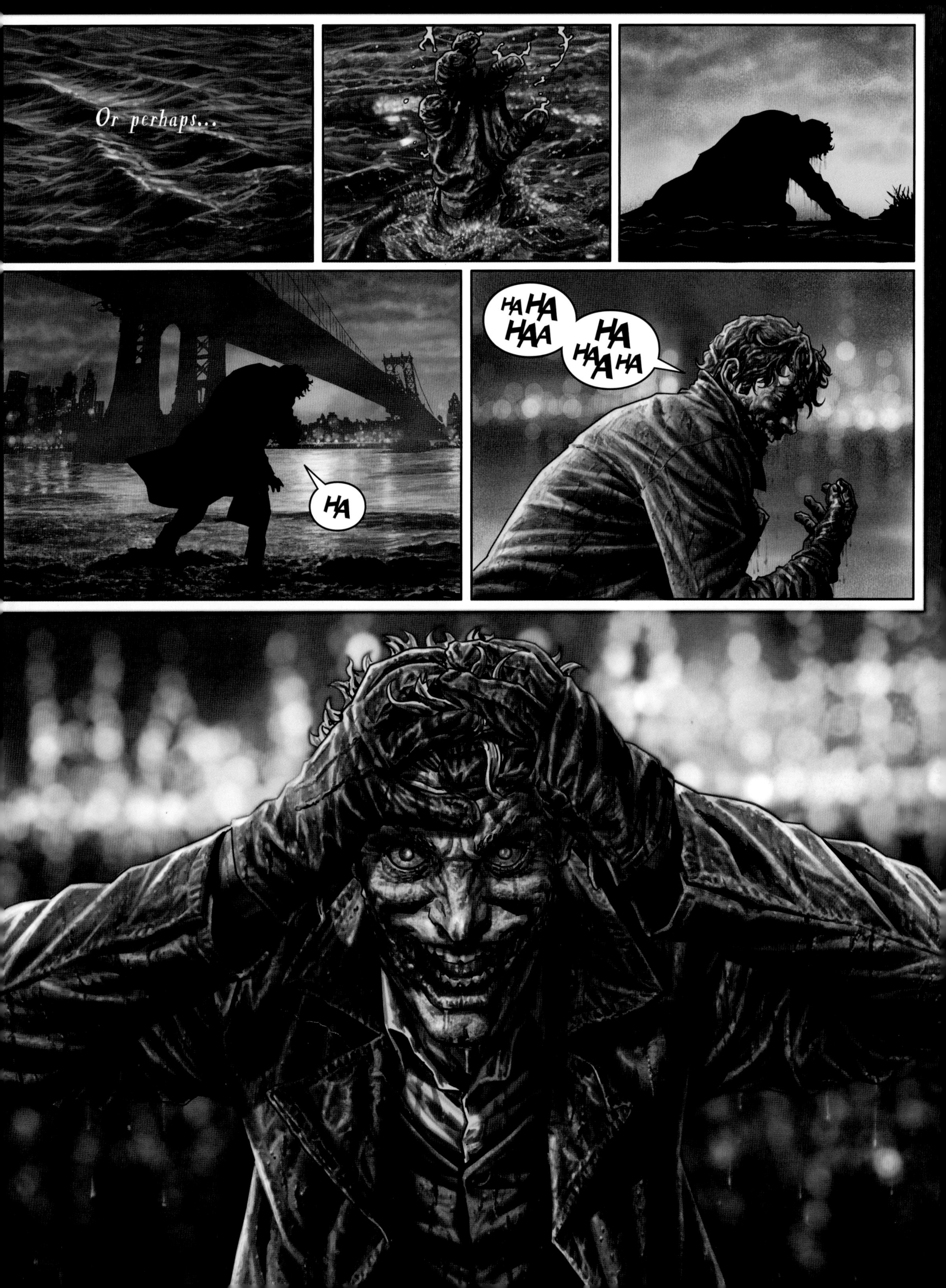
Or perhaps...
HA
HA HA HAA
HA HAA HA

It's just the start of another one.

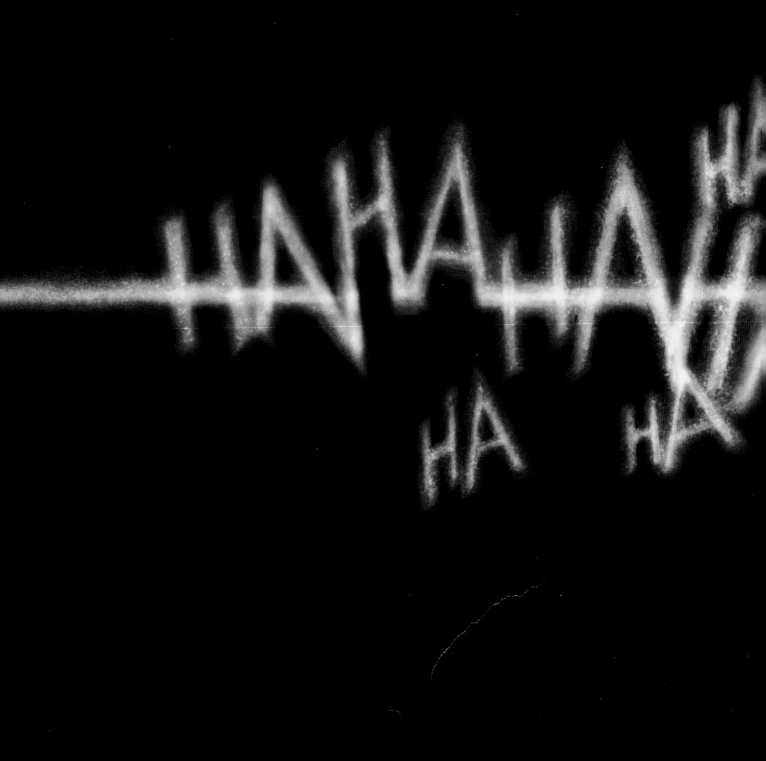

BONUS GALLERY

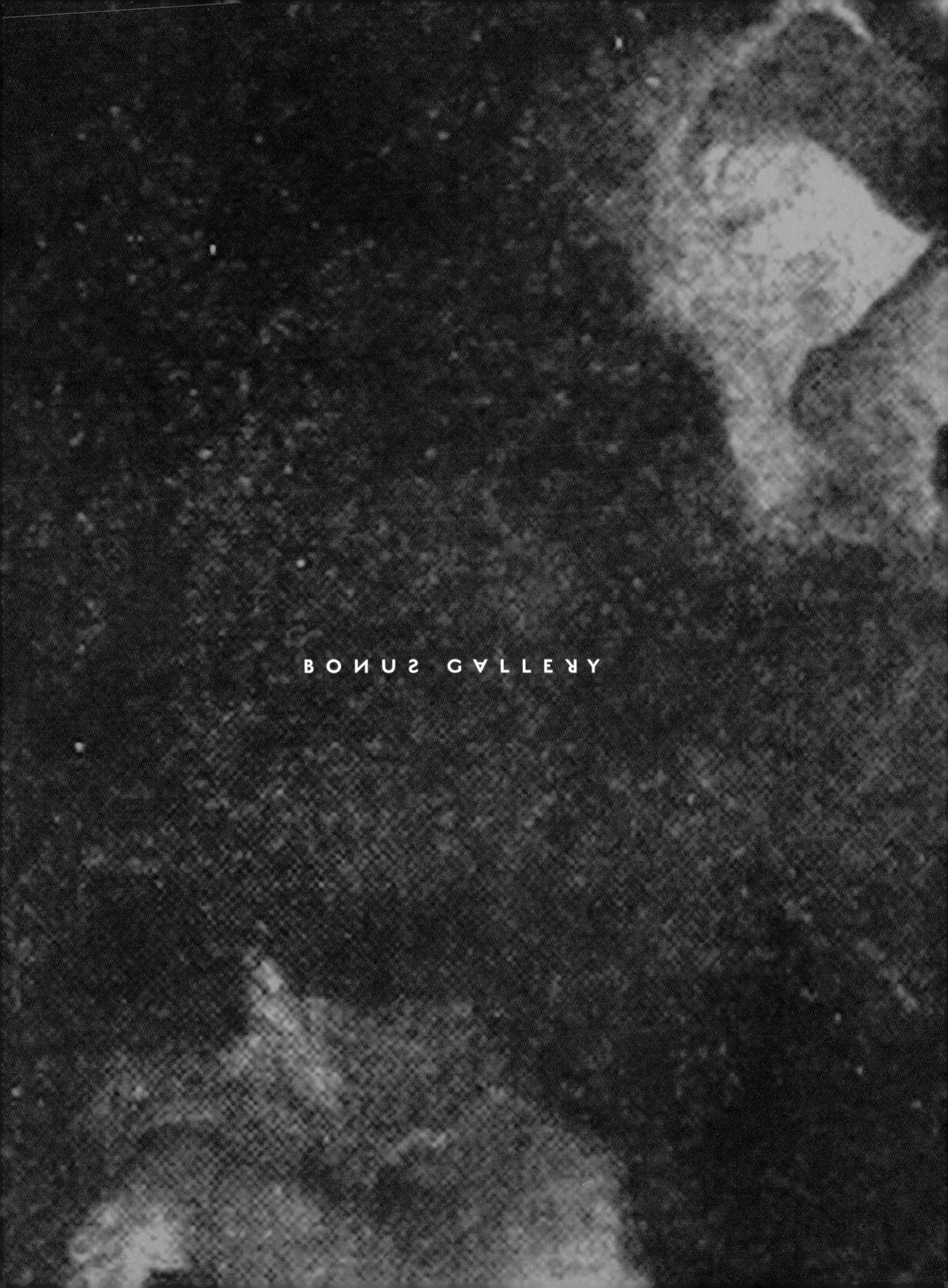

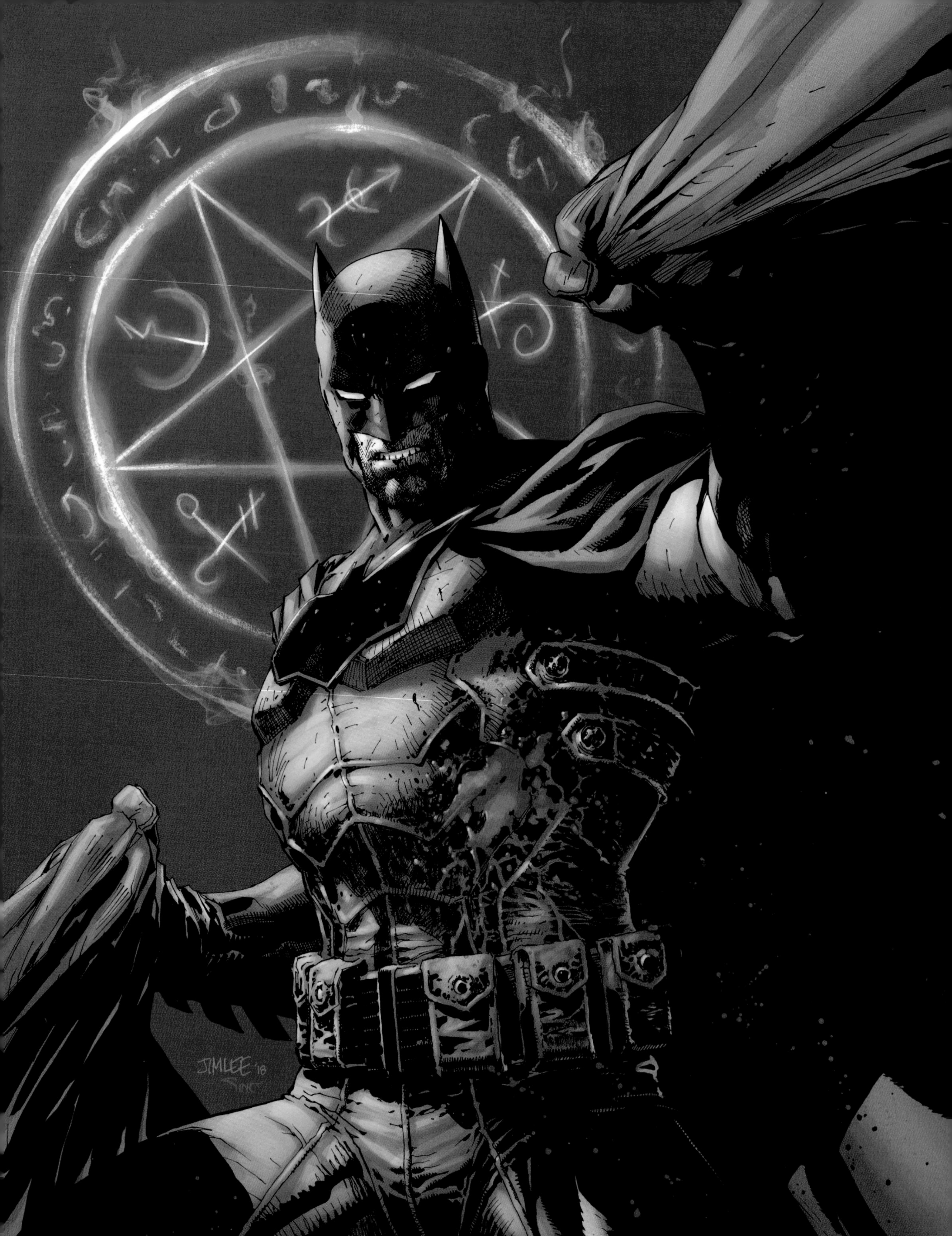
JIM LEE '18

BATMAN: DAMNED №1 variant cover by JIM LEE and ALEX SINCLAIR

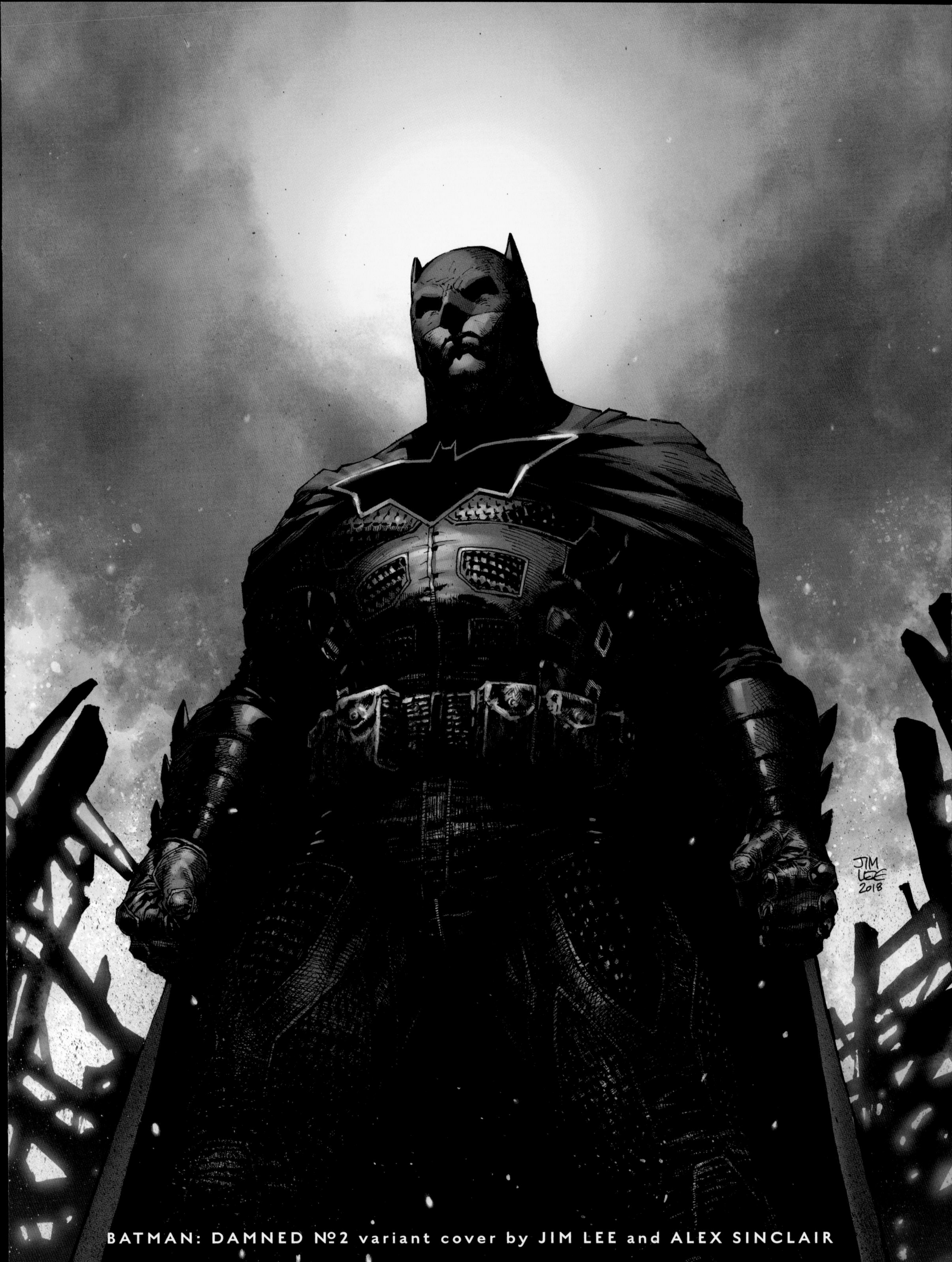
JIM
LEE
2018

BATMAN: DAMNED №2 variant cover by JIM LEE and ALEX SINCLAIR

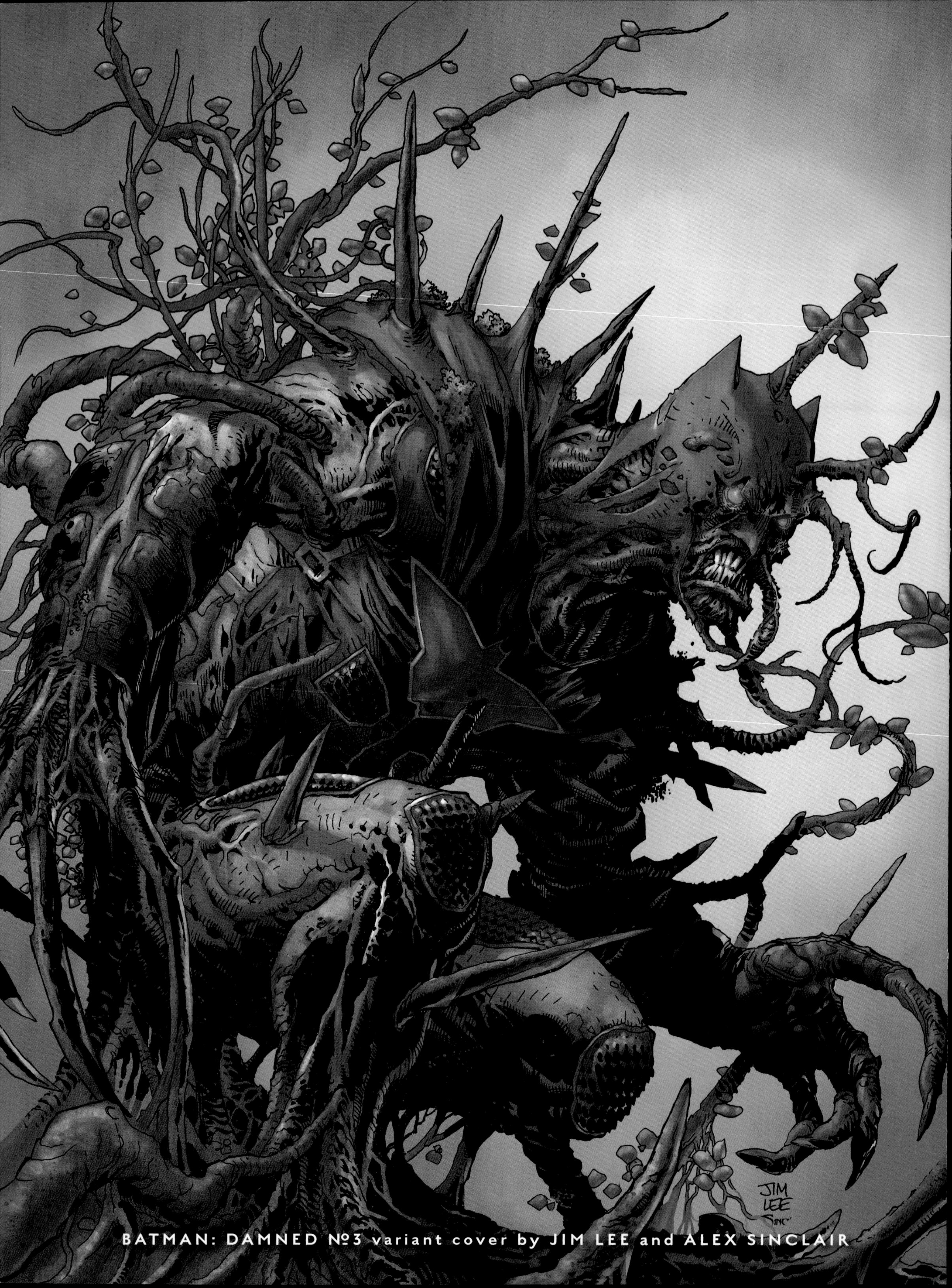
JIM
LEE

BATMAN: DAMNED №3 variant cover by JIM LEE and ALEX SINCLAIR

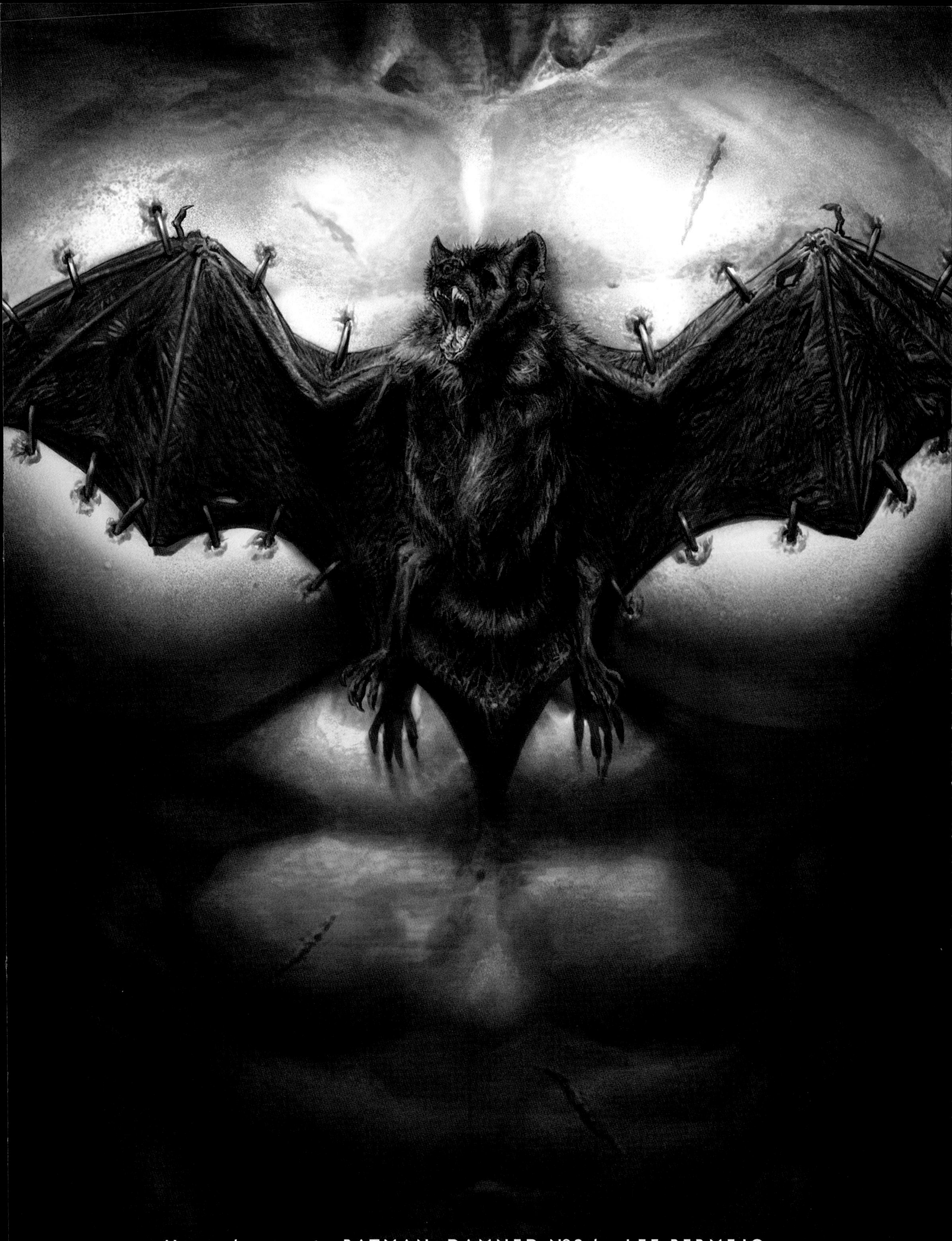

Unused cover to BATMAN: DAMNED №2 by LEE BERMEJO

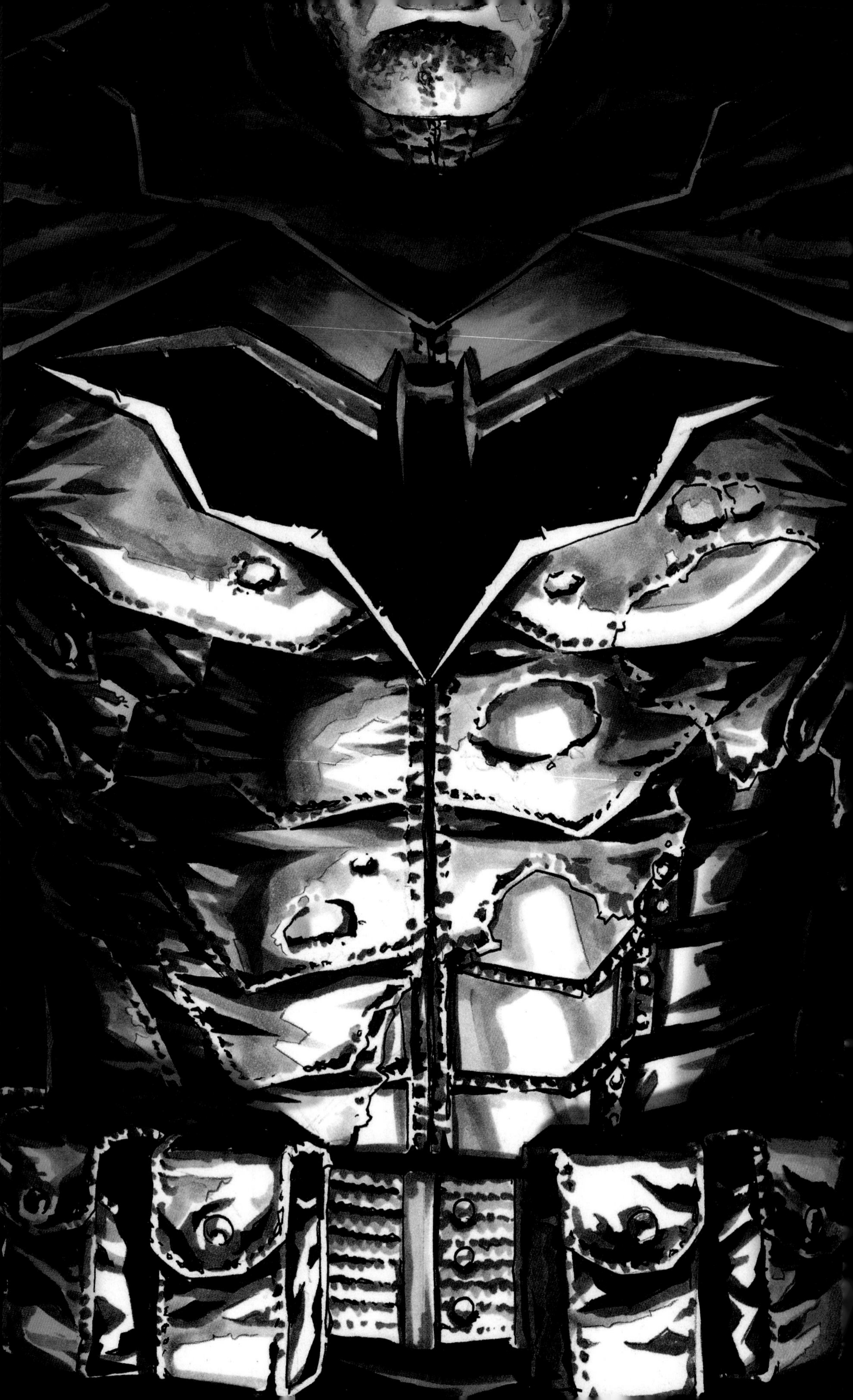

BATMAN character sketch by LEE BERMEJO

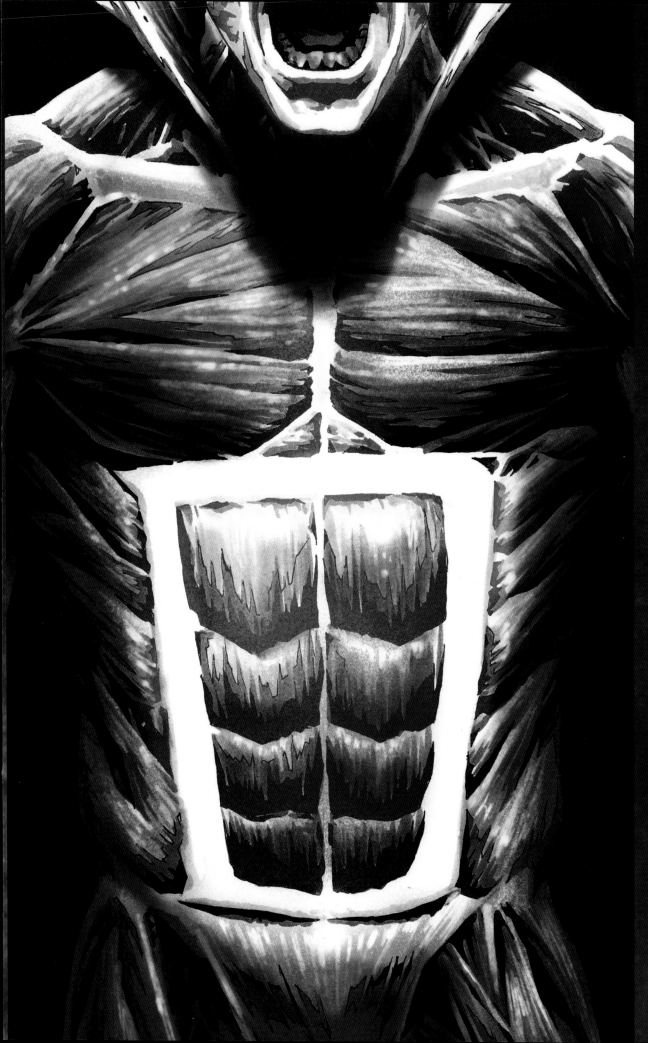

DEADMAN character sketch by LEE BERMEJO

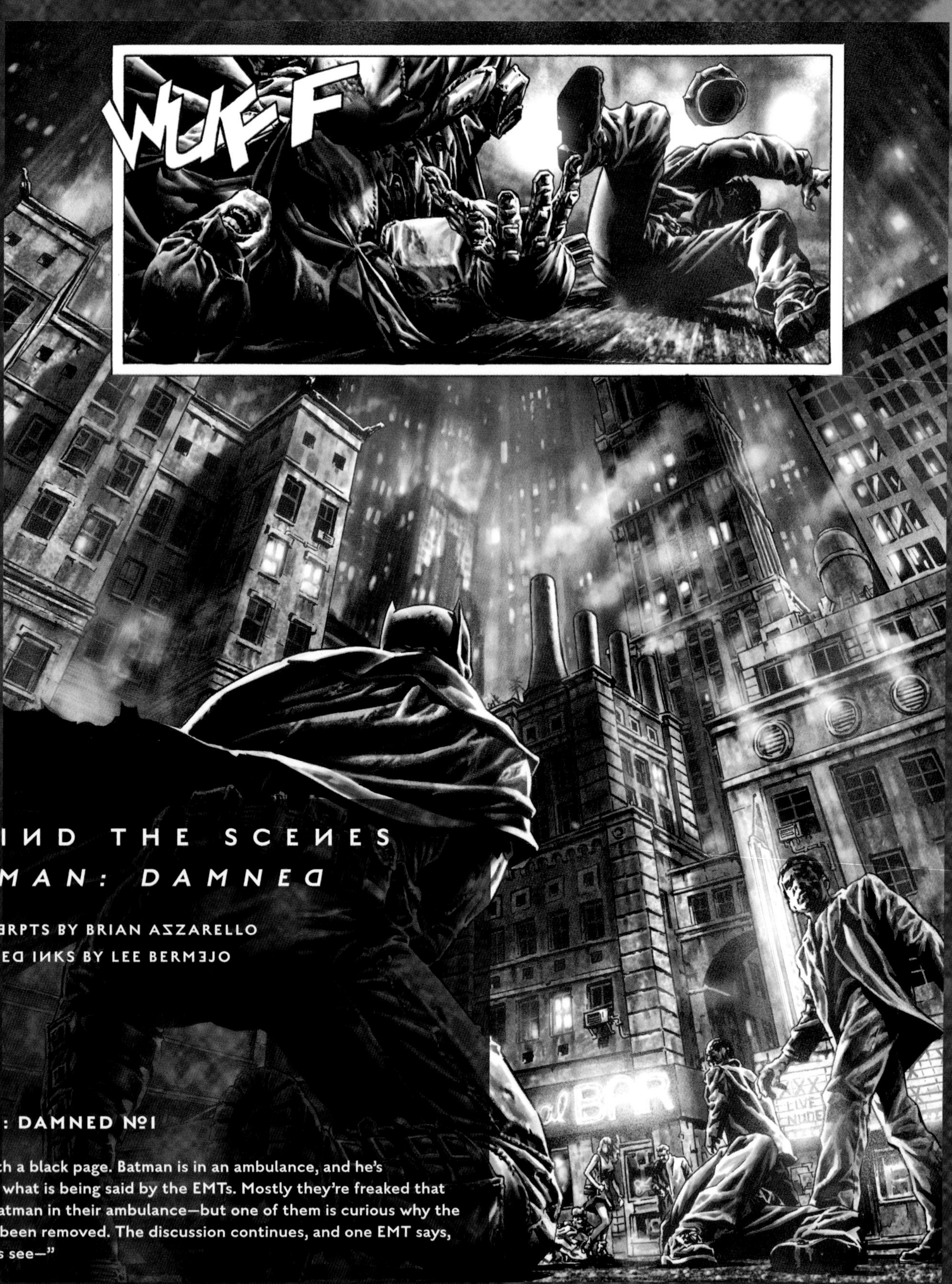
WUFF
BAR

BEHIND THE SCENES
BATMAN: DAMNED

PLOT EXCERPTS BY BRIAN AZZARELLO
UNCOLORED INKS BY LEE BERMEJO

BATMAN: DAMNED №1

We open with a black page. Batman is in an ambulance, and he's overhearing what is being said by the EMTs. Mostly they're freaked that they have Batman in their ambulance—but one of them is curious why the mask hasn't been removed. The discussion continues, and one EMT says, "Fuck it, let's see—"

Batman's eyes spring open while the EMT is trying to take his mask off, and he immediately—and savagely—springs to action. IVs are pulled/yanked off as he incapacitates the EMTs. There's a cop in the back of the ambulance too. He raises his gun and Batman kicks open the door...

And falls out into the equivalent of Gotham's Times Square. He tumbles to the ground, bleeding and snarling. A crowd of people stand and stare... maybe for an instant their faces look a bit off...

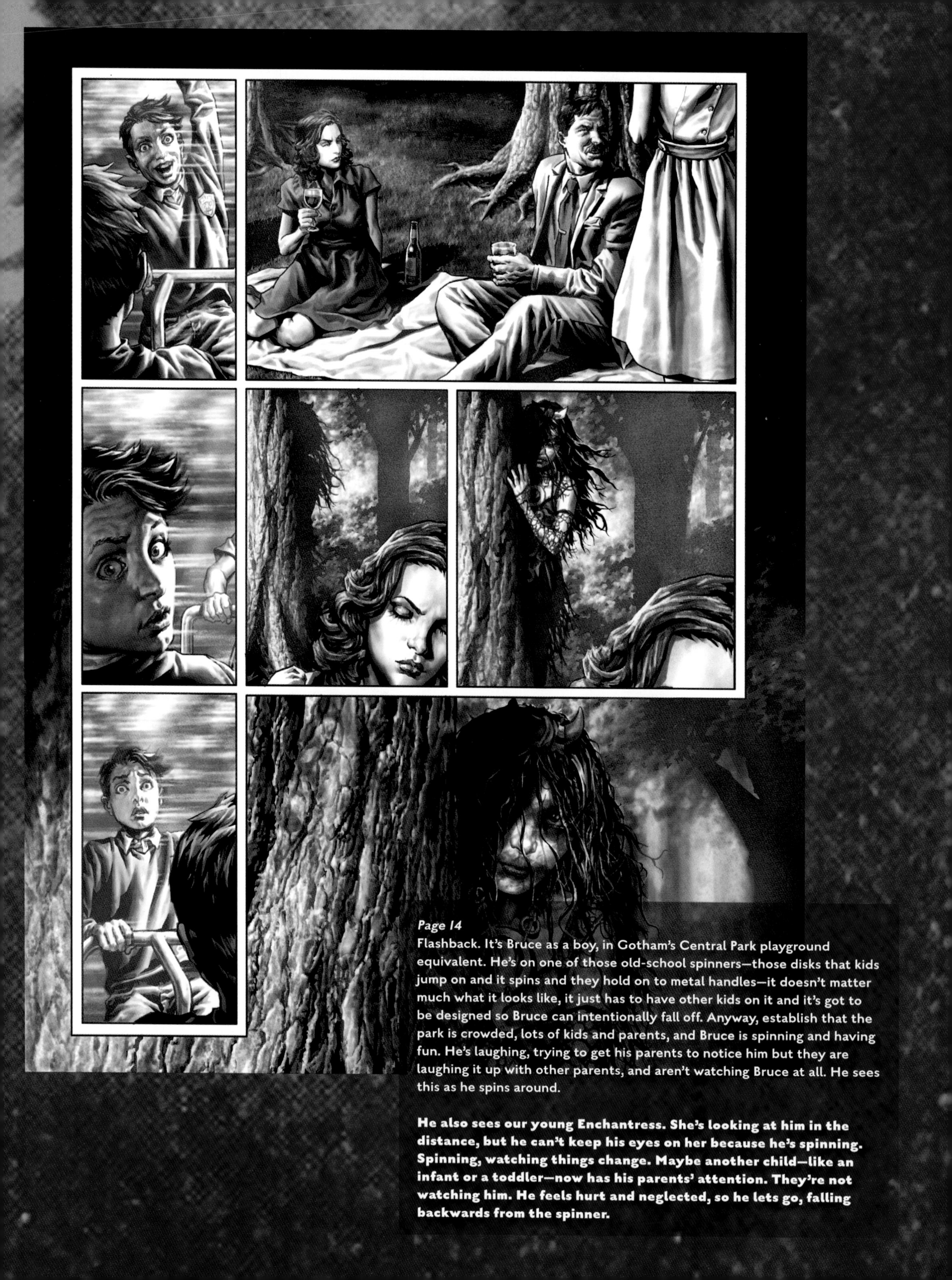

Page 14
Flashback. It's Bruce as a boy, in Gotham's Central Park playground equivalent. He's on one of those old-school spinners—those disks that kids jump on and it spins and they hold on to metal handles—it doesn't matter much what it looks like, it just has to have other kids on it and it's got to be designed so Bruce can intentionally fall off. Anyway, establish that the park is crowded, lots of kids and parents, and Bruce is spinning and having fun. He's laughing, trying to get his parents to notice him but they are laughing it up with other parents, and aren't watching Bruce at all. He sees this as he spins around.

He also sees our young Enchantress. She's looking at him in the distance, but he can't keep his eyes on her because he's spinning. Spinning, watching things change. Maybe another child—like an infant or a toddler—now has his parents' attention. They're not watching him. He feels hurt and neglected, so he lets go, falling backwards from the spinner.

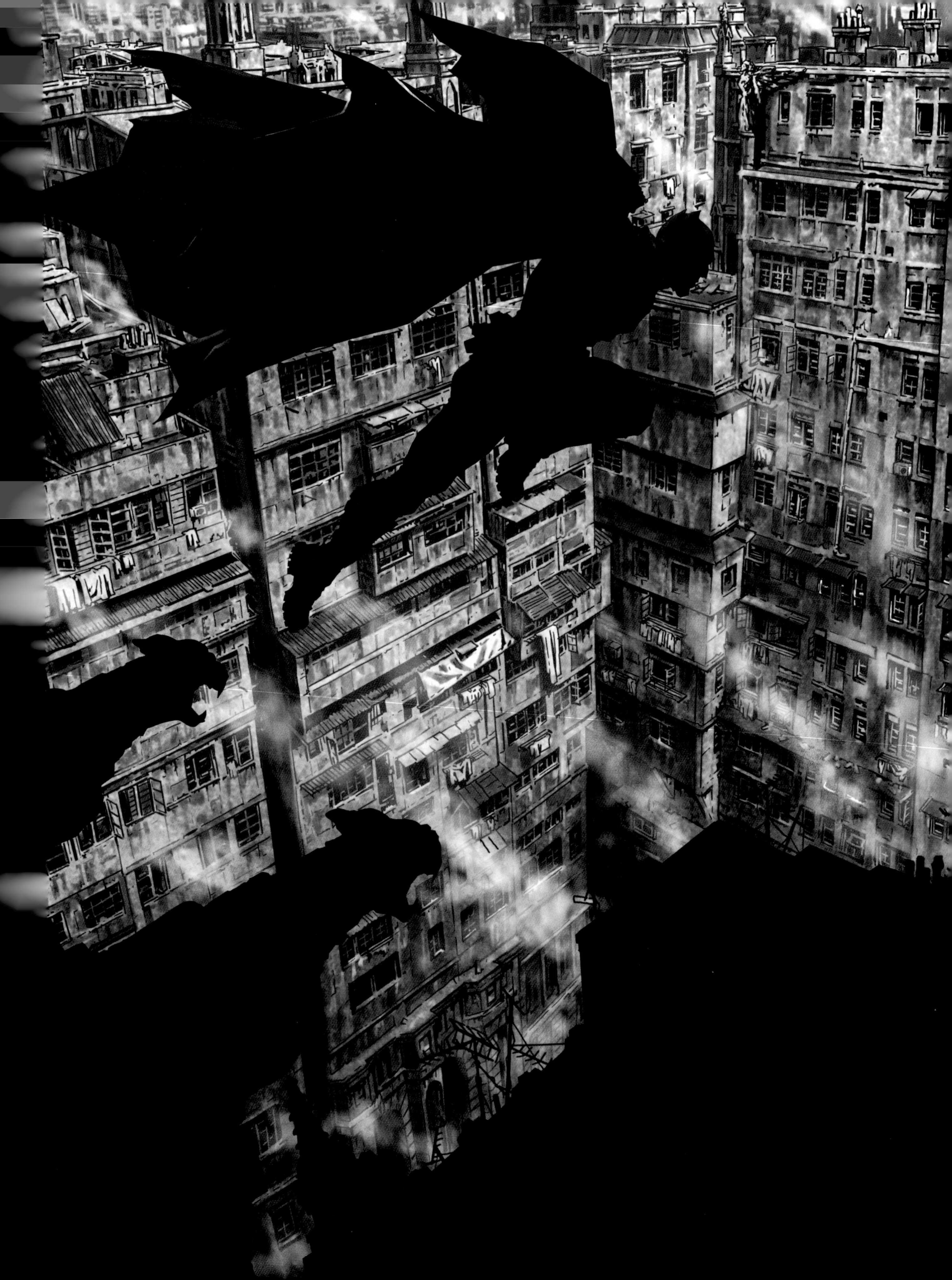

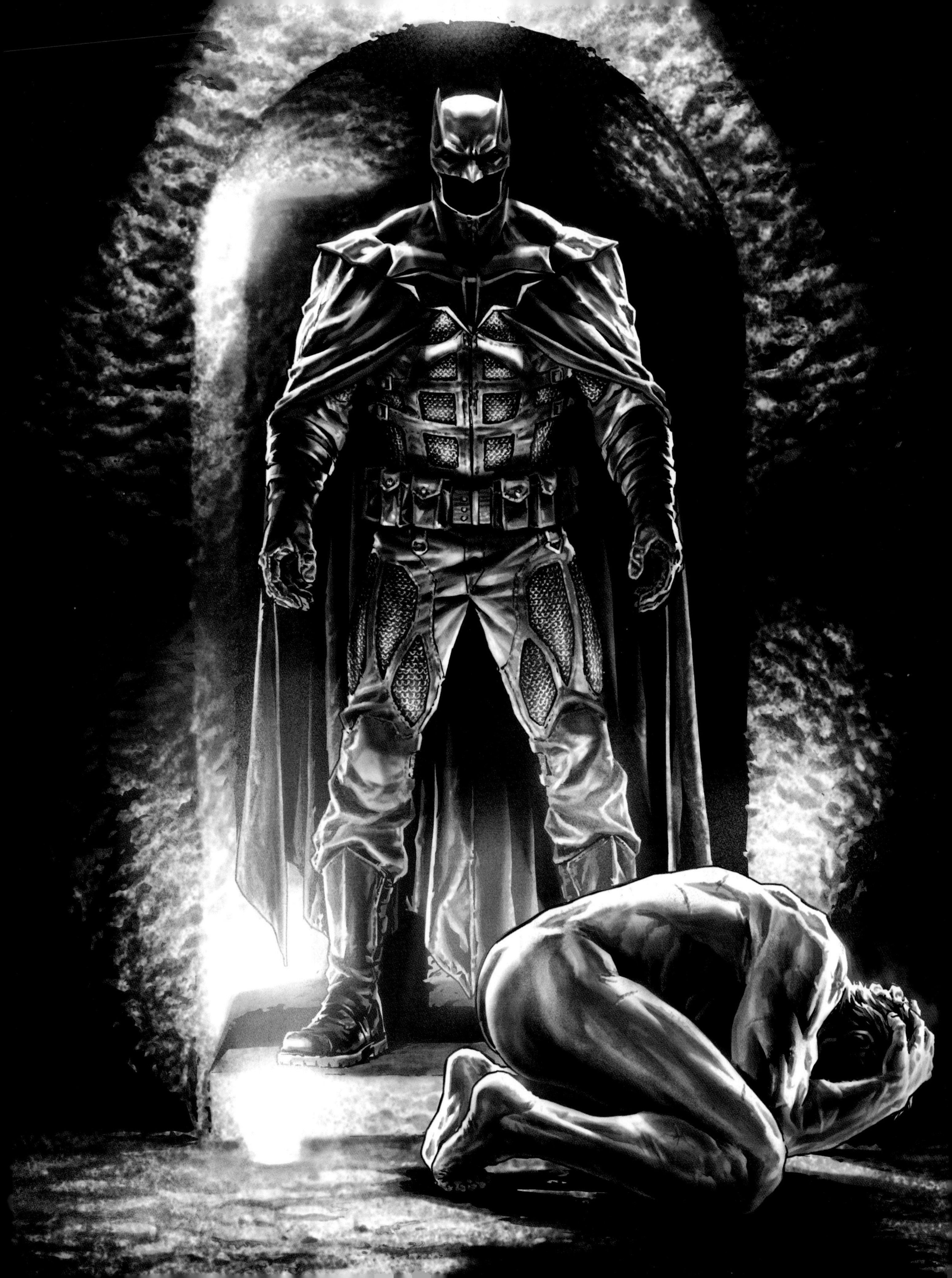

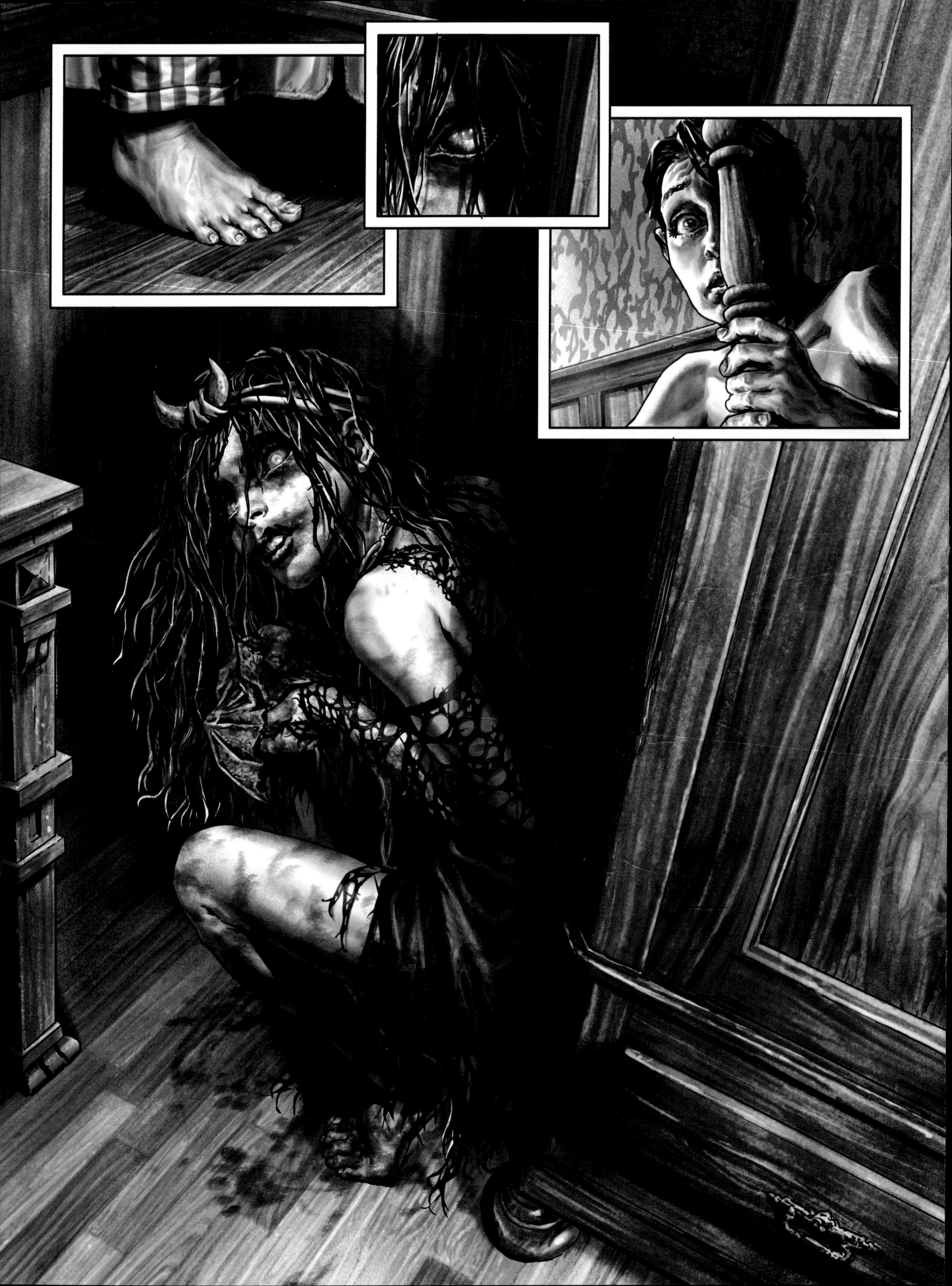

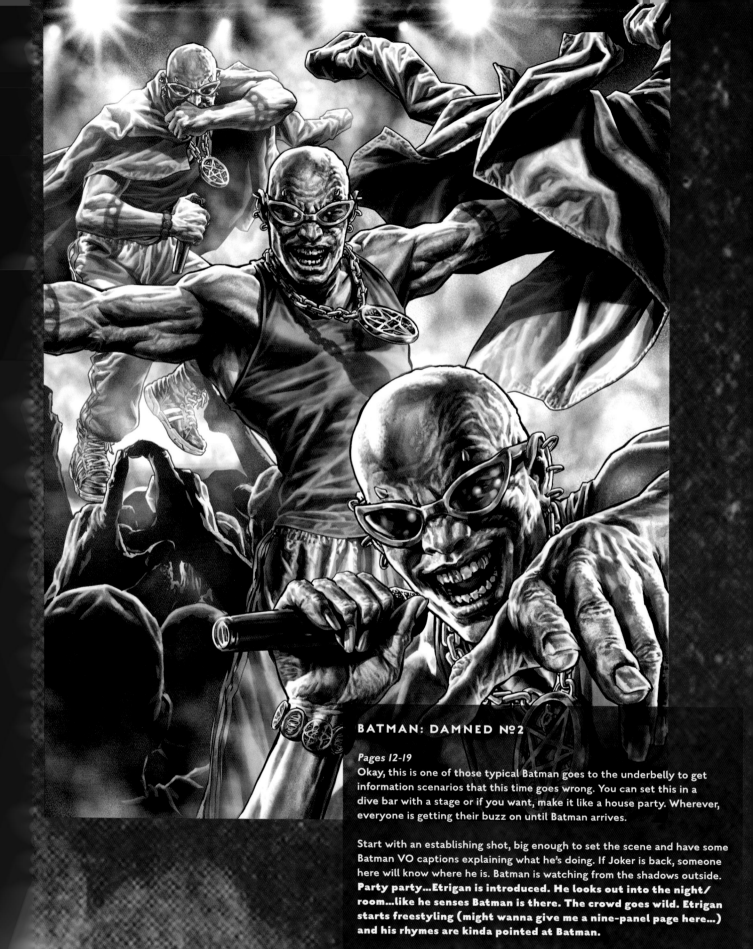

BATMAN: DAMNED Nº2

Pages 12-19

Okay, this is one of those typical Batman goes to the underbelly to get information scenarios that this time goes wrong. You can set this in a dive bar with a stage or if you want, make it like a house party. Wherever, everyone is getting their buzz on until Batman arrives.

Start with an establishing shot, big enough to set the scene and have some Batman VO captions explaining what he's doing. If Joker is back, someone here will know where he is. Batman is watching from the shadows outside. **Party party...Etrigan is introduced. He looks out into the night/ room...like he senses Batman is there. The crowd goes wild. Etrigan starts freestyling (might wanna give me a nine-panel page here...) and his rhymes are kinda pointed at Batman.**

Let's have Batman enter, just walk into the fray like king of all badasses, maybe POV from Batman, so we see the crowd part and their tense reaction. When Batman shows it means trouble. Etrigan jumps into the crowd, still rhyming. As stoic as Batman is, Etrigan is kinetic and animated.

When he finishes his rhyme he's right in Batman's face. Batman asks for Joker's whereabouts. He threatens Etrigan. Grabbing him. Guns are pulled...like many...and all are pointed at Batman. Batman sneers. He knows they won't shoot—they'd hit Etrigan too.

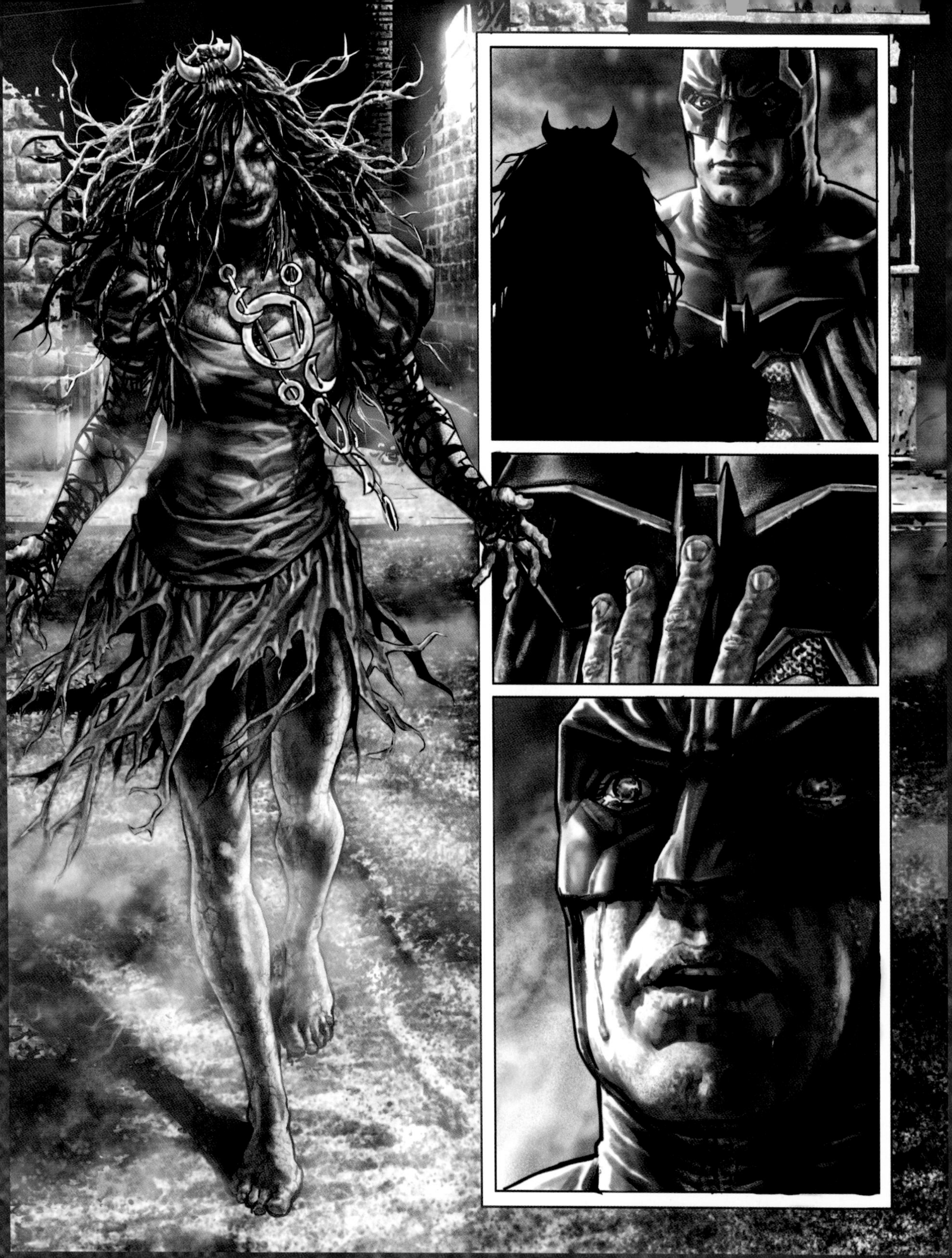

Page 24
Suddenly, Enchantress is standing behind and over Batman...

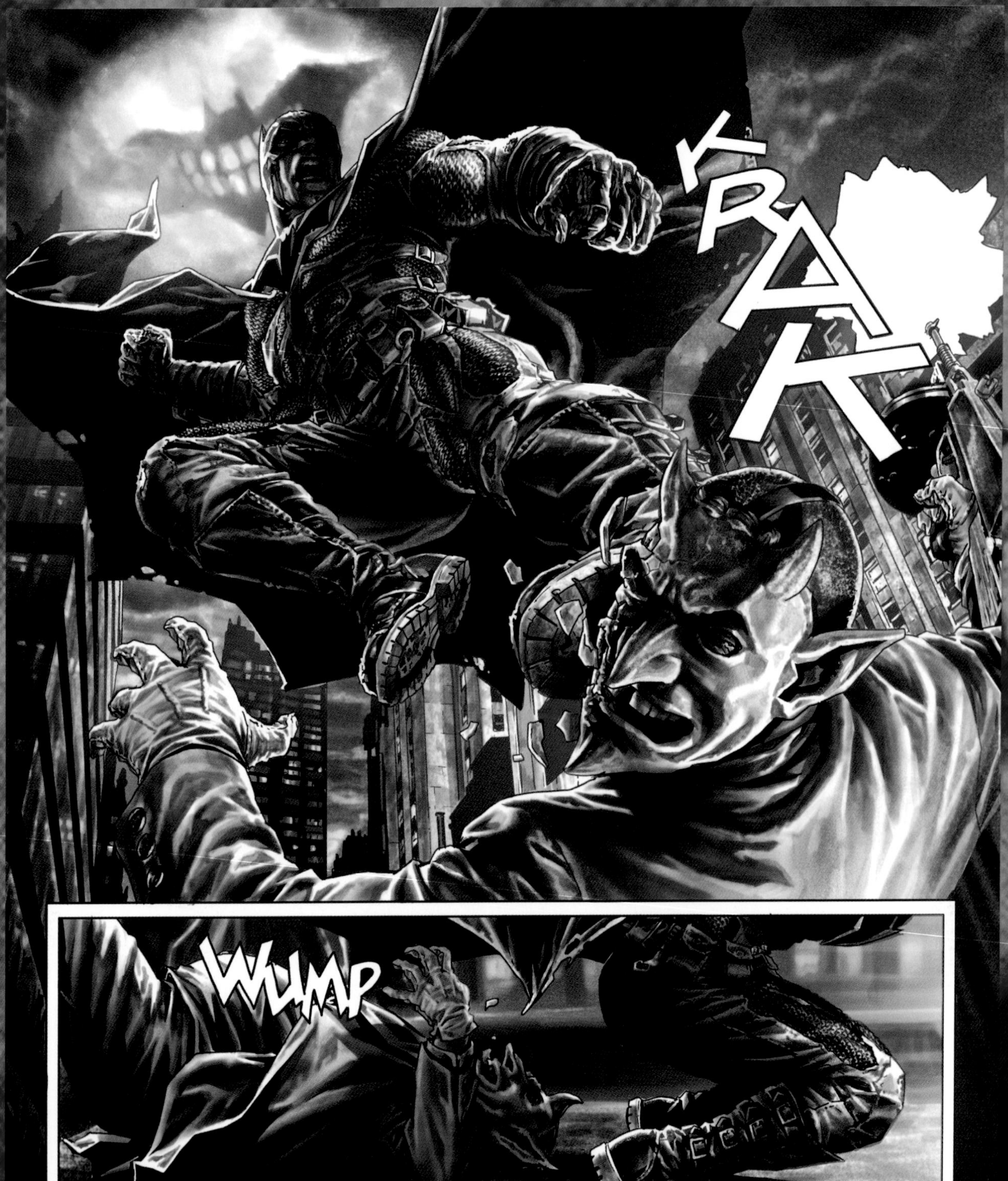
KRAK
WUMP

Pages 33-45
Gordon and the cops pinned down by Harley (still believed to be Joker), who's on the roof with the Batsignal. She has some goons with her, and they all have tommy guns a-blazing. **Dress the goons in Olde Time Devil costumes.**

As they fire at the cops, **Batman arrives. He takes out a goon immediately, and the others turn to him.** As he takes out the last one he's hit with a barbed-wire baseball bat, and we all learn that it's Harley who's orchestrating this attack on Gotham, not Joker.

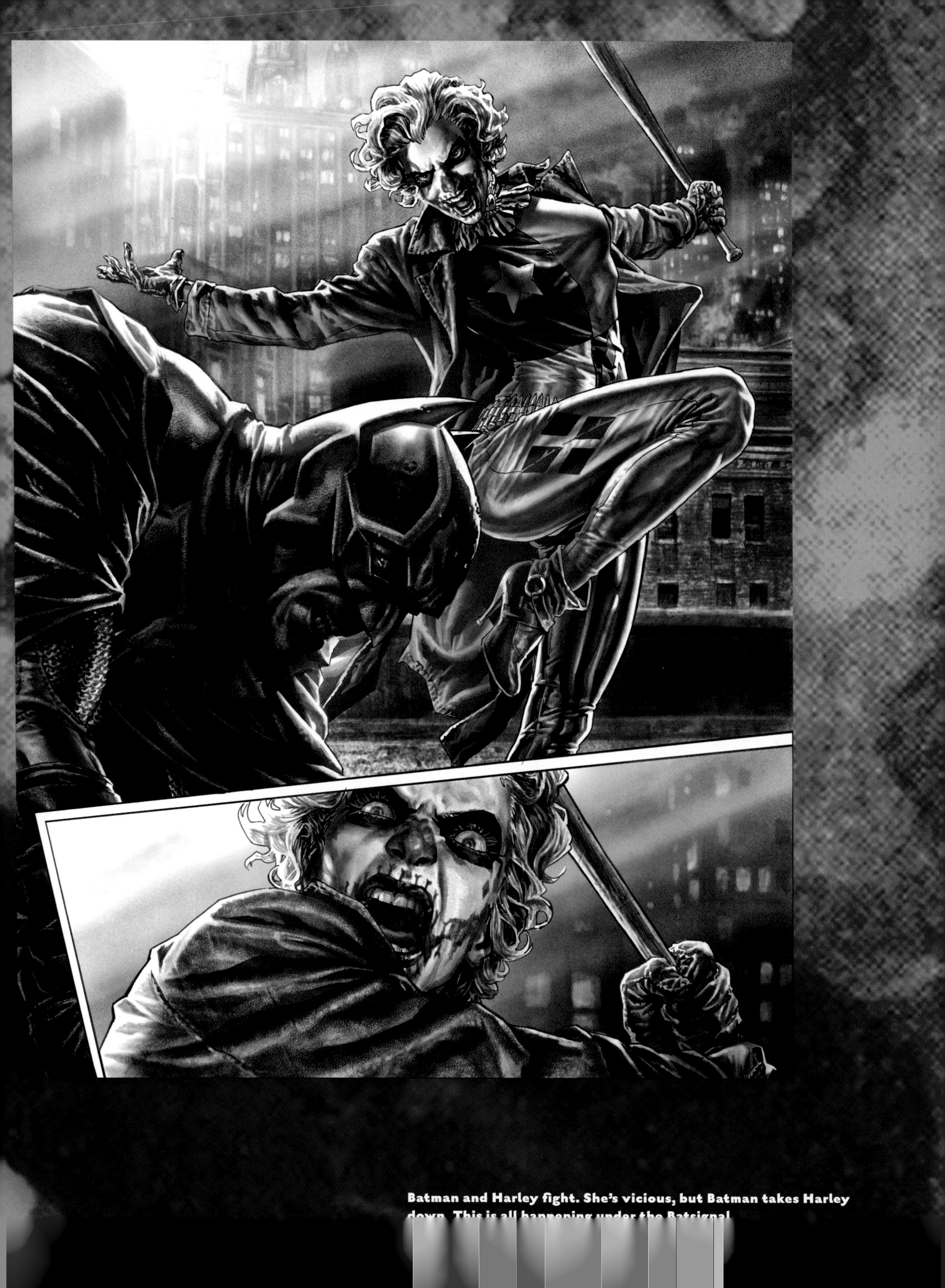

Batman and Harley fight. She's vicious, but Batman takes Harley down. This is all happening under the Batsignal.

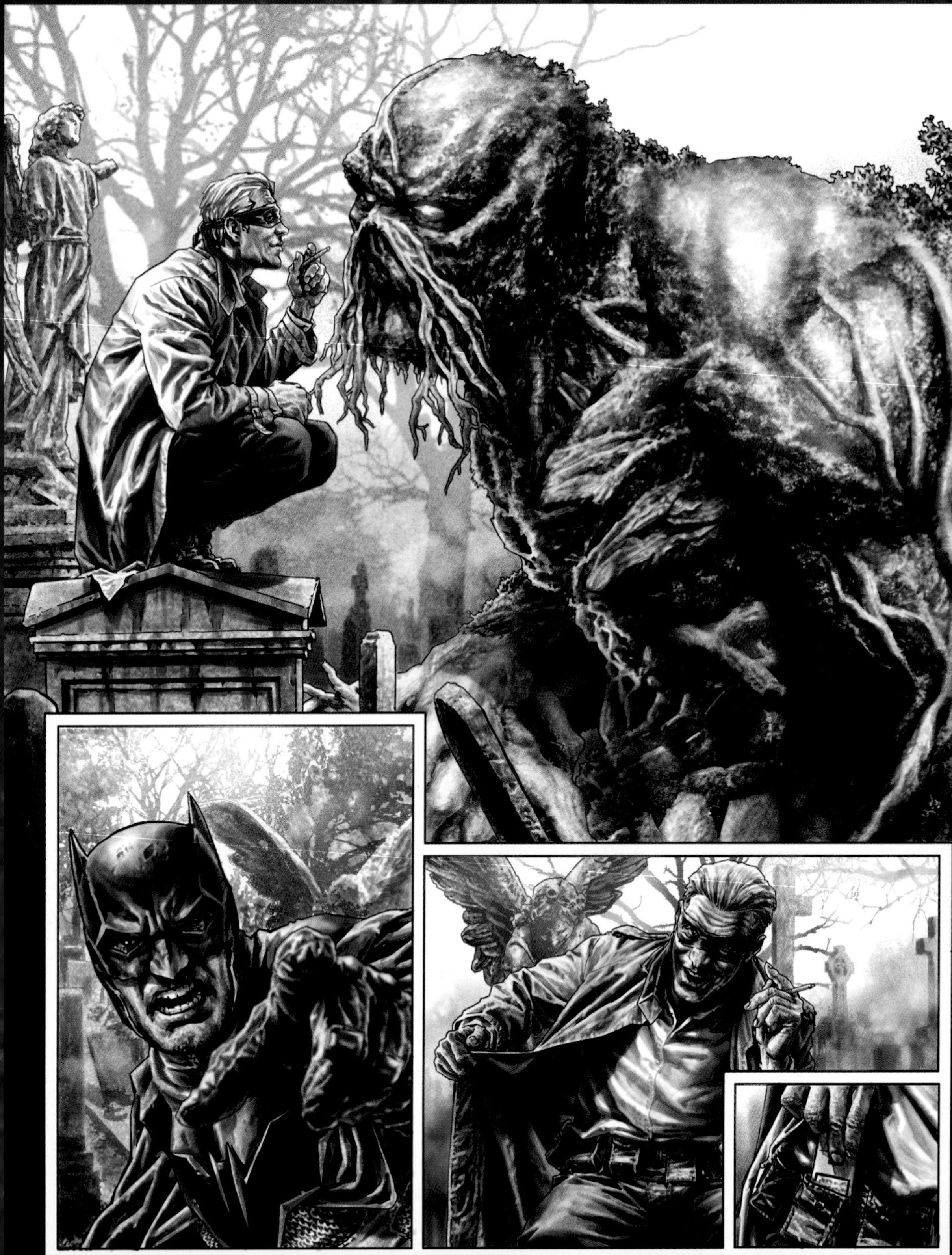

BATMAN: DAMNED №3

Pages 8-9

Swamp Thing warns Batman that the stakes here are not life or death, but for his soul. John quips that can't be; he doesn't have one. Swamp Thing also warns Batman not to trust John, that John is not his friend. He turns his attention to John, wondering why he's involved in this. John's reply is telling: that while the world may need a Superman, humanity needs the Batman. What motivates humanity is fear, not love. He mocks Swamp Thing.

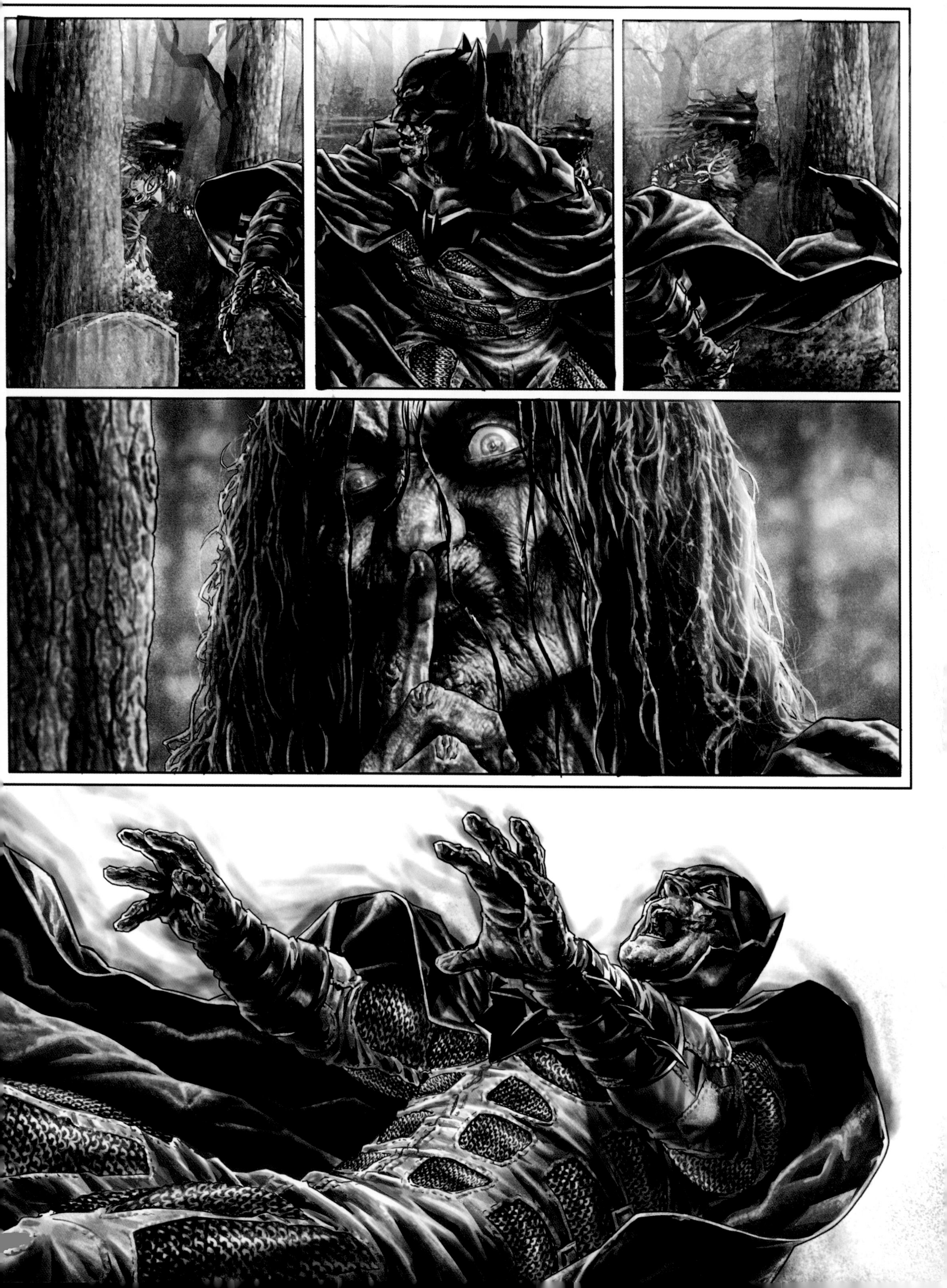

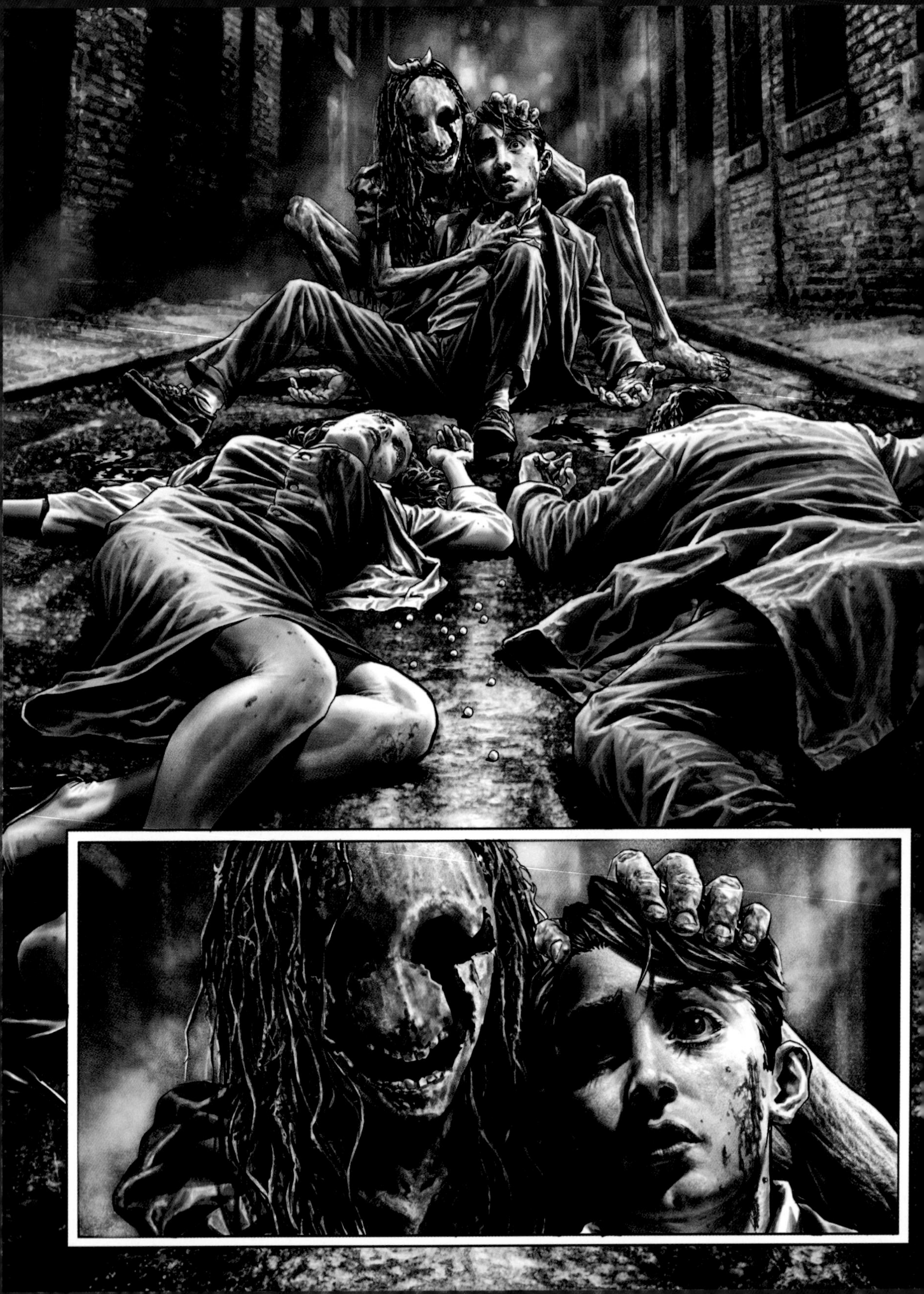

Page 32
We see Enchantress, but now she's a saggy, sore-covered old woman and she holds young Bruce.

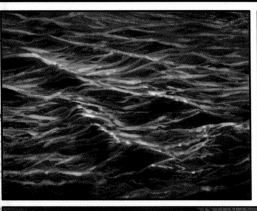

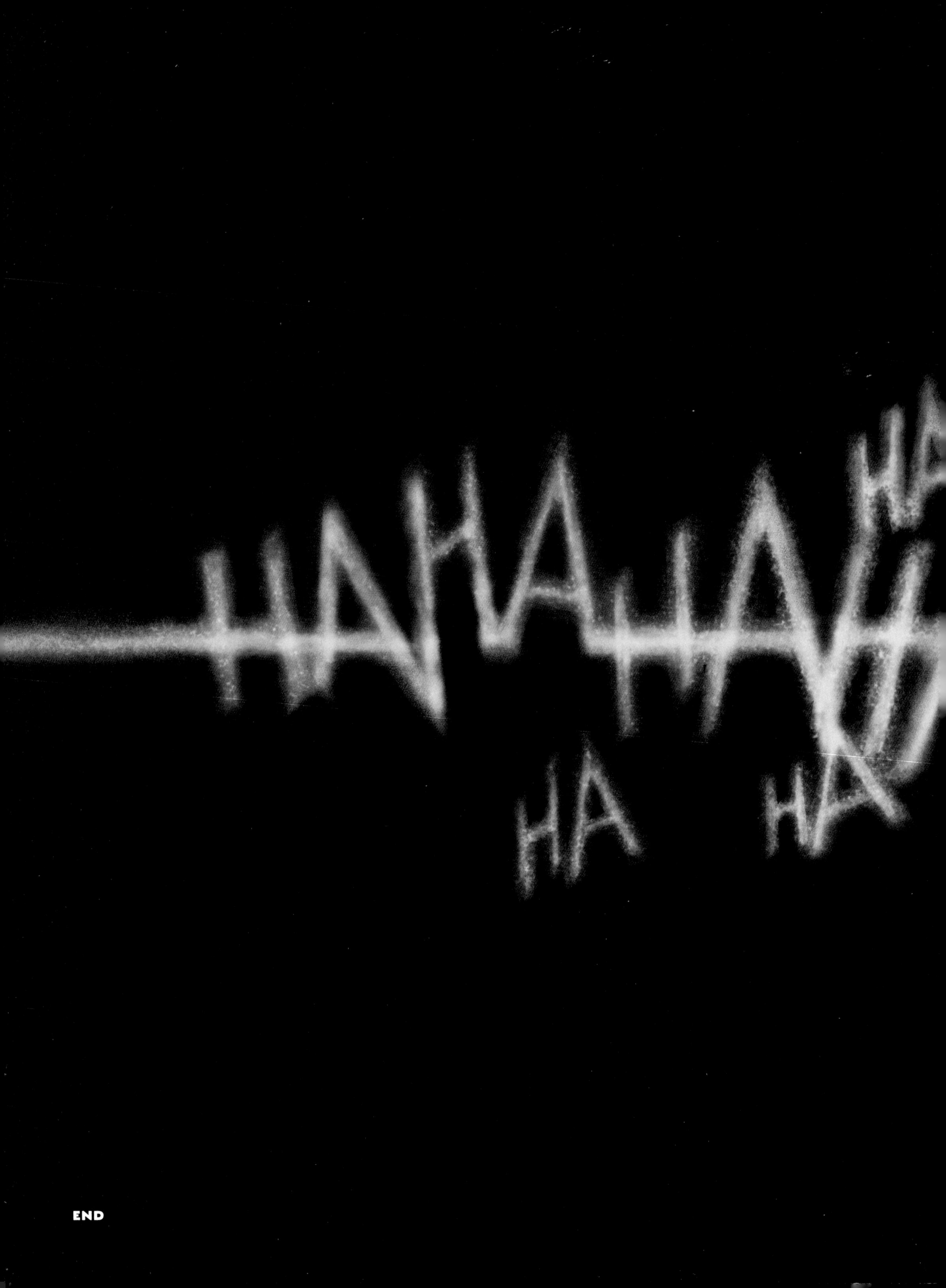
HAHAHAHA
HA
HA
HA

END

DAMNED 'CAUSE WE DO

Creating this book has been an experience...

What BATMAN: DAMNED was meant to be when originally conceived and what it grew up to be are radically different. Of course they are.

The seeds for this book were planted a decade before it was published, when DC was completely surprised by the hit JOKER turned out to be. And they were unprepared. I'm not referring to the print run selling out, but editorially. There was nothing to follow it with, to give readers more of what they wanted. This led Will Dennis and Mark Doyle (two Vertigo editors whom Lee and I have worked with loyally throughout our careers) to brainstorm...the Jokerverse. To take the world that we had created and tell more stories in it, with reinterpretations of other characters—recognizable, but slightly off. A more mature vision of what DC could be—the Black Label. The idea had some traction for a while.

And then it didn't.

And then it did again, rising from the embers of an aborted DCU event that I'd been part of. DAMNED was a supernatural adventure story then, Batman in JUSTICE LEAGUE DARK, a little hell-on-Earth thing. It never gelled the way it could have (lucky us), mainly because I was coming at it from my Vertigo perspective; the story had a lot of adult themes. I remember talking with Lee about it when it didn't work out; it was full of characters we both thought would be interesting to ground in a Batman story. Jim Lee saw something more; he saw a project that could spearhead Black Label.

So there I was in Dallas, in a hotel room, and looking out a window from which I could see the grassy knoll in the distance. I don't know why that's an important detail, but it is. Lee and I were talking on the phone, and we were excited, mature-readers excited. And format excited—Jim was giving us the opportunity to create a unique comic book experience (I've always considered this form of storytelling to be experienced—not just read), so naturally we were going to be ambitious and push the envelope. (Not just Lee and I either. When Jared got involved later in the lettering, he took chances and crafted something really special.)

So we'd exorcised JUSTICE LEAGUE DARK out of DAMNED, but the characters as supernatural/occult entities remained. And it was morphing into a horror story, with Batman and his myth in the center. Our approach was disorienting: a detective story where reality can't be trusted. As fate would have it (yes, I believe in that), Mark Doyle was in Dallas then, too. That evening, on the grassy knoll, I pitched him our... knightmare.

It all came together in Turin, home of the eponymous shroud, and of Lee at the time. Also, it's a city steeped in the occult. It's purported to be one of the vertices of the black magic triangle. Pentagrams adorn more than one statue's head, and legend has the gates to hell located in Piazza Statuto. I was there so we could break our story. We had all the elements, all the characters, all the quirks. All the blood, and the sweat...but not the tears—we were missing our gut punch, and we were beating ourselves up over it. In every story we've told, sometime during the difficult birth something emerges that makes it part of a bigger picture. I guess that's its soul? Is that presumptuous of me?

Anyway, said soul was hiding, being elusive...We'd just had lunch and were back at Lee's studio—a truly inspiring place. We were talking about how the ending would play out, staging it, elliptically walking back to the beginning...

And then a glimpse, a question asked...and a soul larger than life stepped from the shadows and blotted out the sun.

Or maybe it wasn't the shadows. Maybe it came out of those gates I mentioned earlier.

Maybe...it just needed to be experienced.

BRIAN AZZARELLO
June 2019

BRIAN AZZARELLO

BRIAN AZZARELLO HAS BEEN WRITING COMICS
PROFESSIONALLY SINCE THE MID-1990S. HE IS THE
NEW YORK TIMES BEST-SELLING AUTHOR OF **BATMAN**,
JONNY DOUBLE, **SPACEMAN**, *MOONSHINE* AND THE
GROUNDBREAKING, HARVEY AND EISNER AWARD-
WINNING SERIES **100 BULLET**S, ALL CREATED IN
COLLABORATION WITH ARTIST EDUARDO RISSO. HIS
OTHER WORKS INCLUDE **HELLBLAZER** AND **LOVELESS**
(BOTH WITH MARCELO FRUSIN), **SUPERMAN: FOR
TOMORROW** (WITH JIM LEE), **JOKER**, **LUTHOR** AND
BEFORE WATCHMEN (ALL WITH LEE BERMEJO), A
CHARACTER-DEFINING THREE-YEAR RUN ON **WONDER
WOMAN** (WITH CLIFF CHIANG), AS WELL AS **DARK
KNIGHT III: THE MASTER RACE** (WITH FRANK MILLER
AND ANDY KUBERT). HE HAILS FROM CHICAGO.

LEE BERMEJO

AWARD-WINNING ARTIST LEE BERMEJO IS THE
ILLUSTRATOR OF THE GRAPHIC NOVELS **BATMAN/
DEATHBLOW**, **LUTHOR**, **BEFORE WATCHMEN:
RORSCHACH** AND THE *NEW YORK TIMES* BEST-SELLING
JOKER, ALL OF WHICH WERE DONE IN COLLABORATION
WITH WRITER BRIAN AZZARELLO.

BERMEJO'S OTHER WORK FOR DC INCLUDES THE
TITLES **GLOBAL FREQUENCY** (WITH WARREN ELLIS),
SUPERMAN/GEN 13 (WITH ADAM HUGHES) AND
HELLBLAZER (WITH MIKE CAREY), AS WELL AS
SEVERAL DOZEN PAINTED COVERS. HE ALSO WROTE
AND ILLUSTRATED THE BEST-SELLING GRAPHIC NOVELS
BATMAN: NOËL AND **SUICIDERS** FOR VERTIGO.
BERMEJO LIVES AND WORKS IN A SMALL TOWN IN ITALY.